Hampshire County Marriages of the 1800s

Compiled by

Vicki Bidinger Horton

CLEARFIELD

Originally printed by The Hampshire Review
Romney, West Virginia
1994

Reprinted for Clearfield Company by
Genealogical Publishing Company
Baltimore, Maryland
2011

ISBN 978-0-8063-4870-4

Made in the United States of America

Hampshire County Marriages
of the 1800's

Compiled by Vicki Bidinger Horton

These marriage records have been compiled as an aid to genealogists. The records are listed in an alphabetical order by both the groom's and bride's name. When available, the age of the individual follows the name. Following the name is the date of marriage, or, in some cases, the date of bond or license. The asterisk (*) indicates a license or bond date. The last column is the source for the marriage record.

Hampshire County's marriage records prior to 1866 were lost or destroyed during the Civil War, except for one marriage bond book covering the years 1824-1828. The records in this compilation were drawn from several primary sources in an attempt to help the genealogist locate marriage records prior to 1866. The marriages from 1866 to 1900 are recorded in two books in the County Clerk's office. The Virginia State Archives, Richmond, Virginia has a book of Hampshire County marriages for the years 1853 to 1860. However, there has been considerable water damage to this book. The few marriages that are legible have been included in this compilation.

An attempt was made to copy names as they appeared in the record, but due to illegible writing, poor spelling, etc. names may be spelled in an unfamiliar way. It is advisable to check for variable spellings. Duplicates are included if any of the data varied from one source to another.

SOURCE CODES

(1) The South Branch Intelligencer Newspaper (Issue Date)
(2) Virginia Argus and Hampshire Advertiser Newspaper (Issue Date)
(3) Diary of Christian Streit as published in This Heritage by William Edward Eisenberg, published by the Trustees of Grace Evangelical Lutheran Church, Winchester, VA 1954, Page 362.
(4) Hampshire County Marriage Book (Book Number/Page Number; Book #3 Marriage Bonds 1824-1828)
(5) Marriages from THE OWL PRINT
(6) Marriages performed by Reverend William Welch, a compilation by M Cupler, 1978.
(7) North River Meeting Church Book, Rio, WV 1849-1889
(8) Hebron Luthern Church Records; Marriages performed by P Miller
(9) St James Luthern Church Records
(10) Virginia State Archives - Hampshire County Marriages 1853-1860

Name #1	Name #2	Date	Source
Abe Amanda Melvina 24	Largent Charles Edward 25	20 Dec 1896	(4) 2/38
Abe John Adam 53	Sowers Sarah Margaret 43	25 Nov 1897	(4) 2/39
Abe Lacey Ann 26	Whitacre Alpheus Jerome 26	25 Mar 1896	(4) 2/37
Abell Charles F 23	Davis Sarah Odwolt 19	11 Mar 1894	(4) 2/33
Abell Edith Virginia 18	Hott Kirk George 19	3 July 1894	(4) 2/34
Abell Nannie Lee 21	Heare Alfred Joseph Snyder 25	8 May 1895	(4) 2/35
Abernathy Elizabeth	Good Philip	*10 Dec 1825	(4) 3/73
Abernathy Elizabeth	Good Phillip	15 Dec 1825	(6)
Abernathy Marg	Lore Henry	22 Dec 1839	(6)
Abernathy Margaret	Lore Henry	22 Dec 1840	(5)
Abernathy N J	McCormick George	26 Aug 1850	(5)
Abernathy N J	McCormick G	26 Aug 1852	(6)
Abernathy Robert	Sharpless A	21 July 1842	(6)
Abernathy William	Stump Elizabeth D W	*8 Jan 1825	(4) 3/5
Abernathy William	Lore R	14 Aug 1828	(6)
Abrel Margaret 24	Noll Joseph Calvin 25	27 Oct 1867	(4) 1/5
Abrell Clara Bell 25	McNamee Marion 27	5 Sept 1895	(4) 2/36
Abrell Emma M 19	Whitacre George William 24	25 Sept 1894	(40 2/34
Abrell George William 23	Thompson Sarah Virginia 19	5 May 1891	(4) 2/29
Abrell Lemuel 21	Whitacre Sarah E 18	22 Nov 1866	(4) 1/4
Abrell Sarah E 29	Adams James M 50	1 Feb 1900	(4) 2/42
Abrill Amanda Elizabeth 25	Whitacre Lycurgus M 23	21 Nov 1895	(4) 2/36
Abrill David Jackson 22	Kidwell Frances Ann 23	29 Oct 1879	(4) 2/13
Abrill Eliza Jane 38	Chilcote Amos 48	*1 Dec 1875	(4) 2/8
Abrill John Wesley 23	Marston Emma Susan 19	*15 Mar 1877	(4) 2/10
Abrill William E 25	Whitacre Ann Z 20	28 Mar 1867	(4) 1/5
Adams Catharine Elizabeth 21	Pownall William Marshall 24	4 Nov 1896	(4) 2/38
Adams George W 32	Swisher Ann Ziletta 23	28 Apr 1875	(4) 2/7
Adams Jacob Long 32	Grace Sarah Ellen 28	24 Sept 1867	(4) 1/5
Adams James M 50	Abrell Sarah E 29	1 Feb 1900	(4) 2/42
Adams Jno Wm 29	Carder Malinda 20	27 Feb 1866	(4) 1/3
Adams Robert Lee 27	Harmison Martha Wood 26	31 Oct 1888	(4) 2/25
Adams Simon Philip 46	Iliff Virginia Elizabeth 24	21 Apr 1892	(4) 2/30
Adams William 31	Lewis Rosa Ellen 23	19 Nov 1896	(4) 2/38
Albaugh Emma Elizabeth 21	Kerns Isaac Jefferson 31	5 May 1892	(4) 2/31
Albaugh Margaret 33	Light Charles Holliday 34	14 Apr 1886	(4) 2/22
Albaugh Margery Alice 28	Harrison Charles William 26	14 Apr 1886	(4) 2/22
Albaugh Mary F 26	Kerns John Sanford 37	28 Aug 1873	(4) 2/4
Albaugh Nimrod 24	Fletcher Frances 19	7 Jan 1891	(4) 2/29
Albin Elizabeth 25	Schnibbe Lewis 24	11 Oct 1866	(4) 1/3
Albin Mary Jane 32	Flory John Michael 33	10 Aug 1875	(4) 2/7
Albright Cora Bell 20	Carder John Foreman 27	21 Nov 1894	(4) 2/35
Albright Lewis 23	Rudolph ? 26	24 Nov 1860	(10)
Albright Lydia Adeline 20	Wolford John Martin 21	26 Feb 1889	(4) 2/26
Albright Mary Jane 24	Haines Peter Abraham 30	8 Dec 1885	(4) 2/21
Albright Mary Virginia 27	Haines Stephen 51	24 Apr 1883	(4) 2/18
Albright Sarah Ellen 19	Orndorff William Thompson 29	27 Jan 1886	(4) 2/21
Albright Sarah S A 16	Starne Machir I 22	4 Dec 1872	(4) 2/4
Albright Susan Ann 22	Haines George Washington 29	5 Jan 1882	(4) 2/17
Albright William Edward 26	High Hannah Catharine 19	9 Feb 1881	(4) 2/15
Aldereton William	Edward Margaret	3 May 1786	(3)
Alderton Barbara 34	Brelsford J F E 34	*11 Jan 1872	(4) 2/3

Name #1	Name #2	Date	Source
Alderton Edward 23	Slane Nancy E 20	31 May 1876	(4) 2/8
Alderton Francis Marion 25	Noland Cora Lee 18	18 Mar 1890	(4) 2/27
Alderton Isaac 29	Slane Lucinda 26	15 Oct 1872	(4) 2/3
Alderton Joseph 22	Easter Arah Elsie 22	19 May 1875	(4) 2/7
Alderton Martha Jane 40	Patterson Charles Randolph 50	5 Sept 1895	(4) 2/36
Alderton Perry L 20	Kidwell Verdie Blanche 21	8 July 1897	(4) 2/39
Alderton Sarah Catharine 23	Largent Edward Trickle 35	2 Nov 1879	(4) 2/13
Alderton Wm H 23	Vanosdall Rebecca F 16	20 July 1868	(4) 1/6
Alen Rhoda M	Greenwade Moss T	1850	(5)
Alexander Albert 23	Bush Nancy Jane 23	19 Aug 1874	(4) 1/39
Alexander Joseph 50	Howard Milly 34	29 Apr 1869	(4) 1/38
Alexander Mary E 20	Whalen Thomas Edward 23	15 June 1895	(4) 1/41
Alger John Alvahase 23	Miller Rebecca Jane 23	21 Nov 1867	(4) 1/5
Alkire Elizabeth M 35	Shanholtzer Charles W 22	29 Oct 1895	(4) 2/36
Alkire Hiram Welton 24	Scanlan Elizabeth Ellen 21	24 Dec 1878	(4) 2/12
Alkire Jennie Lee 23	Roberson John Alexander 23	15 Aug 1888	(4) 2/25
Alkire Mahala A	Neff Thompson	15 Nov 1839	(1) 5 Dec 1839
Alkire Mahala Catharine 18	Hardy Charles Martin 28	8 Feb 1882	(4) 2/17
Alkire Nimrod 51	Reese Mary Elizabeth 33	5 Sept 1865	(4) 1/1
Alkire Peter	Howard Alcinda		(1) 29 Sept 1838
Alkire Peter	Smoot Rebecca A	20 Apr 1853	(1) 29 Apr 1853
Alkire Sarah 26	Shanholtzer Anthony 27	20 Apr 1871	(4) 2/2
Allamong Fannie Lynch 17	Wolford John William 22	9 Nov 1885	(4) 2/21
Allamong Jerry Arthur 24	Arnold Merand Isabella 24	25 Mar 1879	(4) 2/13
Allamong Lewella Elizabeth 29	Swisher John Wesley 24	16 June 1895	(4) 2/35
Allamong Sarah Catherine 22	Baker Sanford Levi 24	21 Oct 1879	(4) 2/13
Allamong Thomas Brandon 21	Maloney Minnie H 20	28 Nov 1891	(4) 2/30
Allemong Alice Virginia 22	Morris Alexanda 24	10 Mar 1874	(4) 2/6
Allemong Martha Jane 22	Swisher Asa Sine 22	*20 Nov 1880	(4) 2/15
Allemong Mary Christine 26	Arnold Evan Corsey 25	21 Feb 1878	(4) 2/11
Allen ? 24	Dieffendorffer John 25	28 July 1859	(10)
Allen Andrew Fenton 23	Bohrer Eliza Elizabeth 21	9 Oct 1890	(4) 2/28
Allen Elizabeth 21	Santemires Emanuel T 22	4 Oct 1877	(4) 2/10
Allen Frank Page 37	Hartman Lydia Ann 25	24 June 1897	(4) 2/39
Allen Isabella	Hannas Stephen	*14 Mar 1825	(4) 3/22
Allen Jacob 62	Thornton Samantha 40	2 Mar 1898	(4) 1/41
Allen James	Hiett Sarah	*20 Feb 1826	(4) 3/10
Allen Jane 26	Whitfield John Amos 23	23 Sept 1880	(4) 1/40
Allen Kitty 47	Redmond James Sanford 23	23 Sept 1880	(4) 1/40
Allen Margaret 22	StMyer John 23	21 Aug 1884	(4) 2/19
Allen Mary Eliza 20	Coleman Isaac Johnson 28	31 Dec 1890	(4) 1/41
Allen R M	Greenwade M T	3 Apr 1851	(6)
Allen Sallie Ann 22	Morgan Samuel Lewis 23	2 Oct 1890	(4) 1/41
Allen Sarah M 24	Moorhead Robt E 24	20 Sept 1866	(4) 1/3
Allen Susan Elizabeth 28	Pugh Robert James 34	4 Oct 1876	(4) 2/9
Allen Viola 28	Coleman John David 28	2 Oct 1893	(4) 1/41
Allen Virginia 22	Bailey Henry 23	23 Sept 1874	(4) 1/39
Allen William	Case Sarah	*25 June 1824	(4) 3/35
Allender John Thomas 30	Largent Emily Ann 19	17 Dec 1867	(4) 1/6
Allender John William 21	Spurling Margaret Lane 23	3 Oct 1888	(4) 2/25
Allender Mary	Johnson Amos	*5 May 1828	(4) 3/11
Allender Mary Ellen 18	Powell James Julius Walter 20	26 May 1881	(4) 2/16

Name #1	Name #2	Date	Source
Allender Thomas Neavitt 22	Schoroley Mary 28	20 Oct 1896	(4) 2/37
Alloway Hiram	Unglesby Rebecca	*29 Mar 1827	(4) 3/24
Alverson Mary Frances 28	Poland David Granville 21	18 July 1881	(4) 2/16
Ambler James 35	Smith Margaret C 23	19 Dec 1865	(4) 1/2
Ambler William C	Byrd Frances Ann		(1) 10 Apr 1857
Ambler Wm C	Byrd Frances Ann		(2) 9 Apr 1857
Ambrose William Cyrus 24	Hiett Mary 23	22 Mar 1900	(4) 2/42
Ammick Franklin	Orndorff Mary D 28	*3 Spet 1884	(4) 2/19
Amon Mary	Park John	*18 Aug 1828	(4) 3/21
Anderson Alfred S 26	Hook Francis 21	28 Dec 1865	(4) 1/2
Anderson Alice May 18	Cooper Julius Bell 21	14 Dec 1882	(4) 2/18
Anderson Amanda V 22	Washington Henry W 21	20 Aug 1888	(4) 1/40
Anderson Ann Eliza 22	Dunlap Randolph Tucker 24	*27 May 1876	(4) 2/8
Anderson Aranintha May 20	Lafollette Brondell 24	21 Dec 1887	(4) 2/24
Anderson Cornelius George 28	Brill Sarah Ellen 22	7 Jan 1875	(4) 2/6
Anderson Daniel Luther 25	White Mary Elizabeth Ann 24	1 May 1883	(4) 2/18
Anderson David	Earnholt Rebecca	28 June 1842	(5)
Anderson Delilah M 20	Zeiler Edward Newton 29	24 Sept 1891	(4) 2/29
Anderson Elizabeth N 22	Creswell Evan P 25	*8 Oct 1877	(4) 2/10
Anderson Elizabeth	Junkins John	20 June 1816	(5)
Anderson Emma C 26	Brill Harvey P M 24	5 July 1888	(4) 2/25
Anderson Fanny Eliz Victoria 19	Grubbs George William 25	16 Oct 1895	(4) 2/36
Anderson Gertrude Frances 23	? 25	20 Dec 1883	(4) 2/18
Anderson Hattie Malinda 26	Lafollette Elias Elkanah 32	13 Apr 1876	(4) 2/8
Anderson James	James Mary	25 Apr 1819	(5)
Anderson James	Junkins Margaret	23 Mar 1820	(5)
Anderson James	Junkins Mary	23 Mar 1820	(6)
Anderson James H 24	Shoemaker Eliza Ellen 18	4 Apr 1877	(4) 2/10
Anderson Jesse	Harvey Annie	7 Feb 1822	(6)
Anderson Lloyd	Sharpless H	28 Jan 1841	(6)
Anderson Martha M 21	Schaffnaker John Frederick 21	31 Dec 1890	(4) 2/28
Anderson Mary Jane 23	Smith Henry Baker 24	13 Dec 1892	(4) 2/31
Anderson Melissa J 29	Pugh George 53	22 Oct 1896	(4) 2/37
Anderson Mollie M 24	Miller D F 29	13 Apr 1868	(4) 1/6
Anderson Morgan Julius 35	Johnson Florence Virginia 25	26 Jan 1887	(4) 2/23
Anderson Nancy C 23	Arnold Lemuel S 23	11 Jan 1866	(4) 1/2
Anderson Russell Carter 20	Long Lillie 22	27 Apr 1887	(4) 2/23
Anderson Samuel Edward 21	Johnson Melissa Jane 22	26 Mar 1891	(4) 2/29
Anderson Sarah Angelina 21	Spaid Nicholas Leatherman 27	26 Mar 1874	(4) 2/6
Anderson Ulyssis S 21	Larrick Cordelia Sophia 20	28 Dec 1893	(4) 2/33
Anderson Willis 21	Dandridge Margaret 22	25 Dec 1867	(4) 1/6
Anderson Willis 26	Baker Cynthia Margaret 16	20 Mar 1873	(4) 2/4
Ansell Elmer Woodward 24	Blue Mary Virginia 27	12 Sept 1887	(4) 2/24
Arm Catherine	Jenkins Benjamin	9 Jan 1838	(1) 27 Jan 1838
Armstrong David Gibson 25	Gibson Hannah 25	12 Dec 1865	(4) 1/1
Armstrong Edward	Pancake Hannah		(1) 9 Sept 1837
Armstrong Elizabeth McCarty 22	Kidd Robert B 36	14 Mar 1867	(4) 1/4
Armstrong Sidney 22	Jones Allen 28	25 Jan 1876	(4) 1/39
Arnholt Andrew	Bosley Alice	*3 July 1824	(4) 3/38
Arnold Abigail	Woodward George W	17 Jan 1859	(5)
Arnold Albert Smith 30	Pennington Janie 25	25 Dec 1895	(4) 2/36
Arnold Archibald	Groves Mary	*22 Aug 1827	(4) 3/44

Name #1	Name #2	Date	Source
Arnold Barbary	Baker Thornton	3 Dec 1837	(5)
Arnold Benjamin Franklin 22	Sulser Mary Jamima 19	9 Feb 1881	(4) 2/15
Arnold C	Leatherman Nicholas	23 Sept 1846	(6)
Arnold Catherine	Watkins Harrison	*23 Apr 1824	(4) 3/26
Arnold Charles William 30	Huffman Christina 25	19 May 1867	(4) 1/5
Arnold Charlotte 37	Stump Wm Baldwin 40	17 Mar 1875	(4) 2/7
Arnold Chas	Hiett Asa	22 Nov 1855	(6)
Arnold Dan	Ludwick Sallie	14 Dec 1859	(6)
Arnold Daniel 41	Tutwiler Mary Ann Keys 26	10 Mar 1880	(4) 2/14
Arnold David A 24	Snider Anna M 21	21 Nov 1877	(4) 2/10
Arnold Edward 23	Leatherman Susan Elizabeth 22	19 Dec 1877	(4) 2/11
Arnold Edward Daily 23	Edwards Annie Catharine 19	6 Aug 1896	(4) 2/37
Arnold Edward T 27	Lafollette Nellie Jemima 22	25 Nov 1886	(4) 2/22
Arnold Evan Corsey 25	Allemong Mary Christine 26	21 Feb 1878	(4) 2/11
Arnold Geo Benjamin 22	Shelly Maggie B 20	16 Aug 1870	(4) 2/2
Arnold George Edward 26	Whiteman Annie Virginia 19	9 May 1888	(4) 2/25
Arnold George Statton 28	Simpson Hannah Catharine 22	8 Mar 1876	(4) 2/8
Arnold George Washington 23	Cheshir Margaret Ann 22	23 Feb 1871	(4) 2/2
Arnold Hannah	Leatherman Solmon	26 Dec 1841	(5)
Arnold Hannah Catharin 20	Taylor Isaac 25	8 Sept 1875	(4) 2/7
Arnold Harriet Jane 24	Davey Isaac 24	11 Dec 1878	(4) 2/12
Arnold Hester A 22	Shoemaker Edward Holland 26	20 Mar 1877	(4) 2/10
Arnold J S	Riley J C	20 Dec 1854	(6)
Arnold Jacob M 30	? Harriett	1 May 1873	(4) 2/3
Arnold John Wesley 22	Oats ? 19	29 Mar 1860	(10)
Arnold Joseph	Sloane Elizabeth	*20 Jan 1827	(4) 3/8
Arnold Joseph Robert 29	Saville Nancy Irene 18	18 Sept 1895	(4) 2/36
Arnold Joshua R 26	Haines Mary H 30	13 Dec 1867	(4) 1/6
Arnold Laura Catharine 18	Shanholtzer Charles Lupton 21	2 Jan 1889	(4) 2/26
Arnold Laura May 18	Wolford David Markwood 27	12 Feb 1888	(4) 2/24
Arnold Laura V B 20	Lederer Herman 25	2 Sept 1889	(4) 2/26
Arnold Lemuel S 23	Anderson Nancy C 23	11 Jan 1866	(4) 1/2
Arnold Letitia 18	Larrick Lemuel Howard 23	29 Apr 1890	(4) 2/28
Arnold Louisa J 22	Pennington Isaac J 38	10 Jan 1859	(10)
Arnold Mary	Urice Geo	22 Dec 1841	(6)
Arnold Mary 26	Pancake Silas Reese 24	15 Jan 1867	(4) 1/4
Arnold Mary C 22	Brill Emanuel 26	15 Nov 1866	(4) 1/4
Arnold Mary Frances V 20	Lafollette Tiberry Streit 24	13 Apr 1876	(4) 2/8
Arnold Mary Lydia 17	McGee Charles Arthur 21	4 Mar 1896	(4) 2/37
Arnold Mary Susan 21	Shoemaker Jasper 22	14 Sept 1866	(4) 1/3
Arnold Merand Isabella 24	Allamong Jerry Arthur 24	25 Mar 1879	(4) 2/13
Arnold Michael	Sloan Sarah	*16 Feb 1828	(4) 3/3
Arnold Miller Washington 22	Cooper Catharine Magdeliene 18	8 Oct 1871	(4) 2/3
Arnold Minnie Jane 17	Carder Jeremiah Caleb 26	29 Dec 1891	(4) 2/30
Arnold Mollie Chistena 30	Montgomery Eugene 30	1 June 1882	(4) 2/17
Arnold Peter 25	Kelley Martha Ann 23	9 Jan 1866	(4) 1/2
Arnold Rachel	Kline Samuel J	16 Sept 1842	(5)
Arnold Rebecca 43	Roderick Abraham 58	27 Mar 1866	(4) 1/3
Arnold Rob't	Shoemaker T	14 Feb 1839	(6)
Arnold Robert	Shoemaker Tirzah	14 Feb 1840	(5)
Arnold Robert H 24	Shoemaker Maggie A 19	4 July 1872	(4) 2/3
Arnold Samuel	Parker Nancy		(1) 20 Jan 1838

Name #1	Name #2	Date	Source
Arnold Sarah Ann 19	Collins James Perry 27	14 July 1885	(4) 2/20
Arnold Sarah Jane 19	Shanholtzer William Jasper 28	14 Mar 1878	(4) 2/11
Arnold Sol	Leatherman P	18 Nov 1841	(6)
Arnold Solomon	Wine Susan	17 Jan 1839	(1) 1 Feb 1839
Arnold Solomon	Triplett Margaret	9 Apr 1833	(5)
Arnold Susan	Flanigan Dan	7 Jan 1840	(6)
Arnold Susan	Flanagan Daniel	7 Jan 1841	(5)
Arnold Syntha Ann 17	Copp John Russell 24	26 May 1891	(4) 2/29
Arnold Taylor 22	Daugherty Lucinda V 18	18 Oct 1871	(4) 2/3
Arnold William	Spade Mahalah	*31 Dec 1827	(4) 3/63
Aronhalt Wm	Bosley Priscilla	28 Oct 1851	(6)
Arrent Frederick	Hawk Sarah	*19 Apr 1824	(4) 3/25
Artz James Peter 28	Poland Cedena Catharine 21	6 Oct 1873	(4) 2/4
Asbury Mary	Shearer William	*1 Mar 1824	(4) 3/14
Ash Michael	Hass Sarah		(1) 18 Aug 1838
Ashby Bettie	Green George M	23 Nov 1848	(1) 15 Dec 1848
Ashby Mary	Hawley Andrew	21 June 1835	(5)
Ashby Myra Taylor 24	Huffman Jacob Vanmeter 39	1 Dec 1886	(4) 2/22
Ashfield John H 25	Trentor Harriet A 19	19 Jan 1866	(4) 1/2
Ashton Sidney A 20	Pennington William Josephus 25	18 June 1885	(4) 2/20
Athey Amy	Tracy Samuel		(1) 8 Sept 1838
Athey Elizabeth	Tucker William	5 Apr 1827	(5)
Athey Elizabeth	Critton Isaac	*25 Aug 1826	(4) 3/32
Athey John W	Ward Elizabeth		(1) 3 Feb 1838
Athey Joseph	Martin Lavilla	5 Mar 1843	(5)
Athey Nancy	Martin Christopher	22 Jan 1833	(5)
Athey Newton David 30	Shewalter Marietta 21	20 Dec 1876	(4) 2/9
Athey Rachel Virginia 21	Purgit Nashville Summerfield 22	10 Apr 1878	(4) 2/11
Athey Sarah	Deleplain Owen	10 Dec 1828	(5)
Athey Sarah Jane 33	Ludwick James Carter 35	1 Dec 1875	(4) 2/8
Athey Susanna	Tucker Isaac	24 Mar 1830	(5)
Athey Thomas	Frederick Maria	1 Jan 1843	(5)
Athey Thomas Brant 23	Mytinger Caroline Virginia 23	28 Nov 1877	(4) 2/10
Atkins Virginia 19	Davis Robt 24	24 Dec 1872	(4) 2/4
Ault Ida J 26	High John F 28	10 Dec 1899	(4) 2/42
Ault Sarah Alice 24	Flemming James Wilson 44	2 Nov 1898	(4) 2/41
Austin Cornelius Allen 26	Banks Mary 21	17 Dec 1896	(4) 1/41
Austin Henry 24	Mouser Amanda 27	18 Jan 1870	(4) 2/1
Austin Sterling James 25	Fowler Lucy F 23	22 Nov 1882	(4) 1/40
Austin Violet Fleming 16	Warner William 25	24 Feb 1874	(4) 1/38
Ayers Ruth Ann 20	Fisher Richard 29	17 Sept 1874	(4) 1/39
B? Elizabeth Adelphia 18	Pennington Norman F 18	29 Aug 1900	(4) 2/43
Babb Samuel	Johnson Catherine	9 Apr 1838	(5)
Bacon?art Charles	Smith Angeline	16 Sept 1852	(2) 7 Oct 1852
Bacorn Sarah	Height James	30 Dec 1823	(5)
Bacorn William	Likins Hannah	19 June 1838	(5)
Bageant James William 37	Gardner Mary Regina 25	21 Dec 1892	(4) 2/31
Bailey Cora Edith 16	Pultz Albert Fahs 22	11 May 1893	(4) 2/32
Bailey Edgar Tippett 24	Hott Lilly Mabel 24	19 Oct 1893	(4) 2/33
Bailey Edw	McCauley Mary	30 Aug 1821	(6)
Bailey Edward	McCauley Mary	20 Aug 1821	(5)
Bailey Eleanor	Kelly John	30 Aug 1827	(6)

Name #1	Name #2	Date	Source
Bailey Eleanor	Kelly John	*20 Aug 1827	(4) 3/41
Bailey Henry 23	Allen Virginia 22	23 Sept 1874	(4) 1/39
Bailey J W	Whip Elizabeth A	15 June 1848	(6)
Bailey Jacob	Flick Susan	19 Apr 1849	(6)
Bailey James Peter 32	Sanders Milissa Kereebeck 28	18 Sept 1894	(4) 2/34
Bailey Lilly Kate 23	Hines Linley 22	17 June 1897	(4) 2/39
Bailey Robert G 27	Hines Mollie Maloney 22	28 Dec 1899	(4) 2/42
Bailey Thornton	Rotruck M	4 Dec 1856	(6)
Bailey Thornton 62	Iser Della Lee 23	26 Oct 1897	(4) 2/39
Bailey William Warren 24	Hannas Minnie Ray 20	22 July 1891	(4) 2/29
Baily Edward Wright 23	Shoemaker Emma Catherine 20	7 Feb 1894	(4) 2/33
Baird William Nelson 34	Daily Sarah Cornelia 32	21 May 1889	(4) 2/25
Baker ? 38	Strauderman Elizabeth 23	21 Nov 1883	(4) 2/18
Baker Aaron Levi 68	Parrish Mary 54	9 Sept 1879	(4) 2/13
Baker Aaron Levi 72	Hahn Ann 54	4 Nov 1887	(4) 2/24
Baker Albert C 29	Donaldson Catharine R 29	17 May 1882	(4) 2/17
Baker Amanda F 18	Short James D 21	Jan 1857	(10)
Baker Berzealious Honian 23	Wolford Matilda Virginia 21	20 Nov 1873	(4) 2/5
Baker Charles 20	Rosebrough Sallie Rebecca 22	9 Apr 1897	(4) 2/39
Baker Clarisa	Metcalf Hiram	6 Jan 1831	(6)
Baker Cynthia Margaret 16	Anderson Willis 26	20 Mar 1873	(4) 2/4
Baker De Boarnay 21	Harris Bertie 18	25 Dec 1890	(4) 2/28
Baker E C	Long Henry	12 Sept 1848	(6)
Baker Eleanor	Prickett Levi	*22 Oct 1824	(4) 3/48
Baker Eliza Ann 29	Baker Warran 28	29 Dec 1866	(4) 1/4
Baker Enoch	Long Lucy	8 Nov 1836	(6)
Baker Frances 21	Frye James Mason 28	4 Oct 1893	(4) 2/33
Baker Geo	Lyon Ann	21 Feb 1828	(6)
Baker Hezekiah Clagett 24	Saville Rebecca Ann 21	29 Jan 1874	(4) 2/5
Baker Jacob A 35	Clayton Margaret H 25	17 Dec 1867	(4) 1/6
Baker Jacob V 28	Parrill Hannah M 19	12 Apr 1870	(4) 2/1
Baker Jessee	Marshall Rachael	*11 Apr 1826	(4) 3/15
Baker John	McCauley Parthenia	*4 Dec 1826	(4) 3/44
Baker John	Junkins Elizabeth	2 Jan 1823	(6)
Baker John B 28	Emmart Elmira Virginia 18	2 Oct 1873	(4) 2/4
Baker John B 29	Hott Ida 24	3 Feb 1901	(4) 2/44
Baker Joseph	Smith Millie	19 Jan 1837	(6)
Baker Joshua	Smith Mary Ann	5 Mar 1829	(5)
Baker Julia E	Boyd McKendree	12 May 1857	(1) 22 May 1857
Baker Lucy	Short William	*31 July 1827	(4) 3/40
Baker Malinda Lydia 21	Carder John Adam 21	9 Jan 1895	(4) 2/35
Baker Marg Luc Rosetta Lee 18	Parrill Joseph Henry 21	17 Aug 1893	(4) 2/33
Baker Margaret Elizabeth 24	McKee John William 36	2 Feb 1876	(4) 2/8
Baker Mary Catherine 35	Seeders George Washintgon 31	14 Aug 1867	(4) 1/5
Baker Mary Eliza Virginia 21	Oats Thomas Edward 25	13 Nov 1898	(4) 2/41
Baker Millie	Rudy Joshua	21 Feb 1819	(6)
Baker Millie	Mudy Joseph	21 Feb 1819	(5)
Baker R	Martin Joseph	19 July 1855	(10)
Baker Rachael	Culp John	*12 June 1826	(4) 3/25
Baker Rachel	Culp John	15 June 1826	(6)
Baker Rebecca	Wilt John M	11 Sept 1845	(6)
Baker Richard	Martin Mary	10 Mar 1825	(5)

Name #1	Name #2	Date	Source
Baker Richard	Martin Mary	*7 Mar 1825	(4) 3/19
Baker Sanford Levi 24	Allamong Sarah Catherine 22	21 Oct 1879	(4) 2/13
Baker Sarah	Smith Joseph M		(1) 13 Jan 1860
Baker Sarah	Likins William	24 Feb 1828	(5)
Baker Sarah 19	Smith Joseph M 21	5 Jan 1860	(10)
Baker Sarah Ellen	Seeders Ebenezer	19 Mar 1857	(1) 27 Mar 1857
Baker Sarah Ellen 19	Seeders Ebenezer 22	Mar 1857	(10)
Baker Sarah Rebecca 20	Sine Floyd Holmes 27	24 Mar 1897	(4) 2/38
Baker Thornton	Arnold Barbary	3 Dec 1837	(5)
Baker Virginia C 24	Pownell F M 27	26 Oct 1868	(4) 1/7
Baker Warran 28	Baker Eliza Ann 29	29 Dec 1866	(4) 1/4
Baker Wm A 30	Delinger Liza 21	28 Feb 1872	(4) 2/3
Baldwin Laura F 16	Ganoe Thomas Wesley 21	22 Nov 1892	(4) 2/31
Baldwin William 33	Melon Victory 21	25 Dec 1865	(4) 1/2
Ball Frances Elizabeth 25	Jones John Clay 45	19 Oct 1898	(4) 2/41
Bane Abner	Whip Elizabeth	*21 Feb 1826	(4) 3/13
Bane Abner	Long Elizabeth	18 Dec 1834	(6)
Bane Elizabeth	Davis Alfred	30 Nov 1843	(6)
Bane Geo	Thrush Mary	26 June 1828	(6)
Bane George	Head Sarah C	15 Jan 1850	(6)
Bane George	Harison Cathleen	26 June 1828	(5)
Bane George	Head Sarah C	15 Jan 1846	(5)
Bane George	Thrash Margaret	*23 June 1828	(4) 3/16
Bane Zimri	Fink Hester A	6 Dec 1849	(6)
Bank Rhoda 26	Washington John 25	14 Aug 1880	(4) 1/39
Banks Emily 24	Singleton Alexander 25	16 June 1874	(4) 1/39
Banks Emma 17	Coleman John David 21	29 Apr 1884	(4) 1/40
Banks Ewing 24	Jackson Nellie 18	14 Apr 1894	(4) 1/41
Banks Isaac 26	Magruder Mary 28	14 Dec 1892	(4) 1/41
Banks Marshall 32	Jackson L R 18	16 Sept 1868	(4) 1/7
Banks Mary 21	Austin Cornelius Allen 26	17 Dec 1896	(4) 1/41
Banks Mary 25	Goshorn Robert 25	23 Oct 1884	(4) 1/40
Banks Mary 31	Moore Richard Henry 32	25 June 1885	(4) 1/40
Banks Robert 26	Kerr Emma 20	20 June 1895	(4) 1/41
Banlon Ann Eliz 26	Whiting Alfred 37	23 Nov 1865	(4) 1/1
Barb Elizabeth 26	Boughman Levi 35	19 Dec 1865	(4) 1/2
Barb Franklin Columbus 22	Shoemaker Anna 18	8 Dec 1880	(4) 2/15
Barb William Henry 26	Shoemaker Mary Elizabeth 19	31 Dec 1891	(4) 2/30
Barger Michael C 32	Lewis Elmira M 21	8 Mar 1866	(4) 1/3
Bark Adam	Kernawbashaw Maria	8 Oct 1818	(5)
Barker John	Junkins Elizabeth	2 Jan 1823	(5)
Barnes Alexander Monroe 22	Ely Frances Della 21	25 Dec 1889	(4) 2/27
Barnes Barbara Ellen 27	Lewis Thomas Jefferson 22	22 Jan 1878	(4) 2/11
Barnes Delilah	Powelson Robert	*13 June 1825	(4) 3/44
Barnes Frank Pirce 26	Hardy Alberta Elizabeth 21	13 May 1879	(4) 2/13
Barnes George William 27	Carder Mary Jane 27	22 Dec 1896	(4) 2/38
Barnes Ida Lee 25	Hamilton George Riley 27	4 Jan 1893	(4) 2/32
Barnes Isabella May 22	Hannas James William 27	16 Feb 1886	(4) 2/21
Barnes James Newton 25	Haines Debbie Virginia 19	17 Jan 1882	(4) 2/17
Barnes Judson Davis 22	Haines Lorena L 19	15 Mar 1899	(40 2/41
Barnes Laverta Ellen 19	McBride Isaac William 22	13 June 1888	(4) 2/25
Barnes Mary Elizabeth 20	Shanholtzer Lorenza Edgar 29	24 Apr 1901	(4) 2/44

Name #1	Name #2	Date	Source
Barnes Minerva Jane 19	Householder Thomas Walker 23	13 May 1877	(4) 2/10
Barnes Oceanna 21	Saville Isaac Johnson 25	30 May 1888	(4) 2/25
Barnes Peter Wording 37	Bowman Matilda Jane 19	7 Mar 1867	(4) 1/4
Barnett Mary	Lyon John	8 Mar 1827	(5)
Barnhouse Andrew	Smith R	17 Nov 1831	(6)
Barnhouse Elizabeth	Green John	25 Aug 1841	(5)
Barnhouse Elizabeth	Green John	25 Aug 1840	(6)
Barnhouse F A	Kisner Bar'y	4 Sept 1845	(6)
Barnhouse L	Purnel Samuel	2 Oct 1851	(6)
Barnhouse Lavina	Purnel Samuel	2 Oct 1850	(5)
Barnhouse M	Tasker Isaac	15 Oct 1839	(6)
Barnhouse M P	Myers Jane	24 Oct 1849	(6)
Barnhouse Mariam	Tacker Isaac	15 Oct 1840	(5)
Barr John Martin 23	Sirbaugh Mary Elizabeth 18	21 Aug 1888	(4) 2/25
Barrack George	Paris Elizabeth		(1) 28 Feb 1839
Barrack Mary	Dixon Thos	5 Sept 1833	(6)
Barrett Charlotte	Eaton John		(1) 7 July 1838
Barrett Eleanor	Slonaker Michael	*16 aPR 1827	(4) 3/26
Barrett Florence C 28	Whitlock Darius Minor 49	19 Sept 1895	(4) 2/36
Barrett Henry Preston 23	Hawkins Margaret Ann 21	*21 Nov 1870	(4) 2/2
Barrett Rebecca Elizabeth 19	Shanholtzer Martin 28	17 Feb 1869	(4) 1/38
Barrett Samuel Worthington 23	Powell Elizabeth 16	6 Mar 1877	(4) 2/9
Barrett William Scott 17	Powell Mary Alverty 19	17 Oct 1876	(4) 2/9
Barrick Caroline	Ryan Jas	3 Oct 1859	(6)
Barrick Caroline	Ryan James	3 Oct 1860	(5)
Barrick Jacob	Tasker M J	29 Nov 1848	(6)
Barrick John	Kabrick Reb'a	12 Apr 1843	(6)
Barrick Matilda	Frazier Fred	25 Aug 1843	(6)
Barrick Susan	Smith Peter	20 Mar 1817	(6)
Barrott Rhoda	Shivers John	*17 Jan 1825	(4) 3/9
Barrott Samuel	Slane Milly	*23 Aug 1825	(4) 3/55
Barthlow J P		4 Sept 1828	(5)
Bartlett John 24	Smith Rosa 23	3 Feb 1875	(4) 1/39
Bartlett R F B 28	Carder John 21	23 Dec 1869	(4) 1/38
Bartlett Thos	Cundiff Sarah	23 Dec 1821	(6)
Bartlett Vincent 21	Brumball Katie 23	8 Dec 1872	(4) 2/4
Bartlow Eunice	Wallace Charles	21 Aug 1822	(6)
Bartlow J P	Harrison C	4 Sept 1828	(5)
Batsen Daniel L 24	Fields Margaret Henrietta 24	26 Feb 1890	(4) 2/27
Batt John W 52	Sechrist Margaret C 49	30 June 1898	(4) 2/40
Bauer Frederick William 25	Parker Nannie 28	25 Mar 1896	(4) 2/37
Bauer Peter	Poland M A	13 Apr 1859	(6)
Bauers Arthalinda 33	Duffey John W 54	17 Oct 1865	(4) 1/1
Baxter R B	Whip Sarah	23 Sept 1851	(6)
Baxter R B	Whipp Sarah	23 Sept 1850	(5)
Baylis Sanford 37	Rudolph Emanda E 22	13 Mar 1869	(4) 1/38
Beall Ella V 27	Stackhouse Stephen P 38	31 Oct 1871	(4) 2/3
Beals John	George Maria	20 Aug 1845	(5)
Beals Virginia	Moody William	21 Mar 1846	(5)
Beals Virginia	Moody Wm	21 Mar 1850	(6)
Bean Aaron Leslie 26	Bean Lucy M 17	5 Feb 1896	(4) 2/36
Bean Amos Seymour 22	Howdyshell Bertha Ann 18	1 Mar 1896	(4) 2/37

Name #1	Name #2	Date	Source
Bean Andrew	Roberts Eleanor	24 Feb 1820	(6)
Bean Ann Rebecca 23	Garard Wm H 28	15 Mar 1866	(4) 1/3
Bean Bennet	Marshall Ann	*15 Sept 1827	(4) 3/46
Bean Catherine	Buckaloo Jas	28 Oct 1827	(6)
Bean Chloa Ann Virginia 24	Whiteman Charles Bradford 35	18 May 1892	(4) 2/31
Bean Christian 20	Selden William Henry 23	10 Apr 1888	(4) 2/25
Bean Edward Thomas 28	Roberson Fannie Eleanora 23	27 Dec 1893	(4) 2/33
Bean Elizabeth	Burgess Jas	27 June 1824	(6)
Bean Elizabeth	Burgess James	*25 June 1824	(4) 3/36
Bean Erasmus 58	McKeever Mollie 35	2 Oct 1884	(4) 2/20
Bean Frederick Wellington 23	Haines Rebecca Jane 18	21 Jan 1869	(4) 1/38
Bean George Welby 24	Frye Nora Ellen 19	25 Dec 1889	(4) 2/27
Bean Harriet Elizabeth 40	Moton Joseph 57	30 May 1893	(4) 2/32
Bean Henry	Bosley Julia	18 Dec 1831	(6)
Bean Henry Franklin 28	Haines Della C 26	23 Dec 1897	(4) 2/40
Bean John 48	Howdyshell Rebecca E 34	4 July 1886	(4) 2/22
Bean John Warren 56	Orndorff Harriet Elizabeth 35	10 Nov 1885	(4) 2/21
Bean Joseph 28	Garrett Matilda J 25	19 Apr 1866	(4) 1/3
Bean Lucy M 17	Bean Aaron Leslie 26	5 Feb 1896	(4) 2/36
Bean Luther Arnold 21	Hines Sarah 23	21 Mar 1893	(4) 2/32
Bean Lydia	Bosley David	14 Aug 1845	(6)
Bean Mary	Bosley John C	18 Mar 1827	(6)
Bean Mary	Bosley J	30 Dec 1847	(6)
Bean Mary	Bosely John C	*16 Mar 1827	(4) 3/18
Bean Rebecca	Ryan William	3 August 1837	(1) 19 Aug 1937
Bean Samuel Bell 29	Loy Minerva Charlotte 23	27 Dec 1899	(4) 2/42
Bean Sol	Shillingburg Eliz	19 Jan 1837	(6)
Bean Vinora 18	Whiteman Robert Elijah 26	30 July 1890	(4) 2/28
Bean William Harvey 20	Lee Francelia Antoinette 19	7 June 1893	(4) 2/32
Bean Wm	Bosley Priscilla	21 Feb 1854	(6)
Beatty Abraham 32	Shingleton Elizabeth 33	8 Nov 1899	(4) 2/42
Beatty Hugh 25	Starns Nancy Ann 21	20 Feb 1878	(4) 2/11
Beatty Isaac 22	Pownall Rosa Virginia 19	9 Feb 1887	(4) 2/23
Beatty John Henry 33	Haines Sarah C 25	20 Mar 1884	(4) 2/19
Beaver John E 25	Shearwood Ida 20	8 Sept 1886	(4) 2/22
Beaver William	Blackburn	14 Aug 1828	(5)
Beaver Wm	Blackburn E	21 Aug 1828	(6)
Bedinger Christina Margaret 20	Shanholtzer Noah 28	17 Nov 1873	(4) 2/5
Bedinger Joseph Bennett 27	Daugherty Mary Elizabeth 18	21 Oct 1885	(4) 2/21
Been Cathleen	Bucklew James	28 Oct 1827	(5)
Beery Elizabeth C 25	Largent Benj Offutt 39	13 Dec 1866	(4) 1/4
Beery Jacob Deneal 23	Haines Zulema Hester 22	28 Apr 1874	(4) 2/6
Beery Sallie Elizabeth 20	Leith John William 28	20 Dec 1876	(4) 2/9
Beery William Benjamin 23	Loy Mamie Estella 19	11 Apr 1900	(4) 2/42
Belford Mary Ann 38	Ginevan David 56	*16 Apr 1869	(4) 1/38
Belford Mary Ann 38	Ginevan David 56	*16 Apr 1867	(4) 2/1
Belt James S	Strawer Julia Ann		(1) 29 Sept 1838
Benear Belle 31	Short Joseph Calvin 34	5 Aug 1891	(4) 2/29
Bennet James M	Gilbert Eliz	24 Sept 1846	(6)
Bennett Ann Maria 25	Kidwell Jonathan 37	12 Jan 1867	(4) 1/4
Bennett Charles Holland 24	Edwards Mary Cordelia 21	16 Mar 1892	(4) 2/30
Bennett Chas Newton Dill 20	Blaker Nannie Offutt 20	22 Sept 1888	(4) 2/25

Name #1	Name #2	Date	Source
Bennett Edward 22	Largent Mrs Eliza J 26	20 Oct 1892	(4) 2/31
Bennett Helen J 25	Eaton Elijah E 26	14 May 1887	(4) 2/23
Bennett James Arthur 21	Largent Mary Louisa 19	1 Mar 1887	(4) 2/23
Bennett Job 41	Whitacre Elizabeth Ellen 43	24 Mar 1890	(4) 2/27
Bennett John	Grapes Catharine	*19 Dec 1826	(4) 3/47
Bennett John Brundell 29	Whitlock Lottie Gertrude 19	23 Oct 1890	(4) 2/28
Bennett Laura Elizabeth 20	McDonald William Marion 23	5 Oct 1893	(4) 2/33
Bennett Lucy Maria 28	Peasmaker Isaac Newton 35	10 Sept 1885	(4) 2/21
Bennett Margaret 50	Miles John Loy 40	9 Dec 1879	(4) 2/13
Bennett Maria	Grapes John	*13 Dec 1828	(4) 3/45
Bennett Martin Luther 23	Moreland Margaret 20	22 Nov 1860	(10)
Bennett Philip Emanuel 24	Whitacre Mary E 16	22 Mar 1896	(4) 2/37
Bennett S M J J 31	Nelson Jas E 37	9 Apr 1868	(4) 1/6
Bennett Silvanus 36	Roberson Rebecca Ann 35	29 Jan 1867	(4) 1/4
Bennett Virginia Belle 22	Kidwell Deskin Abraham 21	8 Mar 1888	(4) 2/24
Bennett William	Wolford Isabella	*4 Oct 1827	(4) 3/50
Berkheimer Henry L 50	Orndorff Elizabeth Virginia 29	*4 Nov 1878	(4) 2/12
Berkheimer Lillie Elizabeth 17	Pugh Jesse Webster 20	30 Aug 1877	(4) 2/10
Berry Hannah	Salters John	11 Apr 1832	(6)
Berry James	Larimore Rachel	*1 Oct 1827	(4) 3/49
Berry Lessie C 22	Purgit Edgar C 25	26 May 1894	(4) 2/34
Berry Samuel	Larimore Elizabeth	*18 July 1825	(4) 3/48
Berry Thomas	Patch Synthy A	13 Nov 1823	(5)
Berry William	Williamson Mary	*20 Dec 1827	(4) 3/59
Berry William Richard 28	Taylor Maggie Elizabeth 23	22 Feb 1882	(4) 2/17
Betson James W 37	Kidwell Margaret Casandra 30	19 Mar 1889	(4) 2/26
Betson Mary Ann 19	Day Jonathan 27	5 Aug 1875	(4) 2/7
Betterton Margaret	Smoot Norman	*16 Aug 1825	(4) 3/53
Bias Joseph 21	Snigers Milly 19	21 Oct 1865	(4) 1/1
Bias Joseph 26	Smith Ellen 40	13 Apr 1871	(4) 1/38
Bias Joseph 42	Fairfax Hannah 22	30 Aug 1883	(4) 1/40
Bias Maria Ann 22	Feilds Walter 22	*29 Dec 1873	(4) 1/38
Bias Mary 31	Hoard James 54	14 Apr 1870	(4) 1/38
Bidinger C Catharine 18	Kackley Chas P 20	22 Feb 1870	(4) 2/1
Bidinger Sarah Jane 23	Keller Napolen Bonaparte 23	19 Dec 1878	(4) 2/12
Bierkamp Freddie Virginia 20	Davis David Lewis 37	21 June 1899	(4) 2/41
Bigan Esther Jane 21	Webster Joseph 25	22 Apr 1875	(4) 1/39
Billmyre Richard Dabney 27	Slonaker Clara Elizabeth 23	7 June 1883	(4) 2/18
Birch Samuel 22	Ruckman Hannah 19	16 Nov 1868	(4) 1/7
Bird Mary Ann 19	Haines Silas 40	12 Nov 1878	(4) 2/12
Biser Amanda Jane 16	Walker David Frederick 21	30 Jan 1881	(4) 2/15
Biser Charles Henry 21	Hartman Susan Catharine 21	10 Mar 1880	(4) 2/14
Biser Cora Ellen 19	Charlton Mory Lee 22	20 Dec 1899	(4) 2/42
Biser Edward Taylor 22	Foltz Esther Ann 22	14 Oct 1874	(4) 2/6
Biser Hannah 23	Breinig John 28	23 Oct 1877	(4) 2/10
Biser John Wesley 25	Rinker Annie 22	8 Feb 1893	(4) 2/32
Biser Laura Edna 21	White George Solomon 22	31 Oct 1898	(4) 2/41
Biser Martin Miller 21	Foltz Martha Ellen 24	10 May 1882	(4) 2/17
Biser Silas 21	Staggs Mary Elizabeth 18	18 Feb 1874	(4) 2/5
Bisor M A	Culp Wm	29 May 1855	(6)
Bizer John	Stemple Sarah Elizabeth	10 Mar 1859	(1) 1 Apr 1859
Bizer Julia Ann 17	Whiteman Edward W 25	6 Nov 1872	(4) 2/4

Name #1	Name #2	Date	Source
Bizer Mary	Stewart James	*23 June 1826	(4) 3/28
Black John	White Betsey	*27 Sept 1825	(4) 3/61
Blackburn	Beaver William	14 Aug 1828	(5)
Blackburn Bertie Frances 31	Messick Frank 45	10 May 1899	(4) 2/41
Blackburn E	Beaver Wm	21 Aug 1828	(6)
Blackburn E G	Rotruck S M	19 Sept 1839	(6)
Blackburn E G	Rotruck Susan M	19 Sept 1840	(5)
Blackburn Han	Fleming Jas	13 May 1862	(6)
Blackburn Hannah	Fleming James	13 June 1862	(5)
Blackburn James	Spencer Susan E	20 Jan 1853	(6)
Blackburn Jas	Sollars Eliz	8 Oct 1840	(6)
Blackburn Jas	Rotruck S C	26 Dec 1842	(6)
Blackburn John	Rawlings C	18 Nov 1830	(6)
Blackburn M	Gatige Wm	23 Sept 1827	(6)
Blackburn M	Sheets James	30 Mar 1837	(6)
Blackburn Maggie A 24	Hartman Josiah 22	23 Feb 1897	(4) 2/38
Blackburn N	Vandiver John	19 May 1831	(6)
Blackburn S	Idleman Henry	21 Nov 1839	(6)
Blackburn Susan	Idleman Henry	21 Nov 1840	(5)
Blackburn Thomas	Harrison C E	26 Feb 1861	(5)
Blackburn W H	Spencer Eliza	24 Mar 1853	(6)
Blackman David	Slane Rebecka	*3 Jan 1825	(4) 3/2
Blackman James Samuel 26	Kuykendall Mary Hopkins 26	19 Sept 1888	(4) 2/25
Blake John W 23	Heiroumous E C 22	13 Jan 1868	(4) 1/6
Blake Samuel V	Vandiver Nancy Mrs		(2) 9 Apr 1857
Blaker Ada May 17	Orndorff William Wesley 28	28 July 1889	(4) 2/26
Blaker James Fenton 27	Pugh Ida Z 24	16 Oct 1873	(4) 2/5
Blaker Mary E 35	Orndorff Julius Waddle 26	12 Oct 1876	(4) 2/9
Blaker Matilda Catharine 24	Oglesby John Davis 24	26 Dec 1878	(4) 2/12
Blaker Nannie Offutt 20	Bennett Chas Newton Dill 20	22 Sept 1888	(4) 2/25
Blaker Portia Jane 23	Oglesby Daniel Wesley 27	16 Oct 1873	(4) 2/5
Bland James 27	McIlwee Mary Jane 23	14 Nov 1872	(4) 2/4
Blanton Erastus See 27	Snyder Anna 26	21 Dec 1869	(4) 2/1
Bliss Mary Elizabeth 20	Clingerman Isaac 26	3 Apr 1888	(4) 2/24
Bloom Thomas D 22	Offutt Edith 17	22 Jan 1896	(4) 2/36
Bloss Katie Ann 19	Long Adam Henry 26	*14 Dec 1882	(4) 2/18
Bloss William G 21	Roach Eliza E 26	20 Sept 1900	(4) 2/43
Bloxham James William 52	Rudolph Rebecca Susan 42	6 Oct 1897	(4) 2/39
Bloxham Mahala 52	Smith Joseph 71	19 Apr 1866	(4) 1/3
Blue Annie R 21	Blue Marcellus 28	26 Dec 1877	(4) 2/11
Blue Bettie 17	Long Thomas Garret 28	29 Mar 1887	(4) 2/23
Blue Gregg Susan 16	Koerner Frederick Sydenham 27	2 Dec 1880	(4) 2/15
Blue Hannah Kuykendall 20	Hass Thomas Sommerville 24	29 Oct 1872	(4) 2/3
Blue James Henry 33	Washington Sarah Gertrude 26	29 Nov 1881	(4) 2/17
Blue John 33	Fox Ann E 31	18 Jan 1868	(4) 1/6
Blue Julia Ann	Flanagan John	1 Jan 1838	(1) 20 Jan 1838
Blue Kirk 23	Stickley Sarah Virginia 22	30 June 1889	(4) 2/26
Blue Louise 25	Lupton J G F 26	27 Nov 1867	(4) 1/6
Blue Marcellus 28	Blue Annie R 21	26 Dec 1877	(4) 2/11
Blue Mary Virginia 27	Ansell Elmer Woodward 24	12 Sept 1887	(4) 2/24
Blue Mary Virginia 40	Houser David Augustus 40	27 Feb 1896	(4) 2/36
Blue Michael M 47	Sheetz Mary Virginia 30	15 Sept 1886	(4) 2/22

Name #1	Name #2	Date	Source
Blue Mrs Susan 29	Taylor Wm F 31	18 Dec 1877	(4) 2/10
Blue Sallie 24	Herriott Isaac 35	24 Jan 1877	(4) 2/9
Blue Susan E 41	Friut Edward W 50	4 Nov 1873	(4) 2/5
Blue Uriah	Inskeep Rebecca		(1) 8 Sept 1838
Blue Ursula 26	Fox William Vause 30	21 Oct 1874	(4) 2/6
Blue William 44	Harden Catherine 24	27 Sept 1866	(4) 1/4
Blue Zachariah	Ruckman Mary Ann	*20 Feb 1826	(4) 3/11
Bobo Catherine	Liller Emmanuel	8 Mar 1858	(6)
Bobo Ezra Bucy 22	Hartman Estella May 19	17 Apr 1898	(4) 2/40
Bobo George 35	Raines Isabel 18	22 Jan 1873	(4) 2/4
Bobo Herman Faulkner 21	Roadcap Columbia Elizabeth 17	1 Oct 1898	(4) 2/40
Bobo Isaac Gibson 27	High Mary Ellen 24	28 Dec 1881	(4) 2/17
Bobo Jackson 22	Michels Amanda 21	24 Jan 1866	(4) 1/2
Bobo Joseph 26	Cunningham Carroll Rebecca 25	29 Mar 1871	(4) 2/2
Bobo Mary	McNemar Phil	18 Mar 1830	(6)
Bobo Rebecca	Summers John	* 18 Feb 1828	(4) 3/4
Bobo Washington	Liller Sarah	31 Aug 1836	(6)
Bobo William H 21	Robey Rebecca 21	17 June 1860	(10)
Bodine George 26	Long Sarah Francis 17	21 Aug 1865	(4) 1/1
Bogle Peggy	Burgess John	2 Mar 1818	(5)
Bogle Wm	Mills Mary	8 Jan 1846	(6)
Boher Richard Singleton 25	Payne Ellen B 19	27 Sept 1887	(4) 2/24
Boher Thomas Jefferson 26	Brelsford Amanda V Bell 23	21 Jan 1894	(4) 2/33
Boher Thomas Jefferson 21	Crock Margaret Elizabeth 18	15 Aug 1888	(4) 2/25
Boherer Arrete 25	Hook Thomas Edward 29	28 Apr 1897	(4) 2/39
Bohrer Anthony 23	Shanholtzer Mary Martha Jane 22	19 Oct 1893	(4) 2/33
Bohrer Eliza Elizabeth 21	Allen Andrew Fenton 23	9 Oct 1890	(4) 2/28
Bohrer Minnie Ann 22	Milburn William T 23	21 Nov 1897	(4) 2/39
Boley Catherine	Smeltz William	2 Nov 1822	(5)
Boley John William 25	Tower Lidia Frances 21	30 Mar 1880	(4) 2/14
Boley M Ellen 19	Pickering John L	7 May 1873	(4) 2/4
Boling H	Greenwalt Peter	13 Dec 1859	(6)
Boling Henrietta	Greenwalt Peter	13 Dec 1860	(5)
Boman C 44	Hott Geo 56	16 Oct 1868	(4) 1/7
Bond Thomas	Moore Sallie	16 June 1822	(5)
Bond Thos	Moore Sallie	15 June 1822	(6)
Bonham Samuel	Malcom Maria	*25 Dec 1827	(4) 3/60
Bonney Adaline 47	Kreemer Andrew Jackson 65	2 Apr 1889	(4) 2/26
Bonney Martha Jane 24	Whitacre Silas Jeremare 20	3 June 1899	(4) 2/41
Bonny Mary Agnes 22	Herndon George Love 27	12 June 1879	(4) 2/13
Boone James Daniel 32	Swartz Sarah Catharine 26	24 Apr 1892	(4) 2/30
Boor Caroline 20	Hudson Robert B 22	20 Dec 1871	(4) 2/3
Bosely John C	Bean Mary	*16 Mar 1827	(4) 3/18
Bosley Alice	Arnholt Andrew	*3 July 1824	(4) 3/38
Bosley Catherine	Sweltz Wm	28 Nov 1822	(6)
Bosley Daniel	McCauley Anna	8 Mar 1822	(6)
Bosley Daniel	Shields M J	6 Apr 1848	(6)
Bosley David	Bean Lydia	14 Aug 1845	(6)
Bosley David	McCauley Annie	8 Mar 1822	(5)
Bosley Eleanor	Elleburger Thomas	17 June 1828	(5)
Bosley Hanah	Bosley Henry	29 Jan 1839	(6)
Bosley Hannah	Bosley Henry	29 Jan 1840	(5)

Name #1	Name #2	Date	Source
Bosley Henry	Bosley Hannah	29 Jan 1840	(5)
Bosley Henry	Bosley Hanah	29 Jan 1839	(6)
Bosley J	Bean Mary	30 Dec 1847	(6)
Bosley John C	Bean Mary	18 Mar 1827	(6)
Bosley Julia	Bean Henry	18 Dec 1831	(6)
Bosley Nancy	Roberts John	11 June 1829	(6)
Bosley P	Covan Johnson	25 May 1838	(6)
Bosley Phil	Harris Nancy	8 Sept 1839	(5)
Bosley Philip	Harris Nancy	18 Sept 1838	(6)
Bosley Polly	Cononavan Johnson	25 May 1839	(5)
Bosley Priscilla	Bean Wm	21 Feb 1854	(6)
Bosley Priscilla	Aronhalt Wm	28 Oct 1851	(6)
Bosley Priscilla	Earnholt William	28 Oct 1850	(5)
Bosley Robert	James Jemima	6 Jan 1820	(6)
Bosley Solomon	Liller Mary A	15 Apr 1847	(6)
Bosley Tobias	Roberts Elizabeth	1840	(5)
Bosly Adam	Pumory Ruth	13 Sept 1843	(5)
Bosly Nancy	Evans Jacob	22 Sept 1839	(5)
Bosly Phebe	Tevalt Isaac	25 Oct 1832	(5)
Boswell F Reazin Shepherd 37	Milslagle Mary Jane 34	31 Dec 1889	(4) 2/27
Bott George Marion 22	McKee Bertha 20	7 Sept 1895	(4) 2/36
Boughman Levi 35	Barb Elizabeth 26	19 Dec 1865	(4) 1/2
Bovey Henry A	Stine Mary E	14 May 1857	(1) 22 May 1857
Bowen Amelia Whilmina 20	Diehl Louis 30	29 Jan 1867	(4) 1/4
Bowen Chas G	Parsons M C	7 Feb 1853	(6)
Bowen Henry Leaf 24	Iser Hannah Catharine 20	24 May 1880	(4) 2/14
Bowens Joseph 25	Sims Rebecca F 24	15 Oct 1874	(4) 2/6
Bower Charles G	Parsons M C	7 Feb 1853	(5)
Bowers Geo W 23	Hardy Mary C 28	17 Jan 1866	(4) 1/2
Bowers John William 29	Kesner Christina Virginia 20	15 Oct 1891	(4) 2/30
Bowers R I E Melchora	Rudolph Jacob	4 Oct 1864	(8)
Bowles Carrie Belle 19	Ruckman Granville Armstrong 30	12 Feb 1878	(4) 2/11
Bowles Stewart B 26	Smith Henrietta 18	15 Apr 1868	(4) 1/6
Bowley Emma 35	Marpole James Madison 44	19 Dec 1899	(4) 2/42
Bowley James 22	Short Caroline Virginia 17	5 Feb 1880	(4) 2/14
Bowman Andrew	McBride Margaret	*22 Mar 1827	(4) 3/22
Bowman Charles Edward 22	Heare Mrs Minnie Lula 27	10 Sept 1895	(4) 2/36
Bowman Geo	Peatt Rachel	15 Mar 1827	(6)
Bowman George	Peatt Rachael	*13 Mar 1827	(4) 3/17
Bowman George 27	Shingleton Jemima 20	19 Sept 1872	(4) 2/3
Bowman George 31	Sibole ? 32	4 Sept 1860	(10)
Bowman George Washington 27	Sheetz Sallie Ann 28	17 Oct 1871	(4) 2/3
Bowman Hannah Elizabeth 26	Smarr James Lawrence 22	22 Feb 1877	(4) 2/9
Bowman Harriet Ann 26	Ganoe James Marion 34	6 Mar 1889	(4) 2/26
Bowman Isaac Peter 23	Dowman Matilda 24	23 Nov 1881	(4) 2/16
Bowman J Edward 23	Wolford Rosa Lee 23	19 Sept 1894	(4) 2/34
Bowman John Wesley 28	Hines Rosa Belle 22	13 Apr 1893	(4) 2/32
Bowman Margaret Frances 16	Sulser William Henry 23	*14 Nov 1879	(4) 2/13
Bowman Margaret Frances 18	Sulser William Henry 23	17 Sept 1881	(4) 2/16
Bowman Martha Elizabeth 18	Martin John Benjamin 21	24 Feb 1885	(4) 2/20
Bowman Martha Ellen 20	Myers Isaac Solomon 25	31 Mar 1874	(4) 2/6
Bowman Mary Estella 20	Martin Thomas Fallen 22	29 May 1898	(4) 2/40

Name #1	Name #2	Date	Source
Bowman Mary Jane 19	Saville Isaac H 23	11 Apr 1872	(4) 2/3
Bowman Matilda Jane 19	Barnes Peter Wording 37	7 Mar 1867	(4) 1/4
Bowman Matilda Jane 17	Meritt Adam 26	18 Dec 1877	(4) 2/11
Boyce Charles Edward 23	Sutherland Louisa 17	4 July 1896	(4) 2/37
Boyce Noah 23	Poland Anne Lee Bertie 17	26 Apr 1898	(4) 2/40
Boyd McKendree	Baker Julia E	12 May 1857	(1) 22 May 1857
Boyle Eliza	Kitzmiller Jas	29 Oct 1843	(6)
Boyle Peggy	Burgess John	26 Mar 1818	(6)
Bracket Apollos	Nixon E	9 Aug 1821	(6)
Bradfield Charlotte Ann 20	McAtee Elisha James 22	18 Feb 1877	(4) 2/9
Bradfield George Washington 32	Hiett Anne 25	25 Oct 1896	(4) 2/37
Bradfield Jas 40	Simpson C Ann 33	27 Feb 1868	(4) 1/6
Bradfield Keziah M 21	Hardy Edgar 20	30 Sept 1894	(4) 2/34
Bradfield Lydia Margaret 35	Maphis Israel 35	15 Nov 1885	(4) 2/21
Bradfield William Ashby 29	Keiter Mary 25	11 Jan 1894	(4) 2/33
Bradford George	Hyatt Sarah	7 July 1831	(5)
Bradford John	Brian Betsey	6 Aug 1828	(5)
Brady Edna Earl 23	Cornwell John J 24	30 June 1891	(4) 2/29
Brady Jno Copsey 22	Seymour Caroline 21	15 Nov 1865	(4) 1/1
Brady Rebecca S 26	Daily John 28	8 Apr 1857	(10)
Brady Rebecca S	Daily John	8 Apr 1857	(1) 10 Apr 1857
Bragg Maria 41	Warrens John 30	6 Mar 1877	(4) 1/39
Braithwaite Frances Marion 24	Pennington Laura Belle 19	18 Apr 1878	(4) 2/11
Brannan William Grant 22	Kerns Margaret Elizabeth 20	31 July 1898	(4) 2/40
Brannon Frances Elizabeth 22	Sirbaugh Uriah Offutt 24	30 Aug 1893	(4) 2/33
Brannon John William 19	Gardner Tesa Belle 16	11 Oct 1888	(4) 2/25
Brant Elijah P	Knight Sarah	13 Oct 1837	(6)
Brant Elizah P	Kight Sarah	13 Oct 1837	(5)
Brant Jno G	Junkins Marg	8 May 1834	(6)
Brant John	Doman Catharine	*10 Jan 1824	(4) 3/7
Brant John G	Parris Elmira	27 Aug 1852	(6)
Brant John G	Ridings M A	27 Aug 1852	(5)
Breinig John 28	Biser Hannah 23	23 Oct 1877	(4) 2/10
Brelsford Amanda V Bell 23	Boher Thomas Jefferson 26	21 Jan 1894	(4) 2/33
Brelsford Benjamin Blaker 27	Moreland Sarah Isadore 20	29 Mar 1877	(4) 2/10
Brelsford Florence Virginia 21	Kerns Nathanial 28	13 May 1877	(4) 2/10
Brelsford Geo W 33	McDonald Rebecca 28	15 Nov 1860	(10)
Brelsford George Washington 19	Wolford Sarah Elizabeth 22	2 Feb 1887	(4) 2/23
Brelsford J F E 34	Alderton Barbara 34	*11 Jan 1872	(4) 2/3
Brelsford James William 23	Richmond Sidney Elizabeth 19	24 Mar 1881	(4) 2/15
Brelsford Margaret Ester 16	Ginivan George Washington 22	28 Nov 1878	(4) 2/12
Brelsford Mary Elizabeth 23	Poland Amos 75	4 Dec 1894	(4) 2/35
Brian Betsey	Bradford John	6 Aug 1828	(5)
Brian Sarah	Moore John	9 Sept 1824	(5)
Brice Nellie Lewis 19	Stump William 25	29 July 1894	(4) 2/34
Brill Al? Luther 24	Spaid Mariah Elizabeth 21	12 Nov 1896	(4) 2/37
Brill Alice Amanda 22	Mason Charles Edward 22	26 June 1879	(4) 2/13
Brill Almira Virginia 24	Kackly Robert Lee 25	27 Dec 1893	(4) 2/33
Brill Amanda Jane 23	Serbaugh Charles Edward 36	13 Aug 1874	(4) 2/6
Brill Amos T 24	Cole Elizabeth 28	20 Dec 1860	(10)
Brill Asbernia Cordelia 20	Lafollette Theodore Clark 25	28 Jan 1886	(4) 2/21
Brill Champion Trone 40	Stephens Margaret Ellen 21	4 Mar 1896	(4) 2/37

Name #1	Name #2	Date	Source
Brill Diantha	Racy Thomas	12 Jan 1863	(8)
Brill Dorsey Clenton 26	Wilson Hannah A A 29	30 Sept 1886	(4) 2/22
Brill Eleanor	Lafollett Bartholomew	*14 Nov 1825	(4) 3/70
Brill Elias A 23	Pennington Sarah Jane 21	13 Nov 1890	(4) 2/28
Brill Eliza C	Grove Cyrus	1 Nov 1859	(8)
Brill Ellen C 39	Edwards Robert 72	*19 Aug 1879	(4) 2/13
Brill Emanuel 26	Arnold Mary C 22	15 Nov 1866	(4) 1/4
Brill Emma Pheby 36	Wolford William 54	2 May 1878	(4) 2/11
Brill Frances Doyle 21	Dunlap Riley Love 21	23 Apr 1899	(4) 2/41
Brill George Clarence 23	Spaid Nellie Love 19	28 Feb 1900	(4) 2/42
Brill Hampton Jefferson 34	McIntyre Lydia Catharine 26	14 Nov 1878	(4) 2/12
Brill Harrison 30	Nixon Ann Elizabeth 30	*13 Dec 1870	(4) 2/2
Brill Harvey P M 24	Anderson Emma C 26	5 July 1888	(4) 2/25
Brill Howard Lee 27	Davis Fannie May 25	1 Jun 1897	(4) 2/39
Brill Isaac	Riggle Catherine	*21 Mar 1825	(4) 3/24
Brill Isaac	Kelso Jane	*20 May 1828	(4) 3/12
Brill Isaac Perry 28	Lochart Louisa Virginia 19	21 Jan 1872	(4) 2/3
Brill Isaiah Branson 38	Park Louisa Jane 25	6 Mar 1894	(4) 2/33
Brill James Abraham 28	Kelsoe Ida Cornelia 28	14 Apr 1887	(4) 2/23
Brill James William 24	Cline Fanny Bell 25	21 Feb 1884	(4) 2/19
Brill John Wesley 27	Cooper Eva Ellen 27	28 Dec 1876	(4) 2/9
Brill Jonathan Henry 24	Hannum Emma Jane 20	28 Nov 1891	(4) 2/30
Brill Lernon Hilkie 21	Spaid Sarah Eleanora 19	3 Mar 1887	(4) 2/23
Brill Lewis Henry 24	French Susan Taylor 18	24 Dec 1895	(4) 2/36
Brill Lewis Walter 24	Spaid Fannie Hayes 25	14 Nov 1894	(4) 2/35
Brill Lydia Catharine 23	Spaid Jacob Franklin 35	11 Jan 1894	(4) 2/33
Brill Margaret C 22	Spaid Frederick M 24	13 Dec 1866	(4) 1/4
Brill Margaret E	Spaid John W	2 Mar 1865	(8)
Brill Mary C 23	Lafollcttc Baxter 21	20 Dec 1877	(4) 2/11
Brill Maude Littler 22	Michael David William 38	23 Nov 1896	(4) 2/38
Brill Miranda Catharine 38	Pierce Joseph Wilson 48	3 Sept 1885	(4) 2/21
Brill Rachel A	Garvin Mahlon	19 Feb 1861	(8)
Brill Rachel Ann 28	Rudolph Streit Perry 44	9 Apr 1891	(4) 2/29
Brill Richard 27	Saville Ann Mariah 23	13 Oct 1881	(4) 2/16
Brill Robert Franklin 20	Orndorff Mary Elizabeth 19	19 June 1887	(4) 2/23
Brill Sarah Ellen 22	Anderson Cornelius George 28	7 Jan 1875	(4) 2/6
Brill Smith Reed 32	Creswell Bessie Oaida 36	14 Nov 1894	(4) 2/35
Brill Susan A	Park William	13 Sept 1864	(8)
Brill Thomas Benton 34	Sechrist Nancy 48	28 Aug 1884	(4) 2/19
Brill William Arthur 22	Heare Maria Elizabeth Mrs 24	3 Oct 1880	(4) 2/14
Brill William M	? Ellen 23	22 Feb 1860	(10)
Brill Wm Paul 25	Spaid Ann Maria 19	13 Dec 1866	(4) 1/4
Brinks Benj 46	Coleman Hannah 21	23 Nov 1865	(4) 1/1
Broadwater N	Miller Jacob	20 Jan 1832	(6)
Brook Martha Amanda 22	Pugh Zachary Taylor 30	28 Mar 1877	(4) 2/10
Brookhart Rhody	Trevett Joseph	*9 Sept 1825	(4) 3/58
Brooks Annie Bell 24	Latham William Dye 53	11 Jan 1891	(4) 2/29
Brooks Benjamin 28	Keller Lucretia Ellen 24	4 Sept 1865	(4) 1/1
Brooks Charles 45	Stewart Elizabeth 28	9 Oct 1873	(4) 2/4
Brooks Harriett 21	Dandridge Geo Washington 25	27 Dec 1870	(4) 1/38
Brooks Jeremiah Calvin 21	Whitacre Bessie Fernon 15	1 July 1900	(4) 2/42
Brooks Martha 28	Jones Allen 45	Sept 1894	(4) 1/41

Name #1	Name #2	Date	Source
Brooks Samuel David 24	Kline Almira Jamima C 24	9 Feb 1882	(4) 2/17
Brown Amanda B 17	Lewis William Albert 22	8 Aug 1876	(4) 2/8
Brown Ann M	Hansbough	*2 Aug 1828	(4) 3/19
Brown David William 19	Jewell Ida Belle 17	21 Sept 1885	(4) 2/21
Brown Ephraim 20	Didiwick Jennie Savilla 18	23 Mar 1895	(4) 2/35
Brown Francis Marion 24	Stewart Edna Earl 18	13 Nov 1891	(4) 2/30
Brown Frank 47	Webster Harriet 41	16 Sept 1889	(4) 1/40
Brown Frank Marion 30	Moreland Harriet Alverta 19	*16 Sept 1899	(4) 2/42
Brown George Washington 23	Poland Zulema Catharine I 20	1 Nov 1888	(4) 2/25
Brown Hattie Jane 20	Shoemaker James Beckwith 32	7 Jan 1885	(4) 2/20
Brown James	Tasker Mynta	30 Nov 1820	(6)
Brown Jno	Taylor Parentha	13 Sept 1828	(6)
Brown John	Taylor Catherine	*13 Sept 1828	(4) 3/25
Brown Lucinda	Carder William		(1) 8 Sept 1838
Brown Lula 22	Singleton Alexander 20	6 July 1896	(4) 1/41
Brown Marg	Metcalf L R	30 Dec 1837	(6)
Brown Margaret	Metcalf Ludwell		(1) 20 Jan 1838
Brown Mary 21	Taylor Isaac 22	20 Sept 1879	(4) 1/39
Brown Mary F 19	Davis Samuel H 24	29 Apr 1869	(4) 2/1
Brown Mary F 19	Davis Samuel H 24	29 Apr 1869	(4) 1/38
Brown Mary Malinda 20	Lewis Isaac Ferran 25	17 Aug 1875	(4) 2/7
Brown Mary Matilda 21	Hartman Isaac Daniel 25	5 Sept 1888	(4) 2/25
Brown Melissa Caroline 24	Moreland Charles W 23	25 Mar 1896	(4) 2/37
Brown Parthenia	Syms Jas	6 June 1848	(6)
Brown Priscilla Frances 30	Heath Jonathan Seymour 27	15 Apr 1891	(4) 2/29
Brown Sarah Catharine 18	Layton ? Lee 23	10 Aug 1885	(4) 2/20
Brown Thomas Jefferson 25	Poland Elizabeth Jane 19	4 Aug 1886	(4) 2/21
Brown William 22	Iser Jane 19	*1 June 1871	(4) 2/2
Brown William Edward 25	Merritt Sarah Catharine 19	29 Dec 1897	(4) 2/40
Bruce Andrew	Lett Jane	23 Aug 1832	(5)
Bruce Florence Bell 28	Rolls David Powel 27	28 Apr 1897	(4) 1/41
Bruce Harriet 28	Marks Edward 29	17 Mar 1898	(4) 1/41
Bruce Hav	Coats M A	27 Aug 1835	(6)
Bruce Minnie B 23	Peters Benjamin F 23	17 July 1886	(4) 1/40
Bruce Upton	Tyzert Lucinda	8 Aug 1843	(5)
Bruce Wm	Salts Catherine	9 Nov 1828	(6)
Brumback Mandy Jane 21	Williams Thomas 23	19 Oct 1869	(4) 1/38
Brumball Katie 23	Bartlett Vincent 21	8 Dec 1872	(4) 2/4
Bruner George	Reede Maria	*30 Apr 1827	(4) 3/31
Bryan Ann	Hawes John W	14 May 1857	(2) 21 May 1857
Bryan Florence 22	Shannon Jeremiah Chadwick 25	14 Nov 1871	(4) 2/3
Bryan James Abernathy 35	Yost Emma Lee 20	1 May 1889	(4) 2/26
Buckaloo Jas	Bean Catherine	28 Oct 1827	(6)
Buckaloo Rebecca C 24	Smith Asa 23	11 Oct 1857	(10)
Buckbee Elizah	Hickle Jenetta	4 Apr 1861	(5)
Bucklew Elzy Flournoy 19	Smith Maggie Francis 29	5 Nov 1895	(4) 2/36
Bucklew James	Been Cathleen	28 Oct 1827	(5)
Bucklew Mary Catherine 25	Wolford Robert James 22	15 Oct 1876	(4) 2/9
Bucklew Melissa 20	Loy Robert J 29	24 Jan 1889	(4) 2/26
Bucklew Sarah Jane 23	Fitzwaters Elzy 22	26 Feb 1877	(4) 2/9
Bucklew Silas 22	Peer Mary Lee 20	7 Feb 1885	(4) 2/20
Bucklew William Jasper 21	Shanholtzer Sarah Emily Margaret 18	24 Sept 1891	(4) 2/29

Name #1	Name #2	Date	Source
Buckley Annie L 20	Combs Angus Addison 19	11 June 1898	(4) 2/40
Buckley Minnie Bell 18	Dean Isaac Strait 24	25 May 1898	(4) 2/40
Bull Mary	Stockslager Jacob	*3 Nov 1826	(4) 3/38
Bullett Frank 18	Wills Clara Belle 19	13 Dec 1883	(4) 1/40
Bumcrots Landon	Davy Margaret	14 June 1839	(5)
Bumcrotts J A	Kabrick Peter E	4 June 1850	(5)
Bumgarner Elizabeth Ann 21	Shipman ? 36	22 Dec 1859	(10)
Bumgarner Ellen 47	Racey John 53	10 Feb 1870	(4) 2/1
Buncrots Loudon	Davy Marg	14 June 1838	(6)
Buncrotts J A	Kabrick P E	4 June 1851	(6)
Buncrotz Mary	High Geo	14 Dec 1820	(6)
Bunercrotey Mary	High George	14 Dec 1820	(5)
Bunner James Alexander 35	Slonaker Lettie 23	8 Sept 1895	(4) 2/36
Burgess Caroline	Shillingburg Wash	15 Aug 1852	(5)
Burgess James	Bean Elizabeth	*25 June 1824	(4) 3/36
Burgess Jas	Bean Elizabeth	27 June 1824	(6)
Burgess John	Boyle Peggy	26 Mar 1818	(6)
Burgess John	Bogle Peggy	2 Mar 1818	(5)
Burgess John 30	Shurs Harriet 21	20 Feb 1866	(4) 1/2
Burk Catharine 22	Burk Tasco 40	21 Mar 1867	(4) 1/5
Burk Tasco 40	Burk Catharine 22	21 Mar 1867	(4) 1/5
Burke Robert 24	Morgan Cora 19	23 Dec 1890	(4) 1/41
Burke Thomas Gibson 42	Carruthers Sarah E 42	5 May 1885	(4) 2/20
Burket Mary V 24	Patterson I H F 38	7 Dec 1868	(4) 1/7
Burket Rachael	Dowman Henry	*30 Apr 1825	(4) 3/33
Burkett Jno D 30	Rannalls Elmira 28	21 Sept 1868	(4) 1/7
Burkett John Thomas	Swisher ?	28 Feb 1860	(10)
Burkholder Sarah Ann 27	Cline Samuel Franklin 26	26 Mar 1867	(4) 1/5
Burkitt John	Smoot Mariah	*19 Jan 1824	(4) 3/7
Burner Ruth	Starne Thomas	*27 Dec 1824	(4) 3/55
Burnet M	Steerman Rich	4 Nov 1836	(6)
Burns Morgan	Steinback Sarah	*20 July 1824	(4) 3/40
Burnside John Robert 47	Williamson Mary Ann 45	4 Apr 1886	(4) 2/22
Burton Huldah	Culp Geo	17 Dec 1818	(6)
Burwell Joseph Zarrenton 62	Dean Zulemma Virginia 31	28 Oct 1900	(4) 2/43
Busby Ann	Shelton John N	*29 Oct 1828	(4) 3/35
Busby Margaret	Edwards William		(1) 23 May 1839
Bush Nancy Jane 23	Alexander Albert 23	19 Aug 1874	(4) 1/39
Butler John Franklin 28	Windle Mary Susan 26	12 Aug 1891	(4) 2/29
Butt Leonidas 28	Parker Sarah Elizabeth 22	1 Mar 1870	(4) 2/1
Buzzard ?	Sneathen R	1 Dec 1857	(10)
Buzzard J N	Whiteman S A	3 Apr 1854	(6)
Buzzard Jacob N 30	Whiteman Sarah Ann 24	Apr 1854	(10)
Buzzard Jasper Newton 24	Powell Susan M 19	28 Feb 1867	(4) 1/4
Buzzard Mary Rebecca 29	Tutwiler Samuel Benjamin 32	16 Aug 1899	(4) 2/41
Buzzard Rebecca J 28	Haines Isaac N 27	18 Dec 1866	(4) 1/4
Buzzard William Grant 57	Pepper Caroline Matilda 45	21 Oct 1892	(4) 2/31
Byrd Emanuel Thomas 25	Kline Francelia Ellen 18	31 Mar 1892	(4) 2/30
Byrd Frances Ann	Ambler Wm C		(2) 9 Apr 1857
Byrd Frances Ann	Ambler William C		(1) 10 Apr 1857
Cackley Margaret	Sine Christy	*27 Apr 1825	(4) 3/32
Cade Elizabeth	Newman John C	19 June 1817	(6)

Name #1	Name #2	Date	Source
Caldwell Samuel	Stickley Jane		(1) 5 Dec 1839
Caldwell Susan Jane 20	Trout James Henry 31	2 Aug 1865	(4) 1/1
Calvert Judge Lot 25	Creswell Cordelia Elfrida 21	13 July 1885	(4) 2/20
Campbell Geo	Smith Rebecca	21 Feb 1819	(6)
Campbell Henry Wilson 33	Washington Mary 24	19 Sept 1888	(4) 2/25
Cann Jacob	Doyle Jane	*22 Nov 1828	(4) 3/41
Cannon Rufus Buren 24	McBride Babe 22	7 Sept 1887	(4) 2/23
Canon Martha Jane 21	Edwards John Cram 48	23 Sept 1867	(4) 1/5
Carder Albert Lee 26	Watson Elizabeth Jane 18	19 Apr 1894	(4) 2/34
Carder Anna	Park Geroge	*8 Oct 1827	(4) 3/51
Carder Belle Ann 19	Malone Charles Frederick 26	22 Oct 1885	(4) 2/21
Carder Benjamin Franklin 31	Pownall Elizabeth Jane 23	9 Nov 1880	(4) 2/15
Carder Charlotte	Ely William	*7 Mar 1828	(4) 3/6
Carder Elias Edward 35	Patterson Marian Fernadez 23	31 May 1893	(4) 2/32
Carder Elisha Edward 32	Hardy Anne Catharine 22	12 Oct 1875	(4) 2/7
Carder Elizabeth	Joel Wolverton	*3 May 1825	(4) 3/35
Carder Emma 20	Davis James Marion 23	19 Nov 1879	(4) 2/13
Carder George	Hansbough Maria	*9 June 1825	(4) 3/43
Carder James Henry 41	Haines Mrs Margaret Ann 31	16 Nov 1886	(4) 2/22
Carder James Sanford 23	McDonald Mary Elizabeth 18	19 Oct 1887	(4) 2/24
Carder Jeremiah Caleb 26	Arnold Minnie Jane 17	29 Dec 1891	(4) 2/30
Carder John 21	Bartlett R F B 28	23 Dec 1869	(4) 1/38
Carder John Adam 21	Baker Malinda Lydia 21	9 Jan 1895	(4) 2/35
Carder John Foreman 27	Albright Cora Bell 20	21 Nov 1894	(4) 2/35
Carder Joseph Edgar 23	Cheshire Minnie 16	27 Dec 1882	(4) 2/18
Carder Lafaette Ashby 25	Sanders Mary Susan 21	23 Oct 1889	(4) 2/27
Carder Malinda 20	Adams Jno Wm 29	27 Feb 1866	(4) 1/3
Carder Martha Jane 28	Shanholtzer John Newton 38	20 Nov 1889	(4) 2/27
Carder Mary	Poland John	*9 Mar 1825	(4) 3/20
Carder Mary 22	McDonald George Washington 30	2 Dec 1874	(4) 2/6
Carder Mary Jane 27	Barnes George William 27	22 Dec 1896	(4) 2/38
Carder Matilda Belle 21	Losser John Vincent 29	21 Nov 1882	(4) 2/17
Carder Raliegh 26	Smith Nancy C 19	25 Aug 1875	(4) 1/39
Carder Rebecca 40	Yost Henry 60	3 Feb 1878	(4) 2/11
Carder Rebecca Leath 27	Starnes John Thomas 36	26 Apr 1899	(4) 2/41
Carder Sallie V 23	Kidner Jas W 20	22 Aug 1872	(4) 2/3
Carder Sandford 31	Hannahs Rebecca 25	6 May 1869	(4) 1/38
Carder Sanford 30	Pownal Mary 23	20 Oct 1859	(10)
Carder Sanford 31	Hannahs Rebecca 25	6 May 1869	(4) 2/1
Carder Sarah Elizabeth 24	Shank John Lonas 25	18 Mar 1891	(4) 2/29
Carder Sarah Emily 39	Parrill John Columbus 38	4 Sept 1884	(4) 2/19
Carder Susan Elizabeth 34	Lewis John Granville 34	10 Oct 1888	(4) 2/25
Carder Verdie Virginia 21	Parker Isaac Pierson 21	28 Oct 1894	(4) 2/34
Carder William	Brown Lucinda		(1) 8 Sept 1838
Carder William Baker 28	Nichols Febe Jane 19	7 Jan 1896	(4) 2/36
Carelyle Joseph Edward 26	Martin Mary Jane 21	12 Jan 1870	(4) 2/1
Carier Isaac Everett 30	Racey Sarah Jane	16 Dec 1873	(4) 2/5
Carile Benj F 30	Haines Betsy Ann 24	12 Apr 1866	(4) 1/3
Carlile Mary L 20	Cooper Dan'l M 20	3 Mar 1868	(4) 1/6
Carlile William	Mored Rebeca	*20 Mar 1826	(4) 3/14
Carlisle Emma Belle 23	Emmart William Henry 26	26 Apr 1894	(4) 2/34
Carlyle ? May 18	Wolford Robert Richardson 24	3 Mar 1897	(4) 2/38

Name #1	Name #2	Date	Source
Carlyle Isaac Newton 24	Shanholtzer Lydia Marg Ann 19	29 Sept 1870	(4) 2/2
Carlyle James Edward 23	Coffman Caroline V 24	8 Oct 1867	(4) 1/5
Carlyle Jno W 24	Lupton Hannah L 21	12 Aug 1866	(4) 1/3
Carlyle Martha Anna Bell 21	Landacre Wade Hampton 21	21 Dec 1886	(4) 2/22
Carlyle Martha Jane 16	Haines Isaac Henry 30	22 May 1890	(4) 2/28
Carlyle Sarah Virginia 25	Davis Charles Ashby 25	23 Apr 1893	(4) 2/32
Carmichael Hannah	Doran William	*2 May 1825	(4) 3/34
Carmichael Nancy	Ruckman Thomas	4 Jan 1838	(1) 20 Jan 1838
Carnell Adm	Kitzmiller H C	27 Sept 1859	(6)
Carpenter William	McBride Hannah	*16 Feb 1825	(4) 3/15
Carrol Hannah C 21	Whiteman Edward F 41	12 Sept 1871	(4) 2/3
Carroll Sarah E M 28	Leatherman John Wm 24	24 Nov 1886	(4) 2/22
Carruthers Sarah E 42	Burke Thomas Gibson 42	5 May 1885	(4) 2/20
Carskaddon Elizabeth J	Heard? Henry	19 July 1854	(10)
Carskadon J H	Parker R E	19 Nov 1846	(6)
Carter Albert	Thompson Mary	*6 June 1825	(4) 3/42
Carter Calvin Lycurgus 37	Pepper Frances Emily 29	11 Oct 1893	(4) 2/33
Carter Frederick Abott 23	McDonald Margaret Ellen 19	24 Dec 1879	(4) 2/14
Carter Frederick 34	Starnes Sarah 21	27 Feb 1866	(4) 1/3
Carter Jasper Newton 25	Patterson Alcinda Ann 22	11 June 1877	(4) 2/10
Carter John W 22	Showalter Lydia A 25	15 Feb 1868	(4) 1/6
Carter John William 27	Taylor Jemima 26	5 Mar 1873	(4) 2/4
Carter Robert	Peppers Sophiah	*6 June 1825	(4) 3/40
Case Julia Ann	Hardy John J		(1) 27 Oct 1838
Case Sarah	Allen William	*25 June 1824	(4) 3/35
Cassady Masa	Leadman James	3 June 1830	(6)
Cassady William	Lyon Elizabeth	25 June 1845	(5)
Cassidy Sar A	Harvey Wm	27 Aug 1834	(6)
Cassidy Thomas C	Harvey Elizabeth	27 Dec 1827	(6)
Caster John Luther 23	Davis Bettie 19	8 Apr 1879	(4) 2/13
Cather Edward Washington 24	Morris Lizzie 22	12 May 1897	(4) 2/39
Catlett Elisha William 41	Dern Sarah Catharine 42	14 Feb 1878	(4) 2/11
Catlett Ellen 25	Whitacre Harrison Randolph 24	24 Mar 1896	(4) 2/37
Catlett Hanson	Miller Eliza	5 Jan 1824	(6)
Catlett Zina 27	Sine William H 38	30 Dec 1882	(4) 2/18
Caudy Margaret	Stump Peter	*3 May 1827	(4) 3/32
Caudy Mary E 25	Horn John J 30	27 May 1868	(4) 1/6
Caudy Saray	Pugh Ezra	*13 June 1826	(4) 3/26
Cave Robert Lee 21	Herrell Sarah Frances 19	11 Dec 1890	(4) 2/28
Cedars Thomas	Smith Ann Mariah	25 Aug 1822	(5)
Celp John	Baker Rachel	15 June 1826	(5)
Cessna Samuel	Groves Margaret H	*22 Oct 1825	(4) 3/65
Cessney Samuel	Groves Marg	17 Nov 1825	(6)
Chamberline J A R 25	Spade Frances V 24	19 Dec 1868	(4) 1/7
Chaney Alice Maria 24	Reed Edwin Summerfield 22	25 Dec 1878	(4) 2/12
Chaney Amanda Marsella 19	Garland Oliver 20	21 Dec 1876	(4) 2/9
Chaney Mary Elizabeth 28	Starkey John Frederick 20	25 Dec 1876	(4) 2/9
Chaney Nancy Ann 25	Simpson Hugh Soloman 24	9 June 1880	(4) 2/14
Chaney William J 25	Willison Emma B 22	24 Jan 1895	(4) 2/35
Chapman Ann	McCochlin Daniel	3 July 1838	(1) 14 July 1838
Charlton Burwell 29	Link Eliza Ellen 20	4 Nov 1885	(4) 2/21
Charlton Mory Lee 22	Biser Cora Ellen 19	20 Dec 1899	(4) 2/42

Name #1	Name #2	Date	Source
Cheney David Webster 20	Huff Cornelia Elmira 20	21 Oct 1879	(4) 2/13
Cherry Isaac W 22	Hains Mariah 19	27 Jan 1868	(4) 1/6
Cherry James	Walton Louisa A		(1) 1855
Cherry Mary	Fisher Washington		(1) 20 May 1853
Cheshir Margaret Ann 22	Arnold George Washington 23	23 Feb 1871	(4) 2/2
Cheshir Saml B 23	Orndorff Marthy E 22	27 June 1868	(4) 1/6
Cheshire ? Granville 27	Saville Virginia Price 22	11 Mar 1880	(4) 2/14
Cheshire Abraham 26	Daugherty Eliza 25	18 Dec 1877	(4) 2/11
Cheshire Amanda Belle 28	Corbin Job 24	24 Oct 1894	(4) 2/35
Cheshire Amanda Bell 18	Haines Thomas Hillery 23	*4 May 1883	(4) 2/18
Cheshire Bettie Mellisa 27	Hott John David 25	27 Sept 1883	(4) 2/18
Cheshire Burr William 19	Shingleton Catharine 21	7 Dec 1898	(4) 2/41
Cheshire Delilah	Slane Benjamin	*7 June 1824	(4) 3/31
Cheshire Edward Tarryson 23	Howard Mary Eglatine 17	24 Nov 1894	(4) 2/35
Cheshire Emma 41	Heare Jasper Newton 53	20 Sept 1885	(4) 2/21
Cheshire George Washington 23	Shawin Annie Bell 23	19 Nov 1878	(4) 2/12
Cheshire Ida Susan 19	Haines William 25	1 Jan 1885	(4) 2/20
Cheshire James 19	Starnes Mary H 23	4 July 1889	(4) 2/26
Cheshire John	Dicks Mary	*31 Dec 1827	(4) 3/62
Cheshire John Thomas 22	Kline Louisa Jane 21	28 Nov 1886	(4) 2/22
Cheshire Louisa Virginia 18	Starns Isaac Parsons 23	18 May 1880	(4) 2/14
Cheshire Maltilda Jane 20	Starnes John William 23	15 Oct 1867	(4) 1/5
Cheshire Margaret	Pownal Jasper R	9 Mar 1859	(10)
Cheshire Maria 33	Dean Aaron 22	28 Feb 1868	(4) 1/6
Cheshire Mary Susan 30	Shanholtzer James Fahs 23	2 Nov 1898	(4) 2/41
Cheshire Minnie 16	Carder Joseph Edgar 23	27 Dec 1882	(4) 2/18
Cheshire Nancy Jane	Kerns Jacob		(1) 29 Apr 1853
Cheshire P ? Johnson 21	Grapes Anna Maria 23	5 Oct 1882	(4) 2/17
Cheshire Samuel Lupton 21	Haines Abigail Jane 30	12 Jan 1897	(4) 2/38
Cheshire Samuel James Wm 18	Michael Martha Ann 19	17 Mar 1885	(4) 2/20
Cheshire Samuel	Poston Delila	*29 Nov 1824	(4) 3/53
Cheshire Sara Mariah 21	Cline Hiram Sylvester Lee 22	19 Apr 1883	(4) 2/18
Cheshire Uriah Benj 29	Wilson Emma 26	9 Nov 1869	(4) 2/1
Chesnut Charlotte Rebecca 25	Ranck James McNeil 23	17 Jan 1877	(4) 2/9
Chesshire James Robert 19	McDonald Elizabeth Harriet 23	3 Jan 1877	(4) 2/9
Chilcote Amos 48	Abrill Eliza Jane 38	*1 Dec 1875	(4) 2/8
Chilcott Anne 20	Whitlock Edward Augustus 21	13 Dec 1896	(4) 2/38
Chisholm Mary Ann	McClure James	12 Oct 1837	(1) 28 Oct 1837
Chriswell Elizabeth	Pugh Derias		(1) 30 May 1839
Cison Charles Henry 25	Sniggers Anne 31	29 Dec 1885	(4) 1/40
Clark Gracie Valarie 19	Riley Alonzo Vandorn 22	18 July 1900	(4) 2/43
Clark Hendrix	Rinker Hester	4 June 1828	(5)
Clark James Madison 22	Serbaugh Sarah Alverda 22	26 Mar 1889	(4) 2/26
Clark Lavina	Murphy Isaac	25 July 1833	(6)
Clark Sampson B 55	Peacemaker Sarah E 31	31 Oct 1865	(4) 1/1
Clarke John William 32	McCoy Loula Virginia 28	2 Aug 1900	(4) 2/43
Clayton Emma Frances 21	McCarty William Arthur 23	21 June 1893	(4) 2/32
Clayton Margaret H 25	Baker Jacob A 35	17 Dec 1867	(4) 1/6
Clayton Sarah A 22	Fletcher Samuel B 23	20 June 1894	(4) 2/34
Clayton William H 25	Hartman Lillian Jane 17	15 Aug 1894	(4) 2/34
Clem Laura Christina 17	Shelly John Melausthon 18	29 June 1896	(4) 2/37
Clem Mary Emily 21	Jackson Edward Newton 23	23 Nov 1881	(4) 2/16

Name #1	Name #2	Date	Source
Clemm Madison Rector 31	McKeever Margaret 36	5 Jan 1890	(4) 2/27
Clemma Delilah Ann Eliza 21	Nealis John 31	25 Nov 1884	(4) 2/20
Cleve John Michael 31	Simmons Annie 29	6 Oct 1897	(4) 2/39
Click Emma F 21	Taylor J Wm 24	24 Aug 1868	(4) 1/7
Click Susan 22	Pownall Robt J 20	3 Aug 1868	(4) 1/7
Cline Fanny Bell 25	Brill James William 24	21 Feb 1884	(4) 2/19
Cline Hiram Sylvester Lee 22	Cheshire Sara Mariah 21	19 Apr 1883	(4) 2/18
Cline Jacob 23	Largent Nancy Jane 19	25 Aug 1885	(4) 2/21
Cline Madison Rector 21	Saville Druzilla Ann 23	22 Oct 1879	(4) 2/13
Cline Samuel Franklin 26	Burkholder Sarah Ann 27	26 Mar 1867	(4) 1/5
Clingerman Isaac 26	Bliss Mary Elizabeth 20	3 Apr 1888	(4) 2/24
Clingerman Mollie 22	Stottlemyer James 23	*27 Aug 1888	(4) 2/25
Clipstine Mary	Junkins J	23 Sept 1819	(6)
Clipstine Mary Jane	Welch William	27 Aug 1838	(1) 8 Sept 1838
Cnorr James W	Houser Susan S	29 Sept 1852	(2) 7 Oct 1852
Coats M A	Bruce Hav	27 Aug 1835	(6)
Coburn James Miller 29	Letzer Mary Ann 22	17 Feb 1874	(4) 2/5
Cochran William Alexander 33	Dressler Annie Maria 20	28 Mar 1888	(4) 2/24
Coe Wesley	Hook Jane	*19 Aug 1828	(4) 3/22
Coffman Alberta Cordelia 26	Miller Joseph M 25	3 Jan 1878	(4) 2/11
Coffman Caroline V 24	Carlyle James Edward 23	8 Oct 1867	(4) 1/5
Coffman Julius Walter 35	Frye Susan Jennie 23	13 Jan 1881	(4) 2/15
Coffman William Harrison 37	Hott Mary Virginia 30	22 May 1890	(4) 2/28
Coffroth Alex Hamilton Jr 37	Ward Cornelia Gertrude 26	5 May 1886	(4) 2/22
Cogle Ann E	Short George		(1) 13 May 1859
Cokenow Henry	Swisher Catherine	*19 Mar 1827	(4) 3/Page Torn
Colbert Clara	Eddy John	9 May 1828	(5)
Colbert E A	Groves Marcus	10 Aug 1834	(5)
Colbert Fanny I Lacy 25	Ferribee Wellington Pierce 29	3 Sept 1882	(4) 2/17
Colbert Jonathan	Roberts Mary	24 Feb 1823	(5)
Cole Elizabeth 28	Brill Amos T 24	20 Dec 1860	(10)
Cole Jane Eliza Robertson 27	Rudolph David William 28	11 Mar 1880	(4) 2/14
Cole Mary	Roby Isaac	19 Jan 1837	(5)
Coleman Ellen Jane 22	Ward Wm Henry 23	19 Feb 1875	(4) 1/39
Coleman Hannah 21	Brinks Benj 46	23 Nov 1865	(4) 1/1
Coleman Isaac Johnson 28	Allen Mary Eliza 20	31 Dec 1890	(4) 1/41
Coleman John 24	Johnson Susan 18	11 July 1889	(4) 1/40
Coleman John David 21	Banks Emma 17	29 Apr 1884	(4) 1/40
Coleman John David 28	Allen Viola 28	2 Oct 1893	(4) 1/41
Coleman Johnson 21	Thornton Belle 21	10 July 1879	(4) 1/39
Coleman Maria Elizabeth 22	Keys Charles 49	17 Nov 1887	(4) 1/40
Coleman Mary Florence 28	Largent George Washington 28	11 Apr 1878	(4) 2/11
Coleshine E	Harvey Rezin	25 June 1843	(6)
Coleshine John	McCauley Elizabeth	13 May 1817	(5)
Colestine John	McCauly Elizabeth	13 May 1816	(6)
Colley Jacob 27	Smith Charlotte 30	23 Nov 1886	(4) 1/40
Collins Elizabeth Ann 25	Parker William Lee 31	22 June 1898	(4) 2/40
Collins James Perry 27	Arnold Sarah Ann 19	14 July 1885	(4) 2/20
Collins Lavenia	King Alexander		(1) 4 Apr 1839
Collins Moses	Tytus Margaret	*4 Jan 1826	(4) 3/2
Collins Susanna 19	Smith John Wesley 23	28 Aug 1890	(4) 2/28
Combs Abigail 31	Hott William Taylor 41	12 May 1892	(4) 2/31

Name #1	Name #2	Date	Source
Combs Andrew Gibson 20	Shanholtzer Abigal Catharine 21	2 Feb 1882	(4) 2/17
Combs Angus Addison 19	Buckley Annie L 20	11 June 1898	(4) 2/40
Combs Ann Elizabeth Matilda 18	Combs Robert James 30	20 Oct 1887	(4) 2/24
Combs Anne 40	Tharp Samuel Isaac 45	13 Jan 1885	(4) 2/20
Combs Delia Catharine 21	Haines John H F 20	15 Feb 1872	(4) 2/3
Combs Elizabeth 18	Saville Oliver 30	2 May 1860	(10)
Combs Emma Jane 23	Poland Ruben Franklin 21	18 Mar 1897	(4) 2/38
Combs James	Corbin Susan	17 Oct 1838	(1) 3 Nov 1838
Combs James Madison 31	Park Rhoda Ann 31	16 Apr 1889	(4) 2/26
Combs Jno M 21	Peterson Sarah F 22	22 Feb 1866	(4) 1/2
Combs John J	Crawford Susan B		(1) 8 Sept 1838
Combs John Jos 59	Rush Mary 38	13 Oct 1874	(4) 2/6
Combs Maggy Subin 23	Dean Jeremiah Frederick 34	3 Mar 1878	(4) 2/11
Combs Mandy Virginia 18	Poland Franklin M 21	22 Aug 1878	(4) 2/11
Combs Mary Jane 22	Ruckman James Gibson 19	3 Feb 1870	(4) 2/1
Combs Matilda 20	Pownell David G 23	10 Jan 1866	(4) 1/2
Combs Nancy 24	Walker Philip Washington 27	17 Oct 1875	(4) 2/7
Combs Philip 25	Wolford Malinda Catherine 18	9 Jan 1876	(4) 2/8
Combs Rebecca Jane 20	Loy Franklin Pierce 21	18 Nov 1875	(4) 2/7
Combs Robert James 30	Combs Ann Elizabeth Matilda 18	20 Oct 1887	(4) 2/24
Combs Sarah	Starkey John	*Jan/Feb 1824	(4) 3/8
Combs Sarah Catherine 28	Linthicum John David Keller 20	14 Oct 1875	(4) 2/7
Combs Sarah Catharine 17	Heare James Fontaine 33	17 Feb 1887	(4) 2/23
Combs Theodore F 26	Fuller Maggie M 25	9 Dec 1872	(4) 2/4
Combs William Ashby 23	Poland Elizabeth Marg Susan 16	1 Nov 1888	(4) 2/25
Combs Wm G 26	Loy Mary M 24	25 Dec 1877	(4) 2/11
Compton Henry C 24	Ruckman Frances Elmira 27	5 May 1885	(4) 2/20
Conard James Edward 20	Michael Regina 20	10 Apr 1890	(4) 2/27
Condon Harriet 44	Maloney James Harrison 43	30 Dec 1879	(4) 2/14
Condon Sarah Catharine 23	Parker John Edward 37	24 Apr 1877	(4) 2/10
Connell Emma S 32	Davy William 39	18 Apr 1894	(4) 2/34
Cononavan Johnson	Bosley Polly	25 May 1839	(5)
Conrad George 20	Rosebaugh Harriet 27	22 Nov 1865	(4) 1/1
Constable Thomas Franklin 45	Shadwell Jennie 21	24 Aug 1890	(4) 2/28
Cook Franklin A 33	Davy Hester 17	3 Dec 1877	(4) 2/10
Cook John Wesley 30	Waddle Alice henderson 25	6 Sept 1883	(4) 2/18
Cookerly John T 21	Parker Lillian 30	4 Dec 1899	(4) 2/42
Cookus Robert Henry 22	Kremer Arabella Frances 24	11 Dec 1877	(4) 2/10
Cool Catherine	Hamilton Elisha	*17 June 1825	(4) 3/46
Cool Eliza Jane 21	Pownell James Marion 24	15 Dec 1869	(4) 2/1
Cool Harrison Bane 28	Dellaplain Mary Ellen 23	18 Oct 1888	(4) 2/25
Cool James Mortimer 24	Malick Mary Malinda 24	28 Dec 1876	(4) 2/9
Cool John Wesley 29	Simpson Jane 21	19 Dec 1875	(4) 2/8
Cool Louisa Catharine 22	Swisher Philip Matthew 23	2 Nov 1876	(4) 2/9
Cool Margaret E 27	Maloney William H 28	24 Apr 1873	(4) 2/4
Cool Martha Ellen 21	Park James Ashford 26	24 Feb 1887	(4) 2/23
Cool Mary Matilda 22	Robinson William 24	21 June 1870	(4) 2/2
Cool Robert Granville 24	Loy Anna Jemima 17	29 Dec 1887	(4) 2/24
Cooper Abram	Murphy R	17 Feb 1846	(6)
Cooper Catharine	Hickle John	*4 Apr 1825	(4) 3/27
Cooper Catharine Magdeliene 18	Arnold Miller Washington 22	8 Oct 1871	(4) 2/3
Cooper Dan'l M 20	Cariile Mary L 20	3 Mar 1868	(4) 1/6

Hampshire County Marriage Records

Name #1	Name #2	Date	Source
Cooper Edwin Rinehart 22	Offutt Sarah Gertrude 23	24 July 1895	(4) 2/35
Cooper Eva Ellen 27	Brill John Wesley 27	28 Dec 1876	(4) 2/9
Cooper Hoppie Jacobs 29	Miller Peter 65	28 Apr 1892	(4) 2/31
Cooper Jacob	Park Anna	*7 Feb 1825	(4) 3/14
Cooper Julius Bell 21	Anderson Alice May 18	14 Dec 1882	(4) 2/18
Cooper Martha Ann 40	McDonald Evan Griffith 41	31 May 1877	(4) 2/10
Cooper Nancy V 22	Kaylor John Edward 24	9 Sept 1896	(4) 2/37
Cooper Sarah Belle 17	Newhouse George Washington 20	20 Mar 1877	(4) 2/10
Copelen Moses R 21	Powelson Ann E 19	11 Dec 1866	(4) 1/4
Copp John Russell 24	Arnold Syntha Ann 17	26 May 1891	(4) 2/29
Corbett Gertrude 26	Parker Isaac Vance 32	3 Aug 1871	(4) 2/3
Corbin ? 22	Spurling Sarah Ann 20	3 Nov 1857	(10)
Corbin Alverda 17	Liller Henry Bradford 23	15 Dec 1878	(4) 2/12
Corbin Charles 22	Orndorff Ellen 22	24 May 1880	(4) 2/14
Corbin Cornelius	White Pathenia	*29 Aug 1825	(4) 3/56
Corbin David	Swier Catharine	*7 Feb 1826	(4) 3/7
Corbin George Thomas 29	Kirby Rachel Beal 17	11 June 1890	(4) 2/28
Corbin Henry 40	McCauley Martha 21	1 Sept 1872	(4) 2/3
Corbin Job 24	Cheshire Amanda Belle 28	24 Oct 1894	(4) 2/35
Corbin John 32	Kidner Harriett 22	2 Mar 1860	(10)
Corbin John Snyder 20	Timbrook Maggie E 17	24 Oct 1894	(4) 2/35
Corbin Joseph 53	Orndorff Rebecca J 18	18 Dec 1866	(4) 1/4
Corbin Joseph William 24	Haines Sallie Bertie 18	7 Nov 1900	(4) 2/43
Corbin Luther 22	Gill Eveline 25	12 Aug 1866	(4) 1/3
Corbin Martha Eliza Mrs 25	Pownell John Christopher 25	7 Apr 1881	(4) 2/15
Corbin Martha Jane 18	Smith Benjamin Wesley 23	31 Oct 1883	(4) 2/18
Corbin Mary 50	Gray William 39	5 Apr 1876	(4) 2/8
Corbin Mary Elizabeth 19	Haines Joseph E 38	19 Jan 1882	(4) 2/17
Corbin Mary Elizabeth 24	Maphis Benjamin Wade Hampton 24	22 Dec 1897	(4) 2/40
Corbin Nancy 23	Lear Thomas 28	1 Aug 1865	(4) 1/1
Corbin Oscalosa 27	Wolford Lutetia 24	13 Oct 1894	(4) 2/34
Corbin Parthenia 23	Secord Samuel Franklin 38	13 Apr 1892	(4) 2/30
Corbin Rufus Jackson 27	Davy Ida Bell 24	18 July 1894	(4) 2/34
Corbin Sarah 21	Turley Charles William 20	15 May 1887	(4) 2/23
Corbin Susan	Combs James	17 Oct 1838	(1) 3 Nov 1838
Corbin Susan 30	Davy George 24	24 Dec 1870	(4) 2/2
Corbin Winney	Doyle Mathew	*16 June 1825	(4) 3/15
Cornwell George Benjamin 25	Poling Dora Susan 23	11 Nov 1896	(4) 2/38
Cornwell Jesse M 29	Kelly Sarah E K 18	25 Dec 1866	(4) 1/2
Cornwell John J 24	Brady Edna Earl 23	30 June 1891	(4) 2/29
Cosner Adam	Michael Rachel	10 Oct 1833	(5)
Cosner Adam	Michael Margaret	11 Dec 1823	(5)
Cosner E A	Idleman John	1 Oct 1841	(5)
Cosner Elizabeth	Lee Fred	1 Dec 1843	(5)
Cosner Mary	Michael Job	15 Feb 1835	(5)
Cosner Samuel	Idleman Mary A	17 Nov 1842	(5)
Covan Johnson	Bosley P	25 May 1838	(6)
Covell Annie Baldwin 26	Heiskell David Hopkins 26	15 June 1886	(4) 2/22
Covell Mary Avery 26	Parsons Garrett Williams 26	12 Nov 1878	(4) 2/12
Cowan Sarah	Dawson Lewis	22 Dec 1829	(5)
Cowgill Alexander C 20	Wolford Fannie Maria 17	11 June 1873	(4) 2/4
Cowgill Carrie Jane 20	Timbrook Francis Elijah 28	20 May 1891	(4) 2/29

Page 23

Name #1	Name #2	Date	Source
Cowgill Frederick Henry 52	Heare Barbara Alice 35	8 Oct 1876	(4) 2/9
Cowgill James William 23	Reigner Electa 16	9 Nov 1879	(4) 2/13
Cowgill Laura Edna Lee 19	Jenkins Elick Jackson 22	23 Nov 1900	(4) 2/43
Cowgill Sarah Catharine 22	Hardy Adam Jeremiah 24	21 Dec 1879	(4) 2/14
Cowgill W B 20	Pownall Joann 24	26 Nov 1868	(4) 1/7
Cox Henry Harrison 50	Miller Ann Rebecca 40	11 Oct 1892	(4) 2/31
Cox Susanna 24	Malcolm Amos William 28	13 Oct 1886	(4) 2/22
Coxe Bathsheba Ellen 21	Ullery Jacob Lemuel 21	15 Jan 1870	(4) 2/1
Coyner David H	Snodgrass Eliza C		(1) 28 Mar 1839
Craigg Robert Lee 23	Poland Ann Rebecca Susan 23	7 July 1897	(4) 2/39
Crane Willis 58	Fletcher Mary Catharine 28	25 Jan 1875	(4) 2/7
Cranston Jane	Linthicum Archibald	*18 Sept 1826	(4) 3/35
Crausner George Ella 21	McAtee John H 25	11 Dec 1865	(4) 1/1
Crawfis Robert R 25	Seders Mary Ann 17	10 Jan 1878	(4) 2/11
Crawford John Thomas 24	Martin Isabella 22	11 Nov 1879	(4) 2/13
Crawford Laura Alice 22	Criser Jacob B 27	28 Sept 1875	(4) 2/7
Crawford Susan B	Combs John J		(1) 8 Sept 1838
Creswell Alverda C 41	McCoy John 51	15 Dec 1896	(4) 2/38
Creswell Bessie Oaida 36	Brill Smith Reed 32	14 Nov 1894	(4) 2/35
Creswell Cordelia Elfrida 21	Calvert Judge Lot 25	13 July 1885	(4) 2/20
Creswell Evan P 25	Anderson Elizabeth N 22	*8 Oct 1877	(4) 2/10
Creswell Mary Luella May 15	Garvin James M 18	11 Mar 1874	(4) 2/6
Creswell Mary V 24	Hook Henson T 23	*30 Jan 1873	(4) 2/4
Creswell Sallie Estella 20	Gray Anthony Hammack 21	27 Feb 1879	(4) 2/13
Creswell Sarah Frances 21	Gray Henry Newton 26	20 May 1886	(4) 2/22
Criser Jacob B 27	Crawford Laura Alice 22	28 Sept 1875	(4) 2/7
Crites Allen 23	Sirk Rosa Florence 21	26 Dec 1899	(4) 2/42
Critton Frances 30	?Kerig Emanuel 33	19 May 1892	(4) 2/30
Critton Isaac	Athey Elizabeth	*25 Aug 1826	(4) 3/32
Critton Mary E 23	Moore Joseph S 34	4 Mar 1868	(4) 1/6
Critton Phoebe 35	Royce Frederick 35	27 Nov 1860	(10)
Crock John Wm 27	Kerns Susan Catharine 16	15 June 1875	(4) 2/7
Crock Margaret Elizabeth 18	Boher Thomas Jefferson 21	15 Aug 1888	(4) 2/25
Crock Mary Jane 35	Shanholtzer Christopher 40	23 Feb 1875	(4) 2/6
Cropper Jesse	McCullock M A	26 Mar 1839	(6)
Cropper Jessee	McCullough Mary Ann		(1) 28 Mar 1839
Crosley Joanna	Smith Sylves	1 Oct 1844	(6)
Crosley Jos	Thresher Mary	11 June 1822	(6)
Cross Christina 19	Haines John Wesley 21	28 Dec 1882	(4) 2/18
Cross Elizabeth Susan 20	Rannells John William 31	7 Apr 1881	(4) 2/15
Cross Elmira Virginia 20	Miles Asa Morgan 23	9 Nov 1886	(4) 2/22
Cross Granville 24	Malcolm Viola Blance May 15	23 Apr 1893	(4) 2/32
Crounse Alexander 36	McGlothery Martha Campbell 26	29 Oct 1889	(4) 2/27
Crozley Joseph	Thresher Mary	11 June 1822	(5)
Culp Ann	Randalls Thos	18 Nov 1830	(6)
Culp Christina	James Thornton	11 Sept 1818	(5)
Culp Christina	James Thorn	18 Sept 1818	(6)
Culp Geo	Burton Huldah	17 Dec 1818	(6)
Culp James	Flick Catherine	5 May 1836	(6)
Culp John	Baker Rachael	*12 June 1826	(4) 3/25
Culp John	Baker Rachel	15 June 1826	(6)
Culp Maria	Ravenscraft John	*17 Dec 1827	(4) 3/58

Name #1	Name #2	Date	Source
Culp Mariah	Ravenscraft John D	18 Dec 1827	(5)
Culp Wm	Bisor M A	29 May 1855	(6)
Cummins Alverda Lee 22	Sanders Alexander Thomas 29	16 Dec 1885	(4) 2/21
Cummins Edward Beall 25	Sanders Margaret Elizabeth 22	2 Dec 1885	(4) 2/21
Cummins George Thomas 26	Orndorff Frances Elizabeth 21	19 Dec 1883	(4) 2/19
Cummins Mary Ann 54	Stickley Tobias 64	23 Sept 1869	(4) 2/1
Cundiff Catherine Nash	Prye John	*19 Dec 1825	(4) 3/75
Cundiff Elisabeth	Hull Jacob	*15 May 1827	(4) 3/33
Cundiff Eliz	Hull Jacob	17 May 1827	(6)
Cundiff Emelia	Cundiff Henry	22 Apr 1824	(6)
Cundiff Henry	Cundiff Milly	*19 Apr 1824	(4) 3/24
Cundiff Henry	Cundiff Emelia	22 Apr 1824	(6)
Cundiff J R	Johnson Sarah	28 Dec 1848	(6)
Cundiff John	McCarthy Eliza	10 Mar 1842	(6)
Cundiff Lucy	Parrill Hugh	15 Oct 1833	(6)
Cundiff M L	Dawson Andrew	2 Mar 1837	(6)
Cundiff Milly	Cundiff Henry	*19 Apr 1824	(4) 3/24
Cundiff Nancy	Worman William	* 2 Apr 1825	(4) 3/26
Cundiff Nancy	Worman Wm	7 Apr 1825	(6)
Cundiff Nancy C	Dye William	26 Mar 1822	(6)
Cundiff Sarah	Bartlett Thomas L	23 Dec 1821	(6)
Cundiff Sarah D	Ward Jesse	13 Oct 1829	(6)
Cundiff Wesley	Dye Nancy	7 Feb 1822	(6)
Cundill Nancy	Workman William	7 Apr 1825	(5)
Cunningham Carroll Rebecca 25	Bobo Joseph 26	29 Mar 1871	(4) 2/2
Cunningham George S	Harness Miss		(1) 18 Nov 1837
Cunningham Jane	Welton F B		(1) 14 Nov 1839
Cunningham John Calvin 22	Leatherman Sarah Catharine 32	26 Dec 1894	(4) 2/35
Cupp Elizabeth 29	Haws James 28	21 Nov 1868	(4) 1/7
Cupp Hannah Elizabeth 35	Powelson Benjamin W 28	7 May 1879	(4) 2/13
Cupp Jacob 29	Loy Mary V 21	1 July 1873	(4) 2/4
Cupp William Arthur 23	Simmons Maude McClung 19	1 Dec 1897	(4) 2/39
Curlett Christina	Long David	*17 July 1827	(4) 3/39
Curlett Mary	Parsons James G	*22 Mar 1825	(4) 3/25
Currey Jean	Heizer John Leonard	*11 Jan 1825	(4) 3/8
Dailey Nelia Dupuy 23	Walker William Laurens 27	1 Nov 1900	(4) 2/43
Daily John 28	Brady Rebecca S 26	8 Apr 1857	(10)
Daily John 39	Hartigan Sarah Elizabeth 25	8 Oct 1867	(4) 1/5
Daily Sarah Cornelia 32	Baird William Nelson 34	21 May 1889	(4) 2/25
Dandridge Geo Washington 25	Brooks Harriett 21	27 Dec 1870	(4) 1/38
Dandridge Isadore 21	Washington Jos C 23	3 Dec 1883	(4) 1/40
Dandridge Margaret 22	Anderson Willis 21	25 Dec 1867	(4) 1/6
Dandridge Rebecca 20	Washington Smith 22	31 Jan 1871	(4) 1/38
Dandridge Silin 17	Edmonson Edward B 23	11 Dec 1879	(4) 1/39
Daniel Daniel J 26	Fleek Christina 23	22 June 1854	(10)
Daniels Dennis	Flick M J	25 Jan 1849	(6)
Darling Elizah	Dean Ann	1824	(5)
Darr Annie Lee 16	Simmons John Henry 25	25 Dec 1888	(4) 2/25
Darr Elizabeth 17	Long Richard Woodridge 24	22 Dec 1898	(4) 2/41
Darr George Philip 26	Nealis Eliza Ann 26	10 May 1881	(4) 2/16
Darr Mary 23	Fairfax David 23	12 June 1868	(4) 1/6
Darr Mary Ellen 20	Edwards James Anthony Porter 25	17 Nov 1885	(4) 2/21

Name #1	Name #2	Date	Source
Darr William Samuel 28	Dorsey Catharine Virginia 21	29 Dec 1886	(4) 2/23
Daubs Martha	Moreland John	8 Apr 1844	(5)
Daugherty Daniel Ashby 20	Sowers Ellen B 17	20 Dec 1882	(4) 2/18
Daugherty Eliza 25	Cheshire Abraham 26	18 Dec 1877	(4) 2/11
Daugherty Harriet Elizabeth 18	Shanholtzer Philip Lemuel 23	19 Aug 1875	(4) 2/7
Daugherty Harvey Berry 26	Queen Margaret Milissa 17	24 Nov 1881	(4) 2/16
Daugherty Ida May 23	Liller William Henry 24	26 Feb 1895	(4) 2/35
Daugherty Lucinda V 18	Arnold Taylor 22	18 Oct 1871	(4) 2/3
Daugherty Martha E 24	Flory William H 25	28 Jan 1873	(4) 2/4
Daugherty Mary Elizabeth 18	Bedinger Joseph Bennett 27	21 Oct 1885	(4) 2/21
Daugherty N I 22	Shanholtz Benj 26	22 Sept 1868	(4) 1/7
Davey Andrew Russell 23	Maphis Isabel 24	24 Feb 1874	(4) 2/5
Davey Anne Catharine 17	McDonald Jonathan James 22	21 Sept 1898	(4) 2/40
Davey Edward 28	Spurling Harriet 26	2 June 1877	(4) 2/10
Davey Elizabeth 26	Timbrook Benjamin Harrison 23	27 Nov 1884	(4) 2/20
Davey Isaac 24	Arnold Harriet Jane 24	11 Dec 1878	(4) 2/12
Davey John 26	Grabill Ann Caroline 25	22 Sept 1880	(4) 2/14
Davey Lotty Ann 22	Wolford Benjamin Thomas 23	2 Mar 1897	(4) 2/38
Davey Lucy Emma 24	High Summerfield 26	15 Apr 1896	(4) 2/37
Davey Lucy Lee 24	Stewart Henry Michael 31	23 Jan 1901	(4) 2/43
Davey Margaret Ellen 21	Rosebough Joseph Philip 33	10 Oct 1900	(4) 2/43
Davey Robert Gideon 24	Wolfe Daisey E 16	28 Apr 1901	(4) 2/44
Davidson Robert 21	Hott Lelia B 22	26 Dec 1900	(4) 2/43
Davilbliss Martha 37	Truax William 50	1 Oct 1888	(4) 2/25
Davis Alfred	Bane Elizabeth	30 Nov 1843	(6)
Davis Aseneth	Tasker George	5 Apr 1832	(6)
Davis Bettie 19	Caster John Luther 23	8 Apr 1879	(4) 2/13
Davis Catherine 21	Trenton ? 23	3 July 1857	(10)
Davis Charity 40	Sexton Patrick 45	30 Jan 1876	(4) 2/8
Davis Charles Ashby 25	Carlyle Sarah Virginia 25	23 Apr 1893	(4) 2/32
Davis Charles Morris 36	Hannas Mary Victoria 24	15 Jan 1879	(4) 2/12
Davis David Lewis 37	Bierkamp Freddie Virginia 20	21 June 1899	(4) 2/41
Davis Dora Edward 20	Timbrook Susie M 21	17 Mar 1897	(4) 2/38
Davis Dr Reuben Samuel 54	Heare Phoebe Lillie 22	14 Feb 1889	(4) 2/26
Davis E	Hendrixon Aramiah	24 Jan 1837	(6)
Davis Eleanor Jane 22	Watkins Lorenzo Edward 22	1 Apr 1888	(4) 2/24
Davis Elias	Doll Catherine	2 Jan 1834	(6)
Davis Elizabeth	Dean Thomas	6 Jan 1820	(6)
Davis Elizabeth	Parker William	23 Nov 1820	(6)
Davis Emily Susan 21	Shanholtz Benjamin Thomas 18	6 May 1867	(4) 1/5
Davis Fannie May 25	Brill Howard Lee 27	1 Jun 1897	(4) 2/39
Davis Felix	Smith Sarah C	*25 July 1825	(4) 3/52
Davis George Franklin 24	Spaid Hannah Caroline 24	11 Dec 1873	(4) 2/5
Davis George Willaim 26	McKewn Almira Virginia 18	2 Dec 1875	(4) 2/8
Davis Granvill Wilson 27	Poling Susie A 29	3 Apr 1872	(4) 2/3
Davis Hampton Ashby 30	Williams Addie 21	4 Jan 1893	(4) 2/32
Davis Ida Virginia 23	Doyle Charles Ashby 23	7 Nov 1886	(4) 2/22
Davis J F	Harrison Orpha	5 Sept 1848	(6)
Davis James	Yates Elenor	*26 Apr 1825	(4) 3/31
Davis James H 25	Keller Harriet Emma 34	4 Dec 1877	(4) 2/10
Davis James Marion 23	Carder Emma 20	19 Nov 1879	(4) 2/13
Davis Jane	Dew William		(1) 14 Nov 1839

Name #1	Name #2	Date	Source
Davis Jane	Duke James	9 Feb 1848	(6)
Davis Jane C 27	Keller Richard B 24	30 Apr 1874	(4) 2/6
Davis Jethro	Parker Emily	23 Feb 1853	(6)
Davis Jno W 23	Spade E A V 18	19 Dec 1868	(4) 1/7
Davis John 23	Orndorf Matilda 17	27 Dec 1853	(10)
Davis John Edgar 29	Mauk Mary Rosetta 20	19 Dec 1895	(4) 2/36
Davis John William 22	Timbrook Hannah Catharine 20	27 Aug 1874	(4) 2/6
Davis Joseph	St Clair Nancy	10 Nov 1833	(6)
Davis Joseph	Duling Mary		(1) 14 Nov 1839
Davis Julius Ceasar 25	Harloe Mary Jane 22	11 Aug 1875	(4) 2/7
Davis Margaret	Taylor Simon		(1) 21 July 1838
Davis Margaret Ellen 24	Keister Alonzo Mandeville 24	16 Jan 1878	(4) 2/11
Davis Margaret Ellen 26	Everett William Isaac 24	4 Dec 1889	(4) 2/27
Davis Margaret E 18	Orndorff Stephen 23	15 Jan 1873	(4) 2/4
Davis Margaret Francis 24	Heatwole Frank S 27	4 Dec 1877	(4) 2/10
Davis Martha 23	Hawkins Isaac 23	30 Nov 1865	(4) 1/1
Davis Mary	Wilson Nat	2 Dec 1816	(6)
Davis Mary	Metcalf J W H	16 July 1840	(6)
Davis Mary	Metcalf J W H	16 July 1841	(5)
Davis Mary Ann	Doll Phil	26 Feb 1829	(6)
Davis Mary C 19	Jackson Henry C 24	5 Jan 1867	(4) 1/4
Davis Mary Elizabeth 18	Howdeyshell Philip 28	5 Dec 1877	(4) 2/10
Davis Miner	Ross Mary	14 Jan 1830	(6)
Davis Minert	Roberts Susan	31 May 1849	(6)
Davis Mivert	Waxler Lethy A	7 Feb 1861	(5)
Davis Nora Clifton 17	Strother Walter Spencer 21	16 Oct 1895	(4) 2/36
Davis Phebe	Murphy Edw	28 Jan 1838	(6)
Davis Phobe	Murphy Dan'l	28 Jan 1839	(5)
Davis R C	Trenter Poland	3 July 1856	(6)
Davis R S 36	Heare Susan F P 26	14 Sept 1871	(4) 2/3
Davis Rebecca	Steerman Dan	21 Sept 1830	(6)
Davis Rebecca	Wilson Nathan	2 Dec 1816	(5)
Davis Robert P 38	Shelly Laura Ellen 24	29 Jan 1895	(4) 2/35
Davis Robt 24	Atkins Virginia 19	24 Dec 1872	(4) 2/4
Davis Samuel H 24	Brown Mary F 19	29 Apr 1869	(4) 1/38
Davis Samuel H 24	Brown Mary F 19	29 Apr 1869	(4) 2/1
Davis Samuel Lupton 20	Orndorff Sarah Jane 16	15 Jan 1885	(4) 2/20
Davis Samuel Sylvester 25	Kelso Anna Roberta 27	28 Aug 1884	(4) 2/19
Davis Sarah Ellen 30	Wilkins Silas 24	3 Apr 1892	(4) 2/30
Davis Sarah Odwolt 19	Abell Charles F 23	11 Mar 1894	(4) 2/33
Davis Susan K	Duling David	2 Nov 1853	(10)
Davis Susan Mary 23	Sheetz Frederick Warin 26	14 Nov 1865	(4) 1/1
Davis Virginia 22	Smith Charles Henry 20	22 Sept 1875	(4) 2/7
Davis William F 30	Poling Isabella 21	30 Mar 1869	(4) 1/38
Davy Ann E 22	Hartman David C 22	8 May 1866	(4) 1/3
Davy Florence Agnes 17	McCauley Albert Newton 21	22 Oct 1895	(4) 2/36
Davy George 24	Corbin Susan 30	24 Dec 1870	(4) 2/2
Davy Hester 17	Cook Franklin A 33	3 Dec 1877	(4) 2/10
Davy Ida Bell 24	Corbin Rufus Jackson 27	18 July 1894	(4) 2/34
Davy Jno Wm 23	Liller Elizabeth C 21	24 Dec 1866	(4) 1/4
Davy John	Shoemaker M J	20 May 1838	(6)
Davy Marg	Buncrots Loudon	14 June 1838	(6)

Name #1	Name #2	Date	Source
Davy Margaret	Bumcrots Landon	14 June 1839	(5)
Davy Mary 24	Spurling Luke 22	7 Sept 1865	(4) 1/1
Davy Washington	Staouther Ann	8 Dec 1838	(1) 22 Dec 1838
Davy William	Hoffman Ann	11 Oct 1838	(1) 20 Oct 1838
Davy William 39	Connell Emma S 32	18 Apr 1894	(4) 2/34
Davy William Henry 21	Liller Sarah Virginia 18	6 Oct 1876	(4) 2/8
Dawney John	Good Mary	9 Nov 1828	(5)
Dawson Andrew	Cundiff M L	2 Mar 1837	(6)
Dawson Andrew	Dawson Mary	19 May 1842	(6)
Dawson Avy	Perkins Jas E	14 Apr 1842	(6)
Dawson Cephas	Leatherman Margaret	24 Aug 1837	(5)
Dawson Eliz	Rolon Evan J	6 Nov 1845	(6)
Dawson Isaac	Hackley Catherine	20 Oct 1825	(6)
Dawson Jacob	Spencer Julia	23 Nov 1854	(6)
Dawson John James 21	Gulick Virginia Lee 18	27 Apr 1893	(4) 2/32
Dawson Lewis	Cowan Sarah	22 Dec 1829	(5)
Dawson Mary	Dawson Andrew	19 May 1842	(6)
Dawson Mary	Flick Adam	25 Apr 1816	(5)
Dawson Mary	Flick Adam	16 Apr 1816	(6)
Dawson Thos	Moore A M	30 June 1842	(6)
Dawson William D 57	Smith Sarah Jane 32	9 Aug 1860	(10)
Dawson Wm	Ravenscroft Sarah	19 Sept 1837	(6)
Day Edward 24	Hardy Eliza 20	31 Dec 1879	(4) 1/39
Day James 21	Green Fannie 23	24 July 1875	(4) 1/39
Day Jennie 23	Fishel Geo 28	24 Sept 1899	(4) 2/42
Day Jonathan 27	Betson Mary Ann 19	5 Aug 1875	(4) 2/7
Day Lucy Bell 21	Durst Robert W? 23	14 Oct 1879	(4) 2/13
Day Nannie 25	Ward Charles 22	28 Sept 1893	(4) 1/41
Day Thomas L 32	Moreland Margaret Ann 24	25 Feb 1873	(4) 2/4
Day William	Pugh Ann	14 June 1824	(4) 3/34
Dayton Elizabeth	Riding Peter	27 Aug 1841	(5)
Dayton Martha	Liller Geo	19 June 1845	(6)
Dayton Valentine	Shrout Nancy	7 Jan 1852	(6)
Dayton William	Kite Theodasia	5 Oct 1839	(5)
Dayton Wm	Kite Theodosia	5 Oct 1838	(6)
Dean Aaron 22	Cheshire Maria 33	28 Feb 1868	(4) 1/6
Dean Ann	Darling Elizah	1824	(5)
Dean Anna	Duling Elijah	12 Feb 1824	(6)
Dean Anne	Duling Elijah	*7 Feb 1824	(4) 3/9
Dean Benjamin Anthony 32	Hannas Sarah Elizabeth 18	6 Mar 1879	(4) 2/13
Dean Isaac Strait 24	Buckley Minnie Bell 18	25 May 1898	(4) 2/40
Dean Jeremiah 22	Tucker Caroline Matilda 22	10 Oct 1865	(4) 1/1
Dean Jeremiah Frederick 34	Combs Maggy Subin 23	3 Mar 1878	(4) 2/11
Dean Thomas	Davis Elizabeth	6 Jan 1820	(6)
Dean Wm	Duling Ruth	26 June 1823	(6)
Dean Zulemma Virginia 31	Burwell Joseph Zarrenton 62	28 Oct 1900	(4) 2/43
Deats Joseph Jefferson 25	Sirbaugh May Catharine 18	*5 Sept 1875	(4) 2/7
Deats Martha 15	Williams Isaac Welton 24	*5 Sept 1875	(4) 2/7
Deaver Christopher 24	Durst Sarah Almeda 18	25 Feb 1879	(4) 2/13
Deaver Frances A 21	Hiett Joseph C 22	22 Feb 1871	(4) 2/2
Deaver Howell Foote 40	Snyder Ida Elizabeth Powell 18	11 Oct 1892	(4) 2/31
Deaver Howell Hook 27	Slane Annie 21	13 Nov 1878	(4) 2/12

Name #1	Name #2	Date	Source
Deaver Sarah E 17	Largent John A 21	8 Feb 1868	(4) 1/6
Deaver Sarah Virginia 27	Pugh Robert Offutt 28	25 Nov 1880	(4) 2/15
Deerdurf Benjamin 50	Pepper Hannah Catharine 40	18 Oct 1876	(4) 2/9
Deever Richard	Deever Susan	*25 May 1824	(4) 3/29
Deever Susan	Deever Richard	*25 May 1824	(4) 3/29
Deffenbaugh George Irving 25	Hessen Martha Virginia 18	20 Oct 1887	(4) 2/24
Dehaven Perry Christy 23	Omps Texanna 25	25 Nov 1897	(4) 2/39
Deitz Mrs Catherine 22	Leach Charles Oliver 24	1 May 1881	(4) 2/16
Delaplain Asa Pirkey 25	Godlove Virginia C 24	30 Mar 1897	(4) 2/38
Delaplain Margaret Elizabeth 20	Hawes William Branson 24	8 Feb 1870	(4) 2/1
Delawder George Washington 43	Doman Armie Maria 38	23 Mar 1898	(4) 2/40
Deleplain Owen	Athey Sarah	10 Dec 1828	(5)
Deleplane Mary 22	Perrill Isaac Perry 39	29 July 1866	(4) 1/3
Deleplane William 29	Haines Susan Margaret 23	26 Jan 1871	(4) 2/2
Delinger Liza 21	Baker Wm A 30	28 Feb 1872	(4) 2/3
Dellaplain John Christopher 28	Hott Sarah Elizabeth 23	25 Dec 1889	(4) 2/27
Dellaplain Mary Ellen 23	Cool Harrison Bane 28	18 Oct 1888	(4) 2/25
Dellinger Amanda Virginia 23	Orndorff George L 24	11 Apr 1891	(4) 2/29
Demmett S	Warnick Henry	7 Feb 1843	(6)
Dern Sarah Catharine 42	Catlett Elisha William 41	14 Feb 1878	(4) 2/11
Devere Aaron	Hesman Melinda	11 Jan 1821	(6)
Dew John	Duling Ann	12 May 1835	(6)
Dew William	Davis Jane		(1) 14 Nov 1839
Dicken Alverretta Clemmons 21	Wigfield Henry Wm 29	24 Oct 1876	(4) 2/9
Dicken Amos Clay 25	Powell Ettie 22	17 Aug 1898	(4) 2/40
Dicken Flora Frances 17	Thomas David 23	8 June 1887	(4) 2/23
Dicken Miranda Catherine 21	Wintling Charles Edward 21	14 Aug 1879	(4) 2/13
Dicken Viola Myrtle 14	Tawzer Wilber Irvin 22	26 July 1896	(4) 2/37
Dicks Mary	Cheshire John	*31 Dec 1827	(4) 3/62
Didawick Benjamin Ashby 29	Haines Minnie J 26	1 Mar 1900	(4) 2/42
Didawick Dorthy Ann 24	Doman William Alfred 32	2 Mar 1897	(4) 2/38
Didawick Mary Aida 18	Stewart John William 40	30 Mar 1893	(4) 2/32
Didiwick Edna Bell 21	Lambert Howard Jesse 24	4 Dec 1895	(4) 2/36
Didiwick Jennie Savilla 18	Brown Ephraim 20	23 Mar 1895	(4) 2/35
Didiwick John William 21	Hook Miss Jennie 25	22 Oct 1895	(4) 2/36
Dieffendorffer John 25	Allen ? 24	28 July 1859	(10)
Diehl Louis 30	Bowen Amelia Whilmina 20	29 Jan 1867	(4) 1/4
Digman Ellen C 20	White Arther Little 20	31 Aug 1870	(4) 2/2
Dimmit Gillah	Jinkins Ensna	11 Feb 1846	(5)
Dimmit Zillah	Jinkins Elisha	22 Feb 1851	(6)
Dixon Elizabeth	Wilson Thomas	16 July 1829	(5)
Dixon Elizabeth	Wilson Thos	16 June 1829	(6)
Dixon Harriet	Miller Wm H	28 Mar 1844	(6)
Dixon James Porter 22	Offner Hannah Catharine 24	24 Feb 1881	(4) 2/15
Dixon Thos	Barrack Mary	5 Sept 1833	(6)
Dobbins Johnson	Miller S E	21 Sept 1847	(6)
Dobbins Thomas	Ravenscraft Nancy	20 Sept 1839	(5)
Dobbins V	Hammock H A	26 Feb 1844	(6)
Dobbins W	Leatherman B A	22 Mar 1832	(6)
Dohrman Herman H 26	Waggoner Martha Ann 21	25 Jan 1866	(4) 1/2
Doll Abraham	Thomas Jane	*11 June 1827	(4) 3/37
Doll Abram	Thomas Jane	14 June 1827	(6)

Name #1	Name #2	Date	Source
Doll Catherine	Davis Elias	2 Jan 1834	(6)
Doll Phil	Davis Mary Ann	26 Feb 1829	(6)
Doman Armie Maria 38	Delawder George Washington 43	23 Mar 1898	(4) 2/40
Doman Catharine	Brant John	*10 Jan 1824	(4) 3/7
Doman Denton Pierce 26	Jewell Eliza Ann 19	3 June 1884	(4) 2/19
Doman Edward F 26	Marshall Emily A J 24	15 Mar 1866	(4) 1/3
Doman Elizabeth Catherine 21	Spurling Luther 28	10 May 1887	(4) 2/23
Doman Etta Virginia 33	Shanholtzer Benjamin 43	25 Apr 1894	(4) 2/34
Doman Ida Malinda 27	Saville Charles Harbert 28	15 Sept 1897	(4) 2/39
Doman J Newton 44	Kerns Rebecca Ann 38	1 Nov 1895	(4) 2/36
Doman Jasper W 23	Whitaker Amanda L 23	3 July 1873	(4) 2/4
Doman John B 29	Stump Mary Ann 29	5 Jan 1886	(4) 2/21
Doman Juliet 22	George Wesley 25	1 July 1880	(4) 2/14
Doman Martha 28	Watsen Gordon John 38	15 Jan 1890	(4) 2/27
Doman Sallie B 29	Rowzee Isaac Newton 20	9 Feb 1898	(4) 2/40
Doman Thomas Lee 25	Spurling Ellen Ashby 25	25 Nov 1888	(4) 2/25
Doman Tobias S 37	Kern Margaret A 25	7 Nov 1866	(4) 1/4
Doman William Alfred 32	Didawick Dorthy Ann 24	2 Mar 1897	(4) 2/38
Doman Wm H F 30	Powelson Mary A 20	21 Oct 1868	(4) 1/7
Donaldson Catharine R 29	Baker Albert C 29	17 May 1882	(4) 2/17
Donaldson L Ella 22	Hanna Walter 32	2 May 1882	(4) 2/17
Donaldson William G 24	Haines Bertha V 20	25 Nov 1891	(4) 2/30
Doran Hannah Elizabeth 19	Lewis George Tacey 26	26 Feb 1880	(4) 2/14
Doran Joseph	Frye Lucy G	*22 Sept 1827	(4) 3/48
Doran Rebecca	Scott James	3 Jan 1837	(5)
Doran Sarah	Moore Thomas	*4 Oct 1824	(4) 3/46
Doran William	Carmichael Hannah	*2 May 1825	(4) 3/34
Dorne Margaret Jane 19	McKee Robert Franklin 22	15 Aug 1878	(4) 2/11
Dorsey Ashby Wise 22	Proctor Clara A 23	13 May 1894	(4) 2/34
Dorsey Catharine Virginia 21	Darr William Samuel 28	29 Dec 1886	(4) 2/23
Dorsey John W 52	Dorsey Sarah Frances 43	8 Feb 1897	(4) 2/38
Dorsey Sarah Frances 43	Dorsey John W 52	8 Feb 1897	(4) 2/38
Doughtery William H 22	Pownall Margaret Ellen 19	22 Nov 1896	(4) 2/38
Douthit Jas	Simmons Pene	24 Sept 1835	(6)
Dove Benjamin Franklin 24	Hartman Elenora 27	12 Dec 1888	(4) 2/25
Dowman Henry	Burket Rachael	*30 Apr 1825	(4) 3/33
Dowman Matilda 24	Bowman Isaac Peter 23	23 Nov 1881	(4) 2/16
Downan Sarah Elizabeth 21	Friddle John Frances 21	16 Sept 1869	(4) 2/1
Downey John	Good Mary	9 Nov 1828	(6)
Downey Sarah F 20	Hutson Henry A 24	9 Jan 1866	(4) 1/2
Doyle Charles Ashby 23	Davis Ida Virginia 23	7 Nov 1886	(4) 2/22
Doyle Harriett Jane 26	Hines Thomas 47	16 Nov 1870	(4) 2/2
Doyle James Philip 35	Timbrook Mary Susan 19	27 Dec 1888	(4) 2/26
Doyle Jane	Cann Jacob	*22 Nov 1828	(4) 3/41
Doyle Mathew	Corbin Winney	*16 June 1825	(4) 3/15
Doyle Matthew 33	Ruckman Harriet Jane 23	23 Mar 1882	(4) 2/17
Doyle Matthew 60	Swisher Harriet 30	19 Oct 1865	(4) 1/1
Doyle Zulemma Margaret 30	Sheetz Daniel Benjamin 31	21 Aug 1889	(4) 2/26
Drace Agnes	Yokum Riley	22 Feb 1832	(5)
Drace Eliza	Jennings William	2 Feb 1826	(5)
Drace Nancy	Powes Peter	30 Dec 1823	(5)
Drace Rebecca	Martin George	15 Feb 1835	(5)

Name #1	Name #2	Date	Source
Dresser Bellinda Todd 17	Martin John Jr 28	3 Nov 1892	(4) 2/31
Dressler Annie Maria 20	Cochran William Alexander 33	28 Mar 1888	(4) 2/24
Duckworth Andrew Marvell 28	Smith Martha Susan Elizabeth 17	30 Nov 1887	(4) 2/24
Duffey John W 54	Bauers Arthalinda 33	17 Oct 1865	(4) 1/1
Duke James	Davis Jane	9 Feb 1848	(6)
Duke Rebecca	Hamilton Thomas	6 Aug 1860	(5)
Duling Achilles	Knabenshoe Sarah	26 Apr 1821	(5)
Duling Ann	Dew John	12 May 1835	(6)
Duling Catherine M	Wineow John	21 June 1837	(1) 1 July 1837
Duling David	Davis Susan K	2 Nov 1853	(10)
Duling Edm	Harrison J M	29 Aug 1849	(6)
Duling Edmond 39	? Martha 38	24 Oct 1860	(10)
Duling Elijah	Dean Anna	12 Feb 1824	(6)
Duling Elijah	Dean Anne	*7 Feb 1824	(4) 3/9
Duling Mary	Davis Joseph		(1) 14 Nov 1839
Duling Nancy	Knabenshue Jacob	*16 Oct 1824	(4) 3/47
Duling Ruth	Dean Wm	26 June 1823	(6)
Duncan Elizabeth 26	Walker David Shelby 60	15 July 1875	(4) 2/7
Dunlap Algernon Wood 33	Lafollette Fannie 19	18 Nov 1880	(4) 2/15
Dunlap Randolph Tucker 24	Anderson Ann Eliza 22	*27 May 1876	(4) 2/8
Dunlap Riley Love 21	Brill Frances Doyle 21	23 Apr 1899	(4) 2/41
Dunn Francis Marion 29	Short Martha Ellen 23	27 Feb 1881	(4)2/15
Durst Albert W? 23	Day Lucy Bell 21	14 Oct 1879	(4) 2/13
Durst John L 26	Rase Catharine 18	23 Dec 1880	(4) 2/15
Durst Louisa Ellen 19	Moore William Henry 28	28 Sept 1876	(4) 2/8
Durst Margaret A 24	Racy Lewis 26	26 May 1880	(4) 2/14
Durst Sarah Almeda 18	Deaver Christopher 24	25 Feb 1879	(4) 2/13
Durst Susan Catherine 19	Roberts John 25	22 Dec 1881	(4) 2/17
Duvall George Washington 36	Everitt Mary Allice 24	25 Mar 1879	(4) 2/13
Dye A M	McNemar Martin	19 Apr 1836	(6)
Dye Capt John	Harrison R	1 Mar 1849	(6)
Dye David	Harrison Sallie	15 Mar 18321	(6)
Dye J W	Taylor Nancy	19 Dec 1860	(5)
Dye J W	Taylor Nancy	19 Dec 1859	(6)
Dye N E	Harrison Theodore	11 Oct 1854	(6)
Dye Nancy	Cundiff Wesley	7 Feb 1822	(6)
Dye William	Cundiff Nancy C	26 Mar 1822	(6)
Dyre Elizabeth 25	Reynolds James Howard 37	3 Oct 1865	(4) 1/1
Earley James O 23	Frey Rachael 23	17 Jan 1866	(4) 1/2
Earnholt Adam	McCauley Sarah	25 Feb 1819	(6)
Earnholt Jane	Murphy F	3 Oct 1822	(6)
Earnholt John	Kitzmiller Mary	5 Dec 1827	(5)
Earnholt Rebecca	Anderson David	28 June 1842	(5)
Earnholt William	Bosley Priscilla	28 Oct 1850	(5)
Earnholt William	McCauley Susan	29 June 1820	(6)
Earsom Nancy	Rizer Matthias	14 Nov 1839	(1) 21 Nov 1839
Easter Arah Elsie 22	Alderton Joseph 22	19 May 1875	(4) 2/7
Easter Elizabeth 25	Haines Henry Walker 25	1 Sept 1874	(4) 2/6
Easter Henry	Flemming Nancy	*12 Apr 1825	(4) 3/29
Easter Ruth Annie Ward 21	Haines Noah Webster 23	18 Sept 1879	(4) 2/13
Eaton Balam 36	Whitlock Lydia Jane 22	28 Mar 1867	(4) 1/5
Eaton Bertha Raivetta 18	Miller Robert Edgar 28	12 July 1900	(4) 2/43

Name #1	Name #2	Date	Source
Eaton D Elmer 22	Miller Annie Elizabeth 24	16 Aug 1900	(4) 2/43
Eaton Elijah E 26	Bennett Helen J 25	14 May 1887	(4) 2/23
Eaton Elijah E 23	Powell Lucinda M 25	29 Mar 1883	(4) 2/18
Eaton Elijah Everett 23	Hawkins Elizabeth Malinda 20	26 Mar 1874	(4) 2/6
Eaton Eliza Ann 17	Whitacre Jordon 31	21 Dec 1871	(4) 2/3
Eaton James William 20	Serbaugh Arminta Belle 22	16 Mar 1898	(4) 2/40
Eaton John	Barrett Charlotte		(1) 7 July 1838
Eaton John Willaim 21	Sirbaugh Annie Cyrena 17	30 May 1878	(4) 2/11
Eaton Levi James 24	Riley Frances Catharine 32	28 Sept 1882	(4) 2/17
Eaton Margaret Laura 20	Pugh Albert David 21	24 Dec 1891	(4) 2/30
Eaton Sarah E 21	Giffin John Robert 27	3 Jan 1878	(4) 2/11
Eaton Sophia Rosella 16	Whitlock William Braxton 22	31 Oct 1890	(4) 2/28
Eddy John	Colbert Clara	9 May 1828	(5)
Edmiston Elizabeth C	Hancher James W	*16 June 1825	(4) 3/45
Edmondson Oswell 21	Stevens Malinda 21	25 Jan 1888	(4) 1/40
Edmondson Robert Allen 23	Woods Catharine Emily 24	16 Dec 1877	(4) 1/39
Edmonson Charley 23	Lewis Annie Bell 22	3 Nov 1892	(4) 1/41
Edmonson Edward B 23	Dandridge Silin 17	11 Dec 1879	(4) 1/39
Edmunds J F	McCord Mary	22 Apr 1830	(6)
Edward Margaret	Aldereton William	3 May 1786	(3)
Edwards Ann	Powell John	*5 Apr 1824	(4) 3/21
Edwards Ann	Sharf George		(1) 13 Jan 1838
Edwards Annie Catharine 19	Arnold Edward Daily 23	6 Aug 1896	(4) 2/37
Edwards Francis Taylor 25	Yost Mary Elizabeth 22	24 Dec 1876	(4) 2/9
Edwards Geo M Dallas 22	Miller Maria M 22	11 Sept 1866	(4) 1/3
Edwards Harriette E 35	Reed Quinites H 20	15 Nov 1881	(4) 2/16
Edwards James Anthony Porter 25	Darr Mary Ellen 20	17 Nov 1885	(4) 2/21
Edwards John Cram 48	Canon Martha Jane 21	23 Sept 1867	(4) 1/5
Edwards Martha	Scott David	*17 Apr 1826	(4) 3/16
Edwards Mary Cordelia 21	Bennett Charles Holland 24	16 Mar 1892	(4) 2/30
Edwards Robert	Hawkins Eve	*27 Nov 1826	(4) 3/42
Edwards Robert 72	Brill Ellen C 39	*19 Aug 1879	(4) 2/13
Edwards Robert William 23	Kidwell Rebecca Ann 19	28 July 1881	(4) 2/16
Edwards Robt F 23	Fink Susan R 21	8 Mar 1866	(4) 1/3
Edwards William	Busby Margaret		(1) 23 May 1839
Eichelberger Webster 39	Hobart Elizabeth Maria 35	9 Dec 1874	(4) 2/6
Eliason Ella 20	Herriott William Vause 47	19 Jan 1876	(4) 2/8
Elifritz George	Jarvis M	29 Dec 1816	(5)
Elifritz Kesia	Umstot Simon	6 Sept 1850	(5)
Elifritz Kesia	Umstot Simon	6 Sept 1851	(6)
Elifritz Phebe	Polon John	23 Sept 1830	(6)
Elifritz Sarah	Liller Henry	1 June 1826	(6)
Elifritz Sol	Sands Hannah	20 Jan 1824	(6)
Elleburger Thomas	Bosley Eleanor	17 June 1828	(5)
Ellifritz Angelina	Rogers James	30 Oct 1845	(6)
Ellifritz Sarah	Liller Henry	*22 May 1826	(4) 3/21
Elligritz Geo	Jarvis M	29 Dec 1816	(6)
Elliott Elizabeth 20	Lineberg Luther 20	1 Oct 1892	(4) 2/31
Ellis David	Farmer Sarah Jane	*29 Sept 1828	(4) 3/28
Ellis Elize	Weaver Franklin	*7 Apr 1828	(4) 3/9
Ely Amanda Susan 21	McCauley Auther Wellington 21	7 Nov 1871	(4) 2/3
Ely Beecher Ulysses 26	Lewis Amanda Hill 26	25 Nov 1889	(4) 2/27

Name #1	Name #2	Date	Source
Ely Benjamin	Powelson Rosannah	*29 Mar 1828	(4) 3/8
Ely Clara Virginia 23	Feller John Henry 22	14 Nov 1888	(4) 2/25
Ely Frances Della 21	Barnes Alexander Monroe 22	25 Dec 1889	(4) 2/27
Ely Mary Catharine 24	Kline Stevanas 54	23 Jan 1884	(4) 2/18
Ely William	Carder Charlotte	*7 Mar 1828	(4) 3/6
Emmart Elmira Virginia 18	Baker John B 28	2 Oct 1873	(4) 2/4
Emmart Jacob H 26	Heare Eliza R V 21	21 Dec 1870	(4) 2/2
Emmart John William 24	Loy Anne Victory 21	8 Jan 1891	(4) 2/29
Emmart Lemuel Parker 24	Malick Ettie Belle 20	13 Dec 1888	(4) 2/25
Emmart Morgan 28	Thomas Mary Florence 22	8 Feb 1893	(4) 2/32
Emmart Mrs Barbara Ann 48	Rives Robert William 48	17 Sept 1889	(4) 2/27
Emmart William Henry 26	Carlisle Emma Belle 23	26 Apr 1894	(4) 2/34
Emmart Wilmith I Columbia 24	Leith Phio C 29	27 Oct 1881	(4) 2/16
Emmerson James	Reese Hannah	*12 Sept 1827	(4) 3/45
Emmerson James	Reese Hannah	13 Sept 1827	(5)
Emmit Jas	Rawlings Mary	19 Sept 1844	(6)
Emsley James Albert 36	Raines Sarah 29	30 May 1894	(4) 2/34
Emsley James Albert 26	Shank Rachel Ann 18	10 Apr 1883	(4) 2/18
Endler Ann Rebecca	Marshall David Alonzo	13 Nov 1863	(4) 2/1
Endler Luranah	Neal Allen	21 Dec 1833	(6)
Engle Hiram	Groves Amilia	*28 Aug 1824	(4) 3/42
Ensminger Elizabeth	Lawrence John G	1 Oct 1822	(5)
Entler Nancy	Smith Jacob	*17 Sept 1828	(4) 3/27
Entler William	Race Sally	*3 June 1826	(4) 3/22
Ernholt Jane	Murphy Frances	3 Oct 1822	(5)
Eskridge Sanford Virgil 20	Pool Louisa Ella 22	3 Jun 1897	(4) 2/39
Evans Alexander	Tharp Ann	*2 Jan 1826	(4) 3/1
Evans Benj 26	Kesill Eliza 22	9 Apr 1866	(4) 1/3
Evans Caleb 25	Ruckman Emily	1854	(10)
Evans Eliza	Michael Eli	10 Feb 1863	(6)
Evans Elizabeth	Mitchael Eli	10 Feb 1862	(5)
Evans Francis Jane 19	Evans John A 33	19 Apr 1866	(4) 1/3
Evans Jacob	Bosly Nancy	22 Sept 1839	(5)
Evans John A 33	Evans Francis Jane 19	19 Apr 1866	(4) 1/3
Evans Nancy	Shillingburg Washington	19 Sept 1842	(5)
Evans Sarah Amanda 25	Rudolph Adam 67	10 Apr 1867	(4) 1/5
Evans William	Kitzmiller Lydia	18 Mar 1842	(5)
Everett A Frances 18	Simpson Samuel A 35	18 Aug 1896	(4) 2/37
Everett Caroline 21	Fisher Richard 21	28 Sept 1865	(4) 1/1
Everett Elizabeth Catharine 21	Stewart Edward 21	16 July 1879	(4) 2/13
Everett George Marion 19	Geno Catharine 21	12 Sept 1872	(4) 2/3
Everett Harriet Elizabeth	Orndorff Henry Hampton	25 Sept 1860	(10)
Everett Harriet E	Orndorff Henry H	25 Apr 1859	(1) 13 May 1859
Everett Hester Elizabeth 24	Pownall Richard Winifield 30	11 Mar 1896	(4) 2/37
Everett Jamima Ann 17	Hines Millard 24	20 Aug 1896	(4) 2/37
Everett John 72	Lambert Margaret Jane 33	21 Aug 1894	(4) 2/34
Everett Julia A 24	Haines Stephen 23	14 Dec 1868	(4) 1/7
Everett Lewis	Liller Catherine	23 Mar 1842	(6)
Everett Lorany Florence 24	Saville Peter Oliver 34	5 Jan 1898	(4) 2/40
Everett Margaret Jane 29	Miller John William 23	17 Oct 1877	(4) 2/10
Everett Mary E 23	Fertig Ira R 23	11 Apr 1872	(4) 2/3
Everett Mary Elizabeth 24	Mull John L 26	13 Sept 1887	(4) 2/24

Name #1	Name #2	Date	Source
Everett Mary Frances 22	Nevitt Robert Emory 29	23 Sept 1885	(4) 2/21
Everett Nancy Jane 37	Malick George Washington 55	12 June 1894	(4) 2/34
Everett Susan 25	Lee Charles 41	9 Oct 1877	(4) 1/39
Everett William Isaac 24	Davis Margaret Ellen 26	4 Dec 1889	(4) 2/27
Everitt Elizabeth Ann 40	French Robert McKinney 52	11 Apr 1871	(4) 2/2
Everitt Enos	Pettit Sarah	*19 Apr 1824	(4) 3/23
Everitt Mary Allice 24	Duvall George Washington 36	25 Mar 1879	(4) 2/13
Everstine Willard 23	Loy Mary Catharine 25	25 Mar 1894	(4) 2/33
Evick Lonie Alice 16	Fravel Charles N 27	27 Dec 1897	(4) 2/40
Ewers Arthur Loudon 26	Johnson Lucy M 24	14 Sept 1887	(4) 2/24
Ewers Catharine Frazier 18	Thompson John Harris 25	8 Dec 1869	(4) 2/1
Ewers Elizabeth Balthis 22	Johnson Zachariah Esrah 22	21 Oct 1891	(4) 2/30
Ewers Luther Carson 21	Swisher Susan Virginia 21	1 Dec 1875	(4) 2/8
Ewers Mary Agnes 22	Watson Albert Taylor 24	9 May 1882	(4) 2/17
Ewing Robert W	Gardner Elizabeth	7 Apr 1857	(2) 23 Apr 1857
Fagle Martin B 26	Oats Mollie 22	1 Feb 1894	(4) 2/33
Fahs Caroline	Ruckman James		(2) 14 May 1857
Fahs Joseph	Slane Maria	*2 Apr 1827	(4) 3/25
Fahs Leah	Martin George	*28 Apr 1827	(4) 3/29
Fairfax ? 38	Rolls Sallie 36	24 Mar 1874	(4) 1/38
Fairfax Bertie 17	Streets John William 22	26 Nov 1889	(4) 1/41
Fairfax David 23	Darr Mary 23	12 June 1868	(4) 1/6
Fairfax Hannah 22	Bias Joseph 42	30 Aug 1883	(4) 1/40
Fairfax James Lanius 22	Fairfax Lena May 17	29 Sept 1897	(4) 1/41
Fairfax Lena May 17	Fairfax James Lanius 22	29 Sept 1897	(4) 1/41
Fairfax Louisa W	Tapscott Newton	*3 Mar 1825	(4) 3/17
Fait Hiram 25	Marshall Rachael 24	6 Apr 1874	(4) 2/6
Farlow Sina	Queen Dennis	19 Nov 1818	(6)
Farmer Frances Virginia 27	Secrist William Miller 30	15 Oct 1885	(4) 2/21
Farmer George William 30	Reid Cordelia Theresa 26	*19 Feb 1877	(4) 2/9
Farmer James Franklin 27	McDonald Mrs Isabel 38	14 May 1882	(4) 2/17
Farmer Samuel	McDonald Ann	4 Jan 1838	(1) 20 Jan 1838
Farmer Sarah Ann 24	Kidwell Francis Marion 23	16 Feb 1869	(4) 1/38
Farmer Sarah Jane	Ellis David	*29 Sept 1828	(4) 3/28
Farmer Virginia Anne 36	Orndorff Joseph A 45	19 Feb 1889	(4) 2/26
Fauver Addison Buchanan 33	Lafollette Emma C 25	17 Dec 1889	(4) 2/27
Fazenbaker J	Hamilton E	20 Dec 1849	(6)
Feaster Annie Gabriella 19	Groves Parsons Skelton 22	14 Dec 1898	(4) 2/41
Fediwick John 24	Parrill Mary Elizabeth 23	25 Mar 1870	(4) 2/1
Feilds Walter 22	Bias Maria Ann 22	*29 Dec 1873	(4) 1/38
Feller John Henry 22	Ely Clara Virginia 23	14 Nov 1888	(4) 2/25
Feller William Luther 26	Mills Mary Rebecca 23	31 Aug 1881	(4) 2/16
Fellers Jennie 27	Taylor Jacob Thomas 41	14 Feb 1893	(4) 2/32
Fergusen William 23	Rinker Rebecca 21	5 Sept 1865	(4) 1/1
Ferguson Robert Gallier 25	White Lucy 26	27 Jan 1876	(4) 2/8
Ferribee Thos	Hull Nancy	30 Nov 1843	(6)
Ferribee Wellington Pierce 29	Colbert Fanny I Lacy 25	3 Sept 1882	(4) 2/17
Ferriman H	White Abram	13 Sept 1846	(6)
Ferryman Francis	Shockey Lydia	*29 Oct 1827	(4) 3/52
Ferryman Rebeckah	McDonald James	*13 Nov 1828	(4) 3/39
Fertig Ira R 23	Everett Mary E 23	11 Apr 1872	(4) 2/3
Fetter John	Fout Charlotte	11 Sept 1817	(6)

Name #1	Name #2	Date	Source
Fetters Penelope	Liller Abs	11 Sept 1856	(6)
Fields Charles Hammond 30	Kinkead Anne Jennie 22	14 Sept 1899	(4) 2/41
Fields Felicia 21	Loyle Harry 26	6 Nov 1877	(4) 1/39
Fields Margaret Henrietta 24	Batsen Daniel W 24	26 Feb 1890	(4) 2/27
Files Barbara Ann	Oats Lorenzo	7 Mar 1839	(1) 21 Mar 1839
Fink Daniel	Jacobs Nancy	27 Dec 1818	(6)
Fink Hester A	Bane Zimri	6 Dec 1849	(6)
Fink Susan R 21	Edwards Robt F 23	8 Mar 1866	(4) 1/3
Finley Cora Williams 21	Gilkeson Edwin Myers 33	4 Sept 1888	(4) 2/25
Finley Nannie Edwards 25	White William Chester 28	1 Dec 1886	(4) 2/22
Fishel Frances Jane 18	Orndorff Robert Johnson 24	1 Oct 1891	(4) 2/29
Fishel Geo 28	Day Jennie 23	24 Sept 1899	(4) 2/42
Fishel George Washington 21	Henderson Margaret Lee 27	17 Dec 1893	(4) 2/33
Fishel Isaac	Paliner Sarah J	21 June 1863	(8)
Fishel Jacob	Orndorff Mary A	5 Jan 1865	(8)
Fishel Margaret Catharine 21	Oats Theodrick Leath 28	*14 Sept 1887	(4) 2/24
Fishel William 24	Lineberg Ella 22	29 Aug 1896	(4) 2/37
Fishell Jacob David 22	Winfield Minnie 20	7 Oct 1896	(4) 2/37
Fishell Sallie Louisa 19	McIntyre George 45	18 Nov 1897	(4) 2/39
Fisher Ann Jemima	Simmons William M		(1) 6 June 1839
Fisher Chas M 23	Hanlin Deba Ellen 16	7 May 1901	(4) 2/44
Fisher Ella 21	Johnson Jerome E 29	4 Apr 1893	(4) 1/41
Fisher Emma Lillian 18	Wilson ? 23	30 Oct 1879	(4) 2/13
Fisher Katie R 24	Mulinix John Luther 22	24 June 1894	(4) 2/34
Fisher Louisa Walton 21	Roberts William Wesley 21	26 Sept 1877	(4) 2/10
Fisher Mary	Miles J D	27 Oct 1825	(5)
Fisher Richard 29	Ayers Ruth Ann 20	17 Sept 1874	(4) 1/39
Fisher Richard 21	Everett Caroline 21	28 Sept 1865	(4) 1/1
Fisher Robert Scott 25	Lewis Jemima 24	24 Sept 1885	(4) 2/21
Fisher Washington	Cherry Mary		(1) 20 May 1853
Fisher Z T 25	Quinn Mary Belle 18	26 Mar 1867	(4) 1/5
Fitzgerald Maria	Wilson Joseph	*15 Sept 1826	(4) 3/34
Fitzgerald Nancy	Plumb John	10 Dec 1826	(5)
Fitzgerald Nancy	Plumb John	*22 Nov 1826	(4) 3/41
Fitzwater Jas	McDonald M	22 Apr 1847	(6)
Fitzwaters Elzy 22	Bucklew Sarah Jane 23	26 Feb 1877	(4) 2/9
Flanagan Daniel	Arnold Susan	7 Jan 1841	(5)
Flanagan John	Blue Julia Ann	1 Jan 1838	(1) 20 Jan 1838
Flanagan William Lambert 49	Thompson Malinda Ann 48	27 Jan 1897	(4) 2/38
Flanigan Dan	Arnold Susan	7 Jan 1840	(6)
Flannigan E	McCormick Pat	18 Nov 1858	(6)
Flannigan John	Reese Ele'r	4 June 1835	(6)
Fleek Christina 23	Daniel Daniel J 26	22 June 1854	(10)
Fleek Peter	Spencer Rachel	*29 Jan 1828	(4) 3/2
Fleming Christina	Kline William S	19 Aug 1819	(5)
Fleming Harriet J 43	McGee Charles Jackson 47	16 Mar 1890	(4) 2/27
Fleming James	Blackburn Hannah	13 June 1862	(5)
Fleming Joseph 53	Rinker Susan Rebecca 33	9 Oct 1890	(4) 2/28
Fleming Mary Elizabeth 22	Miller Benjamin Franklin 24	19 July 1893	(4) 2/32
Fleming Nettie May 19	Hauvermale Clarence Howard 22	22 Aug 1888	(4) 2/25
Fleming Ruehanna 24	High George McCellan 36	20 Jan 1898	(4) 2/40
Flemming Anne	Shurley Lazarus	*14 Mar 1825	(4) 3/23

Name #1	Name #2	Date	Source
Flemming Edward Anderson 28	Jewell Etta Serena 15	23 Dec 1880	(4) 2/15
Flemming James Wilson 44	Ault Sarah Alice 24	2 Nov 1898	(4) 2/41
Flemming Nancy	Easter Henry	*12 Apr 1825	(4) 3/29
Flemming Nancy 28	Rinker Samuel 45	5 Oct 1879	(4) 2/13
Fletcher Alexander Peirce 31	Hoke Sarah Caroline 18	17 June 1891	(4) 2/29
Fletcher Alvin M 20	Shingleton Minnie Florence 22	3 Sept 1895	(4) 2/36
Fletcher Bertha E 21	Oats Ira Clay 28	30 Dec 1895	(4) 2/36
Fletcher Cora Virginia 23	Frye Orean Allen 29	12 Nov 1896	(4) 2/38
Fletcher Elihu Christy 30	Oats Martha Ann 17	18 Oct 1887	(4) 2/24
Fletcher Elijah	Queen Elizabeth	*30 Jan 1826	(4) 3/4
Fletcher Emanuel Lupton 19	Wolford Alice Belle 21	1 Aug 1898	(4) 2/40
Fletcher Flavius Josephus 27	Kump Jemima Elizabeth 27	4 June 1879	(4) 2/13
Fletcher Frances 19	Albaugh Nimrod 24	7 Jan 1891	(4) 2/29
Fletcher Joseph 22	Rieley Elizabeth Jane 22	15 Aug 1869	(4) 2/1
Fletcher Margaret Frances 16	Lewis William Owen 27	27 Dec 1866	(4) 1/4
Fletcher Margaret 23	Sheetz Jacob Dice 29	30 May 1877	(4) 2/10
Fletcher Mary Catharine 28	Crane Willis 58	25 Jan 1875	(4) 2/7
Fletcher Samuel B 23	Clayton Sarah A 22	20 June 1894	(4) 2/34
Flether Susan Ann 21	Powell Benjamin James 31	9 Apr 1874	(4) 2/6
Flick Adam	Dawson Mary	25 Apr 1816	(5)
Flick Adam	Dawson Mary	16 Apr 1816	(6)
Flick Arthur	Umstot Eliz	8 May 1845	(6)
Flick Catherine	Culp James	5 May 1836	(6)
Flick Catherine	Gangus Jacob	28 Dec 1837	(6)
Flick Christina	Daniels D J	22 June 1854	(6)
Flick E H	Urice Sarah	27 Aug 1846	(6)
Flick Elizabeth	Tate James	29 Jan 1840	(5)
Flick Elizabeth	Tate James	29 Jan 1839	(6)
Flick Isaac	Spencer Mary	6 Mar 1828	(6)
Flick Jacob	Spencer Eliz	4 May 1837	(6)
Flick John William 25	Stagg Isabel Lauretta 17	22 Oct 1878	(4) 2/12
Flick M J	Daniels Dennis	25 Jan 1849	(6)
Flick Magdalene	Putman Jacob	*24 Mar 1824	(4) 3/17
Flick Peter	Spencer Rachel	31 Jan 1828	(6)
Flick Rachel	Harsel Peter	9 Mar 1820	(5)
Flick Susan	Bailey Jacob	19 Apr 1849	(6)
Flick Susannah	Lees J B	10 Apr 1829	(6)
Flick Thorn	Stewart H M	27 Nov 1855	(6)
Flick Wm S	Stagg Delilah	19 Sept 1854	(6)
Florey Newton Brown 23	Pugh Martha Jane 22	27 Dec 1876	(4) 2/9
Flory John Michael 33	Albin Mary Jane 32	10 Aug 1875	(4) 2/7
Flory Mary Virginia 21	Wolford Benjamin Franklin 21	12 Apr 1880	(4) 2/14
Flory William H 25	Daugherty Martha E 24	28 Jan 1873	(4) 2/4
Flournoy Samuel Lightfoot 28	White Frances Ann 30	8 Apr 1875	(4) 2/7
Fogel Charlotte	Kervey Benjamin	*4 Sept 1826	(4) 3/33
Fogel Henry	Harsell Lucretia	18 Dec 1823	(6)
Fogle Henry	Harsell Lucretia	25 Dec 1823	(5)
Fogle Julia A	Leatherman A	9 Mar 1848	(6)
Foley Millery	Moore Solomon	*10 Dec 1828	(4) 3/44
Foley S	Lees Wm	6 Apr 1843	(6)
Foley Thomas Winfield Scott 23	High Mary Texas 18	22 Oct 1874	(4) 2/6
Folks Lucy 21	Johnson George 34	24 Sept 1888	(4) 1/40

Name #1	Name #2	Date	Source
Folty Martin 21	Martin Meineiva 20	29 Nov 1871	(4) 2/3
Folty Sardenia Caroline 19	Haines Leven Taylor 24	26 Feb 1878	(4) 2/11
Foltz Benjamin Price 26	Shanholtzer Marg Melissa 17	7 Jan 1879	(4) 2/12
Foltz Catherine	Haynes Philip		(1) 7 Feb 1839
Foltz Elizabeth 25	Smoot Charles Middleton 35	10 Jan 1897	(4) 2/38
Foltz Esther Ann 22	Biser Edward Taylor 22	14 Oct 1874	(4) 2/6
Foltz Francina 23	Hays Jeremiah Wm 33	1 Mar 1883	(4) 2/18
Foltz Henry 47	McBride Chloe Catharine 27	9 Sept 1896	(4) 2/37
Foltz Isaac Newton 30	Hott Barbara Ann 20	9 Dec 1890	(4) 2/28
Foltz Jacob 28	Nealis Margaret Elizabeth 28	*20 Nov 1880	(4) 2/15
Foltz John Wesley 26	Smoot Addie Mabell 21	3 Jan 1888	(4) 2/24
Foltz Joshua I 24	Shanholtzer Amanda E 19	17 Dec 1872	(4) 2/4
Foltz Lacy Ann 21	Miller Jas Wesly P 24	6 Feb 1878	(4) 2/11
Foltz Margaret Ella 40	Haines James Henry 62	13 Dec 1899	(4) 2/42
Foltz Martha Ellen 24	Biser Martin Miller 21	10 May 1882	(4) 2/17
Foltz Mary Ann	Wolford Jonathan	11 Jan 1866	(4) 1/2
Foltz May 16	Smoot Judson 21	24 Feb 1891	(4) 2/29
Foltz Smith Loy 33	Shanholtzer Theresa Jane 33	20 Apr 1890	(4) 2/28
Foltz Susan Mary 20	Hott Daniel Taylor 24	25 Feb 1886	(4) 2/21
Foltz Virginia L 22	Haines Reazin 66	9 Feb 1886	(4) 2/21
Foltz William Winfield 24	Haines Ella May 20	7 Jan 1897	(4) 2/38
Foote Wm H	Gilliam Arabella	31 Oct 1838	(1) 17 Nov 1838
Foreman Amy Virginia May 18	Largent Benjamin Alfred 21	11 Nov 1880	(4) 2/14
Foreman David Henry 32	Largent Hannah Jane 25	27 Apr 1882	(4) 2/17
Forsyth Jacob	Moreland Polly	7 June 1843	(5)
Fout Ann	Liller Isaac	*19 Mar 1827	(4) 3/Page Torn
Fout Charlotte	Fetter John	11 Sept 1817	(6)
Fout Florence Virginia 19	Mahew John Ephraim 24	6 Dec 1893	(4) 2/33
Fout Lydia 20	Timbrook Thomas Wesley 21	1 June 1892	(4) 2/31
Fout Mary	Grayson Benjamin	*30 Apr 1827	(4) 3/30
Fout Mary	Grayson Benjamin	3 May 1827	(5)
Fout Wm	Patengall Mary	8 May 1832	(6)
Fowler Lucy F 23	Austin Sterling James 25	22 Nov 1882	(4) 1/40
Fox Ann E 31	Blue John 33	18 Jan 1868	(4) 1/6
Fox Rebecca 24	Withers Chas B 24	15 Nov 1865	(4) 1/1
Fox Susan Rebecca 26	Parker Alfred Vause 26	6 Nov 1895	(4) 2/36
Fox William Vause 30	Blue Ursula 26	21 Oct 1874	(4) 2/6
Frank Andrew J 37	Reid Frances V A 29	22 Dec 1870	(4) 2/2
Frank Ellen 22	Sirbaugh Jacob 30	24 Dec 1879	(4) 2/14
Frank Martin C 23	Pennington Anna Lee 24	6 Apr 1897	(4) 2/39
Frantz Adam	Steel Lucinda	26 Feb 1828	(5)
Frantz Sophia	Molden William	19 Jan 1823	(5)
Fravel Charles N 27	Evick Lonie Alice 16	27 Dec 1897	(4) 2/40
Fravel Francis Marian 32	Hockman Leah Catherine 23	17 Oct 1869	(4) 2/1
Fravel Lena May 21	McCauley George William 25	9 May 1893	(4) 2/32
Frazier Eleanor	Probasco Jacob	*7 July 1825	(4) 3/47
Frazier Fred	Barrick Matilda	25 Aug 1843	(6)
Frazier M J	Newhouse John	23 Mar 1842	(6)
Frederick Maria	Athey Thomas	1 Jan 1843	(5)
Frederick Rachael A 26	Little William D 27	13 Mar 1866	(4) 1/3
French Charles Edgar 25	Shanholtzer Della May 20	26 Mar 1901	(4) 2/44
French Charles Montgomery 32	Taylor Hannah Elizabeth 26	18 Nov 1873	(4) 2/5

Name #1	Name #2	Date	Source
French Charles Montgomery 34	Taylor Mary Susan 20	16 Feb 1876	(4) 2/8
French Elizabeth Ellen 19	Orndorff James Richen 21	10 Dec 1884	(4) 2/20
French Ida Virginia 20	Malick James Owen 22	24 Oct 1895	(4) 2/36
French John William 21	Peer Sarah Elizabeth 19	14 Oct 1873	(4) 2/5
French Robert McKinney 52	Everitt Elizabeth Ann 40	11 Apr 1871	(4) 2/2
French Sarah Ann Matilda 19	Haines James William 27	25 Aug 1874	(4) 2/6
French Susan Taylor 18	Brill Lewis Henry 24	24 Dec 1895	(4) 2/36
French William	Taylor Susan	*28 May 1825	(4) 3/39
Frey Rachael 23	Earley James O 23	17 Jan 1866	(4) 1/2
Friddle Henry	Kirk Betsy Ann	*10 May 1824	(4) 3/27
Friddle John	Peters Lydia	*11 Jan 1827	(4) 3/4
Friddle John Frances 21	Downan Sarah Elizabeth 21	16 Sept 1869	(4) 2/1
Friddle John Samuel 26	Roberson Sarah Ann 23	19 Dec 1899	(4) 2/42
Friddle Samuel 51	Matthews Mary Elizabeth 24	4 Sept 1867	(4) 1/5
Friut Edward W 50	Blue Susan E 41	4 Nov 1873	(4) 2/5
Fry Jesse	Moody Emily	22 Aug 1854	(6)
Frye Benjamin Hanson 25	Smith Virginia S 19	15 June 1876	(4) 2/8
Frye Catharine 24	Hurd Robert Lee 24	14 Nov 1889	(4) 2/27
Frye Edward Powell 27	Wolf Elta Lyda 23	2 Feb 1888	(4) 2/24
Frye James H	Frye Nancy J	*3 May 1826	(4) 3/18
Frye James Mason 28	Baker Frances 21	4 Oct 1893	(4) 2/33
Frye Jesse 25	Moody Emily 20	22 Aug 1854	(10)
Frye John	McNemara Catherine	2 Nov 1826	(5)
Frye Lucy G	Doran Joseph	*22 Sept 1827	(4) 3/48
Frye Margaret Elizabeth 20	Gest Andy Smith 21	21 Nov 1897	(4) 2/39
Frye Nancy J	Frye James H	*3 May 1826	(4) 3/18
Frye Nora Ellen 19	Bean George Welby 24	25 Dec 1889	(4) 2/27
Frye Orean Allen 29	Fletcher Cora Virginia 23	12 Nov 1896	(4) 2/38
Frye Robert Lee 28	Pepper Hattie Jane 23	7 Sept 1892	(4) 2/31
Frye S V 27	Kimble Richard L 29	20 Feb 1901	(4) 2/44
Frye Sarah Elizabeth 30	Timbrook Isaac Franklin 27	9 Sept 1897	(4) 2/39
Frye Susan Jennie 23	Coffman Julius Walter 35	13 Jan 1881	(4) 2/15
Fuller Maggie M 25	Combs Theodore F 26	9 Dec 1872	(4) 2/4
Fuller William 48	Whitacre Eliza Jane 30	20 Nov 1870	(4) 2/2
Funk Andrew Jackson 21	Pennington Frances Mary 17	5 Sept 1883	(4) 2/18
Funk Marian 33	Rosebough John M 41	28 July 1873	(4) 2/4
Funk Mary Susan 21	Violett James Edmond 46	7 Nov 1884	(4) 2/20
Furr William Robert 23	Hiett Charlotte Ann 19	9 Jan 1877	(4) 2/9
Gangus Jacob	Flick Catherine	28 Dec 1837	(6)
Gannon John Christopher 22	Liller Martha Ann 20	*24 Dec 1881	(4) 2/17
Gannon Strother	Poling M A	3 Apr 1845	(6)
Ganoe ?	McBride Joseph	20 Aug 1859	(10)
Ganoe Altie Mertie 20	Iser David Washington 22	6 June 1900	(4) 2/42
Ganoe Berzelius 22	Shanholtzer Annie Bell 22	24 Nov 1897	(4) 2/39
Ganoe Elizabeth	Smith John	*15 Dec 1828	(4) 3/47
Ganoe Hester E	White George W	13 Apr 1859	(1) 13 May 1859
Ganoe Isaac R D 23	Hines Amy Susan 18	16 Nov 1871	(4) 2/2
Ganoe James Marion 34	Bowman Harriet Ann 26	6 Mar 1889	(4) 2/26
Ganoe James Marion 18	Grapes Rebecca A 17	15 Oct 1873	(4) 2/5
Ganoe Lucy Ellen 23	Malcolm Nathan Ashby 24	24 Dec 1888	(4) 2/26
Ganoe Maggie Jane 20	Smoot John William 21	21 Jan 1895	(4) 2/35
Ganoe Margaret	Kearns Elisha	*8 Jan 1827	(4) 3/1

Name #1	Name #2	Date	Source
Ganoe Margaret Ann 17	Loy David Jackson 33	*29 July 1895	(4) 2/35
Ganoe Mary 27	Iser James Henry 20	11 Apr 1900	(4) 2/42
Ganoe Mary Jane 21	Nealis Joseph 26	15 June 1896	(4) 2/37
Ganoe Mary Victoria 18	Shingleton Absalom Lee 28	23 Aug 1893	(4) 2/33
Ganoe Rebecca Elizabeth 21	Pepper John William 49	30 Apr 1885	(4) 2/20
Ganoe Thomas Wesley 21	Baldwin Laura F 16	22 Nov 1892	(4) 2/31
Garard Wm H 28	Bean Ann Rebecca 23	15 Mar 1866	(4) 1/3
Gardner Annie Lee 17	Oats Jeanie Dow 20	8 Nov 1894	(4) 2/35
Gardner Elizabeth	Ewing Robert W	7 Apr 1857	(2) 23 Apr 1857
Gardner Esau 23	Webster Nancy Jane 23	25 June 1874	(4) 1/39
Gardner Jacob Rosenberger 39	Nixon Jane 47	12 Mar 1895	(4) 2/35
Gardner James 46	Sutton F Annie 37	28 June 1881	(4) 1/40
Gardner Mary Regina 25	Bageant James William 37	21 Dec 1892	(4) 2/31
Gardner Nora Lee 19	Schaffnaker L Nathaniel 22	12 Dec 1893	(4) 2/33
Gardner Silas Wright 30	Larrick Mary Elizabeth 23	4 Mar 1875	(4) 2/7
Gardner Tesa Belle 16	Brannon John William 19	11 Oct 1888	(4) 2/25
Garland Baltzer 22	Seeders Martha Jane 20	8 Oct 1891	(4) 2/29
Garland Oliver 20	Chaney Amanda Marsella 19	21 Dec 1876	(4) 2/9
Garret William Henry 27	Hawkins Philena 19	22 Dec 1886	(4) 2/23
Garrett Ernest Walter 18	Heishman Nellie Grant 19	30 June 1893	(4) 2/32
Garrett Matilda J 25	Bean Joseph 28	19 Apr 1866	(4) 1/3
Garrett Sarah Ellen 28	Lewis William Carroll 23	23 Nov 1870	(4) 2/2
Garvin Elizabeth A 23	Hook Thomas A 24	20 Dec 1869	(4) 2/1
Garvin James M 18	Creswell Mary Luella May 15	11 Mar 1874	(4) 2/6
Garvin Mahlon	Brill Rachel A	19 Feb 1861	(8)
Garvin Maria Lucinda 17	Kline Rienza 22	13 Apr 1870	(4) 2/1
Garvin Minnie Cordelia 24	Muse William Joseph 31	25 June 1896	(4) 2/37
Garvins Allie Ellen 21	Pugh Amos Luther 24	*4 Apr 1877	(4) 2/10
Gates Jemima 22	Johnson George W 22	19 Nov 1871	(4) 1/38
Gates Nancy 23	Lee Joshua 25	9 Oct 1877	(4) 1/39
Gatige William	Blackburn Mary	23 Sept 1827	(5)
Geno Catharine 21	Everett George Marion 19	12 Sept 1872	(4) 2/3
George Anna	Randle David	*15 Nov 1824	(4) 3/52
George John	Rotruck Polly	8 July 1834	(5)
George John F	Martin Ann R	27 Aug 1852	(5)
George Joseph	Shell Clara	23 Dec 1842	(5)
George Maria	Beals John	20 Aug 1845	(5)
George Sarah	Welch William	11 Dec 1844	(5)
George Silas	Wasson Nancy	*19 July 1824	(4) 3/39
George Wesley 25	Doman Juliet 22	1 July 1880	(4) 2/14
George William Henry 23	Taylor Maggie Jane 18	31 Aug 1898	(4) 2/40
Gess Wm Perry 23	Whitacre Phoebe Ann Catharine 17	11 June 1874	(4) 2/6
Gest Andy Smith 21	Frye Margaret Elizabeth 20	21 Nov 1897	(4) 2/39
Gettis John 28	Haydon Mary M L 33	30 June 1881	(4) 2/16
Gettys Sarah Febia 24	Walker James Wright 25	2 Mar 1875	(4) 2/7
Gibson Hannah 25	Armstrong David Gibson 25	12 Dec 1865	(4) 1/1
Gibson Mel 31	Russell Ellen 21	22 Nov 1883	(4) 1/40
Giffin Charles Fenton 35	Moreland Martha M 23	4 Nov 1896	(4) 2/37
Giffin Herbert ONille 21	Mann Amada Virginia 20	29 May 1901	(4) 2/44
Giffin John Robert 27	Eaton Sarah E 21	3 Jan 1878	(4) 2/11
Giffin John Wm 22	Lafollette Cora Rosa 22	8 Mar 1892	(4) 2/30
Giffin Rettie Margaret 23	Long Alexander Somerville 22	30 Dec 1896	(4) 2/38

Name #1	Name #2	Date	Source
Gilbert Eliz	Bennet James M	24 Sept 1846	(6)
Gilbert S H	Shank Wm E	19 Jan 1854	(6)
Gilbert Wm H 23	Ludwick Sarah J 21	2 Mar 1868	(4) 1/6
Gile Sarah 19	Miles William 23	15 Nov 1865	(4) 1/1
Gilicrist James H 24	Streits Sara 21	8 Oct 1879	(4) 1/39
Gilkeson Edwin Myers 33	Finley Cora Williams 21	4 Sept 1888	(4) 2/25
Gilkeson Margaret Vance 32	Pancake John Silas 38	27 Nov 1884	(4) 2/20
Gill Eveline 25	Corbin Luther 22	12 Aug 1866	(4) 1/3
Gill Isadore 22	Seldon Frederick John 26	5 May 1897	(4) 2/39
Gill Lucretia 25	Thompson Charles Eugene 26	19 Feb 1880	(4) 2/14
Gill Martha A 24	Pugh Marion Omer 24	7 Jan 1897	(4) 2/38
Gilliam Arabella	Foote Wm H	31 Oct 1838	(1) 17 Nov 1838
Gilmore Anthony Jacob 22	Johnson Lucy Ann 23	11 Sept 1873	(4) 1/38
Ginevan David 56	Belford Mary Ann 38	*16 Apr 1869	(4) 1/38
Ginevan David 56	Belford Mary Ann 38	*16 Apr 1867	(4) 2/1
Ginevan David Jacob 26	Portmess Zoe Etta 19	12 Jan 1899	(4) 2/41
Ginevan Thomas 27	Watson Emily Jane 18	25 Oct 1860	(10)
Ginivan George Washington 22	Brelsford Margaret Ester 16	28 Nov 1878	(4) 2/12
Ginivan Morris Newton 29	Stump Elizabeth Catharine 20	21 Feb 1872	(4) 2/3
Gladstone John E 33	Pugh Azza M 28	17 Oct 1888	(4) 2/25
Glaize Mary E 28	Wagoner Mora Lin 29	30 May 1893	(4) 2/32
Glaze ? Short 36	Glaze Emily Frances 35	24 Oct 1875	(4) 2/7
Glaze Emily Frances 35	Glaze ? Short 36	24 Oct 1875	(4) 2/7
Glaze William Andrew 20	Jeffries Mary Ellen 24	14 July 1881	(4) 2/16
Gochenour M	Loy William		(1) 28 Apr 1838
Godlove Isaac Calvin 24	Smith Margaret Ann 19	13 Feb 1876	(4) 2/8
Godlove Isaac Calvin 27	Thompson Eva Jane 17	21 Jan 1880	(4) 2/14
Godlove Joseph Rosser 36	Pultz Leah Margaret 31	9 Apr 1901	(4) 2/44
Godlove Joseph Rosser 25	Thompson Emily Maria 20	19 Mar 1890	(4) 2/27
Godlove Lydia Abigail Pownall 20	Smith Nathaniel Seymour 22	* Sept 1879	(4) 2/13
Godlove Rebecca Virginia 22	Wolford Chas E 20	30 Nov 1880	(4) 2/15
Godlove Sarah Catharine 41	Kerns Benjamin Franklin 60	20 May 1890	(4) 2/28
Godlove Savilla Alice 17	Hockman John Wesley 31	3 Jan 1879	(4) 2/12
Godlove Virginia C 24	Delaplain Asa Pirkey 25	30 Mar 1897	(4) 2/38
Godlove William Tucker 42	Robinson Mary Catharine 24	26 Mar 1899	(4) 2/41
Godlove William Henry Tucker 23	Thompson Mary Alwilda 17	29 Oct 1879	(4) 2/13
Goldsboro John Thomas 31	Parker Bettie Ward 17	26 Nov 1890	(4) 2/28
Goldsborough Stephen 25	McBride E Margaret 24	20 Oct 1884	(4) 2/20
Good Mary	Downey John	9 Nov 1828	(6)
Good Philip	Abernathy Elizabeth	*10 Dec 1825	(4) 3/73
Good Phillip	Abernathy Elizabeth	15 Dec 1825	(6)
Goodin Mary Shobe 22	Kenny John William 25	30 Mar 1875	(4) 2/7
Gooding Senora Wills 23	Haynes Wallace Pembroke 29	22 Feb 1876	(4) 2/8
Goos John D	Spaid Margaret	23 Sept 1852	(2) 7 Oct 1852
Gore James C 29	Hannum Minnie B 22	22 Dec 1895	(4) 2/36
Goshorn Robert 25	Banks Mary 25	23 Oct 1884	(4) 1/40
Grabill Ann Caroline 25	Davey John 26	22 Sept 1880	(4) 2/14
Grace Catherine Brady 20	Parker John Hite 24	18 Sept 1867	(4) 1/5
Grace Emma Virginia 20	Pollock Robert Sherrard 33	11 Nov 1885	(4) 2/21
Grace M 19	Parker Joseph Foreman 23	2 May 1860	(10)
Grace Sarah Ellen 28	Adams Jacob Long 32	24 Sept 1867	(4) 1/5
Grant Lemuel Alfred 24	Hiett Susan Ann 30	3 Nov 1870	(4) 2/2

Name #1	Name #2	Date	Source
Grapes Anna Maria 23	Cheshire P ? Johnson 21	5 Oct 1882	(4) 2/17
Grapes Catharine	Bennett John	*19 Dec 1826	(4) 3/47
Grapes Elizabeth Florence 18	Hiett Asa Griffith 23	29 Oct 1888	(4) 2/25
Grapes Emma Irene 21	Shanholtzer Philip Solomon 22	12 Aug 1888	(4) 2/25
Grapes George Walker 29	Piles Rachel Bell 20	12 Jan 1887	(4) 2/23
Grapes George Wesley 26	Saville Mary Jane 23	10 Oct 1889	(4) 2/27
Grapes James Henry 20	Heavener Ursa B 23	25 Mar 1901	(4) 2/44
Grapes John	Bennett Maria	*13 Dec 1828	(4) 3/45
Grapes John Thomas 23	Wolford Sarah Lurena 19	30 Oct 1883	(4) 2/18
Grapes M B 23	Rogers Wm Henry 24	18 Nov 1896	(4) 2/38
Grapes Margaret Ann 20	Smith James William 21	16 Oct 1879	(4) 2/13
Grapes Martha E 35	McDonald James Wm 66	8 Apr 1900	(4) 2/42
Grapes Mary Elizabeth 30	Lear Thomas Taylor 33	*7 July 1870	(4) 2/2
Grapes Rebecca A 17	Ganoe James Marion 18	15 Oct 1873	(4) 2/5
Grapes Robert Henry 23	Hines Mary Hannah C Ambler 19	7 Dec 1874	(4) 2/6
Gray Anthony Hammack 21	Creswell Sallie Estella 20	27 Feb 1879	(4) 2/13
Gray Benjamin Franklin 23	Swisher Mary Virginia 21	16 June 1895	(4) 2/35
Gray Harry 21	Jackson Sidney 18	17 Nov 1879	(4) 1/39
Gray Henry Newton 26	Creswell Sarah Frances 21	20 May 1886	(4) 2/22
Gray Henry Newton 35	Spaid Regina Susanna 34	28 Dec 1893	(4) 2/33
Gray Ida May 20	Wolford Richard Nixon 25	18 Apr 1894	(4) 2/34
Gray James	Rudolph Barbara A	22 Nov 1866	(9)
Gray Jane 19	Jackson Aaron 26	8 Feb 1866	(4) 1/2
Gray Jas K 22	Rudolph Barbara A 24	22 Nov 1866	(4) 1/4
Gray Joseph Early 24	Hook Annie Elizabeth 20	13 Dec 1872	(4) 2/4
Gray Julius H 28	Lee Sarah E Irene 18	25 Oct 1883	(4) 2/18
Gray Mary Elizabeth 22	Herbaugh John Walker 29	8 Sept 1891	(4) 2/29
Gray Morgan 31	Wolfe Catharine 33	6 Oct 1870	(4) 2/2
Gray Mrs Annie E 33	Nixon Caudy John 26	1 Dec 1887	(4) 2/24
Gray Peter 32	Johnson Sarah Francis 21	22 Nov 1871	(4) 2/3
Gray Philip	Haines Rebecca	19 Jan 1865	(9)
Gray Robert Lee 24	Loy Tamer Catharine 25	10 Jan 1889	(4) 2/26
Gray William	Wise Barbara	8 Dec 1866	(9)
Gray William 39	Corbin Mary 50	5 Apr 1876	(4) 2/8
Gray William Bruce 30	Shanholtzer Lula Bertha 23	14 Dec 1898	(4) 2/41
Grayson Benjamin	Fout Mary	3 May 1827	(6)
Grayson Benjamin	Fout Mary	*30 Apr 1827	(4) 3/30
Grayson Clara	Moody Jas	10 Oct 1850	(6)
Grayson Cornelia 18	Ravenscroft John 24	28 Dec 1854	(10)
Grayson Elizabeth	Liller Jacob	1 Mar 1821	(6)
Grayson John	Miller Ruth	15 Nov 1849	(6)
Grayson M	Hendrixon Dan	27 May 1835	(6)
Grayson Nancy	Liller John	7 Nov 1816	(6)
Green Fannie 23	Day James 21	24 July 1875	(4) 1/39
Green George M	Ashby Bettie	23 Nov 1848	(1) 15 Dec 1848
Green Jacob 21	Ross Mary 22	9 May 1878	(4) 1/39
Green John	Barnhouse Elizabeth	25 Aug 1841	(5)
Green John	Barnhouse Elizabeth	25 Aug 1840	(6)
Greenland Nathan 28	Rannells Florence Belle 27	7 Feb 1881	(4) 2/15
Greenwade M T	Allen R M	3 Apr 1851	(6)
Greenwade Moss T	Alen Rhoda M	1850	(5)
Greenwait Mar	Rotruck J M	12 Sept 1839	(6)

Name #1	Name #2	Date	Source
Greenwalt J D	McNemar A	23 June 1858	(6)
Greenwalt John	Rotruck E	31 Oct 1844	(6)
Greenwalt Peter	Boling H	13 Dec 1859	(6)
Greenwalt Peter	Boling Henrietta	13 Dec 1860	(5)
Greenwalt William Henry 25	Whiteman Sarah Elizabeth 26	25 June 1891	(4) 2/29
Gregg Amy	Kite Wm	15 Aug 1844	(6)
Greitzner Christian 23	Stickley Mariah J 22	18 Mar 1869	(4) 1/38
Greitzner Louisa H 25	Houser Henry G 26	25 Oct 1866	(4) 1/4
Grenwade Margaret	Rotruck Jacob M	12 Sept 1840	(5)
Grey David	Lowery Ruth	1831	(5)
Grey Jesse Ranson 29	Nealis Maggie E 22	9 Apr 1895	(4) 2/35
Grim Catherine	Offner James	27 Apr 1825	(5)
Grimm Hiram Riley 35	Milslagle Margaret Elizabeth 20	7 Sept 1865	(4) 1/1
Grimm R	Mathias	15 July 1841	(6)
Grimm Susan	Smith Jacob	4 Mar 1841	(6)
Gross Ellen 19	Moreland Christopher Columbus 27	16 Dec 1880	(4) 2/15
Gross James Isaac 30	Kaylor Martha Jane 26	20 Aug 1888	(4) 2/25
Grove Cephas F 19	McCauley Eleanora J 19	19 Sept 1872	(4) 2/3
Grove Cyrus	Brill Eliza C	1 Nov 1859	(8)
Groves Amilia	Engle Hiram	*28 Aug 1824	(4) 3/42
Groves Emma Sophia 26	McCoy John 28	14 Apr 1874	(4) 2/6
Groves Marcus	Colbert E A	10 Aug 1834	(5)
Groves Marg	Cessney Samuel	17 Nov 1825	(6)
Groves Margaret H	Cessna Samuel	*22 Oct 1825	(4) 3/65
Groves Margaret C 19	Herrill John L 24	31 Dec 1872	(4) 2/3
Groves Mary	Arnold Archibald	*22 Aug 1827	(4) 3/44
Groves Parsons Skelton 22	Feaster Annie Gabriella 19	14 Dec 1898	(4) 2/41
Groves Philip	Lafollett Mary	*17 Oct 1825	(4) 3/67
Groves Simeon	Lyons Naomi	6 July 1820	(6)
Groves Simeon	Lyons Naomi	6 June 1820	(5)
Groves William	Kline Barbara	*16 June 1828	(4) 3/14
Grovner William H 22	Shanholtzer E I 21	9 May 1868	(4) 1/6
Grubb Margaret Olive 25	Haines Henry Walker 27	12 Mar 1878	(4) 2/11
Grubbs George William 25	Anderson Fanny Eliz Victoria 19	16 Oct 1895	(4) 2/36
Grymm Isabella	Ward John	*25 Nov 1828	(4) 3/42
Guard Sarah	Pugh John	*16 Aug 1824	(4) 3/41
Gulick Ivy May 23	Payne Travis Fenton 25	23 Sept 1896	(4) 2/37
Gulick John Nathaniel 20	Lewis Martha Jane 23	22 Mar 1887	(4) 2/23
Gulick Mary Alice 29	Householder Thomas Walker 33	2 Feb 1887	(4) 2/23
Gulick Nancy E 22	Pownell Jasper R 38	30 Nov 1865	(4) 1/1
Gulick Virginia Lee 18	Dawson John James 21	27 Apr 1893	(4) 2/32
Gulick William Taylor 25	Sanders Vallie Rosa 17	23 Sept 1896	(4) 2/37
Guthrie Elizabeth French 19	Harmison Frank Lupton 30	11 Dec 1900	(4) 2/43
Guthrie William Newton 25	Kuykendall Susan 18	14 Apr 1875	(4) 2/7
Haas Wm	High M A	17 Apr 1861	(6)
Hackley Catherine	Dawson Isaac	20 Oct 1825	(6)
Hackuylot T	Metcalf Wm	17 May 1832	(6)
Hager Susan	Speelman David	14 Nov 1822	(6)
Haggerty Daniel Frederick 27	Heigh Elizabeth 20	15 May 1889	(4) 2/26
Haggerty Elizabeth Catharine 16	Leatherman Daniel Frederick 24	6 Mar 1878	(4) 2/11
Haggerty Mary Bell 15	Shoemaker Charles Wallace 21	17 June 1884	(4) 2/19
Haggerty Sarah Ann 24	Heigh Michael Lee 23	13 Dec 1887	(4) 2/24

Name #1	Name #2	Date	Source
Hahn Ann 54	Baker Aaron Levi 72	4 Nov 1887	(4) 2/24
Hahn James Wm Gilmer 20	Hurd Cora Alice 24	17 Sept 1891	(4) 2/29
Haines Abigail Jane 30	Cheshire Samuel Lupton 21	12 Jan 1897	(4) 2/38
Haines Alcinda 19	Shanholtzer Taylor Franklin 19	10 Mar 1870	(4) 2/1
Haines Amanda Elizabeth 20	Largent George W 24	8 Jan 1880	(4) 2/14
Haines Amanda Milissa 23	Poland Abner Newton 23	16 Oct 1881	(4) 2/16
Haines Ambrose Clayton 27	Shanholtzer Chloe Margaret 23	11 Mar 1884	(4) 2/19
Haines Anna Jane 33	Poland David Fairfax 34	24 May 1900	(4) 2/42
Haines Benjamin M 26	Offutt Nancy E 21	1 Jan 1867	(4) 1/4
Haines Benjamin Taylor 28	Shanholtzer Margaret Rose 18	25 Feb 1879	(4) 2/12
Haines Benjamin Franklin 24	Shanholtzer Miranda Catharine 19	10 Jan 1878	(4) 2/11
Haines Bertha Frances 24	Shanholtzer Hamilton Temple 23	12 June 1901	(4) 2/44
Haines Bertha V 20	Donaldson William G 24	25 Nov 1891	(4) 2/30
Haines Betsy Ann 24	Carile Benj F 30	12 Apr 1866	(4) 1/3
Haines Carrie Bell 24	Kerns Smauel Granville 23	3 Jan 1901	(4) 2/43
Haines Charles Henry 27	Shanholtzer Phoebe Jane 31	3 Mar 1886	(4) 2/22
Haines Charles Page 21	Shawen Lydia Bell 18	24 Aug 1898	(4) 2/40
Haines Charles William 29	Monroe Sarah Elizabeth 23	31 Jan 1893	(4) 2/32
Haines Charles William 26	Powell Nora May 27	28 May 1900	(4) 2/42
Haines Chloe Margaret 18	Smith Benjamin Taylor 23	28 Feb 1877	(4) 2/9
Haines David E 26	Starns Mary Parker 22	26 Oct 1881	(4) 2/16
Haines David M 21	Lokhner Catherine 24	13 Nov 1866	(4) 1/4
Haines David Wilson 25	Howard Anna Bell 27	17 Oct 1900	(4) 2/43
Haines Debbie Virginia 19	Barnes James Newton 25	17 Jan 1882	(4) 2/17
Haines Della C 26	Bean Henry Franklin 28	23 Dec 1897	(4) 2/40
Haines Eliza	Savill Abraham	*9 June 1827	(4) 3/35
Haines Elizabeth F 18	Malick Geo W 27	11 Dec 1866	(4) 1/4
Haines Elizabeth Susan 23	McGill Edward Glen 30	23 Feb 1893	(4) 2/32
Haines Elizabeth 42	Shingleton James Raymond 44	11 Feb 1886	(4) 2/21
Haines Ella 22	Wagoner George Henry 25	1 Apr 1891	(4) 2/29
Haines Ella May 20	Foltz William Winfield 24	7 Jan 1897	(4) 2/38
Haines Ellen Elizabeth 19	Sanders John Henry 26	1 Mar 1877	(4) 2/9
Haines Fannie 18	Hannas James Granville 21	27 Oct 1897	(4) 2/39
Haines Flora Margreat 17	Steward Elihu G 29	*4 Mar 1892	(4) 2/30
Haines Geo M 20	Starns Abigal A 20	10 Feb 1868	(4) 1/6
Haines Geo Washington 35	Martin Martha Virginia 17	12 Aug 1874	(4) 2/6
Haines George M 44	Peasmaker Susan Frances 32	24 Nov 1892	(4) 2/31
Haines George Middleton 20	Hockman Martha Ann 19	7 Jan 1880	(4) 2/14
Haines George Washington 29	Albright Susan Ann 22	5 Jan 1882	(4) 2/17
Haines Hanson Powers 23	Malcolm Harriett Jane 20	12 Apr 1899	(4) 2/41
Haines Hariett Elizabeth 17	Slonaker William 24	14 Apr 1859	(10)
Haines Henry Walker 25	Easter Elizabeth 25	1 Sept 1874	(4) 2/6
Haines Henry Walker 27	Grubb Margaret Olive 25	12 Mar 1878	(4) 2/11
Haines Ida May 24	Oats Jefferson Davis 25	13 Aug 1896	(4) 2/37
Haines Isaac Hampton 21	Iser Ida Sedan 19	17 Dec 1889	(4) 2/27
Haines Isaac Henry 30	Carlyle Martha Jane 16	22 May 1890	(4) 2/28
Haines Isaac Minor 25	Orndorff Margaret Elizabeth 18	17 Mar 1874	(4) 2/6
Haines Isaac N 27	Buzzard Rebecca J 28	18 Dec 1866	(4) 1/4
Haines Jacob Walker 39	Hiett Virginia 24	22 Mar 1894	(4) 2/33
Haines James Edward 19	Wolford Lucinda Elizabeth 18	19 Nov 1876	(4) 2/9
Haines James Henry 62	Foltz Margaret Ella 40	13 Dec 1899	(4) 2/42
Haines James Henry 22	Orndorff Hannah 19	13 Mar 1860	(10)

Name #1	Name #2	Date	Source
Haines James William 27	French Sarah Ann Matilda 19	25 Aug 1874	(4) 2/6
Haines Jas Wm 24	Hott Martha 23	18 Dec 1866	(4) 1/4
Haines Jasper Franklin P 28	Poland Belle Abigail 18	22 Nov 1881	(4) 2/16
Haines Jno W 22	Smith Sarah C 19	13 Sept 1866	(4) 1/3
Haines John Alexander 28	Nealis Mary Matilda 26	22 Nov 1882	(4) 2/17
Haines John H F 20	Combs Delia Catharine 21	15 Feb 1872	(4) 2/3
Haines John Henry 26	Shank Lucretia 20	13 Nov 1873	(4) 2/5
Haines John L 26	Payne Nettie Catherine 21	13 Dec 1893	(4) 2/33
Haines John Maddison 21	Malick Matilda Virginia 25	29 Mar 1871	(4) 2/2
Haines John Madison 22	McGuire Marg Anne Virginia 18	2 Dec 1873	(4) 2/5
Haines John Sensery 25	Powell Louisa M 23	14 Nov 1878	(4) 2/12
Haines John Wesley 21	Cross Christina 19	28 Dec 1882	(4) 2/18
Haines Joseph E 38	Corbin Mary Elizabeth 19	19 Jan 1882	(4) 2/17
Haines Julia Ann 20	Shank John Harbert 28	27 Nov 1884	(4) 2/20
Haines Laura Belle Ella 21	Shawen James Ashby 25	24 Nov 1886	(4) 2/22
Haines Leven Taylor 24	Folty Sardenia Caroline 19	26 Feb 1878	(4) 2/11
Haines Lorena L 19	Barnes Judson Davis 22	15 Mar 1899	(40 2/41
Haines Maggie E 18	Kitchen Clina Ransom 26	8 Feb 1870	(4) 2/1
Haines Mandeville 24	Hott Mintie High 24	5 Sept 1900	(4) 2/43
Haines Margaret Ann 21	Vandergrift Wm Leonard 36	29 May 1879	(4) 2/13
Haines Martha 31	Oats Christopher 69	11 Feb 1884	(4) 2/19
Haines Mary 30	Timbrook Gibson 45	18 Mar 1875	(4) 2/7
Haines Mary 32	Wolfe Alexander Jackson 31	7 Dec 1890	(4) 2/28
Haines Mary Alice 21	Heatwole Lawrence Early 41	19 Oct 1898	(4) 2/41
Haines Mary E 20	Smaltz Robert Lee 24	10 Apr 1901	(4) 2/44
Haines Mary Elizabeth 22	Wolford Joseph Marion 19	27 Nov 1890	(4) 2/28
Haines Mary Ellen 17	Whitacre Vance Elwood 23	27 Mar 1901	(4) 2/44
Haines Mary H 30	Arnold Joshua R 26	13 Dec 1867	(4) 1/6
Haines Mary Parker 23	Piles Samuel Jefferson 21	30 Dec 1884	(4) 2/20
Haines Minnie J 26	Didawick Benjamin Ashby 29	1 Mar 1900	(4) 2/42
Haines Mrs Margaret Ann 31	Carder James Henry 41	16 Nov 1886	(4) 2/22
Haines Nancy 28	Shingleton Absalom 36	1856	(10)
Haines Noah 28	Oats Elizabeth Drusilla 16	4 Feb 1879	(4) 2/12
Haines Noah Webster 23	Easter Ruth Annie Ward 21	18 Sept 1879	(4) 2/13
Haines Ollie 19	Reed David Riley 22	27 May 1890	(4) 2/28
Haines Peter Abraham 30	Albright Mary Jane 24	8 Dec 1885	(4) 2/21
Haines Rachel 21	Lupton Jesse George 22	27 Dec 1866	(4) 1/4
Haines Reazin 66	Foltz Virginia L 22	9 Feb 1886	(4) 2/21
Haines Rebecca	Gray Philip	19 Jan 1865	(9)
Haines Rebecca Frances 22	Shanholtzer Daniel Tucker 25	21 Jan 1869	(4) 1/38
Haines Rebecca Jane 18	Bean Frederick Wellington 23	21 Jan 1869	(4) 1/38
Haines Rosalia Price 19	Hiett Charles Nelson 26	10 Dec 1874	(4) 2/6
Haines Ruth Ann 18	Johnson Joseph Henry 19	15 Jan 1900	(4) 2/42
Haines Salema Jane 29	Ruckman Thomas McDonald 33	3 Dec 1878	(4) 2/12
Haines Sallie Bertie 18	Corbin Joseph William 24	7 Nov 1900	(4) 2/43
Haines Samuel Taylor 28	Shanholtzer Eliza Jane 26	7 Feb 1878	(4) 2/11
Haines Sarah C 25	Beatty John Henry 33	20 Mar 1884	(4) 2/19
Haines Sarah Catherine 20	McDonald James Clark 22	27 Mar 1890	(4) 2/27
Haines Sarah E 22	Orndorff Robert Calvin 23	21 Apr 1892	(4) 2/30
Haines Sarah Frances 19	Lambert Isaac Welton 23	27 Jan 1892	(4) 2/30
Haines Sarah Jane 25	Hott Charles Wilton 22	16 Dec 1896	(4) 2/38
Haines Silas 40	Bird Mary Ann 19	12 Nov 1878	(4) 2/12

Name #1	Name #2	Date	Source
Haines Stephen 23	Everett Julia A 24	14 Dec 1868	(4) 1/7
Haines Stephen 51	Albright Mary Virginia 27	24 Apr 1883	(4) 2/18
Haines Stephen Wheeler 26	Rowzee Mary Elizabeth 22	6 Apr 1884	(4) 2/19
Haines Susan 25	Poland Joseph S 25	27 Feb 1866	(4) 1/3
Haines Susan 25	Pugh Walter Lee 22	13 Jan 1897	(4) 2/38
Haines Susan Margaret 23	Deleplane William 29	26 Jan 1871	(4) 2/2
Haines Theodore Bailey 28	Peer Mary Catharine 21	21 Mar 1900	(4) 2/42
Haines Thomas Hillery 23	Cheshire Amanda Bell 18	*4 May 1883	(4) 2/18
Haines Victoria E 15	Nelson Robert Beauregard 24	10 Nov 1885	(4) 2/21
Haines Virginia Catharine 22	Mitchell Ashmire Hamilton 24	9 June 1874	(4) 2/6
Haines Virginia Isadore 20	Poland James Wesley 22	26 Dec 1876	(4) 2/9
Haines Virginia Belle 23	Pownall Charles Wilbert 21	7 Sept 1892	(4) 2/31
Haines William 25	Cheshire Ida Susan 19	1 Jan 1885	(4) 2/20
Haines William Brithard 21	Iser Etta May 18	29 Mar 1899	(4) 2/41
Haines William Davis 28	Shorb Florence Lee 28	21 Sept 1892	(4) 2/31
Haines William Hill 25	Shull Florence Minnie May 18	23 Feb 1898	(4) 2/40
Haines William Henry 35	Wilson Rebecca 28	13 Dec 1896	(4) 2/38
Haines William Jasper 25	Lewis Ida Lee 26	1 Mar 1893	(4) 2/32
Haines William Lupton 21	Timbrook Cora Lee 19	18 Dec 1890	(4) 2/28
Haines Zulema Hester 22	Beery Jacob Deneal 23	28 Apr 1874	(4) 2/6
Hainey Dan	Miller Barbary	1 Feb 1820	(6)
Hains Mariah 19	Cherry Isaac W 22	27 Jan 1868	(4) 1/6
Hains Rachael	Larimore Thomas	*6 Aug 1825	(4) 3/49
Haley James D	Harvey Elizabeth	1 Oct 1826	(6)
Hall Harriett 34	Webster John 33	10 Nov 1885	(4) 1/40
Hall M E	Leatherman A	12 Feb 1846	(6)
Hall Sarah	Mott Randolph	12 Apr 1836	(6)
Hall William 48	Ward Margaret E 36	23 Dec 1873	(4) 2/5
Hamill Archibald Chisholm 48	Oats Harriet E 25	26 June 1889	(4) 2/26
Hamilton E	Fazenbaker J	20 Dec 1849	(6)
Hamilton Elisha	Cool Catherine	*17 June 1825	(4) 3/46
Hamilton Ella Bell 33	Leatherman Isaac Robert 30	6 June 1894	(4) 2/34
Hamilton George Riley 27	Barnes Ida Lee 25	4 Jan 1893	(4) 2/32
Hamilton George Riley 32	Nealis Fannie Lorenia 31	8 Dec 1897	(4) 2/39
Hamilton James William 24	Violet Della Roberson 21	26 Jan 1887	(4) 2/23
Hamilton Margaret Ann 21	Marks Ralph 33	21 Nov 1867	(4) 1/5
Hamilton Mary	Wilson John	11 Nov 1841	(6)
Hamilton Samuel	Shafer Hannah	*29 Sept 1825	(4) 3/62
Hamilton Thomas	Duke Rebecca	6 Aug 1860	(5)
Hamilton Wilber 22	Washington Fanny 23	8 Dec 1883	(4) 1/40
Hammack Ella 34	Scruggs Henry 28	29 Aug 1889	(4) 2/26
Hammack J	Moore Marcus	10 Dec 1844	(6)
Hammack Mary E 26	Kister John C 29	13 Oct 1870	(4) 2/2
Hammack S E Ashby 19	Lee Jasper Cather 26	20 May 1880	(4) 2/14
Hammack Sarah A 20	Hiett Jeremiah W 21	30 Oct 1866	(4) 1/4
Hammock B C 26	Paskel M L 29	19 Oct 1868	(4) 1/7
Hammock H A	Dobbins V	26 Feb 1844	(6)
Hammock William 45	Savill Mariah Margaret 18	17 Feb 1869	(4) 1/38
Hamounis ? 28	Racey John 37	13 Nov 1855	(10)
Hancher James W	Edmiston Elizabeth C	*16 June 1825	(4) 3/45
Haness Alverda 21	Humphrey Elias 35	31 Aug 1887	(4) 1/40
Hanlin Deba Ellen 16	Fisher Chas M 23	7 May 1901	(4) 2/44

Name #1	Name #2	Date	Source
Hanna Walter 32	Donaldson L Ella 22	2 May 1882	(4) 2/17
Hannahs Rebecca 25	Carder Sandford 31	6 May 1869	(4) 1/38
Hannahs Rebecca 25	Carder Sanford 31	6 May 1869	(4) 2/1
Hannas Charity	Ruckman Wilson	*14 Oct 1828	(4) 3/31
Hannas Charles Dougal 22	Wright Margaret Ellen 21	29 Oct 1891	(4) 2/30
Hannas Elmira Virginia 28	Iser Isaac Martin 19	7 Oct 1879	(4) 2/13
Hannas James Granville 21	Haines Fannie 18	27 Oct 1897	(4) 2/39
Hannas James William 27	Barnes Isabella May 22	16 Feb 1886	(4) 2/21
Hannas John D 22	Ray Mary Florence 26	30 Apr 1892	(4) 2/31
Hannas John William 43	Lewis Elmira Virginia 27	8 Jan 1878	(4) 2/11
Hannas Leah Catharine 22	McBride William Ashby 25	9 Feb 1887	(4) 2/23
Hannas Mary Victoria 24	Davis Charles Morris 36	15 Jan 1879	(4) 2/12
Hannas Minnie Ray 20	Bailey William Warren 24	22 July 1891	(4) 2/29
Hannas Sarah Elizabeth 18	Dean Benjamin Anthony 32	6 Mar 1879	(4) 2/13
Hannas Sarah Elizabeth 20	Starnes William Absalom 32	23 Feb 1887	(4) 2/23
Hannas Solomon 28	Shanholtzer Mary Ann 20	31 Jan 1888	(4) 2/24
Hannas Stephen	Allen Isabella	*14 Mar 1825	(4) 3/22
Hannum Dabney Ball 20	Lafollett Sarah M 22	5 Dec 1867	(4) 1/6
Hannum Emma Jane 20	Brill Jonathan Henry 24	28 Nov 1891	(4) 2/30
Hannum Laura Belle 19	Kump Samuel James 43	15 Feb 1888	(4) 2/24
Hannum Madison F 65	Pifer Barbara 50	19 Nov 1895	(4) 2/36
Hannum Minnie B 22	Gore James C 29	22 Dec 1895	(4) 2/36
Hansbough	Brown Ann M	*2 Aug 1828	(4) 3/19
Hansbough Maria	Carder George	*9 June 1825	(4) 3/43
Hanshaw W	Kuykendall S	26 Oct 1841	(6)
Harden Catherine 24	Blue William 44	27 Sept 1866	(4) 1/4
Hardy Adam Jeremiah 24	Cowgill Sarah Catharine 22	21 Dec 1879	(4) 2/14
Hardy Albert Franklin 22	Trenton Emily Jane 21	27 Mar 1867	(4) 1/5
Hardy Alberta Elizabeth 21	Barnes Frank Pirce 26	13 May 1879	(4) 2/13
Hardy Anne Catharine 22	Carder Elisha Edward 32	12 Oct 1875	(4) 2/7
Hardy Boyd 27	Smith Rosa Lee 24	2 Aug 1887	(4) 1/40
Hardy Charles Martin 28	Alkire Mahala Catharine 18	8 Feb 1882	(4) 2/17
Hardy Edgar 20	Bradfield Keziah M 21	30 Sept 1894	(4) 2/34
Hardy Eliza 20	Day Edward 24	31 Dec 1879	(4) 1/39
Hardy Elizabeth Jane 30	Largent John Thomas 28	3 Sept 1867	(4) 1/5
Hardy Harriett 27	Webster John 29	25 Dec 1872	(4) 1/38
Hardy John J	Case Julia Ann	(1) 27 Oct 1838	
Hardy Louisa Marian 25	McCool John S 23	26 Mar 1876	(4) 2/8
Hardy Martha 21	Nixon James E 22	11 Nov 1872	(4) 2/4
Hardy Mary 25	Llowndes Saul 22	19 Nov 1874	(4) 1/39
Hardy Mary C 28	Bowers Geo W 23	17 Jan 1866	(4) 1/2
Hardy Sarah Elizabeth 21	Smoot John William 20	30 Oct 1873	(4) 2/5
Harison Cathleen	Bane George	26 June 1828	(5)
Harloe Laura Rebecca 21	Slonaker Arthur Clinton 23	24 Mar 1881	(4) 2/15
Harloe Mary Jane 22	Davis Julius Ceasar 25	11 Aug 1875	(4) 2/7
Harloe Wm E 23	Kelsoe Sarah Virginia 21	20 May 1873	(4) 2/4
Harmison Alice 34	Keller John Foman 36	13 Apr 1881	(4) 2/16
Harmison Blanche 26	Hathaway Charles Gustavis 31	1 June 1881	(4) 2/16
Harmison Charles Chilton 31	Stump Lena Elizabeth 23	12 Oct 1892	(4) 2/31
Harmison Frank Lupton 30	Guthrie Elizabeth French 19	11 Dec 1900	(4) 2/43
Harmison John 37	Lewis Virginia Gertrude 20	9 Dec 1891	(4) 2/30
Harmison Lucy Ellen 25	Whitacre Amos Bushrod Currell 25	3 June 1885	(4) 2/20

Name #1	Name #2	Date	Source
Harmison Malcolm Gerstell 24	Parsons Mary Catharine 22	4 Feb 1891	(4) 2/29
Harmison Martha Wood 26	Adams Robert Lee 27	31 Oct 1888	(4) 2/25
Harmon Catherine	Ruckman Gibson	22 Aug 1854	(10)
Harness Annie Pearl 25	Smellie James Wilson 47	14 Apr 1897	(4) 2/39
Harness Joseph	Welton Ann Elizabeth		(1) 11 Nov 1837
Harness Miss	Cunningham George S		(1) 18 Nov 1837
Harness William	Holiday Jane		(1) 15 Dec 1848
Harper Anna	Little John	28 Aug 1828	(6)
Harper Eliza Jane 21	Strawder Wm A 39	1 Jan 1866	(4) 1/2
Harper Myra Ann 27	Sheetz James 53	15 June 1869	(4) 2/1
Harper Nancy M 21	Pattie Champ W 30	20 Oct 1869	(4) 2/1
Harper R	Thatcher Sarah	14 Apr 1816	(6)
Harper Rachel	Houghman Jacob	9 Jan 1823	(6)
Harper Rhody	Thatcher Sarah	18 Apr 1816	(5)
Harper William 58	Kane Sallie Lee	22 Oct 1867	(4) 1/5
Harris Bertie 18	Baker De Boarnay 21	25 Dec 1890	(4) 2/28
Harris C M 23	Kabrick David S 32	20 Mar 1866	(4) 1/3
Harris Hannah	Harris John	22 Dec 1831	(5)
Harris John	Harris Hannah	22 Dec 1831	(5)
Harris John	Likens Sarah	16 May 1837	(6)
Harris John	Likins Sarah	30 Mar 1837	(5)
Harris Joseph R 21	Powell Susan E 26	10 Aug 1876	(4) 2/8
Harris Louisa 18	Liking Isaac 26	23 Jan 1866	(4) 1/2
Harris Lucy Ann 21	Hill Loyd 25	4 Nov 1874	(4) 1/39
Harris Nancy	Bosley Phil	8 Sept 1839	(5)
Harris Nancy	Bosley Philip	18 Sept 1838	(6)
Harris Sanford Simmons 27	Scott Jemima 25	24 Sept 1865	(4) 1/1
Harris William	Marquis Rebecca	21 Apr 1825	(5)
Harrison B F	Mott Nancy	6 Jan 1829	(6)
Harrison C	Bartlow J P	4 Sept 1828	(5)
Harrison C E	Blackburn Thomas	26 Feb 1861	(6)
Harrison Charles William 26	Albaugh Margery Alice 28	14 Apr 1886	(4) 2/22
Harrison E A	Hull Martin	26 Oct 1848	(6)
Harrison F B	Hull Eliza	30 Sept 1857	(6)
Harrison Hettie Claudie 22	Iser Isaac Martin 21	29 May 1898	(4) 2/40
Harrison J C	Harrison Pen	28 Oct 1823	(6)
Harrison J M	Duling Edm	29 Aug 1849	(6)
Harrison John C	Harrison Penelope	20 Nov 1823	(5)
Harrison Lucretia	Mott Marcus	24 Nov 1859	(10)
Harrison M C	Hull J P	25 Dec 1855	(6)
Harrison M I	Harrison N D	16 Mar 1841	(6)
Harrison N D	Harrison M I	16 Mar 1841	(6)
Harrison Orpha	Davis J F	5 Sept 1848	(6)
Harrison Orpha	Head John	*7 May 1825	(4) 3/36
Harrison Penelope	Harrison John C	28 Oct 1823	(6)
Harrison Penelope	Harrison John C	20 Nov 1823	(5)
Harrison R	Dye Capt John	1 Mar 1849	(6)
Harrison Sallie	Dye David	15 Mar 18321	(6)
Harrison Theodore	Dye N E	11 Oct 1854	(6)
Harsel Peter	Flick Rachel	9 Mar 1820	(5)
Harsel Peter	Junkins Mary	9 Mar 1820	(6)
Harsell Lucretia	Fogel Henry	18 Dec 1823	(6)

Name #1	Name #2	Date	Source
Harsell Lucretia	Fogle Henry	25 Dec 1823	(5)
Hartigan Sarah Elizabeth 25	Daily John 39	8 Oct 1867	(4) 1/5
Hartman David C 22	Davy Ann E 22	8 May 1866	(4) 1/3
Hartman David Columbus 51	Wilson Mary Elizabeth 51	24 Nov 1897	(4) 2/39
Hartman Elenora 27	Dove Benjamin Franklin 24	12 Dec 1888	(4) 2/25
Hartman Estella May 19	Bobo Ezra Bucy 22	17 Apr 1898	(4) 2/40
Hartman George Thomas 23	West Margaret Catharine 26	22 Sept 1880	(4) 2/14
Hartman Isaac Daniel 25	Brown Mary Matilda 21	5 Sept 1888	(4) 2/25
Hartman Josiah 22	Blackburn Maggie A 24	23 Feb 1897	(4) 2/38
Hartman Lillian Jane 17	Clayton William H 25	15 Aug 1894	(4) 2/34
Hartman Lydia Ann 25	Allen Frank Page 37	24 June 1897	(4) 2/39
Hartman Margaret C 24	McGee Charles J 22	20 Dec 1865	(4) 1/2
Hartman Margaret	Schockey Joseph	*1 Nov 1828	(4) 3/36
Hartman Phil	Patton Rebecca	15 Mar 1828	(6)
Hartman Phoebe Jane 19	Whetzel Anthony 30	4 Feb 1895	(4) 2/35
Hartman Rebecca 27	High William H 27	1 Jan 1866	(4) 1/2
Hartman Susan Catharine 21	Biser Charles Henry 21	10 Mar 1880	(4) 2/14
Harvey Annie	Anderson Jesse	7 Feb 1822	(6)
Harvey D	Wycoff Moses	1 May 1828	(6)
Harvey Drusia	Lower Wm	8 Jan 1829	(6)
Harvey Eliz	Haley Jas D	1 Oct 1826	(6)
Harvey Eliza	White Henry	24 Mar 1836	(6)
Harvey Elizabeth	Cassidy Thomas C	27 Dec 1827	(6)
Harvey Elizabeth	Haley James D	1 Oct 1826	(5)
Harvey H R	Lee Catherine	5 Nov 1841	(5)
Harvey Hester	Moon Benjamin	14 Nov 1840	(5)
Harvey Hester	Moore Benj	14 Nov 1839	(6)
Harvey J W	Sharpless E	9 Dec 1847	(6)
Harvey Jas B	Junkins Mary	22 Sept 1833	(6)
Harvey Jeremiah	Irons Nancy	5 Nov 1841	(5)
Harvey John L	Junkins Ruth	8 May 1845	(6)
Harvey Lucinda	King Jesse	20 Jan 1842	(6)
Harvey Mariah	Tasker H F	4 Feb 1836	(6)
Harvey Rezin	Coleshine E	25 June 1843	(6)
Harvey Sam	Shillingburg S	22 Nov 1821	(6)
Harvey Sam	Shillingburg Sarah	2 Nov 1821	(5)
Harvey Susan	Sharpless Wm	14 Oct 1841	(6)
Harvey William	Wilson Elizabeth	11 Sept 1823	(5)
Harvey Wm	Cassidy Sar A	27 Aug 1834	(6)
Harwood William Green 27	Taylor Alberta Lee 22	20 Jan 1885	(4) 2/20
Hase Mary	Hassel Adam	10 Dec 1850	(6)
Hasha Sarah Ann 22	Lahman Jacob 22	1 Mar 1866	(4) 1/3
Hass Catharine	Mayberry Israel	*27 Mar 1827	(4) 3/23
Hass David A 21	McMahin Elizabeth H 20	28 Sept 1870	(4) 2/2
Hass Mary	Hassel Adam	Dec 1846	(5)
Hass Sarah	Ash Michael		(1) 18 Aug 1838
Hass Sarah Arnold 27	Stump James Adam 25	4 Aug 1886	(4) 2/22
Hass Thomas Sommerville 24	Blue Hannah Kuykendall 20	29 Oct 1872	(4) 2/3
Hass William	High A M	17 Apr 1861	(5)
Hassel Adam	Hase Mary	10 Dec 1850	(6)
Hassel Adam	Hass Mary	Dec 1846	(5)
Hathaway Charles Gustavis 31	Harmison Blanche 26	1 June 1881	(4) 2/16

Name #1	Name #2	Date	Source
Haun Samuel 25	Kline Lydia M 19	25 Oct 1866	(4) 1/3
Haus Sarah Jane 19	Peer Hampton Wesley 22	12 Sept 1865	(4) 1/1
Hause E Taylor 28	?Hoka Mollie Frances 22	28 Mar 1897	(4) 2/38
Hauvermale Clarence Howard 22	Fleming Nettie May 19	22 Aug 1888	(4) 2/25
Hawes John W	Bryan Ann	14 May 1857	(2) 21 May 1857
Hawes William Branson 24	Delaplain Margaret Elizabeth 20	8 Feb 1870	(4) 2/1
Hawk Isaac	High Jane	*10 Apr 1826	(4) 3/23
Hawk Sarah	Arrent Frederick	*19 Apr 1824	(4) 3/25
Hawkins David	Kidwell Mary	*1 Oct 1825	(4) 3/63
Hawkins Elizabeth Malinda 20	Eaton Elijah Everett 23	26 Mar 1874	(4) 2/6
Hawkins Elizabeth Ann 44	Kidwell Randolph Hawkins 57	28 Mar 1882	(4) 2/17
Hawkins Elizabeth Jane 21	Riley George William 28	14 Oct 1891	(4) 2/29
Hawkins Eve	Edwards Robert	*27 Nov 1826	(4) 3/42
Hawkins George C 25	Patterson Zilla Anne 21	11 Nov 1891	(4) 2/30
Hawkins Henry 35	Slonaker Louisa L 25	3 Mar 1868	(4) 1/6
Hawkins Isaac 23	Davis Martha 23	30 Nov 1865	(4) 1/1
Hawkins Margaret Ann 21	Barrett Henry Preston 23	*21 Nov 1870	(4) 2/2
Hawkins Martha Cordelia 17	McDonald John Alexander 19	11 Feb 1879	(4) 2/12
Hawkins Martha Virginia 20	Shanholtzer Robert Harris 24	15 May 1889	(4) 2/26
Hawkins Mary A 19	Sirbaugh Julius A 18	25 Dec 1877	(4) 2/11
Hawkins Mary Florence 19	McDonald Edward Luther 28	25 Dec 1894	(4) 2/35
Hawkins Philena 19	Garret William Henry 27	22 Dec 1886	(4) 2/23
Hawley Andrew	Ashby Mary	21 June 1835	(5)
Haws Euphennia 18	Wolford William Ryland 23	26 Aug 1884	(4) 2/19
Haws James 28	Cupp Elizabeth 29	21 Nov 1868	(4) 1/7
Haws Lydia Ann 18	Stewart John William 35	12 July 1888	(4) 2/25
Haws Margaret Ann 32	Martin Levi 33	9 June 1873	(4) 2/4
Hayden Annie	Ross Abraham Isaac	17 Apr 1884	(4) 1/40
Haydon Mary M L 33	Gettis John 28	30 June 1881	(4) 2/16
Hayes Rebecca	Stallaberger Mathew	*18 Dec 1826	(4) 3/46
Haynes John	Larimore Nancy	*13 Apr 1825	(4) 3/30
Haynes Philip	Foltz Catherine		(1) 7 Feb 1839
Haynes Wallace Pembroke 29	Gooding Senora Wills 23	22 Feb 1876	(4) 2/8
Hays Annie	Powell James B	26 Nov 1845	(5)
Hays C G	Ingmire Mary	9 June 1829	(6)
Hays Charles G	Ingmore Margaret	19 June 1829	(5)
Hays Jeremiah Wm 33	Foltz Francina 23	1 Mar 1883	(4) 2/18
Hays R	Stullenbarger Mat	19 Dec 1826	(6)
Head Eliza	Hendrixon John	15 Oct 1835	(6)
Head Geo	Van Meter Ann R	18 May 1848	(6)
Head John	Harrison Orpha	*7 May 1825	(4) 3/36
Head Martha	Tucker Jacob	10 May 1848	(6)
Head Sarah C	Bane George	15 Jan 1846	(5)
Head Sarah C	Bane George	15 Jan 1850	(6)
Hear Sedenia	Loy Daniel	12 Sept 1839	(1) 26 Sept 1839
Heard? Henry	Carskaddon Elizabeth J	19 July 1854	(10)
Heare Abigail Virginia 23	Riggleman Joseph 21	8 Nov 1877	(4) 2/10
Heare Abigal Jane 24	Hott George Hunter 32	19 May 1881	(4) 2/16
Heare Alfred Joseph Snyder 25	Abell Nannie Lee 21	8 May 1895	(4) 2/35
Heare Augusta Florence 27	Ringer George Washington 27	2 Nov 1892	(4) 2/31
Heare Barbara Alice 35	Cowgill Frederick Henry 52	8 Oct 1876	(4) 2/9
Heare David Hott 25	Saville Maria Elizabeth 17	11 Dec 1873	(4) 2/5

Name #1	Name #2	Date	Source
Heare Eliza R V 21	Emmart Jacob H 26	21 Dec 1870	(4) 2/2
Heare Emsey Jane 25	Riggleman John Robert 19	6 Jan 1878	(4) 2/11
Heare George Lock 20	Loy Ettie Jane 16	16 Dec 1888	(4) 2/25
Heare Gracie Ann 25	Hott William Taylor 26	25 Nov 1875	(4) 2/8
Heare Isaac James Todd 43	Park Mary Ellen 27	24 Sept 1867	(4) 1/5
Heare Jacob W 34	Poland Martha Jane 21	25 Sept 1881	(4) 2/16
Heare James Fontaine 33	Combs Sarah Catharine 17	17 Feb 1887	(4) 2/23
Heare Jasper Newton 53	Cheshire Emma 41	20 Sept 1885	(4) 2/21
Heare John L	Powelson Eliza	*20 Oct 1828	(4) 3/33
Heare Lillie Estella 21	McCauley Charles Edward 27	9 Aug 1887	(4) 2/23
Heare Lucy Catharine Imboden 17	Ruckman Wright Welton 26	6 Sept 1880	(4) 2/14
Heare Maria Elizabeth 24	Brill William Arthur 22	3 Oct 1880	(4) 2/14
Heare Martha Abigail 20	Pepper James Anthony 27	14 Mar 1867	(4) 1/5
Heare Mary Elizabeth 30	Ludwick Amos Christopher 24	23 May 1884	(4) 2/19
Heare Mathew	Powelson Mary Ann	*12 Nov 1825	(4) 3/69
Heare Mrs Minnie Lula 27	Bowman Charles Edward 22	10 Sept 1895	(4) 2/36
Heare Paran 23	Ruckman Martha E 22	1 Dec 1869	(4) 2/1
Heare Peter Loy 22	Hott Minnie Lulie Lee 19	28 Feb 1887	(4) 2/23
Heare Phoebe Lillie 22	Davis Dr Reuben Samuel 54	14 Feb 1889	(4) 2/26
Heare Susan F P 26	Davis R S 36	14 Sept 1871	(4) 2/3
Heare Tamar Rosella C 23	Ludwick Arthur Wellington 30	28 Sept 1884	(4) 2/20
Heath James Clinton 37	Moreland Chloey 31	1 Dec 1897	(4) 2/39
Heath Jonathan Seymour 27	Brown Priscilla Frances 30	15 Apr 1891	(4) 2/29
Heatwole Barbara Etta 20	Sanders Mayberry G 30	28 Dec 1887	(4) 2/24
Heatwole Charles Elliott 25	Kremer Helen Virginia 20	16 Jan 1877	(4) 2/9
Heatwole Frank S 27	Davis Margaret Francis 24	4 Dec 1877	(4) 2/10
Heatwole Laura Louisa 24	Slonaker Wesley 48	4 Apr 1882	(4) 2/17
Heatwole Lawrence Early 41	Haines Mary Alice 21	19 Oct 1898	(4) 2/41
Heatwole Marquis Lafayette 23	Oats Frances Virginia 24	5 Nov 1884	(4) 2/20
Heavener Ursa B 23	Grapes James Henry 20	25 Mar 1901	(4) 2/44
Heigh Elizabeth 20	Haggerty Daniel Frederick 27	15 May 1889	(4) 2/26
Heigh Michael Lee 23	Haggerty Sarah Ann 24	13 Dec 1887	(4) 2/24
Height James	Bacorn Sarah	30 Dec 1823	(5)
Heinzman Elizabeth	Sea Adam	*6 Jan 1825	(4) 3/4
Heironimus Harry Beuten 27	Long Clara Ellen 28	10 Sept 1895	(4) 2/36
Heiroumous E C 22	Blake John W 23	13 Jan 1868	(4) 1/6
Heishman Abraham Lincoln 27	Spaid Martha 21	13 Oct 1892	(4) 2/31
Heishman Angus Wood 32	Poland Emsey Abigail 20	2 Sept 1886	(4) 2/22
Heishman Arta M 32	Heishman Tilbury 33	13 Sept 1900	(4) 2/43
Heishman Nellie Grant 19	Garrett Ernest Walter 18	30 June 1893	(4) 2/32
Heishman Tilberry 25	Kline Bessie 21	27 Oct 1892	(4) 2/31
Heishman Tilbury 33	Heishman Arta M 32	13 Sept 1900	(4) 2/43
Heiskell Catherine	Vance James	*31 July 1826	(4) 3/31
Heiskell David Hopkins 26	Covell Annie Baldwin 26	15 June 1886	(4) 2/22
Heiskell Edgar Sensency 40	Scanlan Ella Pauline 26	22 Apr 1891	(4) 2/29
Heiskell Eleanora Grace 23	Streby Joseph Clarence 23	10 June 1891	(4) 2/29
Heitt Osie	Richardson John	31 Aug 1834	(5)
Heizer John Leonard	Currey Jean	*11 Jan 1825	(4) 3/8
Helman Frederick Hinnbiord 24	Shoemaker Sarah Catharine 26	*15 Sept 1875	(4) 2/7
Helman James Samuel 23	Leatherman Rosa May 21	15 Mar 1900	(4) 2/42
Heltzel Franklin Davis 25	Timbrook Malinda Melissa 20	14 Nov 1878	(4) 2/12
Hemilright Rachel Ann 22	Orndorff Joseph Atwell 32	30 Jan 1878	(4) 2/11

Name #1	Name #2	Date	Source
Hemilwright Nancy A M 22	Kump William N 24	21 July 1895	(4) 2/35
Henderson Elizabeth	Junkins John	25 Apr 1816	(6)
Henderson Elizabeth Caroline 19	Shanholtzer William Robert 21	26 Sept 1870	(4) 2/2
Henderson Jam	James Mary	25 Apr 1819	(6)
Henderson Laskin Harris Lane 26	Ruckman Sarah Virginia 23	16 Dec 1879	(4) 2/14
Henderson Margaret Lee 27	Fishel George Washington 21	17 Dec 1893	(4) 2/33
Henderson Mary Matilda 21	Hott Samuel William 24	17 Nov 1870	(4) 2/2
Henderson Richard Thomas 45	Royce Anne Virginia 25	31 Dec 1889	(4) 2/27
Henderson Sarah	Perry Charles	27 Mar 1838	(1) 14 Apr 1838
Henderson Thomas R 21	McBride Jane 21	30 Nov 1865	(4) 1/1
Henderson Virna 40	Poling James Wm 63	29 Nov 1899	(4) 2/42
Hendrixon Aramiah	Davis E	24 Jan 1837	(6)
Hendrixon Dan	Grayson M	27 May 1835	(6)
Hendrixon Eliz	Rinker Elizah	10 Sept 1835	(5)
Hendrixon John	Head Eliza	15 Oct 1835	(6)
Hendrixon Margaret	Smith Greenbury	17 Mar 1836	(5)
Henline Joseph	Hilky Ruth	31 Oct 1842	(5)
Henline Sari	Ruckman John	6 Oct 1853	(6)
Henry David Alexander 22	Hesser Toluloh Francis 18	27 Oct 1881	(4) 2/16
Herbaugh Ettie 23	Taylor Dora D 40	25 Jan 1899	(4) 2/41
Herbaugh Florence M 18	Hott Silas Lemuel 37	25 Nov 1886	(4) 2/22
Herbaugh John Walker 29	Gray Mary Elizabeth 22	8 Sept 1891	(4) 2/29
Herbaugh William Victonus 36	McBride Sarah Elizabeth 29	28 Mar 1893	(4) 2/32
Herell Charles Edward 35	Kern Rachel Ellen 19	20 Aug 1867	(4) 1/5
Heriott Ephraim	Reese Eliza	13 Nov 1827	(5)
Herndon George Love 27	Bonny Mary Agnes 22	12 June 1879	(4) 2/13
Herrell Sarah Frances 19	Cave Robert Lee 21	11 Dec 1890	(4) 2/28
Herrill John L 24	Groves Margaret C 19	31 Dec 1872	(4) 2/3
Herriott Ephraim	Reese Eliza	*10 Nov 1827	(4) 3/54
Herriott Ephraim	Reese Eliza	13 Nov 1827	(6)
Herriott Isaac 35	Blue Sallie 24	24 Jan 1877	(4) 2/9
Herriott J J	Parker D E	12 Sept 1855	(6)
Herriott Mary Isabell 32	Rinehart Stephen Chandler 46	13 Jan 1867	(4) 1/4
Herriott William Vause 47	Eliason Ella 20	19 Jan 1876	(4) 2/8
Hershey James	Trenter Cathleen	11 Jan 1838	(5)
Heskett Susan Caroline 49	Hockman Philip 55	11 Oct 1881	(4) 2/16
Hesman Melinda	Devere Aaron	11 Jan 1821	(6)
Hessen Martha Virginia 18	Deffenbaugh George Irving 25	20 Oct 1887	(4) 2/24
Hesser Toluloh Francis 18	Henry David Alexander 22	27 Oct 1881	(4) 2/16
Hickle Elizabeth	Moore Isaac	*25 Sept 1826	(4) 3/36
Hickle Jenetta	Buckbee Elizah	4 Apr 1861	(5)
Hickle John	Cooper Catharine	*4 Apr 1825	(4) 3/27
Hicks Edward Martin 22	Johnson Sarah Margaret 19	11 June 1890	(4) 2/28
Hiett Allis Jane 27	Williamson Silas William 33	19 Feb 1874	(4) 2/5
Hiett Anne 25	Bradfield George Washington 32	25 Oct 1896	(4) 2/37
Hiett Anne Bell 35	Short J Wesley 54	13 Mar 1900	(4) 2/42
Hiett Asa	Arnold Chas	22 Nov 1855	(6)
Hiett Asa Griffith 23	Grapes Elizabeth Florence 18	29 Oct 1888	(4) 2/25
Hiett Charles Nelson 26	Haines Rosalia Price 19	10 Dec 1874	(4) 2/6
Hiett Charlotte Ann 19	Furr William Robert 23	9 Jan 1877	(4) 2/9
Hiett Dorothy 35	Smith Giles Jenkins 40	30 Mar 1875	(4) 2/7
Hiett Edward P 27	Offutt Margaret Ellen 26	24 Oct 1894	(4) 2/34

Name #1	Name #2	Date	Source
Hiett Evan Peter 26	Smith Annie Lee 18	23 Aug 1899	(4) 2/41
Hiett Evan Terrin 23	Wolford Sarah Virginia 19	11 Dec 1873	(4) 2/5
Hiett George Washington 23	McCoole Elizabeth Anne 22	*28 July 1879	(4) 1/13
Hiett Henry Harrison 35	McDonald Frederica A Rebecca 25	17 Apr 1877	(4) 2/10
Hiett Jeremiah W 21	Hammack Sarah A 20	30 Oct 1866	(4) 1/4
Hiett John Luther 25	Wills Jane 26	23 Mar 1871	(4) 2/2
Hiett Joseph C 22	Deaver Frances A 21	22 Feb 1871	(4) 2/2
Hiett Joseph William 25	McDonald Margaret S 21	20 Jan 1867	(4) 1/4
Hiett Laura Ann 25	Smith Charles William 31	4 June 1895	(4) 2/35
Hiett Mary 23	Ambrose William Cyrus 24	22 Mar 1900	(4) 2/42
Hiett Samuel Leonidas 24	Slonaker Olive Edith 17	28 Nov 1892	(4) 2/31
Hiett Samuel Marion 28	Power Lillie Florance 18	25 May 1893	(4) 2/32
Hiett Sarah	Allen James	*20 Feb 1826	(4) 3/10
Hiett Susan Ann 30	Grant Lemuel Alfred 24	3 Nov 1870	(4) 2/2
Hiett Virginia 24	Haines Jacob Walker 39	22 Mar 1894	(4) 2/33
Hiett Zebulon Montgomery 30	Wolford Anne Belle 22	13 Nov 1888	(4) 2/25
Hietto Alexander	Martin Polly	24 Sept 1835	(5)
Higgins Joseph C	Parker Mary		(1) 21 Nov 1839
Higgins Patsy	Taylor Charles S	*10 June 1826	(4) 3/24
High A M	Hass William	17 Apr 1861	(5)
High Alonzo Tecumseh 31	Rinker Ann Jemima 29	4 Feb 1883	(4) 2/18
High Amelia Frances 16	Huffman Ulyses Saville Grant 21	27 July 1890	(4) 2/28
High Ann 19	Pancake Andrew 43	16 Nov 1859	(10)
High Annie Elizabeth 27	High Edward Dekalb 32	9 Aug 1893	(4) 2/33
High Christena Kale 17	Veach Abel Seymour 25	17 Oct 1878	(4) 2/12
High Cora Sciota 22	Racey Calvin Jackson 24	21 Aug 1895	(4) 2/36
High Curtis William 24	Huffman Bertie Mary 23	25 Dec 1890	(4) 2/28
High Cuthbert Elijah 28	Purgit Grace Olive 18	24 Oct 1900	(4) 2/43
High Dorothy Ann 19	Shoemaker Lionel Franklin 21	2 June 1891	(4) 2/29
High Edward Dekalb 32	High Annie Elizabeth 27	9 Aug 1893	(4) 2/33
High Elijah 63	Susan White 34	18 Mar 1869	(4) 1/38
High Emely	Rinker Sam'l	18 Oct 1836	(6)
High Emily 28	Rinker Sylvester 25	19 June 1878	(4) 2/11
High Francis 23	Smith William George 23	7 Aug 1889	(4) 2/26
High Geo	Buncrotz Mary	14 Dec 1820	(6)
High George	Bunercrotey Mary	14 Dec 1820	(5)
High George McCellan 36	Fleming Ruehanna 24	20 Jan 1898	(4) 2/40
High Hannah Catharine 19	Albright William Edward 26	9 Feb 1881	(4) 2/15
High Hariet Jane 22	Leatherman Isaac D 21	1 May 1878	(4) 2/11
High Hiram	Ingmine Susan	30 Oct 1827	(6)
High J F	Ludwick M E	9 Mar 1848	(6)
High Jane	Hawk Isaac	*10 Apr 1826	(4) 3/23
High Jno C 23	Tucker Eliza C 23	16 Dec 1868	(4) 1/7
High John F 28	Ault Ida J 26	10 Dec 1899	(4) 2/42
High Jonathan	Shoemaker S	15 Sept 1836	(6)
High M A	Haas Wm	17 Apr 1861	(6)
High M A	Taylor W J	26 Oct 1853	(6)
High Martha I 21	Rotruck Robert Elmer 27	15 Nov 1899	(4) 2/42
High Mary	Ludwick George	*29 Aug 1825	(4) 3/57
High Mary Ellen 24	Bobo Isaac Gibson 27	28 Dec 1881	(4) 2/17
High Mary Susan 25	High Tiffis Osceola 36	23 Sept 1885	(4) 2/21
High Mary Susan 33	Tarr Oliver Harrison 27	13 Sept 1893	(4) 2/33

Name #1	Name #2	Date	Source
High Mary Texas 18	Foley Thomas Winfield Scott 23	22 Oct 1874	(4) 2/6
High Miss	Taylor Joseph		(1) 22 Dec 1838
High Nancy	Ridgeway Jacob	15 Sept 1839	(1) 26 Sept 1839
High Northman 22	Liller Mary Ellen 18	14 Jan 1878	(4) 2/11
High Olphus 33	Loyed Sarah A 22	28 Jan 1866	(4) 1/2
High Sarah D 18	Markwood Charles A 28	31 Mar 1897	(4) 2/39
High Sarah Louisa 26	Whiteman Charles David 29	20 Jan 1886	(4) 2/21
High Summerfield 26	Davey Lucy Emma 24	15 Apr 1896	(4) 2/37
High Susan Catharine 23	Hottinger William Seymour 29	30 Nov 1890	(4) 2/28
High Susan Elizabeth 17	Rinker Joshua 35	24 Oct 1867	(4) 1/5
High Tiffis Osceola 36	High Mary Susan 25	23 Sept 1885	(4) 2/21
High William H 27	Hartman Rebecca 27	1 Jan 1866	(4) 1/2
High William H 29	Liller Margaret Ann 25	25 Aug 1867	(4) 1/5
High William H 54	Smith Jemima	17 Feb 1892	(4) 2/30
High William Randolph 24	Liller N C 20	21 July 1897	(4) 2/39
Hilbrant John 34	Pugh Effie May 24	15 May 1894	(4) 2/34
Hilkey Eliz	McNemar J H	6 Apr 1848	(6)
Hilkey Jacob	Michael A E	30 Dec 1847	(6)
Hilky Elanor	Michael Adam	9 Dec 1841	(5)
Hilky Elizabeth	Simmons Josiah	4 Nov 1844	(5)
Hilky Ruth	Henline Joseph	31 Oct 1842	(5)
Hill Loyd 25	Harris Lucy Ann 21	4 Nov 1874	(4) 1/39
Hill William Barger 24	Walaker Mary Catherine 20	8 Mar 1866	(4) 1/3
Himelwright Florence Edna A 22	Hottle Marcus Lee 29	27 Dec 1900	(4) 2/43
Himelwright Jane C 22	Triplett Bush 26	2 Sept 1875	(4) 2/7
Himelwright John William 25	Orndorff Nora Virginia 16	17 Jan 1889	(4) 2/26
Hines Amy Susan 18	Ganoe Isaac R D 23	16 Nov 1871	(4) 2/2
Hines James Randolph 21	Shank Melissa 21	18 Apr 1877	(4) 2/10
Hines Linley 22	Bailey Lilly Kate 23	17 June 1897	(4) 2/39
Hines Mary Hannah C Ambler 19	Grapes Robert Henry 23	7 Dec 1874	(4) 2/6
Hines Millard 24	Everett Jamima Ann 17	20 Aug 1896	(4) 2/37
Hines Mollie Maloney 22	Bailey Robert G 27	28 Dec 1899	(4) 2/42
Hines Rebecca C 26	Shank Philip S 25	15 Jan 1872	(4) 2/3
Hines Rosa Belle 22	Bowman John Wesley 28	13 Apr 1893	(4) 2/32
Hines Sarah 23	Bean Luther Arnold 21	21 Mar 1893	(4) 2/32
Hines Thomas	McBride Nancy	*25 Nov 1825	(4) 3/72
Hines Thomas 47	Doyle Harriett Jane 26	16 Nov 1870	(4) 2/2
Hinkle Lewis	Wagoner Julian	2 Aug 1838	(1) 11 Aug 1838
Hinkle Mausie Lewis Davis 50	Smith Mary Elizabeth 36	3 Jan 1867	(4) 1/4
Hiper Elizabeth	Smith John	12 Aug 1832	(5)
Hite George William 35	Taylor Mary Ellen 30	19 May 1885	(4) 2/20
Hite Lucy Annie Bell 16	Pugh Charles Newton 24	18 Nov 1886	(4) 2/22
Hix John William 30	Pennington Elizabeth E 41	21 Jan 1884	(4) 2/19
Hoard James 54	Bias Mary 31	14 Apr 1870	(4) 1/38
Hobart Elizabeth Maria 35	Eichelberger Webster 39	9 Dec 1874	(4) 2/6
Hobson Jane	Monroe Sylvester	*15 Dec 1828	(4) 3/46
Hockman Harvey Milton 21	King Margaret Ellen 19	31 Oct 1878	(4) 2/12
Hockman John Wesley 31	Godlove Savilla Alice 17	3 Jan 1879	(4) 2/12
Hockman Leah Catherine 23	Fravel Francis Marian 32	17 Oct 1869	(4) 2/1
Hockman Martha Ann 19	Haines George Middleton 20	7 Jan 1880	(4) 2/14
Hockman Mary Frances 30	McDonald Evan 27	1 May 1882	(4) 2/17
Hockman Philip 55	Heskett Susan Caroline 49	11 Oct 1881	(4) 2/16

Name #1	Name #2	Date	Source
Hodgson I H W 26	Parker Roberta S 22	16 Oct 1872	(4) 2/3
Hoffman Ann	Davy William	11 Oct 1838	(1) 20 Oct 1838
Hoffman Elizabeth	Smoot Samuel	*24 May 1825	(4) 3/41
Hoffman Martha Ann 23	Taylor Seymour Rudolph 30	16 May 1888	(4) 2/25
Hoffman Martie Rizer 38	Williamson Nannie M 36	12 Sept 1876	(4) 2/8
Hoffman Sarah	Swisher Henry	*12 Feb 1827	(4) 3/11
Hoka? Mollie Frances 22	Hause E Taylor 28	28 Mar 1897	(4) 2/38
Hoke John Levi 37	Simpson Mary Ellen 22	14 Sept 1884	(4) 2/19
Hoke Sarah Caroline 18	Fletcher Alexander Peirce 31	17 June 1891	(4) 2/29
Holiday Jane	Harness William		(1) 15 Dec 1848
Hollenbach Catherine	Umstott Samuel	23 Aug 1860	(5)
Hollenbach Mariah	Rhinehart Ellis	17 July 1823	(5)
Hollenback Catharine 23	Umstott ?	1 Aug 1860	(10)
Hollenback E	Lawrence D	28 Aug 1817	(6)
Hollenback E	Leatherman J	12 Oct 1843	(6)
Hollenback E	Rinehart Ellis	26 June 1823	(6)
Hollenback M	Meese John M	25 June 1846	(6)
Holliday Angus M D	Vandiver Susan	*20 Dec 1824	(4) 3/54
Holt Dan'l 27	Johnson Caroline 22	23 Sept 1868	(4) 1/7
Holt Phillis 40	Robinson John Wesley 58	11 Feb 1885	(4) 1/40
Hook Annie Elizabeth 20	Gray Joseph Early 24	13 Dec 1872	(4) 2/4
Hook Florence Virginia 24	Wotring James Abraham 28	9 Feb 1886	(4) 2/21
Hook Francis 21	Anderson Alfred S 26	28 Dec 1865	(4) 1/2
Hook Henson T 23	Creswell Mary V 24	*30 Jan 1873	(4) 2/4
Hook Isaiah Proctor 60	Smaltz Lewella 32	1 Jan 1901	(4) 2/43
Hook Jane	Coe Wesley	*19 Aug 1828	(4) 3/22
Hook Joseph Samuel 26	McCarty Anna Maria 17	14 Mar 1887	(4) 2/23
Hook Laura Virginia 21	Pease John W 28	9 Nov 1886	(4) 2/22
Hook Martha Anne E 22	Riley Fenton Butler 32	21 Aug 1890	(4) 2/28
Hook McCullough Branden 23	Lafollette Martha Abalona 16	24 Nov 1892	(4) 2/31
Hook Miss Jennie 25	Didiwick John William 21	22 Oct 1895	(4) 2/36
Hook Robert Calvin 25	McDonald Sarah Elizabeth 20	23 Jan 1890	(4) 2/27
Hook Thomas A 24	Garvin Elizabeth A 23	20 Dec 1869	(4) 2/1
Hook Thomas Edward 29	Boherer Arrete 25	28 Apr 1897	(4) 2/39
Hook? William 31	Leith Elizabeth 25	25 May 1854	(10)
Hooke Eliza B 17	Mcdonald Charles B 33	25 Jan 1866	(4) 1/2
Hoopengarner Samuel Sheridan 25	Smith Mary Jane 20	1 Jan 1889	(4) 2/26
Hoopingarner Wilson 21	Whiteman Sallie 21	*3 May 1879	(4) 2/13
Hoover Sarah	Stern George	*2 Sept 1828	(4) 3/23
Hopkins Maria	Scamp Abraham		(1) 1 July 1837
Horn Elizabeth	King William	*3 Apr 1824	(4) 3/19
Horn George	Park Samuel Jr	*27 Mar 1824	(4) 3/18
Horn George Jun	Pugh Hannah	27 Dec 1786	(3)
Horn Henry Jackson 28	Lewis Virzilla Ann 28	27 Mar 1889	(4) 2/26
Horn John J 30	Caudy Mary E 25	27 May 1868	(4) 1/6
Horn Mary Bell 21	Jones Charles Edward 27	12 July 1881	(4) 2/16
Horner Thomas Rankin 31	Leath ? Leberta 19	27 Mar 1879	(4) 2/13
Horner William Anderson 31	Pugh Martha A 21	2 Jan 1901	(4) 2/43
Hott Alberta 21	McKee John Wm Tilden 24	30 Jan 1901	(4) 2/44
Hott Barbara Ann 20	Foltz Isaac Newton 30	9 Dec 1890	(4) 2/28
Hott Belsora Jane 17	Hott Isaac Washington 24	28 Dec 1880	(4) 2/15
Hott Benjamin Franklin 25	Timbrook Martha Elizabeth 20	16 Feb 1888	(4) 2/24

Name #1	Name #2	Date	Source
Hott Catharine 21	Swisher Stephen 24	29 May 1860	(10)
Hott Catharine A 21	Piles Benjamin 18	24 Mar 1896	(4) 2/37
Hott Charles Tilden 24	Poland Sallie Catharine 28	26 Sept 1900	(4) 2/43
Hott Charles Wilton 22	Haines Sarah Jane 25	16 Dec 1896	(4) 2/38
Hott Daniel Taylor 24	Foltz Susan Mary 20	25 Feb 1886	(4) 2/21
Hott David Aaron 24	Payne Fanny Belle 21	26 Dec 1894	(4) 2/35
Hott David Gibson 25	Messick Mary Ellen 22	15 Dec 1879	(4) 2/14
Hott David Jasper 35	Miller Daisy M 17	10 Jan 1897	(4) 2/38
Hott Eliza Jane 22	Shank Abraham 25	6 Dec 1874	(5) 2/6
Hott Elizabeth 19	Seville William 25	24 Mar 1859	(10)
Hott Emma 22	Lewis Luther Alexander 25	26 Dec 1888	(4) 2/26
Hott Fowler Canfield 23	Shanholtzer Sarah 18	26 Mar 1874	(4) 2/6
Hott Geo 56	Boman C 44	16 Oct 1868	(4) 1/7
Hott George 27	Riley Mary Cordelia 19	21 Oct 1880	(4) 2/14
Hott George Hunter 32	Heare Abigal Jane 24	19 May 1881	(4) 2/16
Hott George Wash Jefferson 23	Saville Lucinda Catherine 18	30 Aug 1883	(4) 2/18
Hott Ida 24	Baker John B 29	3 Feb 1901	(4) 2/44
Hott Isaac 24	Hott Sarah 25	29 Dec 1870	(4) 2/2
Hott Isaac Washington 24	Hott Belsora Jane 17	28 Dec 1880	(4) 2/15
Hott James Arthur 26	Maphis Mary Susan 14	17 Sept 1885	(4) 2/21
Hott James Henry 24	Sowers Martha Susan 21	26 Sept 1876	(4) 2/8
Hott Jemima E 19	Hott John William 25	22 June 1876	(4) 2/8
Hott John David 25	Cheshire Bettie Mellisa 27	27 Sept 1883	(4) 2/18
Hott John William 25	Hott Jemima E 19	22 June 1876	(4) 2/8
Hott Joseph Franklin 22	Iser Amanda Jane 19	30 May 1900	(4) 2/42
Hott Kirk George 19	Abell Edith Virginia 18	3 July 1894	(4) 2/34
Hott Laura Ann 18	Shane Charles Wesley 22	6 Nov 1879	(4) 2/13
Hott Leanna 24	Miller Algemon 43	8 July 1890	(4) 2/28
Hott Lelia B 22	Davidson Robert 21	26 Dec 1900	(4) 2/43
Hott Lilly Mabel 24	Bailey Edgar Tippett 24	19 Oct 1893	(4) 2/33
Hott Louisa Belle Agnes 25	Loy Benjamin Bane 25	23 Feb 1898	(4) 2/40
Hott Martha 23	Haines Jas Wm 24	18 Dec 1866	(4) 1/4
Hott Mary Anna 22	Peters James William 19	31 Oct 1876	(4) 2/9
Hott Mary Catharine 20	Iser Absolin 23	12 Feb 1880	(4) 2/14
Hott Mary Elizabeth 21	Poland Edward T 23	26 July 1871	(4) 2/3
Hott Mary Virginia 30	Coffman William Harrison 37	22 May 1890	(4) 2/28
Hott Matilda Jane 23	Parrill John Columbus 28	24 Nov 1873	(4) 2/5
Hott Minnie Lulie Lee 19	Heare Peter Loy 22	28 Feb 1887	(4) 2/23
Hott Mintie High 24	Haines Mandeville 24	5 Sept 1900	(4) 2/43
Hott Nancy Catharine 20	Loy David Jackson 22	27 Mar 1884	(4) 2/19
Hott Nora Jemima C 18	Shanholtzer Benjamin Lee 22	31 Dec 1891	(4) 2/30
Hott Ollie Vernon 18	Williamson Otis 21	11 Nov 1896	(4) 2/38
Hott Ora E 18	Shingleton James Holister 28	14 Dec 1898	(4) 2/41
Hott Rachel 20	Saville Joseph 21	29 May 1860	(10)
Hott Rachel Susan 29	Shank David 69	20 Dec 1885	(4) 2/21
Hott Rebecca Lavina 20	Loy William Henry 21	20 Jan 1881	(4) 2/15
Hott Samuel Albert 27	McDonald Charlotte Ellen 19	11 Feb 1896	(4) 2/36
Hott Samuel William 24	Henderson Mary Matilda 21	17 Nov 1870	(4) 2/2
Hott Sarah 22	McBride Shelton Ashby 27	5 Apr 1894	(4) 2/34
Hott Sarah 25	Hott Isaac 24	29 Dec 1870	(4) 2/2
Hott Sarah Elizabeth 23	Dellaplain John Christopher 28	25 Dec 1889	(4) 2/27
Hott Silas Lemuel 37	Herbaugh Florence M 18	25 Nov 1886	(4) 2/22

Name #1	Name #2	Date	Source
Hott Silas Lemuel 32	Patterson Frances Howard 19	11 Aug 1878	(4) 2/11
Hott Susan Ann 30	Shelley Philip 45	6 Mar 1877	(4) 2/9
Hott William 68	Shanholtzer Elizabeth 29	31 Jan 1871	(4) 2/2
Hott William Taylor 41	Combs Abigail 31	12 May 1892	(4) 2/31
Hott William Taylor 26	Heare Gracie Ann 25	25 Nov 1875	(4) 2/8
Hottinger Noah 27	Ludwick Demersa Biser 28	17 Jan 1882	(4) 2/17
Hottinger Silas 24	Leatherman Ann Mariah 21	9 Aug 1882	(4) 2/17
Hottinger William Seymour 29	High Susan Catharine 23	30 Nov 1890	(4) 2/28
Hottle Marcus Lee 29	Himelwright Florence Edna A 22	27 Dec 1900	(4) 2/43
Houghman Jacob	Harper Rachel	9 Jan 1823	(6)
House Amon	Lawson Catherine	*Aug 1827	(4) 3/43
House Daniel 29	Loy Mary Elizabeth 30	20 June 1894	(4) 2/34
House Samuel	Lawson Nancy	*16 Apr 1827	(4) 3/27
Householder Mary	Jones Moses	4 Mar 1825	(6)
Householder Mary	Jones Moses	*3 Mar 1825	(4) 3/18
Householder Thomas Walker 23	Barnes Minerva Jane 19	13 May 1877	(4) 2/10
Householder Thomas Walker 33	Gulick Mary Alice 29	2 Feb 1887	(4) 2/23
Householder William Robert 24	Swisher Minnie L 21	27 Dec 1894	(4) 2/35
Housell John Luther 23	Shank Cordelia 25	25 Apr 1900	(4) 2/42
Houser Charles Stewart 24	Sperrow Bertha Evaline 16	30 Jan 1895	(4) 2/35
Houser David Augustus 40	Blue Mary Virginia 40	27 Feb 1896	(4) 2/36
Houser Henry G 26	Greitzner Louisa H 25	25 Oct 1866	(4) 1/4
Houser Susan S	Cnorr James W	29 Sept 1852	(2) 7 Oct 1852
Howard Alcinda	Alkire Peter		(1) 29 Sept 1838
Howard Anna Bell 27	Haines David Wilson 25	17 Oct 1900	(4) 2/43
Howard Clemy 65	Wood Daniel 66	19 Aug 1865	(4) 1/1
Howard Eveline	Paugh J B	19 Sept 1839	(6)
Howard Eveline	Pugh James B	19 Sept 1840	(5)
Howard Helen Frances 19	Whitacre Sydnon McClellan 27	31 Oct 1889	(4) 2/27
Howard Mary Eglatine 17	Cheshire Edward Tarryson 23	24 Nov 1894	(4) 2/35
Howard Milly 34	Alexander Joseph 50	29 Apr 1869	(4) 1/38
Howard Virginia 27	Miller William 57	3 Oct 1892	(4) 2/31
Howdeyshell Philip 28	Davis Mary Elizabeth 18	5 Dec 1877	(4) 2/10
Howdyshell Bertha Ann 18	Bean Amos Seymour 22	1 Mar 1896	(4) 2/37
Howdyshell Malinda Catharine 19	Mowrey Isaac Randolph 30	17 Nov 1880	(4) 2/15
Howdyshell Rebecca E 34	Bean John 48	4 July 1886	(4) 2/22
Howdyshell Sarah Jane 21	Ludwig Joseph 23	16 Feb 1879	(4) 2/12
Hudson Robert B 22	Boor Caroline 20	20 Dec 1871	(4) 2/3
Hudson Susan	Lees William	8 Apr 1819	(5)
Huff Cornelia Elmira 20	Cheney David Webster 20	21 Oct 1879	(4) 2/13
Huff Margaret Savannah 19	Lease Jacob Thomas 20	26 Dec 1885	(4) 2/21
Huff Nora Lee 19	Lease John Henry 25	22 July 1886	(4) 2/22
Huffman Amos 64	Saville Mrs Mary Catharine 53	8 Aug 1889	(4) 2/26
Huffman Bertie Mary 23	High Curtis William 24	25 Dec 1890	(4) 2/28
Huffman Catharine 44	Shoemaker Elijah 59	17 July 1887	(4) 2/23
Huffman Christina 25	Arnold Charles William 30	19 May 1867	(4) 1/5
Huffman Daniel Frederick 27	Whiteman Anne Elizabeth 26	28 Feb 1900	(4) 2/42
Huffman Jacob Seymour 25	Whiteman Hattie Ethel 21	25 May 1900	(4) 2/42
Huffman Jacob Vanmeter 39	Ashby Myra Taylor 24	1 Dec 1886	(4) 2/22
Huffman John Samuel 28	Whiteman Francis High 20	25 Nov 1891	(4) 2/30
Huffman Mary Catharine 34	Sharp Thomas Elwell 44	25 Dec 1878	(4) 2/12
Huffman Ulyses Saville Grant 21	High Amelia Frances 16	27 July 1890	(4) 2/28

Name #1	Name #2	Date	Source
Hull Eliza	Harrison F B	30 Sept 1857	(6)
Hull Eliza J	Parker Adde'm	29 Oct 1846	(6)
Hull Isaac	Myers Catherine Ann		(1) 24 June 1837
Hull J P	Harrison M C	25 Dec 1855	(6)
Hull Jacob	Cundiff Elisabeth	*15 May 1827	(4) 3/33
Hull Jacob	Cundiff Elizabeth	17 May 1827	(6)
Hull John	Miller Margaret	15 Dec 1831	(6)
Hull Louisa	Wilson Peter	29 Jan 1843	(6)
Hull Martin	Harrison E A	26 Oct 1848	(6)
Hull Nancy	Ferribee Thos	30 Nov 1843	(6)
Hull Ruth	Sailor Wm	19 Feb 1847	(6)
Hull Sarah Catharine 17	Sinclair John M 22	1 Mar 1866	(4) 1/3
Hull Stephen	Utla Catherine	15 Feb 1835	(6)
Hull William H	Thrush Sarah	27 Oct 1850	(5)
Hull Wm F	Thrush Sarah	27 Oct 1851	(6)
Hulver George W 29	Moreland Misty May 18	18 Dec 1894	(4) 2/35
Humes Nancy	Rannells William	*20 Sept 1824	(4) 3/44
Humphrey Elias 35	Haness Alverda 21	31 Aug 1887	(4) 1/40
Hunter John	Roberts Dorcas	24 May 1827	(5)
Hurbert Robert Cline 25	McDonald Mary Catharine 32	4 Sept 1879	(4) 2/13
Hurd Charles	Maphis Sarah A	31 Dec 1863	(7)
Hurd Cora Alice 24	Hahn James Wm Gilmer 20	17 Sept 1891	(4) 2/29
Hurd Robert Lee 24	Frye Catharine 24	14 Nov 1889	(4) 2/27
Hurd Sarah Ann 35	Orndorff Martin Vanburan 45	19 Nov 1885	(4) 2/21
Hurshey Auther Wm 26	Newhouse Mattie 35	19 June 1901	(4) 2/44
Huskins Mary Jane 24	Mathews John William 25	12 May 1897	(4) 1/41
Hutcheson Jonathan 30	Sirbaugh Ida 20	23 Jan 1901	(4) 2/43
Hutcheson Sarah Fanny 46	Lynch Joseph 41	31 July 1866	(4) 1/3
Hutson Henry A 24	Downey Sarah F 20	9 Jan 1866	(4) 1/2
Hyatt Sarah	Bradford George	7 July 1831	(5)
Idleman Elizabeth	McNemar Joseph	18 Mar 1823	(5)
Idleman Henry	Blackburn Susan	21 Nov 1839	(6)
Idleman John	Cosner E A	1 Oct 1841	(5)
Idleman Mary A	Cosner Samuel	17 Nov 1842	(5)
Iliff Elias Harrison 40	Poland Hannah Susan 28	26 May 1874	(4) 2/6
Iliff Margaret	Shope Elias	*5 Apr 1824	(4) 3/20
Iliff Virginia Elizabeth 24	Adams Simon Philip 46	21 Apr 1892	(4) 2/30
Ingmin Susan	Nigh Hiram	30 Oct 1827	(5)
Ingmine Susan	High Hiram	30 Oct 1827	(6)
Ingmire Mary	Hays C G	9 June 1829	(6)
Ingmore Margaret	Hays Charles G	19 June 1829	(5)
Inskeep Ann Elizabeth 19	Washington George 23	4 Oct 1870	(4) 2/2
Inskeep Isaac A	King Margaret V	*12 Dec 1825	(4) 3/74
Inskeep John J 24	Washington Bettie M 23	4 Mar 1869	(4) 1/38
Inskeep Mary Elizabeth 28	Vance John Thomas 36	20 Oct 1869	(4) 2/1
Inskeep Rachel	Schrock Geo	27 Sept 1832	(6)
Inskeep Rebecca	Blue Uriah		(1) 8 Sept 1838
Inskeep Sallie Wright 24	Pancake Joseph Samuel 40	3 Mar 1897	(4) 2/38
Inskeep William 31	Lyle Pauline Isabel 24	19 Dec 1882	(4) 2/18
Irons Nancy	Harvey Jeremiah	5 Nov 1841	(5)
Iser Absolin 23	Hott Mary Catharine 20	12 Feb 1880	(4) 2/14
Iser Amanda Jane 19	Hott Joseph Franklin 22	30 May 1900	(4) 2/42

Name #1	Name #2	Date	Source
Iser David Washington 22	Ganoe Altie Mertie 20	6 June 1900	(4) 2/42
Iser Della Lee 23	Bailey Thornton 62	26 Oct 1897	(4) 2/39
Iser Etta 19	Thompson John 74	17 Oct 1894	(4) 2/34
Iser Etta May 18	Haines William Brithard 21	29 Mar 1899	(4) 2/41
Iser George Walter 21	Poland Aida Louise Elizabeth 17	14 Nov 1894	(4) 2/35
Iser Gustie May 19	Malcolm James William 34	4 Nov 1900	(4) 2/43
Iser Hannah Catharine 20	Bowen Henry Leaf 24	24 May 1880	(4) 2/14
Iser Ida Sedan 19	Haines Isaac Hampton 21	17 Dec 1889	(4) 2/27
Iser Isaac Martin 19	Hannas Elmira Virginia 28	7 Oct 1879	(4) 2/13
Iser Isaac Martin 21	Harrison Hettie Claudie 22	29 May 1898	(4) 2/40
Iser James Henry 20	Ganoe Mary 27	11 Apr 1900	(4) 2/42
Iser John 53	Leatherman Rachel Jane 25	1 Nov 1867	(4) 1/5
Iser Rachel J 48	Sulser Mortimer 53	2 Mar 1892	(4) 2/30
Iser Silas 53	White Christina 30	20 Jan 1898	(4) 2/40
Jackson Aaron 26	Gray Jane 19	8 Feb 1866	(4) 1/2
Jackson Agnes 16	Mathews Harry 22	16 July 1874	(4) 1/39
Jackson Caroline 25	Marks Aaron 36	10 Aug 1876	(4) 1/39
Jackson Clark 37	Jackson Martha 23	21 Oct 1880	(4) 1/40
Jackson Edward Newton 23	Clem Mary Emily 21	23 Nov 1881	(4) 2/16
Jackson Harriett 21	Mathews Daniel 23	9 Dec 1869	(4) 1/38
Jackson Henry Byrne 23	Shelley Hannah May 18	22 Dec 1891	(4) 2/30
Jackson Henry C 24	Davis Mary C 19	5 Jan 1867	(4) 1/4
Jackson Joseph 60	Johnson Ida 20	2 Nov 1882	(4) 1/40
Jackson Kate 19	Washington Lewis 45	*23 June 1869	(4) 1/38
Jackson L R 18	Banks Marshall 32	16 Sept 1868	(4) 1/7
Jackson Martha 23	Jackson Clark 37	21 Oct 1880	(4) 1/40
Jackson Mary 17	Strawden Geo W 27	20 May 1884	(4) 1/40
Jackson Mary V 21	Richardson Henry Harrison 26	15 Oct 1885	(4) 1/40
Jackson Nellie 18	Banks Ewing 24	14 Apr 1894	(4) 1/41
Jackson Richard 22	Johnson Eliza 24	28 Feb 1876	(4) 1/39
Jackson Sarah 23	Seleleton Archibald H 23	18 Dec 1886	(4) 1/40
Jackson Sidney 18	Gray Harry 21	17 Nov 1879	(4) 1/39
Jacob Granville 23	Washington Rebecca Cordelia 18	13 Jan 1880	(4) 1/39
Jacobs Catherine 24	Moore Benj F 27	14 Dec 1865	(4) 1/2
Jacobs Nancy	Fink Daniel	27 Dec 1818	(6)
James Jemima	Bosley Robert	6 Jan 1820	(6)
James Mary	Anderson James	25 Apr 1819	(5)
James Mary	Henderson Jam	25 Apr 1819	(6)
James Thorn	Culp Christina	18 Sept 1818	(6)
James Thornton	Culp Christina	11 Sept 1818	(5)
Jane Moreland 26	Stewart James Henry 25	16 Feb 1869	(4) 1/38
Janney Rachel	Smith Sol	19 Dec 1840	(5)
Janney Rachel	Smith Sol	19 Dec 1839	(6)
Janny Wm	Jinkins Mary	6 July 1835	(6)
Jarvis M	Ellifritz George	29 Dec 1816	(6)
Jeffers Delila 35	Merrit William 59	14 Apr 1874	(4) 2/6
Jeffries Mary Ellen 24	Glaze William Andrew 20	14 July 1881	(4) 2/16
Jeffries Sarah Louisa 28	Jewell John Peter 22	3 Mar 1881	(4) 2/15
Jenkins Benjamin	Arm Catherine	9 Jan 1838	(1) 27 Jan 1838
Jenkins Elick Jackson 22	Cowgill Laura Edna Lee 19	23 Nov 1900	(4) 2/43
Jenkins H P	Roberts Hannah	3 Sept 1850	(5)
Jenkins James	Clipstine	23 Sept 1819	(5)

Name #1	Name #2	Date	Source
Jenkins Mary	Powell James L	*13 May 1824	(4) 3/28
Jenkins Mary	Tasker George	*26 Sept 1825	(4) 3/60
Jenkins William Henry 22	Simmons? Millie Dorothy 21	*26 Dec 1892	(4) 2/31
Jennings William	Drace Eliza	2 Feb 1826	(5)
Jewell Eliza Ann 19	Doman Denton Pierce 26	3 June 1884	(4) 2/19
Jewell Etta Serena 15	Flemming Edward Anderson 28	23 Dec 1880	(4) 2/15
Jewell Ida Belle 17	Brown David William 19	21 Sept 1885	(4) 2/21
Jewell John Peter 22	Jeffries Sarah Louisa 28	3 Mar 1881	(4) 2/15
Jewell Mary C 18	Shoemaker Thomas Nicholas 22	1 Aug 1893	(4) 2/32
Jewell Mary Jane 20	Minshall John 38	7 June 1881	(4) 2/16
Jewett Ellen M	White John K	19 Nov 1839	(1) 5 Nov 1839
Jinkins Elisha	Dimmit Zillah	22 Feb 1851	(6)
Jinkins Ensna	Dimmit Gillah	11 Feb 1846	(5)
Jinkins H P	Roberts Hannah	3 Sept 1851	(6)
Jinkins Mary	Janny Wm	6 July 1835	(6)
Joel Wolverton	Carder Elizabeth	*3 May 1825	(4) 3/35
Johnson Abraham 30	Sutton Charlotte 35	30 Nov 1865	(4) 1/1
Johnson Abram	Parker S M	20 Mar 1844	(6)
Johnson Amos	Allender Mary	*5 May 1828	(4) 3/11
Johnson Anne 21	Peterson Andrew Jackson 24	18 Dec 1889	(4) 1/41
Johnson Bazel	McVicker Jane	*13 June 1826	(4) 3/27
Johnson Benjamin	Means Mariah	*20 Feb 1826	(4) 3/12
Johnson Benjamin	Means Mariah	9 Mar 1826	(6)
Johnson Bessie 22	Peterson Andrew 33	10 May 1899	(4) 1/42
Johnson Caroline 22	Holt Dan'l 27	23 Sept 1868	(4) 1/7
Johnson Catherine	Babb Samuel	9 Apr 1838	(5)
Johnson Charles 39	Marshall Annie Frances 16	4 Nov 1886	(4) 1/40
Johnson E	Welton Wright	31 May 1836	(6)
Johnson Eliza 24	Jackson Richard 22	28 Feb 1876	(4) 1/39
Johnson Ella May 25	Mellen William 34	14 Sept 1887	(4) 2/24
Johnson Florence Virginia 25	Anderson Morgan Julius 35	26 Jan 1887	(4) 2/23
Johnson George 34	Folks Lucy 21	24 Sept 1888	(4) 1/40
Johnson George W 22	Gates Jemima 22	19 Nov 1871	(4) 1/38
Johnson H A	Reese Wm D	4 Sept 1845	(6)
Johnson Henry 27	Williams Sarah E 23	23 Aug 1866	(4) 1/3
Johnson Henry 65	Woods Ellen 42	25 July 1891	(4) 1/41
Johnson Ida 20	Jackson Joseph 60	2 Nov 1882	(4) 1/40
Johnson James Henry 22	Larrick Flashie Alice 21	18 May 1882	(4) 2/17
Johnson James W 24	Nelson Joanna S 28	9 Mar 1870	(4) 2/1
Johnson Jerome E 29	Fisher Ella 21	4 Apr 1893	(4) 1/41
Johnson Jesse 47	Rice Mary Jane 35	1 May 1871	(4) 2/2
Johnson John	Powell Isab	30 Apr 1843	(6)
Johnson Joseph Henry 19	Haines Ruth Ann 18	15 Jan 1900	(4) 2/42
Johnson Lena 21	Tharp Jackson 28	25 Aug 1897	(4) 2/39
Johnson Lucy Ann 23	Gilmore Anthony Jacob 22	11 Sept 1873	(4) 1/38
Johnson Lucy M 24	Ewers Arthur Loudon 26	14 Sept 1887	(4) 2/24
Johnson Lula G 21	Kackley Charles M L 22	25 Dec 1895	(4) 2/36
Johnson Malors Hamilton 23	Keller Elizabeth Alberta 21	1 Feb 1872	(4) 2/3
Johnson Mary 19	Matthews Brandson 23	16 Jan 1870	(4) 1/38
Johnson Mary Jane 23	Lafollette Charles Cephas 23	25 Dec 1894	(4) 2/35
Johnson Melissa Jane 22	Anderson Samuel Edward 21	26 Mar 1891	(4) 2/29
Johnson N Walter 20	Kiblin Martha J 22	26 Apr 1869	(4) 1/38

Name #1	Name #2	Date	Source
Johnson Richard Menter 33	Larrick Sallie Jane 18	12 Feb 1874	(4) 2/5
Johnson Sarah	Cundiff J R	28 Dec 1848	(6)
Johnson Sarah F 17	Lewis Solomon 22	3 May 1888	(4) 1/40
Johnson Sarah Francis 21	Gray Peter 32	22 Nov 1871	(4) 2/3
Johnson Sarah Margaret 19	Hicks Edward Martin 22	11 June 1890	(4) 2/28
Johnson Sol Loundes Vesta 22	Nelson Alice Virginia 18	15 Oct 1898	(4) 1/41
Johnson Susan	Pomeroy Johnson	12 June 1860	(10)
Johnson Susan 18	Coleman John 24	11 July 1889	(4) 1/40
Johnson Susan Jane 24	Selvey Harrison 26	5 Sept 1890	(4) 2/28
Johnson Walter N 20	Kibler Martha I 22	26 Apr 1869	(4) 2/1
Johnson William	Ward Abigal	*17 Jan 1825	(4) 3/10
Johnson Zachariah Esrah 22	Ewers Elizabeth Balthis 22	21 Oct 1891	(4) 2/30
Jones Allen 28	Armstrong Sidney 22	25 Jan 1876	(4) 1/39
Jones Allen 45	Brooks Martha 28	Sept 1894	(4) 1/41
Jones Charles Edward 27	Horn Mary Bell 21	12 July 1881	(4) 2/16
Jones Jesse	Stonebreaker Ruth	21 May 1834	(5)
Jones John Clay 45	Ball Frances Elizabeth 25	19 Oct 1898	(4) 2/41
Jones Mary	Levings Caleb	*25 Oct 1828	(4) 3/34
Jones Moses	Householder M	4 Mar 1825	(6)
Jones Moses	Householder Mary	*3 Mar 1825	(4) 3/18
Jones Thomas	Ward Elizabeth	22 Aug 1823	(5)
Jones Thomas	Ward Elizabeth	17 July 1823	(6)
Jordan Robert 35	Swisher Mary Virginia 21	15 Feb 1866	(4) 1/2
Judy Adam 22	Yokum Mary Jane 23	21 Mar 1866	(4) 1/3
Junkins Elizabeth	Baker John	2 Jan 1823	(6)
Junkins J	Clipstine Mary	23 Sept 1819	(6)
Junkins Jane	Knabenshew John	29 Oct 1835	(5)
Junkins John	Anderson Elizabeth	20 June 1816	(5)
Junkins John	Henderson Elizabeth	25 Apr 1816	(6)
Junkins Lucinda	Wilson Jas	25 Dec 1832	(6)
Junkins Marg	Brant Jno G	8 May 1834	(6)
Junkins Margaret	Anderson James	23 Mar 1820	(5)
Junkins Mary	Tasker George	29 Sept 1825	(6)
Junkins Mary	Harsel Peter	9 Mar 1820	(6)
Junkins Mary	Harvey Jas B	22 Sept 1833	(6)
Junkins Mary	Lockridge James	22 Nov 1839	(5)
Junkins N	Lockbridge Jas	22 Nov 1838	(6)
Junkins Ruth	Harvey John L	8 May 1845	(6)
Junkins Thoas	Smith Eliz	24 Apr 1849	(6)
Ka? Joseph Robert 21	Orndorff Alice 21	14 Jan 1901	(4) 2/43
Kabrick David S 32	Harris C M 23	20 Mar 1866	(4) 1/3
Kabrick P E	Buncrotts J A	4 June 1851	(6)
Kabrick Peter E	Bumcrotts J A	4 June 1850	(5)
Kabrick Reb'a	Barrick John	12 Apr 1843	(6)
Kabrick Wm W	Liller M C	23 Sept 1858	(6)
Kackley Charles M L 22	Johnson Lula G 21	25 Dec 1895	(4) 2/36
Kackley Chas P 20	Bidinger C Catharine 18	22 Feb 1870	(4) 2/1
Kackley Minnie Bell 21	Sirbaugh Samuel Harvey 25	26 Dec 1889	(4) 2/27
Kackley Minnie G 17	Whitacre William Washington 23	21 May 1896	(4) 2/37
Kackly Robert Lee 25	Brill Almira Virginia 24	27 Dec 1893	(4) 2/33
Kail Christiana	Thompson Elijah	*4 Apr 1825	(4) 3/28
Kail Elizabeth	Taylor Robert	*30 Jan 1825	(4) 3/11

Name #1	Name #2	Date	Source
Kalbauga Alex	Trentor M C	8 Oct 1846	(5)
Kalbaugh Alex	Tasker M C	8 Oct 1850	(6)
Kane Lydia I 28	Parker Isaac P 50	3 Jan 1866	(4) 1/2
Kane Sallie Lee	Harper William 58	22 Oct 1867	(4) 1/5
Kave Isaac Ashby 21	Maphis Ida Alverta 16	8 Aug 1889	(4) 2/26
Kave James Albert 29	Whitacre Alice Virginia 22	*14 Nov 1895	(4) 2/36
Kaylor Andrew 28	Miles Catharine 16	14 Sept 1865	(4) 1/1
Kaylor James Wesley 30	Montgomery Elizabeth A 25	24 Oct 1889	(4) 2/27
Kaylor John Edward 24	Cooper Nancy V 22	9 Sept 1896	(4) 2/37
Kaylor Martha Jane 26	Gross James Isaac 30	20 Aug 1888	(4) 2/25
Kaylor Thomas William 24	Miller Sarah 25	30 May 1890	(4) 2/28
Kearns Elisha	Ganoe Margaret	*8 Jan 1827	(4) 3/1
Keckley Cephas Dr 75	Offutt Mary Margaret 40	22 Dec 1900	(4) 2/43
Keckley Harrison Lot 29	Stephens Sarah 19	26 Dec 1888	(4) 2/26
Keckley Rosa C Catharine 21	Rogers John Benjamin 22	26 May 1892	(4) 2/31
Keister Alonzo Mandeville 24	Davis Margaret Ellen 24	16 Jan 1878	(4) 2/11
Keister Emma Elizabeth 22	Ruckman Arthur Jackson 23	3 Mar 1896	(4) 2/37
Keister Katie 22	Scruggs William Franklin 30	5 May 1887	(4) 2/23
Keister Minnie 21	Schnibbe George Wesley 22	6 May 1890	(4) 2/28
Keister Robert Lee 22	Kline Emma Virginia 18	7 Mar 1894	(4) 2/33
Keiter Esther	Templar John L	29 Mar 1838	(1) 7 Apr 1838
Keiter Mary 25	Bradfield William Ashby 29	11 Jan 1894	(4) 2/33
Keller Charles	Price Elmira	*28 Jan 1826	(4) 3/3
Keller Elizabeth Alberta 21	Johnson Malors Hamilton 23	1 Feb 1872	(4) 2/3
Keller Harriet Emma 34	Davis James H 25	4 Dec 1877	(4) 2/10
Keller John Foman 36	Harmison Alice 34	13 Apr 1881	(4) 2/16
Keller Lucretia Ellen 24	Brooks Benjamin 28	4 Sept 1865	(4) 1/1
Keller Maggie Bell 19	Sirbaugh James 19	22 Feb 1899	(4) 2/41
Keller Martha V 22	Worden Horatia N 24	14 Mar 1866	(4) 1/3
Keller Napolen Bonaparte 23	Bidinger Sarah Jane 23	19 Dec 1878	(4) 2/12
Keller Peter 45	Shelton Margaret Ann 30	*29 Nov 1871	(4) 2/3
Keller Richard B 24	Davis Jane C 27	30 Apr 1874	(4) 2/6
Keller Sarah Catharine 30	Soles Edward Eli 30	9 Mar 1881	(4) 2/15
Kelley Edward 22	Whitacre Rhoda Ellen 20	6 June 1876	(4) 2/8
Kelley Elizabeth 20	Shoemaker John 22	26 Mar 1857	(10)
Kelley Etta Fanny 31	Smith George Renic 31	3 Oct 1900	(4) 2/43
Kelley George Wesley 23	Link Elizabeth Catharine 21	23 Feb 1881	(4) 2/15
Kelley Hiram Nelson 52	Purgit Susan Jane 39	14 June 1899	(4) 2/41
Kelley Isaac Patrick 32	Whitacre Lydia F 24	12 Feb 1884	(4) 2/19
Kelley Isabelle	Riley Alexander	29 Mar 1827	(5)
Kelley John	McWaine Jerusia	27 June 1824	(5)
Kelley Martha Ann 23	Arnold Peter 25	9 Jan 1866	(4) 1/2
Kelley Sarah Frances 17	Malcolm Harry 23	12 Oct 1891	(4) 2/29
Kelly Alverda Jeannetta 22	Leatherman Daniel Thomas 24	14 Sept 1875	(4) 2/7
Kelly E	Shoemaker John	26 Mar 1856	(6)
Kelly Isabel	Riley Alex	26 Mar 1827	(6)
Kelly Isabella	Riley Alexander	*19 Mar 1827	(4) 3/19
Kelly Isabelle	Ward John	27 Nov 1828	(6)
Kelly James	Logue Rebecca K	23 June 1844	(6)
Kelly John	Bailey Eleanor	*20 Aug 1827	(4) 3/41
Kelly John	Bailey Eleanor	30 Aug 1827	(6)
Kelly Joseph A 23	Stickley Mary Margaret 22	18 June 1867	(4) 1/5

Name #1	Name #2	Date	Source
Kelly S A	Shoemaker W H	29 June 1848	(6)
Kelly Sarah E K 18	Cornwell Jesse M 29	25 Dec 1866	(4) 1/2
Kelso Anna Roberta 27	Davis Samuel Sylvester 25	28 Aug 1884	(4) 2/19
Kelso Carter Gilbert 24	Spaid Elin May 20	19 Mar 1891	(4) 2/29
Kelso Jane	Brill Isaac	*20 May 1828	(4) 3/12
Kelso Mahlon Lore 30	Slonaker Molly Delila 22	22 Dec 1891	(4) 2/30
Kelsoe Florence Roberta 22	Martin Anderson Amby 28	27 Apr 1896	(4) 2/37
Kelsoe Ida Cornelia 28	Brill James Abraham 28	14 Apr 1887	(4) 2/23
Kelsoe Lillie B 34	Sine Alfred L 33	6 Mar 1895	(4) 2/35
Kelsoe Martha Malinda 24	Lafollette Edgar Lee 33	12 Jan 1898	(4) 2/40
Kelsoe Sarah Virginia 21	Harloe Wm E 23	20 May 1873	(4) 2/4
Kendall Laura Lowring 19	Smith James Franklin 26	10 Oct 1881	(4) 2/16
Kenney Virginia Ann 22	Reynolds William Frank 28	18 Jan 1877	(4) 2/9
Kenney William H 31	Miller Martha Allie 22	29 Oct 1878	(4) 2/12
Kenny John William 25	Goodin Mary Shobe 22	30 Mar 1875	(4) 2/7
Keplinger Christian 36	Whitacre Mary Matilda 30	31 Aug 1874	(4) 2/6
Kerig? Emanuel 33	Critton Frances 30	19 May 1892	(4) 2/30
Kern David	Leatherman M A	11 July 1853	(6)
Kern David	Leatherman M A	1 July 1853	(5)
Kern H E	Leatherman W L	30 Apr 1857	(6)
Kern Margaret A 25	Doman Tobias S 37	7 Nov 1866	(4) 1/4
Kern Rachel Ellen 19	Herell Charles Edward 35	20 Aug 1867	(4) 1/5
Kern? Martha Fannie 21	Monroe Joseph 25	2 Jan 1894	(4) 2/33
Kernawbashaw Maria	Bark Adam	8 Oct 1818	(5)
Kerne Elisha	Noel Martha Jane	21 Sept 1852	(2) 7 Oct 1852
Kerns A 24	Seaton K 48	6 Feb 1859	(10)
Kerns Andrew Jacob 22	Moreland Evaline 24	21 Feb 1894	(4) 2/33
Kerns Benjamin Franklin 60	Godlove Sarah Catharine 41	20 May 1890	(4) 2/28
Kerns Elizabeth Florence 20	Sirbaugh Wm Joshua 24	25 Feb 1892	(4) 2/30
Kerns Frank Perry 27	Pool Lyda Hennietta 28	27 Aug 1889	(4) 2/26
Kerns Harris Ephraim 24	Miller Mary Frances 22	3 June 1896	(4) 2/37
Kerns Isaac Jefferson 31	Albaugh Emma Elizabeth 21	5 May 1892	(4) 2/31
Kerns Jacob	Cheshire Nancy Jane		(1) 29 Apr 1853
Kerns John Lewis 25	Yost Maria Flory 18	15 Oct 1867	(4) 1/5
Kerns John Sanford 37	Albaugh Mary F 26	28 Aug 1873	(4) 2/4
Kerns John William 34	Kline Emma Elizabeth 23	24 May 1888	(4) 2/25
Kerns John William 24	Mason Lethe May 17	28 Mar 1899	(4) 2/41
Kerns Laura Belle 22	Snyder Richard Martin 23	8 Nov 1888	(4) 2/25
Kerns Lewis Kennison 33	Shanholtzer Mary 35	25 Dec 1873	(4) 2/5
Kerns Margaret Elizabeth 20	Brannan William Grant 22	31 July 1898	(4) 2/40
Kerns Margary Isabell 18	Miller ? Henry 22	11 July 1880	(4) 2/14
Kerns Mary Almeda A 22	Koontz William Henry 32	23 Oct 1884	(4) 2/20
Kerns Mary Jane 21	Rineheart Jeremiah 27	3 July 1873	(4) 2/4
Kerns Nancy Elizabeth 22	Stickley ? Tobias 22	24 Feb 1874	(4) 2/5
Kerns Nathanial 28	Brelsford Florence Virginia 21	13 May 1877	(4) 2/10
Kerns O Bell 18	Mason A Clayton 20	1 July 1897	(4) 2/39
Kerns Rachel C 28	Shambaugh Jos Jasper Mathew 38	24 Apr 1901	(4) 2/44
Kerns Rebecca Ann 38	Doman J Newton 44	1 Nov 1895	(4) 2/36
Kerns Robert W 45	Whitacre Virginia 23	21 Aug 1898	(4) 2/40
Kerns Samuel Nathan 30	Wright Mary Cordelia 16	5 June 1894	(4) 2/34
Kerns Smauel Granville 23	Haines Carrie Bell 24	3 Jan 1901	(4) 2/43
Kerns Susan Catharine 16	Crock John Wm 27	15 June 1875	(4) 2/7

Name #1	Name #2	Date	Source
Kerns Thomas Good 41	Prior Fanny Agnes 29	3 Apr 1897	(4) 2/35
Kerr Emma 20	Banks Robert 26	20 June 1895	(4) 1/41
Kervey Benjamin	Fogel Charlotte	*4 Sept 1826	(4) 3/33
Kesill Eliza 22	Evans Benj 26	9 Apr 1866	(4) 1/3
Kesner Christina Virginia 20	Bowers John William 29	15 Oct 1891	(4) 2/30
Kesner Mahala Jane 17	Shrout William Lewis 25	7 Nov 1891	(4) 2/30
Kessel Charley Anderson 23	Taylor Mary Ellen 18	27 Feb 1895	(4) 2/35
Kester Elias	Probst Anna	17 Dec 1831	(6)
Ketterman Barbara A 27	Parsons Adam H 39	15 Feb 1866	(4) 1/2
Keys Charles 49	Coleman Maria Elizabeth 22	17 Nov 1887	(4) 1/40
Keys Edith 23	Smith William Brown 28	30 Nov 1894	(4) 1/41
Keys Maria 22	Quarles Joseph 24	22 Apr 1891	(4) 1/41
Keyser Abram	Moreland Sarah	19 Oct 1844	(5)
Kibler Isaac Newton 30	Racey Olive Bell 19	25 May 1896	(4) 2/37
Kibler Martha I 22	Johnson Walter N 20	26 Apr 1869	(4) 2/1
Kiblin Martha J 22	Johnson N Walter 20	26 Apr 1869	(4) 1/38
Kidd Robert B 36	Armstrong Elizabeth McCarty 22	14 Mar 1867	(4) 1/4
Kidd Virginia B 35	Snyder John M 49	28 Aug 1873	(4) 2/4
Kidner Harriett 22	Corbin John 32	2 Mar 1860	(10)
Kidner Jas W 20	Carder Sallie V 23	22 Aug 1872	(4) 2/3
Kidner Mary Elizabeth 21	Kidwell William Ashford 26	23 Dec 1873	(4) 2/5
Kidner Wm Franklin 20	Pyles Mollie 21	1 Nov 1899	(4) 2/42
Kidwell ? 25	Patterson Charles 25	8 Mar 1860	(10)
Kidwell Albert R 24	Shanholtzer Marg L Catherine 17	25 Aug 1893	(4) 2/33
Kidwell Alice Jane 15	White Thomas Edward 24	30 Dec 1873	(4) 2/5
Kidwell Benjamin Alexander 22	Moreland Sarah Ellen 20	26 Mar 1880	(4) 2/14
Kidwell Delia 21	Kidwell Joseph M 23	17 Dec 1874	(4) 2/6
Kidwell Deskin Abraham 21	Bennett Virginia Belle 22	8 Mar 1888	(4) 2/24
Kidwell Emma C 17	Kidwell James Robert 22	15 Mar 1877	(4) 2/10
Kidwell Frances Ann 23	Abrill David Jackson 22	29 Oct 1879	(4) 2/13
Kidwell Francis Marion 23	Farmer Sarah Ann 24	16 Feb 1869	(4) 1/38
Kidwell George Washington 28	Slane Julia Ann 26	12 Apr 1876	(4) 2/8
Kidwell James 67	Largent Elizabeth Ann 50	18 July 1871	(4) 2/3
Kidwell James Robert 22	Kidwell Emma C 17	15 Mar 1877	(4) 2/10
Kidwell John Newton 35	Largent Louisa Catharine 23	23 Feb 1875	(4) 2/7
Kidwell Jonathan 37	Bennett Ann Maria 25	12 Jan 1867	(4) 1/4
Kidwell Joseph M 23	Kidwell Delia 21	17 Dec 1874	(4) 2/6
Kidwell Lorenzo William 22	Kidwell Lucinda Florence 21	27 Feb 1877	(4) 2/9
Kidwell Lucinda Florence 21	Kidwell Lorenzo William 22	27 Feb 1877	(4) 2/9
Kidwell Malinda Jane 22	Shanholtzer George William 22	25 Mar 1886	(4) 2/22
Kidwell Margaret Casandra 30	Betson James W 37	19 Mar 1889	(4) 2/26
Kidwell Martha Jane 33	King Isaac Warner 27	7 Dec 1876	(4) 2/9
Kidwell Mary	Hawkins David	*1 Oct 1825	(4) 3/63
Kidwell Mary Ellen 24	Riley James Robert 31	15 Mar 1877	(4) 2/10
Kidwell Mary V 18	McDonald Jas H M 31	5 Apr 1866	(4) 1/3
Kidwell Randolph Hawkins 26	Proctor Rebecca Frances 18	22 May 1877	(4) 2/10
Kidwell Randolph Hawkins 57	Hawkins Elizabeth Ann 44	28 Mar 1882	(4) 2/17
Kidwell Rebecca Ann 19	Edwards Robert William 23	28 July 1881	(4) 2/16
Kidwell Robert Senseny 24	Largent Sarah Elizabeth 18	30 Nov 1882	(4) 2/18
Kidwell Verdie Blanche 21	Alderton Perry L 20	8 July 1897	(4) 2/39
Kidwell William Ashford 26	Kidner Mary Elizabeth 21	23 Dec 1873	(4) 2/5
Kight Caleb	Tasker L S	25 Dec 1850	(5)

Name #1	Name #2	Date	Source
Kight Sarah	Brant Elizah P	13 Oct 1837	(5)
Kimble Alice Eveline 17	Pool Lloyd Logan 24	7 Jan 1879	(4) 2/12
Kimble Clara Eugenie 18	Pool Joseph Asbury 27	7 Jan 1879	(4) 2/12
Kimble Richard L 29	Frye S V 27	20 Feb 1901	(4) 2/44
Kimble Sylvester 25	Orndorff Ella Barbara 25	2 June 1881	(4) 2/16
King Alexander	Collins Lavenia		(1) 4 Apr 1839
King Benjamin Franklin 34	Pultz Lydia Margaret 22	10 Feb 1885	(4) 2/20
King Emily Laura 21	Stephens Beverly Nash 29	20 Oct 1896	(4) 1/41
King Greenberry	McCormick Mary	4 Mar 1824	(5)
King Isaac Warner 27	Kidwell Martha Jane 33	7 Dec 1876	(4) 2/9
King Jesse	Harvey Lucinda	20 Jan 1842	(6)
King John	Norman Lucy	*17 Oct 1825	(4) 3/68
King Margaret Ann 39	Milleson Peter Marion 38	31 May 1893	(4) 2/32
King Margaret Ellen 19	Hockman Harvey Milton 21	31 Oct 1878	(4) 2/12
King Margaret V	Inskeep Isaac A	*12 Dec 1825	(4) 3/74
King Mary Catharine 22	McKee ? 40	6 Nov 1883	(4) 2/18
King Sarah Isabelle 24	Martin Jasper Newton 29	19 Mar 1878	(4) 2/11
King Thomas Earl 26	Vanosdel Martha Ann 21	23 Dec 1875	(4) 2/8
King Thorn A	Kite Armin	28 Mar 1839	(6)
King Thornton A	Kite Armitha	28 Mar 1840	(5)
King Wesley	St Clair Marjory	16 Nov 1820	(5)
King William	Horn Elizabeth	*3 Apr 1824	(4) 3/19
Kinkead Anne Jennie 22	Fields Charles Hammond 30	14 Sept 1899	(4) 2/41
Kirby Edward Walter 27	Saville Harriet Jane 17	28 Sept 1886	(4) 2/22
Kirby Rachel Beal 17	Corbin George Thomas 29	11 June 1890	(4) 2/28
Kirby William 56	Wagoner Elizabeth 55	10 July 1894	(4) 2/34
Kirk Betsy Ann	Friddle Henry	*10 May 1824	(4) 3/27
Kisner Bar'y	Barnhouse F A	4 Sept 1845	(6)
Kister John C 29	Hammack Mary E 26	13 Oct 1870	(4) 2/2
Kitchen Clina Ransom 26	Haines Maggie E 18	8 Feb 1870	(4) 2/1
Kite Armin	King Thorn A	28 Mar 1839	(6)
Kite Armitha	King Thornton A	28 Mar 1840	(5)
Kite Henry	Sharpless Sarah	20 Aug 1816	(5)
Kite Henry	Sharpless Sarah	20 June 1816	(6)
Kite Nancy	Sharps Wash	19 Jan 1843	(6)
Kite Theodasia	Dayton William	5 Oct 1839	(5)
Kite Theodosia	Dayton Wm	5 Oct 1838	(6)
Kite Wm	Gregg Amy	15 Aug 1844	(6)
Kite Wm	McCormick Nancy	8 Jan 1835	(6)
Kitzmiller Gasper	Ward Millie	13 Dec 1821	(6)
Kitzmiller Gasper	Ward Minnie	13 Dec 1821	(5)
Kitzmiller H	Stuttenbarger E	8 May 1856	(6)
Kitzmiller H C	Carnell Adam	27 Sept 1859	(6)
Kitzmiller Jas	Boyle Eliza	29 Oct 1843	(6)
Kitzmiller Joseph	Sollars Mary	20 Jan 1831	(6)
Kitzmiller Lewis	Paugh M	20 Jan 1831	(6)
Kitzmiller Lydia	Evans William	18 Mar 1842	(5)
Kitzmiller Mary	Earnholt John	5 Dec 1827	(5)
Kitzmiller William H	Shields Mary	27 Nov 1836	(5)
Kline Almira Jamima C 24	Brooks Samuel David 24	9 Feb 1882	(4) 2/17
Kline Amanda Alice 19	Lincoln John Edward 23	22 Oct 1878	(4) 2/12
Kline Annie Rebecca 22	Lafollette Elias Miller 31	4 Dec 1894	(4) 2/35

Name #1	Name #2	Date	Source
Kline Barbara	Groves William	*16 June 1828	(4) 3/14
Kline Bessie 21	Heishman Tilberry 25	27 Oct 1892	(4) 2/31
Kline Dora 18	Peer Elmore Roy 19	22 May 1899	(4) 2/41
Kline Edward Luther 25	Saville Mary Jane 16	7 Feb 1889	(4) 2/26
Kline Emma Elizabeth 23	Kerns John William 34	24 May 1888	(4) 2/25
Kline Emma Virginia 18	Keister Robert Lee 22	7 Mar 1894	(4) 2/33
Kline Francelia Ellen 18	Byrd Emanuel Thomas 25	31 Mar 1892	(4) 2/30
Kline H Lee 33	Piles Hannah 39	11 Apr 1893	(4) 2/32
Kline James 35	Sheriff Nancy V 20	29 June 1868	(4) 1/6
Kline James N 24	Saville Eliza 19	22 Sept 1885	(4) 2/21
Kline John 27	Saville Sarah Catharine 20	11 Apr 1889	(4) 2/26
Kline John Jr 26	Peer Herriet 22	15 Sept 1868	(4) 1/7
Kline John Wesley 24	Swisher Sarah Belle 17	1 Sept 1881	(4) 2/16
Kline Joseph 28	Swisher Pruda Dara D 15	31 Dec 1876	(4) 2/9
Kline Julius Calvin 28	Stewart Margaret Elizabeth 40	30 Dec 1880	(4) 2/15
Kline Louisa Jane 21	Cheshire John Thomas 22	28 Nov 1886	(4) 2/22
Kline Lydia M 19	Haun Samuel 25	25 Oct 1866	(4) 1/3
Kline Martha Elizabeth 19	McBride Lorenzo Beauregard 20	27 Dec 1881	(4) 2/17
Kline Mary 18	Lafollette William Carson 27	20 Apr 1893	(4) 2/32
Kline Minnie Belle 19	Oates George William 28	28 Oct 1897	(4) 2/39
Kline Philip	Spaid Elisabeth	*21 Feb 1827	(4) 3/15
Kline Philip 50	Swisher Ann Rebecca 35	2 Nov 1873	(4) 2/5
Kline Rienza 22	Garvin Maria Lucinda 17	13 Apr 1870	(4) 2/1
Kline Samuel J	Arnold Rachel	16 Sept 1842	(5)
Kline Stevanas 54	Ely Mary Catharine 24	23 Jan 1884	(4) 2/18
Kline Virginia Frances 21	Oats Daniel 26	28 Nov 1871	(4) 2/3
Kline William S	Fleming Christina	19 Aug 1819	(5)
Klinedinsts Augustive 42	Whiteman Margaret Isabel 28	21 May 1879	(4) 2/13
Knabenshew John	Junkins Jane	29 Oct 1835	(5)
Knabenshoe Sarah	Duling Achilles	26 Apr 1821	(5)
Knabenshue Jacob	Duling Nancy	*16 Oct 1824	(4) 3/47
Knee E Lester 28	Slonaker Dora E 22	10 Oct 1900	(4) 2/43
Knight Caleb	Tasker L S	30 Oct 1851	(6)
Knight Sarah	Brant Elijah P	13 Oct 1837	(6)
Koerner Frederick Sydenham 27	Blue Gregg Susan 16	2 Dec 1880	(4) 2/15
Koontz William Henry 32	Kerns Mary Almeda A 22	23 Oct 1884	(4) 2/20
Kramer Margaret	Marshall Richard	31 Oct 1839	(1) 14 Nov 1839
Kreemer Andrew Jackson 65	Bonney Adaline 47	2 Apr 1889	(4) 2/26
Kreemer Emma Catharine 26	Taylor John of Thos 37	28 Oct 1886	(4) 2/22
Kremer Arabella Frances 24	Cookus Robert Henry 22	11 Dec 1877	(4) 2/10
Kremer Helen Virginia 20	Heatwole Charles Elliott 25	16 Jan 1877	(4) 2/9
Kremes George Thomas 22	Speelman Mollie V 18	10 Aug 1871	(4) 2/3
Kuhn John 26	Vishon Whitley 30	8 Mar 1866	(4) 1/3
Kump Benjamin Franklin 35	Rudolph Margaret Frances 34	15 June 1875	(4) 2/7
Kump Chas M S 21	Oates Emma 22	6 May 1900	(4) 2/42
Kump Jacob	Millslagle Julia Ann	25 Jan 1838	(1) 10 Feb 1838
Kump Jemima Elizabeth 27	Fletcher Flavius Josephus 27	4 June 1879	(4) 2/13
Kump John H 23	Lafollette Ursula Ellen 22	24 Oct 1893	(4) 2/33
Kump Samuel James 43	Hannum Laura Belle 19	15 Feb 1888	(4) 2/24
Kump William N 24	Hemilwright Nancy A M 22	21 July 1895	(4) 2/35
Kuykendall Fannie B 24	Taylor Isaac 29	5 Mar 1867	(4) 1/4
Kuykendall Isaac	Williams Susan	29 Sept 1852	(2) 7 Oct 1852

Name #1	Name #2	Date	Source
Kuykendall James Lawson 38	McGlothery Ida Raymond 28	5 Oct 1887	(4) 2/24
Kuykendall Joseph 26	Smith Mary Jane 20	2 Dec 1900	(4) 2/43
Kuykendall Luke	Welch Elizabeth	13 Nov 1828	(6)
Kuykendall Luke	Welch Elizabeth	*10 Nov 1828	(4) 3/38
Kuykendall Mary Hopkins 26	Blackman James Samuel 26	19 Sept 1888	(4) 2/25
Kuykendall S	Hanshaw W	26 Oct 1841	(6)
Kuykendall Susan 18	Guthrie William Newton 25	14 Apr 1875	(4) 2/7
Kuykendall Thomas 28	McGill Kate 24	5 June 1883	(4) 2/18
Lafollett Bartholomew	Brill Eleanor	*14 Nov 1825	(4) 3/70
Lafollett Jemima 18	McCauly James Henry 20	14 Mar 1867	(4) 1/5
Lafollett Julius 37	McIlwee Judith Rebecca 27	24 July 1884	(4) 2/19
Lafollett Lillie Eleanora 18	Lafollett Richard Turner 25	24 Nov 1887	(4) 2/24
Lafollett Mary	Groves Philip	*17 Oct 1825	(4) 3/67
Lafollett Richard Turner 25	Lafollett Lillie Eleanora 18	24 Nov 1887	(4) 2/24
Lafollett Sarah M 22	Hannum Dabney Ball 20	5 Dec 1867	(4) 1/6
Lafollette Asbury 26	McIlwee Sarah 26	*3 Mar 1873	(4) 2/4
Lafollette Baxter 21	Brill Mary C 23	20 Dec 1877	(4) 2/11
Lafollette Brondell 24	Anderson Aranintha May 20	21 Dec 1887	(4) 2/24
Lafollette Charles Cephas 23	Johnson Mary Jane 23	25 Dec 1894	(4) 2/35
Lafollette Cora Rosa 22	Giffin John Wm 22	8 Mar 1892	(4) 2/30
Lafollette Edgar Lee 33	Kelsoe Martha Malinda 24	12 Jan 1898	(4) 2/40
Lafollette Elias Elkanah 32	Anderson Hattie Malinda 26	13 Apr 1876	(4) 2/8
Lafollette Elias Miller 31	Kline Annie Rebecca 22	4 Dec 1894	(4) 2/35
Lafollette Emma C 25	Fauver Addison Buchanan 33	17 Dec 1889	(4) 2/27
Lafollette Fannie 19	Dunlap Algernon Wood 33	18 Nov 1880	(4) 2/15
Lafollette Florence E 21	McKee Clinton C 22	7 Nov 1888	(4) 2/25
Lafollette Gegirtha Frances 18	Spaid Jeremiah James 25	12 Apr 1899	(4) 2/41
Lafollette Hannah J 20	Miller William T 27	5 Dec 1872	(4) 2/4
Lafollette Martha Abalona 16	Hook McCullough Branden 23	24 Nov 1892	(4) 2/31
Lafollette Mullen 25	Stephens Lillie B 24	16 Apr 1895	(4) 2/35
Lafollette Nellie Jemima 22	Arnold Edward T 27	25 Nov 1886	(4) 2/22
Lafollette Rosa Estella 19	Larrick John Will 23	2 Mar 1898	(4) 2/40
Lafollette Theodore Clark 25	Brill Asbernia Cordelia 20	28 Jan 1886	(4) 2/21
Lafollette Tiberry Streit 24	Arnold Mary Frances V 20	13 Apr 1876	(4) 2/8
Lafollette Ursula Ellen 22	Kump John H 23	24 Oct 1893	(4) 2/33
Lafollette William Carson 27	Kline Mary 18	20 Apr 1893	(4) 2/32
Lahman Jacob 22	Hasha Sarah Ann 22	1 Mar 1866	(4) 1/3
Lambert Abraham H 42	Shelton Mary Jane 30	25 Mar 1869	(4) 1/38
Lambert Benjamin Stickley 24	Lambert Grace Alice 18	18 Oct 1879	(4) 2/13
Lambert Catharine Regina 24	Runyon Levi Ashby 21	28 May 1885	(4) 2/10
Lambert Grace Alice 18	Lambert Benjamin Stickley 24	18 Oct 1879	(4) 2/13
Lambert Howard Jesse 24	Didiwick Edna Bell 21	4 Dec 1895	(4) 2/36
Lambert Isaac Welton 23	Haines Sarah Frances 19	27 Jan 1892	(4) 2/30
Lambert Margaret Jane 33	Everett John 72	21 Aug 1894	(4) 2/34
Lambert Rebecca Wiltmuth 21	Peer James Harrison 25	7 July 1875	(4) 2/7
Lambert Sallie Ann 23	Perrill Edward Ashby 21	5 Feb 1883	(4) 2/18
Landacre Wade Hampton 21	Carlyle Martha Anna Bell 21	21 Dec 1886	(4) 2/22
Lanham Dennie	Nixon Nancy	*6 Nov 1826	(4) 3/39
Largent Benj Offutt 39	Beery Elizabeth C 25	13 Dec 1866	(4) 1/4
Largent Benjamin Alfred 21	Foreman Amy Virginia May 18	11 Nov 1880	(4) 2/14
Largent Charles Edward 25	Abe Amanda Melvina 24	20 Dec 1896	(4) 2/38
Largent Dan'l H 22	Largent Louisa 21	18 Dec 1868	(4) 1/7

Name #1	Name #2	Date	Source
Largent Edward Trickle 35	Alderton Sarah Catharine 23	2 Nov 1879	(4) 2/13
Largent Eliza J Mrs 26	Bennett Edward 22	20 Oct 1892	(4) 2/31
Largent Elizabeth Ann 50	Kidwell James 67	18 July 1871	(4) 2/3
Largent Emily Ann 19	Allender John Thomas 30	17 Dec 1867	(4) 1/6
Largent George W 24	Haines Amanda Elizabeth 20	8 Jan 1880	(4) 2/14
Largent George Washington 28	Coleman Mary Florence 28	11 Apr 1878	(4) 2/11
Largent Hannah Jane 25	Foreman David Henry 32	27 Apr 1882	(4) 2/17
Largent John A 21	Deaver Sarah E 17	8 Feb 1868	(4) 1/6
Largent John Thomas 28	Hardy Elizabeth Jane 30	3 Sept 1867	(4) 1/5
Largent Joseph Sanford 22	Saville Sarah Elizabeth 21	1 Jan 1867	(4) 1/4
Largent Louisa 21	Largent Dan'l H 22	18 Dec 1868	(4) 1/7
Largent Louisa Catharine 23	Kidwell John Newton 35	23 Feb 1875	(4) 2/7
Largent Mary Elizabeth 22	Offutt Robert James 21	23 Nov 1875	(4) 2/8
Largent Mary Louisa 19	Bennett James Arthur 21	1 Mar 1887	(4) 2/23
Largent Nancy Jane 19	Cline Jacob 23	25 Aug 1885	(4) 2/21
Largent Robert Benjamin 26	Malcolm Clara E 21	23 July 1890	(4) 2/28
Largent Sarah Elizabeth 18	Kidwell Robert Senseny 24	30 Nov 1882	(4) 2/18
Larimore Elizabeth	Berry Samuel	*18 July 1825	(4) 3/48
Larimore Nancy	Haynes John	*13 Apr 1825	(4) 3/30
Larimore Rachel	Berry James	*1 Oct 1827	(4) 3/49
Larimore Thomas	Hains Rachael	*6 Aug 1825	(4) 3/49
Larrick Cordelia Sophia 20	Anderson Ulyssis S 21	28 Dec 1893	(4) 2/33
Larrick David Lee 22	Oats Rettie Elizabeth 16	19 June 1890	(4) 2/28
Larrick Flashie Alice 21	Johnson James Henry 22	18 May 1882	(4) 2/17
Larrick Frederick 22	Oats Sarah Eliz 22	28 Aug 1872	(4) 2/3
Larrick Hattie L 23	Loftin Lemuel Lee 25	9 Nov 1898	(4) 2/41
Larrick John Will 23	Lafollette Rosa Estella 19	2 Mar 1898	(4) 2/40
Larrick Lemuel Howard 23	Arnold Letitia 18	29 Apr 1890	(4) 2/28
Larrick Mary Elizabeth 23	Gardner Silas Wright 30	4 Mar 1875	(4) 2/7
Larrick Sallie Jane 18	Johnson Richard Menter 33	12 Feb 1874	(4) 2/5
Larrick Theodore F 23	Wilson Martha F 21	14 Dec 1872	(4) 2/4
Larrick Zachariah Taylor 23	Wilson Sarah Jane 16	16 June 1870	(4) 2/2
Larrimore Jane 25	Shawen Daniel M 22	1857	(10)
Latham William Dye 53	Brooks Annie Bell 24	11 Jan 1891	(4) 2/29
Latherman Susan	Sion Adam	6 Oct 1840	(5)
Laudaen Hannah 25	Robison Jacob R 30	12 Dec 1865	(4) 1/2
Laurence John Thomas 23	Sirbough Servanah 17	27 Jan 1881	(4) 2/15
Lawrence D	Hollenback E	28 Aug 1817	(6)
Lawrence John G	Ensminger Elizabeth	1 Oct 1822	(5)
Lawson Catherine	House Amon	*Aug 1827	(4) 3/43
Lawson Nancy	House Samuel	*16 Apr 1827	(4) 3/27
Layton ? Lee 23	Brown Sarah Catharine 18	10 Aug 1885	(4) 2/20
Leach Charles Oliver 24	Deitz Mrs Catherine 22	1 May 1881	(4) 2/16
Leadman James	Cassady Masa	3 June 1830	(6)
Leapley John	McDonald Elizabeth	*17 May 1826	(4) 3/20
Lear James Granville 20	Martin Mary Jane 22	15 July 1891	(4) 2/29
Lear Jefferson Davis 22	Saville Lucy Ann 16	28 Feb 1884	(4) 2/19
Lear Jefferson Davis 30	Smith Sarah Francis 22	21 June 1892	(4) 2/31
Lear Mary Catharine 20	Spurling William 39	24 Mar 1886	(4) 2/22
Lear Thomas 28	Corbin Nancy 23	1 Aug 1865	(4) 1/1
Lear Thomas Taylor 33	Grapes Mary Elizabeth 30	*7 July 1870	(4) 2/2
Lease Jacob	Lyons Julian	22 Apr 1839	(1) 9 May 1839

Name #1	Name #2	Date	Source
Lease Jacob Thomas 20	Huff Margaret Savannah 19	26 Dec 1885	(4) 2/21
Lease John Henry 25	Huff Nora Lee 19	22 July 1886	(4) 2/22
Leath ? Leberta 19	Horner Thomas Rankin 31	27 Mar 1879	(4) 2/13
Leatherman A	Fogle Julia A	9 Mar 1848	(6)
Leatherman A	Hall M E	12 Feb 1846	(6)
Leatherman Ann Mariah 21	Hottinger Silas 24	9 Aug 1882	(4) 2/17
Leatherman B	Rannell E	9 Feb 1826	(6)
Leatherman B A	Dobbins W	22 Mar 1832	(6)
Leatherman B F	Painter E J	24 Sept 1846	(5)
Leatherman B F	Palmer E J	24 Sept 1850	(6)
Leatherman Benjamin	Rannell Elizabeth	*6 Feb 1826	(4) 3/6
Leatherman Benjamin	Rannell Elizabeth	9 Feb 1826	(5)
Leatherman D	Stagg Frank	1 Feb 1844	(6)
Leatherman Dan	Stagg Elizabeth	25 Aug 1822	(6)
Leatherman Dan	Rotruck E	28 Dec 1846	(6)
Leatherman Dan'l Robt 23	Ludwick Emily J 22	23 Jan 1868	(4) 1/6
Leatherman Daniel Frederick 24	Haggerty Elizabeth Catharine 16	6 Mar 1878	(4) 2/11
Leatherman Daniel Thomas 24	Kelly Alverda Jeannetta 22	14 Sept 1875	(4) 2/7
Leatherman Elizabeth	Spade John	24 Nov 1836	(6)
Leatherman Geo W	Whip M L	30 July 1857	(6)
Leatherman George L 22	Ludwick Catharine Elizabeth 19	26 Nov 1878	(4) 2/12
Leatherman Isaac Robert 30	Hamilton Ella Bell 33	6 June 1894	(4) 2/34
Leatherman Isaac D 21	High Hariet Jane 22	1 May 1878	(4) 2/11
Leatherman J	Hollenback E	12 Oct 1843	(6)
Leatherman J L	Parmer E	2 Oct 1851	(6)
Leatherman J L	Parmer Eleanor	2 Oct 1850	(5)
Leatherman Jane Ann 24	Whiteman John Henry 22	31 Nov 1867	(4) 1/6
Leatherman John	Wilson Nancy	23 Apr 1829	(6)
Leatherman John Wm 24	Carroll Sarah E M 28	24 Nov 1886	(4) 2/22
Leatherman John William 26	Liller Armelia Alice 24	24 Dec 1888	(4) 2/26
Leatherman John Nicholas 27	Liller Martha Ann 23	15 Sept 1885	(4) 2/21
Leatherman John Frederick 21	Whiteman Cora Ada 19	12 Aug 1891	(4) 2/29
Leatherman M A	Kern David	11 July 1853	(6)
Leatherman M A	Kern David	1 July 1853	(5)
Leatherman Maggie J 20	Veach Henson W 25	18 Apr 1887	(4) 2/23
Leatherman Margaret	Dawson Cephas	24 Aug 1837	(6)
Leatherman Martha Ellen 20	Millar Michael Adam 20	5 Apr 1893	(4) 2/32
Leatherman N J	Parmer J T	4 Dec 1850	(5)
Leatherman Nicholas	Arnold C	23 Sept 1846	(6)
Leatherman P	Arnold Sol	18 Nov 1841	(6)
Leatherman Peter	Smarr P	16 May 1833	(6)
Leatherman Polly	Roberts Benjamin	3 Jan 1826	(6)
Leatherman Polly	Roberts Benjamin	*28 Dec 1825	(4) 3/76
Leatherman Rachel Jane 25	Iser John 53	1 Nov 1867	(4) 1/5
Leatherman Rosa May 21	Helman James Samuel 23	15 Mar 1900	(4) 2/42
Leatherman S	Long James	15 Nov 1826	(6)
Leatherman Sarah Catharine 32	Cunningham John Calvin 22	26 Dec 1894	(4) 2/35
Leatherman Sarah	Roberts Thomas	5 Dec 1843	(5)
Leatherman Solmon	Arnold Hannah	26 Dec 1841	(5)
Leatherman Susan Elizabeth 22	Arnold Edward 23	19 Dec 1877	(4) 2/11
Leatherman Susanah	Long James	*13 Nov 1826	(4) 3/40
Leatherman Susanna	Long James	16 Nov 1826	(5)

Name #1	Name #2	Date	Source
Leatherman Susan	Sion Adam	6 Oct 1839	(6)
Leatherman W L	Kern H E	30 Apr 1857	(6)
Leavens Caleb	Parker Sarah E	22 Oct 1846	(5)
Lederer Herman 25	Arnold Laura V B 20	2 Sept 1889	(4) 2/26
Lee Catherine	Harvey H R	5 Nov 1841	(5)
Lee Catherine	Spencer Arthur	9 Dec 1819	(6)
Lee Charles 41	Everett Susan 25	9 Oct 1877	(4) 1/39
Lee Emma Jane 24	Poland Jasper Newton 39	19 Apr 1893	(4) 2/32
Lee Francelia Antoinette 19	Bean William Harvey 20	7 June 1893	(4) 2/32
Lee Fred	Cosner Elizabeth	1 Dec 1843	(5)
Lee Hannah Catharine 46	Ludwig Henry Amos 52	9 Oct 1898	(4) 2/40
Lee Jasper Cather 26	Hammack S E Ashby 19	20 May 1880	(4) 2/14
Lee Jesse Washington 21	Piles Fannie J 21	22 Sept 1898	(4) 2/40
Lee John David 26	Swisher Mary Alice 22	26 Oct 1876	(4) 2/9
Lee John David 38	Stewart Amanda 18	29 Dec 1887	(4) 2/24
Lee Joshua 25	Gates Nancy 23	9 Oct 1877	(4) 1/39
Lee Sarah E Irene 18	Gray Julius H 28	25 Oct 1883	(4) 2/18
Lee William	Hudson Susan	8 Apr 1819	(6)
Lees Cathleen	Spencer Arthur	9 Dec 1819	(6)
Lees Cynthia	McNary William	29 Mar 1821	(6)
Lees Eliz	Lyons D B	17 Jan 1833	(6)
Lees J B	Flick Susannah	10 Apr 1829	(6)
Lees John	Lees Mary	11 Apr 1847	(6)
Lees Mary	Lees John	11 Apr 1847	(6)
Lees Thomas	Scritchfield Sarah	31 May 1827	(6)
Lees William	Hudson Susan	8 Apr 1819	(5)
Lees Wm	Foley S	6 Apr 1843	(6)
Leise Thomas	Schaitepfield Sibil	28 May 1827	(4) 3/34
Leith Elizabeth 25	Hook? William 31	25 May 1854	(10)
Leith John William 28	Beery Sallie Elizabeth 20	20 Dec 1876	(4) 2/9
Leith Phio C 29	Emmart Wilmith I Columbia 24	27 Oct 1881	(4) 2/16
Leith Sarah	Mauzee William	*18 June 1827	(4) 3/38
Leith Sarah Winiford 23	Stuckey Benjamin Allen 28	27 Oct 1881	(4) 2/16
Leright Edm	Welch Susan	17 Mar 1835	(6)
Lett Cabel	Thomas Albt	1 Jan 1835	(5)
Lett Jane	Bruce Andrew	23 Aug 1832	(5)
Lett Stacy	Redman Barnet	4 Sept 1823	(5)
Letzer Mary Ann 22	Coburn James Miller 29	17 Feb 1874	(4) 2/5
Levens Caleb	Parker C E	22 Oct 1850	(6)
Levings Caleb	Jones Mary	*25 Oct 1828	(4) 3/34
Lewis Abraham Franklin 27	McBride Tacey Ann 23	12 Jan 1887	(4) 2/23
Lewis Amanda Hill 26	Ely Beecher Ulysses 26	25 Nov 1889	(4) 2/27
Lewis Ann F 25	Wince Benjamin F 23	19 Aug 1873	(4) 2/4
Lewis Annie Bell 22	Edmonson Charley 23	3 Nov 1892	(4) 1/41
Lewis Charles Kerns 29	Mulledy Otelia 18	3 Mar 1896	(4) 2/37
Lewis David Harris 24	Pownall Margaret A 20	11 Feb 1885	(4) 2/20
Lewis Elmira M 21	Barger Michael C 32	8 Mar 1866	(4) 1/3
Lewis Elmira Virginia 27	Hannas John William 43	8 Jan 1878	(4) 2/11
Lewis Enoch Bert 26	Smith Laura Bell 24	16 Dec 1882	(4) 2/18
Lewis George Tacey 26	Doran Hannah Elizabeth 19	26 Feb 1880	(4) 2/14
Lewis Harriete Elizabeth 23	Poland Jeremiah 23	17 Dec 1878	(4) 2/12
Lewis Ida Lee 26	Haines William Jasper 25	1 Mar 1893	(4) 2/32

Name #1	Name #2	Date	Source
Lewis Isaac Ferran 25	Brown Mary Malinda 20	17 Aug 1875	(4) 2/7
Lewis James William 22	Seymour Belzara 22	12 Jan 1898	(4) 2/40
Lewis Jemima 24	Fisher Robert Scott 25	24 Sept 1885	(4) 2/21
Lewis John Granville 34	Carder Susan Elizabeth 34	10 Oct 1888	(4) 2/25
Lewis John Robert 27	Miller Frances Ann 25	24 Feb 1876	(4) 2/8
Lewis Luther Alexander 25	Hott Emma 22	26 Dec 1888	(4) 2/26
Lewis M	Markwood Conrad	1 Aug 1839	(6)
Lewis Margaret	Markwood Conrad	1 Aug 1840	(5)
Lewis Maria Catharine 18	Shelly Charles William 23	29 Dec 1886	(4) 2/23
Lewis Martha Jane 23	Gulick John Nathaniel 20	22 Mar 1887	(4) 2/23
Lewis Mary Alberta 22	Smith Andrew 23	31 Aug 1896	(4) 1/41
Lewis Mary Elizabeth 22	Mulldey James 22	12 Apr 1875	(4) 2/7
Lewis Mary Francis 20	Powelson Alvin Judson 26	6 Feb 1901	(4) 2/44
Lewis Parthenia Alice 23	Pownall John Albert 23	10 Feb 1886	(4) 2/21
Lewis Philip Alexander 27	Swisher Nettie Rebecca 21	28 Feb 1894	(4) 2/33
Lewis Rosa Ellen 23	Adams William 31	19 Nov 1896	(4) 2/38
Lewis Solomon 22	Johnson Sarah F 17	3 May 1888	(4) 1/40
Lewis Thomas Jefferson 22	Barnes Barbara Ellen 27	22 Jan 1878	(4) 2/11
Lewis Virginia Florence 24	Mulledy Robert Ambrose 29	6 Feb 1884	(4) 2/19
Lewis Virginia Gertrude 20	Harmison John 37	9 Dec 1891	(4) 2/30
Lewis Virzilla Ann 28	Horn Henry Jackson 28	27 Mar 1889	(4) 2/26
Lewis William Albert 22	Brown Amanda B 17	8 Aug 1876	(4) 2/8
Lewis William Carroll 23	Garrett Sarah Ellen 28	23 Nov 1870	(4) 2/2
Lewis William Owen 27	Fletcher Margaret Frances 16	27 Dec 1866	(4) 1/4
Lewwright E M	Loofbourrow Helen		(1) 10 Feb 1838
Light Charles Holliday 34	Albaugh Margaret 33	14 Apr 1886	(4) 2/22
Light Charles Holliday 22	Watson Agnes Elenora 22	19 Feb 1874	(4) 2/5
Light Ethel Minerva 21	Taylor Francis Lemuel 26	10 Sept 1900	(4) 2/43
Light John W 35	Richmond Rebecca E 25	21 Aug 1884	(4) 2/19
Light Joseph Edward 31	McLaughlin Lauranda Jane Ev 31	9 Aug 1877	(4) 2/10
Likens J J	Moody Elizabeth	17 Jan 1854	(6)
Likens James	McNemar Fran	3 Aug 1845	(6)
Likens James 25	Rhoderick Futah C 20	13 Feb 1866	(4) 1/2
Likens M	Van Buskirk M J	11 May 1865	(6)
Likens Mary	Rotruck Jacob	1 Apr 1851	(6)
Likens Michael	Mills Chris	16 Aug 1852	(6)
Likens Sarah	Harris John	16 May 1837	(6)
Likens William	Baker Sarah	24 Feb 1828	(6)
Likens Wm	Van Buskirk S	28 Jan 1863	(6)
Liking Isaac 26	Harris Louisa 18	23 Jan 1866	(4) 1/2
Likins Eliza	Martin Henry	4 May 1826	(5)
Likins George	Rotruck Hannah	14 Apr 1841	(5)
Likins Hannah	Bacorn William	19 June 1838	(5)
Likins James	Rotruck Sarah	3 Nov 1836	(5)
Likins Mary	Rotruck Jacob	1 Apr 1846	(5)
Likins Michael	Mills Christina	16 Aug 1852	(5)
Likins Michael	Van Buskirk M J	11 May 1862	(5)
Likins Sarah	Harris John	30 Mar 1837	(5)
Likins William	Van Buskirk Sarah	20 Jan 1862	(5)
Liller Abs	Fetters Penelope	11 Sept 1856	(6)
Liller Armelia Alice 24	Leatherman John William 26	24 Dec 1888	(4) 2/26
Liller Catherine	Everett Lewis	23 Mar 1842	(6)

Name #1	Name #2	Date	Source
Liller Clara Elizabeth 20	Shoemaker Archibald Jerome 21	22 Mar 1893	(4) 2/32
Liller Elizabeth Belle 22	Spurling Reuben 33	24 Sept 1889	(4) 2/27
Liller Elizabeth C 21	Davy Jno Wm 23	24 Dec 1866	(4) 1/4
Liller Elizabeth	Miller John	25 Mar 1819	(6)
Liller Elizabeth	White Robert	7 Nov 1844	(6)
Liller Emmanuel	Bobo Catherine	8 Mar 1858	(6)
Liller Geo	Dayton Martha	19 June 1845	(6)
Liller Henry	Elifritz Sarah	1 June 1826	(6)
Liller Henry	Elifritz Sarah	1 June 1826	(5)
Liller Henry	Ellifritz Sarah	*22 May 1826	(4) 3/21
Liller Henry Bradford 23	Corbin Alverda 17	15 Dec 1878	(4) 2/12
Liller Hiram	McNemar R E	3 June 1856	(6)
Liller Isaac	Fout Ann	*19 Mar 1827	(4) 3/Page Torn
Liller Jacob	Grayson Elizabeth	1 Mar 1821	(6)
Liller John	Grayson Nancy	7 Nov 1816	(6)
Liller M C	Kabrick Wm W	23 Sept 1858	(6)
Liller M V	Shockey Sam V	24 July 1845	(6)
Liller Maggie Lee 21	Smith Daniel Victor 29	24 May 1883	(4) 2/18
Liller Margaret Ann 25	High William H 29	25 Aug 1867	(4) 1/5
Liller Martha Ann 20	Gannon John Christopher 22	*24 Dec 1881	(4) 2/17
Liller Martha Ann 23	Leatherman John Nicholas 27	15 Sept 1885	(4) 2/21
Liller Mary A	Bosley Solomon	15 Apr 1847	(6)
Liller Mary Ellen 18	High Northman 22	14 Jan 1878	(4) 2/11
Liller N C 20	High William Randolph 24	21 July 1897	(4) 2/39
Liller Sarah	Bobo Washington	31 Aug 1836	(6)
Liller Sarah Virginia 18	Davy William Henry 21	6 Oct 1876	(4) 2/8
Liller Thomas	Shockey Susan	28 Oct 1845	(6)
Liller William Henry 24	Daugherty Ida May 23	26 Feb 1895	(4) 2/35
Linaburg Mary C E 23	Reanser Richard 25	24 Nov 1870	(4) 2/2
Lincoln John Edward 23	Kline Amanda Alice 19	22 Oct 1878	(4) 2/12
Lineberg Ella 22	Fishel William 24	29 Aug 1896	(4) 2/37
Lineberg Luther 20	Elliott Elizabeth 20	1 Oct 1892	(4) 2/31
Link Eliza Ellen 20	Charlton Burwell 29	4 Nov 1885	(4) 2/21
Link Elizabeth Catharine 21	Kelley George Wesley 23	23 Feb 1881	(4) 2/15
Linthicum Archibald	Cranston Jane	*18 Sept 1826	(4) 3/35
Linthicum Benjamin Franklin 33	Poland Rebecca 28	26 Oct 1881	(4) 2/16
Linthicum John David Keller 20	Combs Sarah Catherine 28	14 Oct 1875	(4) 2/7
Linthicum Margaret M 22	Poling Joseph M 21	24 June 1872	(4) 2/3
Linthicum Mary J 22	Maloney B F 29	27 Oct 1868	(4) 1/7
Linthicum Sarah Catharine 25	Parks George 51	4 Sept 1889	(4) 2/26
Linthicum William	Tucker Hannah	24 June 1824	(5)
Linton Elizabeth H 50	Sheridan Campbell 50	4 Aug 1892	(4) 2/31
Little John	Harper Anna	28 Aug 1828	(6)
Little William D 27	Frederick Rachael A 26	13 Mar 1866	(4) 1/3
Llowndes Saul 22	Hardy Mary 25	19 Nov 1874	(4) 1/39
Lloyd Robert Jackson 27	Mingo Rebecca G 23	9 May 1895	(4) 2/35
Lochart Louisa Virginia 19	Brill Isaac Perry 28	21 Jan 1872	(4) 2/3
Lockbridge Jas	Junkins N	22 Nov 1838	(6)
Lockhart Elizabeth	Pugh John	*1 Jan 1825	(4) 3/1
Lockmiller Eliza	Timbrook Hanson	31 May 1853	(1) 10 June 1853
Lockridge James	Junkins Mary	22 Nov 1839	(5)
Loftin Lemuel Lee 25	Larrick Hattie L 23	9 Nov 1898	(4) 2/41

Name #1	Name #2	Date	Source
Lofton Mary Elizabeth 17	Peasmaker Isaac Newton 43	10 May 1893	(4) 2/32
Logue Rebecca K	Kelly James	23 June 1844	(6)
Lokhner Catherine 24	Haines David M 21	13 Nov 1866	(4) 1/4
Long Adam Henry 26	Bloss Katie Ann 19	*14 Dec 1882	(4) 2/18
Long Alexander Somerville 22	Giffin Rettie Margaret 23	30 Dec 1896	(4) 2/38
Long Clara Ellen 28	Heironimus Harry Beuten 27	10 Sept 1895	(4) 2/36
Long Cornelius R	Moseley Elizabeth		(1) 10 Mar 1838
Long David	Curlett Christina	*17 July 1827	(4) 3/39
Long Eliza Jane	Parker Benjamin	*8 Dec 1828	(4) 3/43
Long Elizabeth	Bane Abner	18 Dec 1834	(6)
Long Etta Mary 21	Luttrell Charles Edward 30	27 Sept 1900	(4) 2/43
Long Henry	Baker E C	12 Sept 1848	(6)
Long J W	Welch Harriet C	6 Sept 1849	(6)
Long James	Leatherman S	15 Nov 1826	(6)
Long James	Leatherman Susanah	*13 Nov 1826	(4) 3/40
Long James	Leatherman Susanna	16 Nov 1826	(5)
Long Lillie 22	Anderson Russell Carter 20	27 Apr 1887	(4) 2/23
Long Lucy	Baker Enoch	8 Nov 1836	(6)
Long Mary C 24	Milleson Chas M 21	28 Feb 1866	(4) 1/3
Long Mary Christena 22	Parsons Marshall J 30	16 Oct 1878	(4) 2/12
Long Richard Woodridge 24	Darr Elizabeth 17	22 Dec 1898	(4) 2/41
Long S M	Murphy Jas E	2 June 1847	(6)
Long Sarah Francis 17	Bodine George 26	21 Aug 1865	(4) 1/1
Long Thomas Garret 28	Blue Bettie 17	29 Mar 1887	(4) 2/23
Long Uriah 27	Taylor Hannah Lawson 19	8 Mar 1893	(4) 2/32
Long William 33	Taylor Hattie A 24	4 Mar 1884	(4) 2/18
Longacre Isaac N 26	White Virginia M 19	8 Mar 1866	(4) 1/3
Loofbourrow Helen	Lewwright E M		(1) 10 Feb 1838
Lore Catharine 42	Staup Christopher 35	17 Feb 1870	(4) 2/1
Lore Henry	Abernathy Marg	22 Dec 1839	(6)
Lore Henry	Abernathy Margaret	22 Dec 1840	(5)
Lore R	Abernathy William	14 Aug 1828	(6)
Losser John Vincent 29	Carder Matilda Belle 21	21 Nov 1882	(4) 2/17
Lough Charles 28	Simmons Estella May 18	22 Oct 1899	(4) 2/42
Louthan Mary E	Marvin Joseph B		(1) 26 Sept 1839
Love E	Poland Isaac		(1) 20 Oct 1838
Lovett Albert Alvey 30	Loy Margaret A 20	2 Oct 1877	(4) 2/10
Lovett Albert Ottis 24	Park Susan 22	20 Oct 1869	(4) 2/1
Lowe Mary 16	Rolls George B 23	24 May 1877	(4) 1/39
Lower William	Narvey Drusilla	8 Jan 1829	(5)
Lower Wm	Harvey Drusia	8 Jan 1829	(6)
Lowery Ruth	Grey David	1831	(5)
Lowry Betsy	Redman Isaac	23 Nov 1832	(5)
Loy Adam Clark 24	Miller Mary Jane 26	4 Nov 1869	(4) 2/1
Loy Alverda Catharine 18	Wolford William Lock 23	4 Jan 1887	(4) 2/23
Loy Amanda Jerusha 20	Pugh Evan Preston 23	21 Dec 1876	(4) 2/9
Loy Anna Jemima 17	Cool Robert Granville 24	29 Dec 1887	(4) 2/24
Loy Anne Victory 21	Emmart John William 24	8 Jan 1891	(4) 2/29
Loy Benjamin Bane 25	Hott Louisa Belle Agnes 25	23 Feb 1898	(4) 2/40
Loy Charles Nixon 25	White Indiana 18	3 Feb 1892	(4) 2/30
Loy Daniel	Hear Sedenia	12 Sept 1839	(1) 26 Sept 1839
Loy David Jackson 33	Ganoe Margaret Ann 17	*29 July 1895	(4) 2/35

Name #1	Name #2	Date	Source
Loy David Jackson 22	Hott Nancy Catharine 20	27 Mar 1884	(4) 2/19
Loy Edgar Johnson 23	Ruckman Martha Rosetta 20	30 Apr 1891	(4) 2/29
Loy Ettie Jane 16	Heare George Lock 20	16 Dec 1888	(4) 2/25
Loy Franklin Pierce 21	Combs Rebecca Jane 20	18 Nov 1875	(4) 2/7
Loy James Mordicai 24	Snyder Mary Rebecca Melissa 18	20 Aug 1899	(4) 2/41
Loy James William 27	Peter Rachel 19	9 Nov 1867	(4) 1/5
Loy James William 49	Poland Sarah Ann 40	18 Sept 1889	(4) 2/27
Loy Leah Martha 18	Poling George Washington 27	5 Nov 1889	(4) 2/27
Loy Lemuel Johnson 20	Timbrook Mary Catharine 18	27 Dec 1883	(4) 2/19
Loy Louisa Jane 17	Poland John W 23	16 Sept 1866	(4) 1/3
Loy Mamie Estella 19	Beery William Benjamin 23	11 Apr 1900	(4) 2/42
Loy Margaret A 20	Lovett Albert Alvey 30	2 Oct 1877	(4) 2/10
Loy Mary Ann 26	Park Benjamin 30	29 May 1867	(4) 1/5
Loy Mary Catharine 25	Everstine Willard 23	25 Mar 1894	(4) 2/33
Loy Mary Cordelia 23	Moreland William 22	4 Apr 1871	(4) 2/2
Loy Mary Elizabeth 30	House Daniel 29	20 June 1894	(4) 2/34
Loy Mary M 24	Combs Wm G 26	25 Dec 1877	(4) 2/11
Loy Mary V 21	Cupp Jacob 29	1 July 1873	(4) 2/4
Loy Minerva Charlotte 23	Bean Samuel Bell 29	27 Dec 1899	(4) 2/42
Loy Minnie Belle 20	Saville William Ridgeley 26	18 July 1900	(4) 2/43
Loy Morgan Randolph 21	Timbrook Sarah M Virginia 22	26 Dec 1878	(4) 2/12
Loy Robert J 29	Bucklew Melissa 20	24 Jan 1889	(4) 2/26
Loy Samuel	Martin Lea	*9 June 1828	(4) 3/13
Loy Samuel 40	Yost Elizabeth Ann 25	27 Nov 1866	(4) 1/4
Loy Sarah Catharine 23	? 22	3 Dec 1883	(4) 2/18
Loy Sedema Catharine 17	Saville John Benjamin 21	21 Oct 1886	(4) 2/22
Loy Tamer Catharine 25	Gray Robert Lee 24	10 Jan 1889	(4) 2/26
Loy William	Gochenour M		(1) 28 Apr 1838
Loy William 24	Starkey Rebecca 20	27 Dec 1866	(4) 1/4
Loy William Henry 30	Poland Clerza Ann 20	18 Dec 1889	(4) 2/27
Loy William Henry 21	Hott Rebecca Lavina 20	20 Jan 1881	(4) 2/15
Loyed Sarah A 22	High Olphus 33	28 Jan 1866	(4) 1/2
Loyle Harry 26	Fields Felicia 21	6 Nov 1877	(4) 1/39
Ludwick Amos Christopher 24	Heare Mary Elizabeth 30	23 May 1884	(4) 2/19
Ludwick Arthur Wellington 30	Heare Tamar Rosella C 23	28 Sept 1884	(4) 2/20
Ludwick Catharine Elizabeth 19	Leatherman George L 22	26 Nov 1878	(4) 2/12
Ludwick Catherine	Singleton Wilburn	23 Aug 1860	(5)
Ludwick Demersa Biser 28	Hottinger Noah 27	17 Jan 1882	(4) 2/17
Ludwick E J	Shockey Job	24 Sept 1853	(6)
Ludwick Elizabeth Jane 37	Sulser Mortimore 44	11 Oct 1881	(4) 2/16
Ludwick Emily J 22	Leatherman Dan'l Robt 23	23 Jan 1868	(4) 1/6
Ludwick Emily J	Shockey Job	24 Sept 1853	(5)
Ludwick Fred	Welch Susan	21 Sept 1841	(6)
Ludwick George	High Mary	*29 Aug 1825	(4) 3/57
Ludwick James Carter 35	Athey Sarah Jane 33	1 Dec 1875	(4) 2/8
Ludwick Joseph	Taylor Ann	*10 Sept 1825	(4) 3/59
Ludwick M E	High J F	9 Mar 1848	(6)
Ludwick Mary	Parker Jacob	25 Dec 1823	(6)
Ludwick Sallie	Arnold Dan	14 Dec 1859	(6)
Ludwick Sarah J 21	Gilbert Wm H 23	2 Mar 1868	(4) 1/6
Ludwig Henry Amos 52	Lee Hannah Catharine 46	9 Oct 1898	(4) 2/40
Ludwig John William 28	Stewart Lula 19	31 May 1897	(4) 2/39

Name #1	Name #2	Date	Source
Ludwig Joseph 23	Howdyshell Sarah Jane 21	16 Feb 1879	(4) 2/12
Ludwig Sanford Romanus 30	Shoemaker Martha Virginia 20	18 Sept 1889	(4) 2/27
Lupton Hannah L 21	Carlyle Jno W 24	12 Aug 1866	(4) 1/3
Lupton Harriett Ettie Lee 20	Oats Wesley Edgar Lee 22	18 Jan 1888	(4) 2/24
Lupton J G F 26	Blue Louise 25	27 Nov 1867	(4) 1/6
Lupton Jesse	Oates Elizabeth	7 Sept 1852	(2) 7 Oct 1852
Lupton Jesse George 22	Haines Rachel 21	27 Dec 1866	(4) 1/4
Lupton Josephine E 28	Milleson William Taylor 31	6 Oct 1897	(4) 2/39
Lupton Kate Parsons 19	Schaffer Oliver Wellington 23	15 June 1881	(4) 2/16
Lupton Martha Lizzie 18	Spaid Luther B 24	29 Sept 1897	(4) 2/39
Lupton Rebecca Artiminsta 17	Whitacre ?lorence Edward 21	10 June 1900	(4) 2/42
Lupton William Seims 28	Mauk Eva Amilia 19	18 May 1875	(4) 2/7
Luttrell Charles Edward 30	Long Etta Mary 21	27 Sept 1900	(4) 2/43
Luttrell James Pendleton 28	McCauley Martha E Carlyle 20	1 Sept 1885	(4) 2/21
Lyle Pauline Isabel 24	Inskeep William 31	19 Dec 1882	(4) 2/18
Lynch Joseph 41	Hutcheson Sarah Fanny 46	31 July 1866	(4) 1/3
Lynch Sam	Parrott Margaret	7 Mar 1818	(5)
Lynch Sam	Parrot Marg	17 Mar 1818	(6)
Lynn John Henry 28	Rudolph Cora Victoria 24	14 June 1900	(4) 2/43
Lyon Ann	Baker Geo	21 Feb 1828	(6)
Lyon Elizabeth	Cassady William	25 June 1845	(5)
Lyon John	Smith Mary	*12 Mar 1827	(4) 3/16
Lyon John	Barnett Mary	8 Mar 1827	(5)
Lyon Thomas	Stingley Lydia	6 Mar 1823	(5)
Lyons D B	Lees Eliz	17 Jan 1833	(6)
Lyons Darkas Ann 18	Swainy Thomas 25	23 Sept 1869	(4) 2/1
Lyons John Henry 21	Moreland Amanda Rebecca 21	30 Apr 1877	(4) 2/10
Lyons Julian	Lease Jacob	22 Apr 1839	(1) 9 May 1839
Lyons Naomi	Groves Simeon	6 June 1820	(5)
Lyons Naomi	Groves Simeon	6 July 1820	(6)
Maddox Thos	Welch Nancy	12 Feb 1831	(6)
Madera Anna Bell 21	Spurling Robert 30	14 Feb 1883	(4) 2/18
Magruder Elizabeth 25	Martin Henry 32	24 Mar 1887	(4) 1/40
Magruder Mary 28	Banks Isaac 26	14 Dec 1892	(4) 1/41
Magruder Minnie 17	Rolls Taylor Burton 23	10 Feb 1892	(4) 1/41
Mahew John Ephraim 24	Fout Florence Virginia 19	6 Dec 1893	(4) 2/33
Malcolm Amos William 28	Cox Susanna 24	13 Oct 1886	(4) 2/22
Malcolm Ann Alice 24	Stickley Gabriel Tobias 33	28 June 1885	(4) 2/20
Malcolm Clara E 21	Largent Robert Benjamin 26	23 July 1890	(4) 2/28
Malcolm Harriett Jane 20	Haines Hanson Powers 23	12 Apr 1899	(4) 2/41
Malcolm Harry 23	Kelley Sarah Frances 17	12 Oct 1891	(4) 2/29
Malcolm James William 34	Iser Gustie May 19	4 Nov 1900	(4) 2/43
Malcolm Laura E 19	Snyder Samuel A 21	27 Dec 1893	(4) 2/31
Malcolm Martha Jane 38	Rowzee Samuel Atwell 47	6 May 1883	(4) 2/18
Malcolm Mary Catharine 35	Moreland James 44	30 Aug 1877	(4) 2/10
Malcolm Mary Sabine 25	Moreland Bassil Newton 30	11 Feb 1874	(4) 2/5
Malcolm Nathan Ashby 24	Ganoe Lucy Ellen 23	24 Dec 1888	(4) 2/26
Malcolm Nathan Harrison 43	Martin Lenora 36	13 Jan 1884	(4) 2/19
Malcolm Viola Blance May 15	Cross Granville 24	23 Apr 1893	(4) 2/32
Malcom Elmira Jane 28	Showalter Samuel Brown 36	*17 Apr 1871	(4) 2/2
Malcom James	Watson Jane	*14 Oct 1828	(4) 3/30
Malcom Margaret Lucinda 21	McDonald Philip 22	29 Oct 1867	(4) 1/5

Name #1	Name #2	Date	Source
Malcom Maria	Bonham Samuel	*25 Dec 1827	(4) 3/60
Malcom Robert Gorden 29	Ulery Martha Elizabeth 20	16 Apr 1867	(4) 1/5
Malick Aaron 78	Saville Catharine 69	9 Oct 1879	(4) 2/13
Malick Edward Seymour 23	Piles Susan F 20	1 June 1892	(4) 2/31
Malick Ettie Belle 20	Emmart Lemuel Parker 24	13 Dec 1888	(4) 2/25
Malick Eva Irene 16	Roberson Lewis Ashby 24	16 Oct 1894	(4) 2/34
Malick Geo W 27	Haines Elizabeth F 18	11 Dec 1866	(4) 1/4
Malick George Washington 55	Everett Nancy Jane 37	12 June 1894	(4) 2/34
Malick Hannah Catharine 44	Saville Philip 60	31 Oct 1876	(4) 2/9
Malick James Owen 22	French Ida Virginia 20	24 Oct 1895	(4) 2/36
Malick Mallissa Arabel 24	Saville Philip Holland 31	26 July 1892	(4) 2/31
Malick Mary Malinda 24	Cool James Mortimer 24	28 Dec 1876	(4) 2/9
Malick Matilda Virginia 25	Haines John Maddison 21	29 Mar 1871	(4) 2/2
Malick William Reese 27	Roberson Rebecca Frances 22	2 Mar 1899	(4) 2/41
Malone Charles Frederick 26	Carder Belle Ann 19	22 Oct 1885	(4) 2/21
Maloney B F 29	Linthicum Mary J 22	27 Oct 1868	(4) 1/7
Maloney Charles Franklin 20	Martin Gertrude May 21	25 Mar 1896	(4) 2/37
Maloney James Harrison 43	Condon Harriet 44	30 Dec 1879	(4) 2/14
Maloney Mattie Warren 18	Maphis Wm Edward 21	24 Dec 1888	(4) 2/26
Maloney Minnie H 20	Allamong Thomas Brandon 21	28 Nov 1891	(4) 2/30
Maloney William H 28	Cool Margaret E 27	24 Apr 1873	(4) 2/4
Mann Amada Virginia 20	Giffin Herbert ONille 21	29 May 1901	(4) 2/44
Maphis Benjamin Wade Hampton 24	Corbin Mary Elizabeth 24	22 Dec 1897	(4) 2/40
Maphis Cordelia C Savanah 23	Mauk James Oliver 32	31 Oct 1900	(4) 2/43
Maphis Francis Cordelia 23	McDonald Clifford Ernest 22	21 Mar 1900	(4) 2/42
Maphis George Washington 22	Wilson Virginia 18	17 Aug 1865	(4) 1/1
Maphis Ida Alverta 16	Kave Isaac Ashby 21	8 Aug 1889	(4) 2/26
Maphis Isabel 24	Davey Andrew Russell 23	24 Feb 1874	(4) 2/5
Maphis Israel 35	Bradfield Lydia Margaret 35	15 Nov 1885	(4) 2/21
Maphis Jacob Anthony 18	Shank Frances Elizabeth 21	28 Feb 1884	(4) 2/18
Maphis Lena 18	Mongold David Washington 21	19 Oct 1900	(4) 2/43
Maphis Mary Susan 14	Hott James Arthur 26	17 Sept 1885	(4) 2/21
Maphis Rachel	Wilson Zacharia L	13 Sept 1864	(7)
Maphis Sarah A	Hurd Charles	31 Dec 1863	(7)
Maphis Wm Edward 21	Maloney Mattie Warren 18	24 Dec 1888	(4) 2/26
Marks Aaron 36	Jackson Caroline 25	10 Aug 1876	(4) 1/39
Marks Edward 29	Bruce Harriet 28	17 Mar 1898	(4) 1/41
Marks Ralph 33	Hamilton Margaret Ann 21	21 Nov 1867	(4) 1/5
Markwood Charles A 28	High Sarah D 18	31 Mar 1897	(4) 2/39
Markwood Conrad	Lewis M	1 Aug 1839	(6)
Markwood Conrad	Lewis Margaret	1 Aug 1840	(5)
Markwood George H 22	Pool Mary E 21	8 Feb 1866	(4) 1/2
Markwood Jno W 24	Taylor Lesizah 21	18 Apr 1866	(4) 1/3
Markwood John	Pool S A	3 Mar 1850	(6)
Markwood John	Pool Sarah A	4 Mar 1846	(5)
Marpole James Madison 27	Snyder Virginia Ashley 20	20 Apr 1882	(4) 2/17
Marpole James Madison 44	Bowley Emma 35	19 Dec 1899	(4) 2/42
Marquis Rebecca	Harris William	21 Apr 1825	(5)
Marshall Ann	Bean Bennet	*15 Sept 1827	(4) 3/46
Marshall Annie Frances 16	Johnson Charles 39	4 Nov 1886	(4) 1/40
Marshall David Alonzo	Endler Ann Rebecca	13 Nov 1863	(4) 2/1
Marshall Emily A J 24	Doman Edward F 26	15 Mar 1866	(4) 1/3

Name #1	Name #2	Date	Source
Marshall Florinda Virginia 27	Neel Jerrold Wilber 26	16 Jan 1896	(4) 2/36
Marshall Priscilla Barbra 19	Poland Amos 22	30 Jan 1867	(4) 1/4
Marshall Rachael	Baker Jessee	*11 Apr 1826	(4) 3/15
Marshall Rachael 24	Fait Hiram 25	6 Apr 1874	(4) 2/6
Marshall Richard	Kramer Margaret	31 Oct 1839	(1) 14 Nov 1839
Marston Emma Susan 19	Abrill John Wesley 23	*15 Mar 1877	(4) 2/10
Martin A R	George John F	27 Aug 1852	(6)
Martin Anderson Amby 28	Kelsoe Florence Roberta 22	27 Apr 1896	(4) 2/37
Martin Ann R	George John F	27 Aug 1852	(5)
Martin Annie L 22	Wolford Charles C 21	25 Sept 1894	(4) 2/34
Martin Benj F 22	Queen Jane 22	16 Dec 1866	(4) 1/2
Martin Blakeney Hollis 28	Poland Lulu Ellen 21	18 May 1898	(4) 2/40
Martin Catharine V A 17	Park Ashford 38	1 Sept 1870	(4) 2/2
Martin Charles Edward 23	Miller Nannie Dorcus 25	6 Feb 1879	(4) 2/12
Martin Christopher	Athey Nancy	22 Jan 1833	(5)
Martin Estella May 21	Thompson Charles Taylor 22	*9 May 1901	(4) 2/44
Martin Francis	Urice Marg	22 Dec 1836	(6)
Martin George	Drace Rebecca	15 Feb 1835	(5)
Martin George	Fahs Leah	*28 Apr 1827	(4) 3/29
Martin George S	Roberts Elizabeth J	13 June 1861	(6)
Martin Gertrude May 21	Maloney Charles Franklin 20	25 Mar 1896	(4) 2/37
Martin Henry	Likins Eliza	4 May 1826	(5)
Martin Henry 23	Streets Mary 21	9 May 1878	(4) 1/39
Martin Henry 32	Magruder Elizabeth 25	24 Mar 1887	(4) 1/40
Martin Isabella 22	Crawford John Thomas 24	11 Nov 1879	(4) 2/13
Martin Jasper Newton 29	King Sarah Isabelle 24	19 Mar 1878	(4) 2/11
Martin John	Thompson Ellen	*19 Feb 1827	(4) 3/14
Martin John Benjamin 21	Bowman Martha Elizabeth 18	24 Feb 1885	(4) 2/20
Martin John Jr 28	Dresser Bellinda Todd 17	3 Nov 1892	(4) 2/31
Martin John Robert 33	Shanholtzer Sarah 32	23 Dec 1879	(4) 2/14
Martin Joseph	Baker R	19 July 1855	(10)
Martin Lavilla	Athey Joseph	5 Mar 1843	(5)
Martin Lea	Loy Samuel	*9 June 1828	(4) 3/13
Martin Lenora 36	Malcolm Nathan Harrison 43	13 Jan 1884	(4) 2/19
Martin Levi 33	Haws Margaret Ann 32	9 June 1873	(4) 2/4
Martin Lillie May 22	Wolford Leonard Harper 25	6 Mar 1895	(4) 2/35
Martin Lizzie Lee 18	Wolford John William 35	31 Oct 1899	(4) 2/42
Martin Martha Virginia 17	Haines Geo Washington 35	12 Aug 1874	(4) 2/6
Martin Mary	Baker Richard	*7 Mar 1825	(4) 3/19
Martin Mary	Baker Richard	10 Mar 1825	(5)
Martin Mary Jane 21	Carelyle Joseph Edward 26	12 Jan 1870	(4) 2/1
Martin Mary Jane 22	Lear James Granville 20	15 July 1891	(4) 2/29
Martin Meineiva 20	Folty Martin 21	29 Nov 1871	(4) 2/3
Martin Polly	Hietto Alexander	24 Sept 1835	(5)
Martin Rebecca Ann 35	Moton Joseph 30	3 Sept 1865	(4) 1/1
Martin Richardson Rufus 22	Wolford Malinda Jane 17	17 June 1874	(4) 2/6
Martin Sarah	Pownall John J	*8 Apr 1828	(4) 3/10
Martin Thomas Fallen 22	Bowman Mary Estella 20	29 May 1898	(4) 2/40
Martin Virginia Bell 21	Saville John David 23	18 Dec 1889	(4) 2/27
Martin William Franklin 35	White Christena 28	did not marry	(4) 2/39
Marvin Joseph B	Louthan Mary E		(1) 26 Sept 1839
Mason A Clayton 20	Kerns O Bell 18	1 July 1897	(4) 2/39

Name #1	Name #2	Date	Source
Mason Charles Edward 22	Brill Alice Amanda 22	26 June 1879	(4) 2/13
Mason Lethe May 17	Kerns John William 24	28 Mar 1899	(4) 2/41
Mathews Daniel 23	Jackson Harriett 21	9 Dec 1869	(4) 1/38
Mathews Harry 22	Jackson Agnes 16	16 July 1874	(4) 1/39
Mathews James 42	Washington Miranda 27	3 Oct 1894	(4) 2/34
Mathews John William 25	Huskins Mary Jane 24	12 May 1897	(4) 1/41
Mathias	Grimm R	15 July 1841	(6)
Matthews Brandson 23	Johnson Mary 19	16 Jan 1870	(4) 1/38
Matthews Mary Elizabeth 24	Friddle Samuel 51	4 Sept 1867	(4) 1/5
Mauk Eva Amilia 19	Lupton William Seims 28	18 May 1875	(4) 2/7
Mauk James Oliver 32	Maphis Cordelia C Savanah 23	31 Oct 1900	(4) 2/43
Mauk John Frederick 23	Rosebugh Mary Elizabeth 24	15 Feb 1883	(4) 2/18
Mauk Martha Jane 26	Swisher Joseph Anthony 58	1 Nov 1892	(4) 2/31
Mauk Mary Rosetta 20	Davis John Edgar 29	19 Dec 1895	(4) 2/36
Mauk Thomas William 24	Pultz Virginia May 21	19 Feb 1896	(4) 2/36
Mauzee William	Leith Sarah	*18 June 1827	(4) 3/38
Mauzey William Howard 25	Pool Willie 28	2 Aug 1898	(4) 2/40
Mauzy Emily 19	Oats George 22	8 Apr 1880	(4) 2/14
Mauzy John	Powell Elizabeth	*11 Jan 1825	(4) 3/3
Maxwell John	Wilson Reb'a	27 Dec 1836	(6)
Mayberry Israel	Hass Catharine	*27 Mar 1827	(4) 3/23
Mayer Minnie Bell 20	Shank William Edgar 22	31 Mar 1897	(4) 2/38
Mayhew Benjamin 35	White Mary 27	11 May 1854	(10)
McAtee Elisha James 22	Bradfield Charlotte Ann 20	18 Feb 1877	(4) 2/9
McAtee John H 25	Crausner George Ella 21	11 Dec 1865	(4) 1/1
McBee Alice Maretta 22	Slonaker Wesley Luther 25	5 Oct 1886	(4) 2/22
McBrid Eli 25	Smith Rebecca E 22	3 Feb 1868	(4) 1/6
McBride Alpheus 22	Watkins Harriet J 20	10 Apr 1866	(4) 1/3
McBride Babe 22	Cannon Rufus Buren 24	7 Sept 1887	(4) 2/23
McBride Chloe Catharine 27	Foltz Henry 47	9 Sept 1896	(4) 2/37
McBride E Margaret 24	Goldsborough Stephen 25	20 Oct 1884	(4) 2/20
McBride Emma Jane 32	Montgomery Raymond 22	11 Nov 1900	(4) 2/43
McBride George Washington 22	McCauley Dora A 20	23 Feb 1886	(4) 2/21
McBride Grayson 28	Miller Susan Rebecca 25	1 Nov 1888	(4) 2/25
McBride Hannah	Carpenter William	*16 Feb 1825	(4) 3/15
McBride Isaac William 22	Barnes Laverta Ellen 19	13 June 1888	(4) 2/25
McBride Jane 21	Henderson Thomas R 21	30 Nov 1865	(4) 1/1
McBride John Alexander 23	Sandy Margaret Ann Virginia 20	5 Nov 1878	(4) 2/12
McBride John William 26	Wolford Lucy Ellen 30	29 July 1896	(4) 2/37
McBride Joseph	Ganoe ?	20 Aug 1859	(10)
McBride Lorenzo Beauregard 20	Kline Martha Elizabeth 19	27 Dec 1881	(4) 2/17
McBride Louiza	Swier David	*15 Sept 1828	(4) 3/26
McBride Lydia	Pugh Ezra	*15 Jan 1827	(4) 3/7
McBride Margaret	Bowman Andrew	*22 Mar 1827	(4) 3/22
McBride Martha	Short George	*29 Dec 1828	(4) 3/49
McBride Matilda	White Robert Norvell	13 Feb 1824	(4) 3/10
McBride Nancy	Hines Thomas	*25 Nov 1825	(4) 3/72
McBride Nancy	McBride Robert	*8 Jan 1825	(4) 3/6
McBride Nancy	Patterson Samuel	*24 Nov 1825	(4) 3/71
McBride Robert	McBride Nancy	*8 Jan 1825	(4) 3/6
McBride Samuel 30	?	19 Dec 1854	(10)
McBride Sarah Elizabeth 29	Herbaugh William Victonus 36	28 Mar 1893	(4) 2/32

Name #1	Name #2	Date	Source
McBride Shelton Ashby 27	Hott Sarah 22	5 Apr 1894	(4) 2/34
McBride Tacey Ann 23	Lewis Abraham Franklin 27	12 Jan 1887	(4) 2/23
McBride Virginia Bell 21	Smith Charles Milton 25	11 Apr 1895	(4) 2/35
McBride William Ashby 25	Hannas Leah Catharine 22	9 Feb 1887	(4) 2/23
McBride William 43	Orndorff Rachele 33	21 Apr 1875	(4) 2/7
McCarthy Eliza	Cundiff John	10 Mar 1842	(6)
McCartney R	Parsons Isaac	1 June 1820	(6)
McCarty Anna Maria 17	Hook Joseph Samuel 26	14 Mar 1887	(4) 2/23
McCarty Aquilla B	Sheetz Mary Elizabeth		(1) 10 June 1853
McCarty William Arthur 23	Clayton Emma Frances 21	21 June 1893	(4) 2/32
McCauley Albert Newton 21	Davy Florence Agnes 17	22 Oct 1895	(4) 2/36
McCauley Ann Jemima	Moreland George	1854	(10)
McCauley Anna	Bosley Daniel	8 Mar 1822	(6)
McCauley Annie	Bosley David	8 Mar 1822	(5)
McCauley Auther Wellington 21	Ely Amanda Susan 21	7 Nov 1871	(4) 2/3
McCauley Charles Edward 27	Heare Lillie Estella 21	9 Aug 1887	(4) 2/23
McCauley Dora A 20	McBride George Washington 22	23 Feb 1886	(4) 2/21
McCauley Eleanora J 19	Grove Cephas F 19	19 Sept 1872	(4) 2/3
McCauley Elizabeth	Coleshine John	13 May 1817	(5)
McCauley George William 25	Fravel Lena May 21	9 May 1893	(4) 2/32
McCauley George	Peppers Juliann	*20 Aug 1827	(4) 3/42
McCauley Jesse F 24	Whitlock Margaret Catharine 23	12 Feb 1896	(4) 2/36
McCauley Martha 21	Corbin Henry 40	1 Sept 1872	(4) 2/3
McCauley Martha E Carlyle 20	Luttrell James Pendleton 28	1 Sept 1885	(4) 2/21
McCauley Mary	Bailey Edward	20 Aug 1821	(5)
McCauley Mary	Bailey Edw	30 Aug 1821	(6)
McCauley Mary Ellen 23	Shanholtzer Philip Absalon 26	12 Nov 1878	(4) 2/12
McCauley Parthenia	Baker John	*4 Dec 1826	(4) 3/44
McCauley Rebecca	Simpson John	*11 Dec 1826	(4) 3/45
McCauley Rosetta Florence 21	Saville Joel Jackson 22	16 Jan 1883	(4) 2/18
McCauley S	Earnholt Wm	29 June 1820	(6)
McCauley Sarah	Earnholt Adam	25 Feb 1819	(6)
McCauley Susan	Earnholt William	1820	(5)
McCauly Andrew W 23	Shelly Priscilla C 23	3 Dec 1867	(4) 1/6
McCauly Elizabeth	Colestine John	13 May 1816	(6)
McCauly James Henry 20	Lafollett Jemima 18	14 Mar 1867	(4) 1/5
McClure James	Chisholm Mary Ann	12 Oct 1837	(1) 28 Oct 1837
McClure James	Spicer Ruth	28 Sept 1826	(6)
McCochlin Daniel	Chapman Ann	3 July 1838	(1) 14 July 1838
McCool John S 23	Hardy Louisa Marian 25	26 Mar 1876	(4) 2/8
McCoole Elizabeth Anne 22	Hiett George Washington 23	*28 July 1879	(4) 1/13
McCord Mary	Edmunds J F	22 Apr 1830	(6)
McCormick G	Abernathy N J	26 Aug 1852	(6)
McCormick George	Abernathy N J	26 Aug 1850	(5)
McCormick James	Nally S	24 Sept 1834	(6)
McCormick Mary	King Greenberry	4 Mar 1824	(5)
McCormick Nancy	Kite Wm	8 Jan 1835	(6)
McCormick Pat	Flannigan E	18 Nov 1858	(6)
McCoy John 28	Groves Emma Sophia 26	14 Apr 1874	(4) 2/6
McCoy John 51	Creswell Alverda C 41	15 Dec 1896	(4) 2/38
McCoy Loula Virginia 28	Clarke John William 32	2 Aug 1900	(4) 2/43
McCullock M A	Cropper Jesse	26 Mar 1839	(6)

Name #1	Name #2	Date	Source
McCullough John	Smar Eliza		(1) 18 Aug 1838
McCullough Mary Ann	Cropper Jessee		(1) 28 Mar 1839
McDonald Alvin Elzey 22	Serbaugh Emma Almira 22	25 Dec 1889	(4) 2/27
McDonald Angus	Naylor Leacy Ann	*11 Jan 1827	(4) 3/2
McDonald Ann	Farmer Samuel	4 Jan 1838	(1) 20 Jan 1838
McDonald Anne Bell 20	Smith Aaron Clarence 23	9 Mar 1892	(4) 2/30
McDonald Anthony	Stonebreaker	18 Sept 1836	(5)
McDonald Archibald 26	Roberson Rachael 24	Feb 1866	(4) 1/2
McDonald Benjamin Franklin 27	Merrit Sarah Frances 18	4 Dec 1873	(4) 2/5
McDonald Celia Ellen 53	Nichols Isaac Gibson 66	27 Jan 1885	(4) 2/20
Mcdonald Charles B 33	Hooke Eliza B 17	25 Jan 1866	(4) 1/2
Mcdonald Charles H 22	Sirbaugh Lucy S 18	23 Jan 1901	(4) 2/43
McDonald Charlotte Ellen 19	Hott Samuel Albert 27	11 Feb 1896	(4) 2/36
McDonald Clifford Ernest 22	Maphis Francis Cordelia 23	21 Mar 1900	(4) 2/42
McDonald Edward Luther 28	Hawkins Mary Florence 19	25 Dec 1894	(4) 2/35
McDonald Eleanor	Stickley Benjamin	21 Sept 1826	(5)
McDonald Elizabeth Harriet 23	Chesshire James Robert 19	3 Jan 1877	(4) 2/9
McDonald Elizabeth	Leapley John	*17 May 1826	(4) 3/20
McDonald Esther 20	Serbaugh ? 24	10 Sept 1857	(10)
McDonald Evan 27	Hockman Mary Frances 30	1 May 1882	(4) 2/17
McDonald Evan Griffith 41	Cooper Martha Ann 40	31 May 1877	(4) 2/10
McDonald Frederica A Rebecca 25	Hiett Henry Harrison 35	17 Apr 1877	(4) 2/10
McDonald George Washington 30	Carder Mary 22	2 Dec 1874	(4) 2/6
McDonald George	Miller Marg	*14 July 1828	(4) 3/17
McDonald Isabel Mrs 38	Farmer James Franklin 27	14 May 1882	(4) 2/17
McDonald Jacob 32	Pownall Martha Elizabeth 22	23 Dec 1875	(4) 2/8
McDonald James	Ferryman Rebeckah	*13 Nov 1828	(4) 3/39
McDonald James Clark 22	Haines Sarah Catherine 20	27 Mar 1890	(4) 2/27
McDonald James Wm 66	Grapes Martha E 35	8 Apr 1900	(4) 2/42
McDonald James Wm 31	Messick Lula Bell 20	27 Feb 1901	(4) 2/44
McDonald Jared Andrew 24	Shingleton Mariah 23	22 Dec 1880	(4) 2/15
McDonald Jared Andrew 28	Timbrook Julia Ann 23	5 Mar 1885	(4) 2/20
McDonald Jas H M 31	Kidwell Mary V 18	5 Apr 1866	(4) 1/3
McDonald John Alexander 19	Hawkins Martha Cordelia 17	11 Feb 1879	(4) 2/12
McDonald John Snyder 30	White Alberta Lee 23	12 Dec 1893	(4) 2/33
McDonald John William 24	Swisher Cora Florence 20	2 Sept 1891	(4) 2/29
McDonald Jonathan James 22	Davey Anne Catharine 17	21 Sept 1898	(4) 2/40
McDonald Lydia Ann 24	Milleson William 28	15 Mar 1892	(4) 2/30
McDonald M	Fitzwater Jas	22 Apr 1847	(6)
McDonald Margaret 23	? Soloman J 29	18 Mar 1860	(10)
McDonald Margaret S 21	Hiett Joseph William 25	20 Jan 1867	(4) 1/4
McDonald Margaret Ellen 19	Carter Frederick Abott 23	24 Dec 1879	(4) 2/14
McDonald Martha Jane 22	Ruckman Jacob Calvin 27	13 Nov 1895	(4) 2/36
McDonald Mary Alice 23	Milburn Charles Albert 22	21 Apr 1881	(4) 2/16
McDonald Mary Catharine 32	Hurbert Robert Cline 25	4 Sept 1879	(4) 2/13
McDonald Mary Elizabeth 18	Carder James Sanford 23	19 Oct 1887	(4) 2/24
McDonald Millicent S	Sherrard William	*24 May 1825	(4) 3/38
McDonald P	Miller Rebecca	30 Sept 1859	(6)
McDonald Peter	Miller Rebecca	30 Sept 1860	(5)
McDonald Philip 22	Malcom Margaret Lucinda 21	29 Oct 1867	(4) 1/5
McDonald Rachel Catharine 25	Shingleton Joseph Sibert 23	25 Mar 1884	(4) 2/19
McDonald Rebecca 28	Brelsford Geo W 33	15 Nov 1860	(10)

Name #1	Name #2	Date	Source
McDonald Rebecca 22	Rogers John Thomas 24	18 Oct 1898	(4) 2/41
McDonald Rebecca Josaphine 18	Shingleton Elihue Pownell 23	22 Dec 1880	(4) 2/15
McDonald Samuel	Wolford Elizabeth	7 June 1859	(10)
McDonald Sarah Elizabeth 20	Hook Robert Calvin 25	23 Jan 1890	(4) 2/27
McDonald Sarah Jane 38	Swisher Philip Mathew 30	9 Nov 1882	(4) 2/17
McDonald Susana	Powell John	*16 Aug 1828	(4) 3/20
McDonald Thomas Henry 23	Pownall Melissa Josephine 20	15 Dec 1870	(4) 2/2
McDonald William Marion 23	Bennett Laura Elizabeth 20	5 Oct 1893	(4) 2/33
McDonald William 20	Shanholtzer Linnie 19	18 Aug 1891	(4) 2/29
McDowell Jennie A 19	Sirbaugh Chas Lemuel 25	4 July 1899	(4) 2/41
McDowell Matilda Woodie	Tabb Dougal C		(1) 13 May 1859
McDowell Thomas	Rogers M E	9 Feb 1859	(6)
McFarland Catherine	Sickafoos John	*26 July 1826	(4) 3/30
McFarling Cathleen	Sigafoose J N	6 Aug 1826	(6)
McGee Charles Arthur 21	Arnold Mary Lydia 17	4 Mar 1896	(4) 2/37
McGee Charles J 22	Hartman Margaret C 24	20 Dec 1865	(4) 1/2
McGee Charles Jackson 47	Fleming Harriet J 43	16 Mar 1890	(4) 2/27
McGill Edward Glen 30	Haines Elizabeth Susan 23	23 Feb 1893	(4) 2/32
McGill Ella C 22	Swisher John Arnold Harris 26	17 Oct 1883	(4) 2/18
McGill Kate 24	Kuykendall Thomas 28	5 June 1883	(4) 2/18
McGlothery Ida Raymond 28	Kuykendall James Lawson 38	5 Oct 1887	(4) 2/24
McGlothery Martha Campbell 26	Crounse Alexander 36	29 Oct 1889	(4) 2/27
McGraw Samuel	Shore Margaret	7 Feb 1826	(6)
McGraw Samuel	Shores Margaret	*6 Feb 1826	(4) 3/5
McGruder Martha L E 16	Washington Hite 21	26 Aug 1899	(4) 1/42
McGuire Marg Anne Virginia 18	Haines John Madison 22	2 Dec 1873	(4) 2/5
McIlwee Charles Ashby 26	Williams Frances 32	8 Sept 1887	(4) 2/23
McIlwee George 19	Miller Emma 18	17 July 1878	(4) 2/11
McIlwee Judith Rebecca 27	Lafollett Julius 37	24 July 1884	(4) 2/19
McIlwee Mary Jane 23	Bland James 27	14 Nov 1872	(4) 2/4
McIlwee Sarah 26	Lafollette Asbury 26	*3 Mar 1873	(4) 2/4
McIlwee Sarah Elizabeth	Miers John W		(1) 28 Oct 1837
McIntyre George 45	Fishell Sallie Louisa 19	18 Nov 1897	(4) 2/39
McIntyre Lydia Catharine 26	Brill Hampton Jefferson 34	14 Nov 1878	(4) 2/12
McKee ? 40	King Mary Catharine 22	6 Nov 1883	(4) 2/18
McKee Bertha 20	Bott George Marion 22	7 Sept 1895	(4) 2/36
McKee Clinton C 22	Lafollette Florence E 21	7 Nov 1888	(4) 2/25
McKee Edward Tollison 22	Sirbaugh Frances Ellen 21	22 May 1890	(4) 2/28
McKee Hiram Addison 27	Whitlock Mary Laney 21	28 Jan 1876	(4) 2/8
McKee John William 36	Baker Margaret Elizabeth 24	2 Feb 1876	(4) 2/8
McKee John Wm Tilden 24	Hott Alberta 21	30 Jan 1901	(4) 2/44
McKee Josiah 43	Miller Mary Ann 21	12 Dec 1871	(4) 2/3
McKee Mary Ida 18	Williams H B 26	6 Oct 1897	(4) 2/39
McKee Mary Margaret	Pettit Daniel	3 Aug 1852	(2) 7 Oct 1852
McKee Robert Franklin 22	Dorne Margaret Jane 19	15 Aug 1878	(4) 2/11
McKee Verda Alverda Elizabeth 17	Oates James F 26	20 Apr 1893	(4) 2/32
McKeever Elias 29	Serbaugh Mary Catharine 27	3 Feb 1874	(4) 2/5
McKeever Margaret 36	Clemm Madison Rector 31	5 Jan 1890	(4) 2/27
McKeever Margery Ann 27	Sirbaugh Samuel Harvey 37	24 May 1900	(4) 2/42
McKeever Mollie 35	Bean Erasmus 58	2 Oct 1884	(4) 2/20
McKenzie A	Spencer C C	26 Aug 1849	(6)
McKewn Almira Virginia 18	Davis George Willaim 26	2 Dec 1875	(4) 2/8

Name #1	Name #2	Date	Source
McLaughlin Lauranda Jane Ev 31	Light Joseph Edward 31	9 Aug 1877	(4) 2/10
McLoy Jane Susan 19	Powel Thomas Carskadden 25	14 Nov 1865	(4) 1/1
McMahin Elizabeth H 20	Hass David A 21	28 Sept 1870	(4) 2/2
McMannas Catherine L 22	Peacemaker Alfred P 27	28 Dec 1865	(4) 1/2
McNamee Marion 27	Abrell Clara Bell 25	5 Sept 1895	(4) 2/36
McNary Nim	Robertson N	24 June 1833	(6)
McNary William	Lees Cynthia	29 Mar 1821	(6)
McNeal Banjamin S 57	Porter Margaret 25	26 Sept 1865	(4) 1/1
McNeil John William 23	Pancake Mary McNeil 21	6 Jan 1874	(4) 2/5
McNeil Sydney	Pugh Hannibal	*29 July 1828	(4) 3/18
McNemar A	Greenwalt J D	23 June 1858	(6)
McNemar Ann B	Merit Geo	19 June 1845	(6)
McNemar Anna	Watson Alb	10 Oct 1830	(6)
McNemar Fran	Likens James	3 Aug 1845	(6)
McNemar J H	Hilkey Eliz	6 Apr 1848	(6)
McNemar Joseph	Idleman Elizabeth	18 Mar 1823	(5)
McNemar Lurana	Shirly James	3 Mar 1853	(5)
McNemar Martin	Dye A M	19 Apr 1836	(6)
McNemar Phil	Bobo Mary	18 Mar 1830	(6)
McNemar R E	Liller Hiram	3 June 1856	(6)
McNemar Wesley B	Park Rebecca		(1) 30 May 1839
McNemara Catherine	Frye John	2 Nov 1826	(5)
McRobie John	Murphy M	16 Dec 1838	(6)
McRobie John	Murphy Margaret	6 Dec 1839	(5)
McVicker Isabella	Poston John	*31 Jan 1825	(4) 3/12
McVicker Jane	Johnson Bazel	*13 June 1826	(4) 3/27
McVicker Mary	Poston Ashford	*19 Nov 1827	(4) 3/55
McWaine Jerusia	Kelley John	27 June 1824	(5)
McWycoff Moses	Deborah	1 May 1828	(5)
Means Isaac	Race Elizabeth	5 Oct 1826	(6)
Means Mariah	Johnson Benjamin	9 Mar 1826	(6)
Means Mariah	Johnson Benjamin	*20 Feb 1826	(4) 3/12
Medcalf Fenton	Wolf Lacy Ann	*28 Oct 1826	(4) 3/37
Meese John M	Hollenback M	25 June 1846	(6)
Melin Benjamin Franklin 21	Meritt Henrietta Virginia 18	28 May 1879	(4) 2/13
Mellen William 34	Johnson Ella May 25	14 Sept 1887	(4) 2/24
Mellin Louisa Ann 18	Miller William Luther 27	19 Jan 1875	(4) 2/6
Mellon Elizabeth Catharine 20	Miller John William 26	27 Mar 1888	(4) 2/24
Mellon Marcus Anthony 25	Oats Frances Ellen 27	31 May 1876	(4) 2/8
Mellon Sallie Ester 23	Oats Geo William 38	12 Oct 1897	(4) 2/39
Melon Victory 21	Baldwin William 33	25 Dec 1865	(4) 1/2
Mercer Bertram Longfellow 25	Taylor Mary Elizabeth 26	4 Sept 1895	(4) 2/36
Merit Geo	McNemar Ann B	19 June 1845	(6)
Merit Rebecca	Palmer Artona	9 Mar 1845	(6)
Meritt Adam 26	Bowman Matilda Jane 17	18 Dec 1877	(4) 2/11
Meritt Henrietta Virginia 18	Melin Benjamin Franklin 21	28 May 1879	(4) 2/13
Merrit Sarah Frances 18	McDonald Benjamin Franklin 27	4 Dec 1873	(4) 2/5
Merrit William 59	Jeffers Delila 35	14 Apr 1874	(4) 2/6
Merritt George Washington 28	Shoemaker Rosetta E 18	27 Nov 1889	(4) 2/27
Merritt Hannah 31	Spurling William 51	27 Aug 1857	(10)
Merritt Sarah Catharine 19	Brown William Edward 25	29 Dec 1897	(4) 2/40
Merritt William 58	Vaughn Sarah 30	*8 Mar 1873	(4) 2/4

Name #1	Name #2	Date	Source
Merygold Mary Jane 26	Sites John 31	14 Dec 1865	(4) 1/2
Messick Charles Ward 19	Shawen Mary E C 19	10 Sept 1895	(4) 2/36
Messick Elizabeth Jane 16	Shingleton Absalon Lee 21	19 Jan 1887	(4) 2/23
Messick Emma Susan 20	Saville Hider Washington 28	1 Mar 1899	(4) 2/41
Messick Frank 45	Blackburn Bertie Frances 31	10 May 1899	(4) 2/41
Messick James Albert 24	Rotruck Ida May 18	1 Jan 1884	(4) 2/19
Messick Lula Bell 20	McDonald James Wm 31	27 Feb 1901	(4) 2/44
Messick Mary Ellen 22	Hott David Gibson 25	15 Dec 1879	(4) 2/14
Messick Minnie Bell 16	Payne James Edward 23	11 Dec 1890	(4) 2/28
Messick Thomas Harrison 62	Shingleton Elizabeth Mrs 53	7 Oct 1897	(4) 2/39
Messick Uriah Oliver 25	Timbrook Hannah Tabitha 19	10 Mar 1887	(4) 2/23
Messick William Harrison 22	Vermillion Mary Ellen 17	4 Mar 1886	(4) 2/22
Metcalf Fenton	Wolf Lucy Ann	2 Nov 1826	(6)
Metcalf Hiram	Baker Clarisa	6 Jan 1831	(6)
Metcalf Hiram 21	Owens Sarah 26	9 Aug 1865	(4) 1/1
Metcalf J W H	Davis Mary	16 July 1841	(5)
Metcalf J W H	Davis Mary	16 July 1840	(6)
Metcalf L R	Brown Margaret	30 Dec 1837	(6)
Metcalf Ludwell	Brown Margaret		(1) 20 Jan 1838
Metcalf Wm	Hackuylot T	17 May 1832	(6)
Michael A E	Hilkey Jacob	30 Dec 1847	(6)
Michael Adam	Hilky Elanor	9 Dec 1841	(5)
Michael David	Worth Maria Louisa	19 Sept 1837	(1) 7 Oct 1837
Michael David William 38	Brill Maude Littler 22	23 Nov 1896	(4) 2/38
Michael Eli	Evans Eliza	10 Feb 1863	(6)
Michael Job	Cosner Mary	15 Feb 1835	(5)
Michael John	Smith Lousia	1 Nov 1843	(5)
Michael John 30	Michael Louisa J 22	2 Jan 1868	(4) 1/6
Michael John Henry 20	Spurling Mary Catharine 22	28 May 1879	(4) 2/13
Michael Joseph	Parris Elmira	8 Dec 1852	(5)
Michael Louisa J 22	Michael John 30	2 Jan 1868	(4) 1/6
Michael Margaret	Cosner Adam	11 Dec 1823	(5)
Michael Margaret 26	Pennington Saml J 31	4 Feb 1868	(4) 1/6
Michael Martha Ann 19	Cheshire Samuel James Wm 18	17 Mar 1885	(4) 2/20
Michael Moses	Worth Rebecca Anne	19 Sept 1837	(1) 7 Oct 1837
Michael Rachel	Cosner Adam	10 Oct 1833	(5)
Michael Regina 20	Conard James Edward 20	10 Apr 1890	(4) 2/27
Michael Samuel Hartell 27	Miller Laura May 18	*21 Oct 1878	(4) 2/12
Michael Virginia May 17	Wolford Leonard Harper 21	3 Mar 1891	(4) 2/29
Michels Amanda 21	Bobo Jackson 22	24 Jan 1866	(4) 1/2
Miers John W	McIlwee Sarah Elizabeth		(1) 28 Oct 1837
Miers Mary J 48	Plush Wm 23	17 Oct 1865	(4) 1/1
Milburn Charles Albert 22	McDonald Mary Alice 23	21 Apr 1881	(4) 2/16
Milburn William T 23	Bohrer Minnie Ann 22	21 Nov 1897	(4) 2/39
Miles Asa Morgan 23	Cross Elmira Virginia 20	9 Nov 1886	(4) 2/22
Miles Catharine 16	Kaylor Andrew 28	14 Sept 1865	(4) 1/1
Miles J D	Fisher Mary	27 Oct 1825	(5)
Miles John Loy 40	Bennett Margaret 50	9 Dec 1879	(4) 2/13
Miles Martha Ellen Virginia 18	Saville Isaac Newton 21	28 Aug 1884	(4) 2/19
Miles Sarah Ann 36	Vandegraft John 38	8 Jan 1880	(4) 2/14
Miles William 23	Gile Sarah 19	15 Nov 1865	(4) 1/1
Millar James	Morehead Loreana	*19 Nov 1827	(4) 3/56

Name #1	Name #2	Date	Source
Millar Mary Decker 32	Pancake John Isaac 26	29 June 1887	(4) 2/23
Millar Michael Adam 20	Leatherman Martha Ellen 20	5 Apr 1893	(4) 2/32
Millar William Charles 22	Pancake Etta Virginia 22	23 Sept 1890	(4) 2/28
Millburn George Henry 23	Smith Sarah 21	30 Dec 1875	(4) 1/39
Miller ? 25	Thomas Adda Salina 21	*29 Aug 1882	(4) 2/17
Miller Agnes Jannetta 21	Swisher David Edward 22	21 Dec 1887	(4) 2/24
Miller Algemon 43	Hott Leanna 24	8 July 1890	(4) 2/28
Miller Alverda 28	Tutwiler Joseph Henry 28	10 Dec 1889	(4) 2/27
Miller Amos Wm 21	Sirbaugh Mary Elizabeth 21	24 Mar 1878	(4) 2/11
Miller Ann Eliza 18	Withers Henry Clay 24	26 Aug 1880	(4) 2/14
Miller Ann Rebecca 40	Cox Henry Harrison 50	11 Oct 1892	(4) 2/31
Miller Annie Elizabeth 24	Eaton D Elmer 22	16 Aug 1900	(4) 2/43
Miller Barbary	Hainey Dan	1 Feb 1820	(6)
Miller Benjamin Franklin 24	Fleming Mary Elizabeth 22	19 July 1893	(4) 2/32
Miller Catherine	Rotruck Peter	20 Aug 1816	(6)
Miller Charles F 23	Shoemaker Sarah Frances 29	10 Oct 1877	(4) 2/10
Miller Claudia Shelton 23	Speelman William 23	11 Jan 1897	(4) 2/38
Miller Cora Wills 22	Milleson William Jedson 23	20 July 1892	(4) 2/31
Miller D F 29	Anderson Mollie M 24	13 Apr 1868	(4) 1/6
Miller Daisy M 17	Hott David Jasper 35	10 Jan 1897	(4) 2/38
Miller E C 18	Miller John H 25	13 Oct 1868	(4) 1/7
Miller Eliza	Catlett Hanson	5 Jan 1824	(6)
Miller Elizabeth 21	Vandergriff Jno 22	16 Sept 1868	(4) 1/7
Miller Elizabeth	Price A H	16 Apr 1818	(6)
Miller Ellen 22	Snyder Martin Luther 22	1 Sept 1881	(4) 2/16
Miller Emma 18	McIlwee George 19	17 July 1878	(4) 2/11
Miller Frances Ann 25	Lewis John Robert 27	24 Feb 1876	(4) 2/8
Miller Gilbert Proctor 32	Washington Edna 29	19 Apr 1899	(4) 2/41
Miller Jacob	Roberts Ann	28 Oct 1830	(6)
Miller Jacob	Broadwater N	20 Jan 1832	(6)
Miller Jacob 21	Reynolds Margaret C 19	4 Feb 1866	(4) 1/2
Miller Jas Wesly P 24	Foltz Lacy Ann 21	6 Feb 1878	(4) 2/11
Miller Jeremiah 23	Parrell Mary Ann 23	28 Nov 1872	(4) 2/4
Miller John	Liller Elizabeth	25 Mar 1819	(6)
Miller John H 25	Miller E C 18	13 Oct 1868	(4) 1/7
Miller John William 21	Orndorff Ida May 21	28 Mar 1891	(4) 2/29
Miller John William 26	Mellon Elizabeth Catharine 20	27 Mar 1888	(4) 2/24
Miller John William 23	Everett Margaret Jane 29	17 Oct 1877	(4) 2/10
Miller Joseph M Dr 47	Wilson Mary Taylor 30	14 Nov 1900	(4) 2/43
Miller Joseph M 25	Coffman Alberta Cordelia 26	3 Jan 1878	(4) 2/11
Miller Kesiah	Rannells John	*12 Nov 1824	(4) 3/51
Miller Laura May 18	Michael Samuel Hartell 27	*21 Oct 1878	(4) 2/12
Miller Marg	McDonald George	*14 July 1828	(4) 3/17
Miller Margaret	Hull John	15 Dec 1831	(6)
Miller Maria M 22	Edwards Geo M Dallas 22	11 Sept 1866	(4) 1/3
Miller Martha Allie 22	Kenney William H 31	29 Oct 1878	(4) 2/12
Miller Mary	Spencer John	*10 Nov 1824	(4) 3/50
Miller Mary Ann 21	McKee Josiah 43	12 Dec 1871	(4) 2/3
Miller Mary Elizabeth 21	Snyder Benjamin Franklin 24	2 June 1886	(4) 2/22
Miller Mary Frances 22	Kerns Harris Ephraim 24	3 June 1896	(4) 2/37
Miller Mary Jane 26	Loy Adam Clark 24	4 Nov 1869	(4) 2/1
Miller Mary Virginia	Spaid John H	16 Apr 1857	(10)

Name #1	Name #2	Date	Source
Miller Mich	Rawlings Elizabeth	19 Feb 1828	(6)
Miller Nancy 26	Stump Joseph 42	13 Jan 1870	(4) 2/1
Miller Nannie Dorcus 25	Martin Charles Edward 23	6 Feb 1879	(4) 2/12
Miller Peter	Spencer Julia	26 Feb 1824	(6)
Miller Peter	Urice Elizabeth	28 May 1841	(5)
Miller Peter	Spencer Julia Ann	*21 Feb 1824	(4) 3/11
Miller Peter	Urice Elizabeth	28 May 1840	(6)
Miller Peter 65	Cooper Hoppie Jacobs 29	28 Apr 1892	(4) 2/31
Miller Rebecca	McDonald Peter	30 Sept 1860	(5)
Miller Rebecca	McDonald P	30 Sept 1859	(6)
Miller Rebecca Jane 23	Alger John Alvahase 23	21 Nov 1867	(4) 1/5
Miller Robert Edgar 28	Eaton Bertha Raivetta 18	12 July 1900	(4) 2/43
Miller Rosa Verena 23	Saville John Letcher 24	26 Jan 1886	(4) 2/21
Miller Ruth	Grayson John	15 Nov 1849	(6)
Miller S E	Dobbins Johnson	21 Sept 1847	(6)
Miller Sarah 25	Kaylor Thomas William 24	30 May 1890	(4) 2/28
Miller Susan Rebecca 25	McBride Grayson 28	1 Nov 1888	(4) 2/25
Miller Uriah Lease 38	Walker Amanda Jane 28	27 June 1893	(4) 2/32
Miller W H 23	Poland Mary J 26	18 Nov 1868	(4) 1/7
Miller William 57	Howard Virginia 27	3 Oct 1892	(4) 2/31
Miller William Henry 22	Kerns Margary Isabell 18	11 July 1880	(4) 2/14
Miller William Luther 27	Mellin Louisa Ann 18	19 Jan 1875	(4) 2/6
Miller William T 27	Lafollette Hannah J 20	5 Dec 1872	(4) 2/4
Miller Willie Sarah 21	Pancake Frederick S 25	14 Jan 1886	(4) 2/21
Miller Wm H	Dixon Harriet	28 Mar 1844	(6)
Milleson Chas M 21	Long Mary C 24	28 Feb 1866	(4) 1/3
Milleson Elizabeth	Pugh John	21 Feb 1860	(10)
Milleson John 24	Moreland Sarah C 25	20 Mar 1866	(4) 1/3
Milleson John 35	Sirbaugh Vernie 20	8 Aug 1892	(4) 2/31
Milleson Martha 21	Powell David Sylvester 28	20 Feb 1867	(4) 1/4
Milleson Peter Marion 38	King Margaret Ann 39	31 May 1893	(4) 2/32
Milleson Sarah Virg Bell 22	Portmess John Franklin 26	15 Apr 1886	(4) 2/22
Milleson Silas	Slane Harriett	*19 Feb 1827	(4) 3/12
Milleson William Taylor 31	Lupton Josephine E 28	6 Oct 1897	(4) 2/39
Milleson William 28	McDonald Lydia Ann 24	15 Mar 1892	(4) 2/30
Milleson William Jedson 23	Miller Cora Wills 22	20 July 1892	(4) 2/31
Millineaux Israel	Poland Mary	11 Jan 1821	(5)
Millison Jesse Benjamin 28	White Emma Jane Victoria 19	22 Nov 1899	(4) 2/42
Millison Martha	Williamson Benjamin	*21 Nov 1827	(4) 2/57
Mills Christina	Likins Michael	16 Aug 1852	(5)
Mills Isaac	Smith Sarah	28 Nov 1839	(6)
Mills Isaac	Smith Sarah	28 Nov 1840	(5)
Mills John	Potts Elizabeth	12 Oct 1839	(6)
Mills John	Potts Elizabeth	12 Oct 1840	(5)
Mills Mary	Bogle Wm	8 Jan 1846	(6)
Mills Mary Rebecca 23	Feller William Luther 26	31 Aug 1881	(4) 2/16
Mills Sarah Catharine 20	Taylor Joseph 27	7 Jan 1874	(4) 2/5
Mills Seth	Sharpless Missouri	20 Nov 1850	(6)
Mills Seth	Sharpless Missouri	20 Nov 1846	(5)
Mills Thomas Thompson 45	Stevenson Mary A 48	24 May 1892	(4) 2/31
Millslagle Julia Ann	Kump Jacob	25 Jan 1838	(1) 10 Feb 1838
Milslagle Flora Belle 28	Stewart James Henry 51	11 Oct 1893	(4) 2/33

Name #1	Name #2	Date	Source
Milslagle Hannah	Pennington James	*14 May 1825	(4) 3/37
Milslagle Margaret Elizabeth 20	Grimm Hiram Riley 35	7 Sept 1865	(4) 1/1
Milslagle Mary Jane 34	Boswell F Reazin Shepherd 37	31 Dec 1889	(4) 2/27
Mingo Rebecca G 23	Lloyd Robert Jackson 27	9 May 1895	(4) 2/35
Minshall John 38	Jewell Mary Jane 20	7 June 1881	(4) 2/16
Mintsligie Nancy	Trentor Samuel		(1) 29 July 1837
Mitchael Eli	Evans Elizabeth	10 Feb 1862	(5)
Mitchel Ella Bell 20	Patterson Thomas Ezra 21	9 Jan 1890	(4) 2/27
Mitchel Mary Lincoln 26	Oates George 33	26 Apr 1893	(4) 2/32
Mitchell Ashmire Hamilton 24	Haines Virginia Catharine 22	9 June 1874	(4) 2/6
Molden William	Frantz Sophia	19 Jan 1823	(5)
Mongold David Washington 21	Maphis Lena 18	19 Oct 1900	(4) 2/43
Monroe Alexander 45	Pugh Ephenia 40	26 Jan 1869	(4) 1/38
Monroe Alexander 47	Pugh Margaret E 26	21 Nov 1866	(4) 1/4
Monroe Ellen 22	Tharp Wilber L 28	29 Nov 1899	(4) 2/42
Monroe Hannah 29	Rietbrook Henry 36	Oct 1854	(10)
Monroe James	Pugh Margaret	*8 Nov 1827	(4) 3/53
Monroe Joseph 25	Kern? Martha Fannie 21	2 Jan 1894	(4) 2/33
Monroe Malinda 35	Snapp James C 46	25 Oct 1860	(10)
Monroe Sarah Elizabeth 23	Haines Charles William 29	31 Jan 1893	(4) 2/32
Monroe Sylvester	Hobson Jane	*15 Dec 1828	(4) 3/46
Montgomery ?	Seders John S	20 Dec 1855	(10)
Montgomery Bettie 19	Patterson Wm E 21	1 July 1892	(4) 2/31
Montgomery Charles Henry 21	Oats Nettie Elizabeth 18	5 Oct 1896	(4) 2/37
Montgomery Elizabeth A 25	Kaylor James Wesley 30	24 Oct 1889	(4) 2/27
Montgomery Eugene 30	Arnold Mollie Chistena 30	1 June 1882	(4) 2/17
Montgomery Raymond 22	McBride Emma Jane 32	11 Nov 1900	(4) 2/43
Moody Elizabeth	Likens J J	17 Jan 1854	(6)
Moody Emily 20	Frye Jesse 25	22 Aug 1854	(10)
Moody Jas	Grayson Clara	10 Oct 1850	(6)
Moody M	Ravenscroft Nich	24 Aug 1852	(6)
Moody Mary	Ravenscraft Nicholas	2 Aug 1852	(5)
Moody William	Beals Virginia	21 Mar 1846	(5)
Moody Wm	Beals Virginia	21 Mar 1850	(6)
Moon Benjamin	Harvey Hester	14 Nov 1840	(5)
Moore A M	Dawson Thos	30 June 1842	(6)
Moore Abraham	Stump Sarah	*1 Oct 1828	(4) 3/29
Moore Ann Rebecca 30	Noland John William 36	15 Nov 1870	(4) 2/2
Moore Anna Dawson 35	Short John William 26	3 Feb 1881	(4) 2/15
Moore Benj	Harvey Hester	14 Nov 1839	(6)
Moore Benj F 27	Jacobs Catherine 24	14 Dec 1865	(4) 1/2
Moore Elizabeth J 35	Noland Robt D 35	4 Feb 1868	(4) 1/6
Moore Isaac	Hickle Elizabeth	*25 Sept 1826	(4) 3/36
Moore John	Brian Sarah	9 Sept 1824	(5)
Moore Joseph S 34	Critton Mary E 23	4 Mar 1868	(4) 1/6
Moore Marcus	Hammack J	10 Dec 1844	(6)
Moore Myrtle V 18	Saville William Van Kirk 21	22 June 1898	(4) 2/40
Moore Richard Henry 32	Banks Mary 31	25 June 1885	(4) 1/40
Moore Sallie	Bond Thomas	16 June 1822	(5)
Moore Sallie	Bond Thos	15 June 1822	(6)
Moore Solomon	Foley Millery	*10 Dec 1828	(4) 3/44
Moore Thomas	Doran Sarah	*4 Oct 1824	(4) 3/46

Name #1	Name #2	Date	Source
Moore William Henry 28	Durst Louisa Ellen 19	28 Sept 1876	(4) 2/8
Moorehead Robt Wm 19	Shanholtzer Mary Catharine 21	19 Oct 1865	(4) 1/1
Mooreland Walter	Shell Lucretia	10 Jan 1836	(5)
Moorhead James	Urton Bersheba		(1) 6 Oct 1838
Moorhead Martha	Urton William		(1) 23 May 1839
Moorhead Robt E 24	Allen Sarah M 24	20 Sept 1866	(4) 1/3
Mored Rebeca	Carlile William	*20 Mar 1826	(4) 3/14
Morehead Loreana	Millar James	*19 Nov 1827	(4) 3/56
Moreland Amanda Rebecca 21	Lyons John Henry 21	30 Apr 1877	(4) 2/10
Moreland Bassil Newton 30	Malcolm Mary Sabine 25	11 Feb 1874	(4) 2/5
Moreland Bazil Newton 28	Whitacre Rhoda Ann 25	7 Mar 1880	(4) 2/14
Moreland Charles W 23	Brown Melissa Caroline 24	25 Mar 1896	(4) 2/37
Moreland Chloe E 21	Saville William H 23	31 Jan 1868	(4) 1/6
Moreland Chloey 31	Heath James Clinton 37	1 Dec 1897	(4) 2/39
Moreland Christopher Columbus 27	Gross Ellen 19	16 Dec 1880	(4) 2/15
Moreland Delcie L 20	Shanholtzer James R Luther 20	24 Mar 1901	(4) 2/44
Moreland Eliza	Ponifirt Sam	23 June 1840	(6)
Moreland Eliza	Promfirt Samuel	23 June 1841	(5)
Moreland Elizabeth 44	Offutt Thornton W 44	*21 Apr 1874	(4) 2/6
Moreland Evaline 24	Kerns Andrew Jacob 22	21 Feb 1894	(4) 2/33
Moreland George	McCauley Ann Jemima	1854	(10)
Moreland George William 32	Queen Mary 25	3 Sept 1867	(4) 1/5
Moreland Harriet Alverta 19	Brown Frank Marion 30	*16 Sept 1899	(4) 2/42
Moreland James 44	Malcolm Mary Catharine 35	30 Aug 1877	(4) 2/10
Moreland James Jackson 24	Wolford Sidney Sophia 23	25 Apr 1882	(4) 2/17
Moreland James Price 22	Moreland Sarah Catherine 21	8 Sept 1881	(4) 2/16
Moreland John	Daubs Martha	8 Apr 1844	(5)
Moreland Margaret 20	Bennett Martin Luther 23	22 Nov 1860	(10)
Moreland Margaret Ann 24	Day Thomas L 32	25 Feb 1873	(4) 2/4
Moreland Martha M 23	Giffin Charles Fenton 35	4 Nov 1896	(4) 2/37
Moreland Martha Virginia 18	Stewart Benjamin Franklin 21	22 Dec 1881	(4) 2/17
Moreland Mary	Queen Stephen	*29 Jan 1827	(4) 3/10
Moreland Misty May 18	Hulver George W 29	18 Dec 1894	(4) 2/35
Moreland Polly	Forsyth Jacob	7 June 1843	(5)
Moreland Sadie Jane 19	Parrill William 19	21 Mar 1897	(40 2/38
Moreland Sam	Smith Elizabeth	20 Jan 1831	(6)
Moreland Sarah	Keyser Abram	19 Oct 1844	(5)
Moreland Sarah C 25	Milleson John 24	20 Mar 1866	(4) 1/3
Moreland Sarah Catherine 21	Moreland James Price 22	8 Sept 1881	(4) 2/16
Moreland Sarah Ellen 20	Kidwell Benjamin Alexander 22	26 Mar 1880	(4) 2/14
Moreland Sarah Ellen 20	Saville Jefferson Davis 27	28 May 1890	(4) 2/28
Moreland Sarah Isadore 20	Brelsford Benjamin Blaker 27	29 Mar 1877	(4) 2/10
Moreland William 22	Loy Mary Cordelia 23	4 Apr 1871	(4) 2/2
Moreland William Franklin 31	Rinehart Margaret Ann 19	22 Feb 1887	(4) 2/23
Moreland William Edward 22	Rinehart Virginia Bell 16	17 Feb 1881	(4) 2/15
Morgan Cora 19	Burke Robert 24	23 Dec 1890	(4) 1/41
Morgan Samuel 44	Toliver Sarah Frances 35	*27 Mar 1871	(4) 1/38
Morgan Samuel Lewis 23	Allen Sallie Ann 22	2 Oct 1890	(4) 1/41
Morris Alexanda 24	Allemong Alice Virginia 22	10 Mar 1874	(4) 2/6
Morris Lizzie 22	Cather Edward Washington 24	12 May 1897	(4) 2/39
Moseley Elizabeth	Long Cornelius R		(1) 10 Mar 1838
Moton Joseph 30	Martin Rebecca Ann 35	3 Sept 1865	(4) 1/1

Name #1	Name #2	Date	Source
Moton Joseph 57	Bean Harriet Elizabeth 40	30 May 1893	(4) 2/32
Mott Marcus	Harrison Lucretia	24 Nov 1859	(10)
Mott Nancy	Harrison B F	6 Jan 1829	(6)
Mott Randolph	Hall Sarah	12 Apr 1836	(6)
Mouser Amanda 27	Austin Henry 24	18 Jan 1870	(4) 2/1
Mowrey Isaac Randolph 30	Howdyshell Malinda Catharine 19	17 Nov 1880	(4) 2/15
Moyer Anna Rebecca 19	Shingleton William Jackson 28	21 Apr 1897	(4) 2/39
Mudy James	Staggs Mary	15 Aug 1844	(6)
Mudy Joseph	Baker Millie	21 Feb 1819	(5)
Mulinix John Luther 22	Fisher Katie R 24	24 June 1894	(4) 2/34
Mull John L 26	Everett Mary Elizabeth 24	13 Sept 1887	(4) 2/24
Mullady Milly	Parsons David	*11 Jan 1827	(4) 3/3
Mulldey James 22	Lewis Mary Elizabeth 22	12 Apr 1875	(4) 2/7
Mulledy Otelia 18	Lewis Charles Kerns 29	3 Mar 1896	(4) 2/37
Mulledy Robert Ambrose 29	Lewis Virginia Florence 24	6 Feb 1884	(4) 2/19
Mullineaux Israel	Poland Mary	11 Jan 1821	(6)
Munday Anna Belle 26	Wirgman James Jr 32	24 Feb 1892	(4) 2/30
Murphy Dan'l	Davis Phobe	28 Jan 1839	(5)
Murphy Edw	Davis Phebe	28 Jan 1838	(6)
Murphy Frances	Earnholt Jane	3 Oct 1822	(6)
Murphy Hugh	Mary	11 June 1828	(5)
Murphy Isaac	Clark Lavina	25 July 1833	(6)
Murphy Jas E	Long S M	2 June 1847	(6)
Murphy John	Streets Elizabeth	5 Dec 1844	(6)
Murphy M	McRobie John	16 Dec 1838	(6)
Murphy Margaret	McRobie John	6 Dec 1839	(5)
Murphy Mary E 32	Taylor Charles M 35	18 Jan 1866	(4) 1/2
Murphy R	Cooper Abram	17 Feb 1846	(6)
Murphy Sarah M 26	Taylor Simon D 33	1 Nov 1865	(4) 1/1
Muse William Joseph 31	Garvin Minnie Cordelia 24	25 June 1896	(4) 2/37
Mutte Archibald	Wingfield Susannah	*18 Apr 1826	(4) 3/17
Myers Catherine Ann	Hull Isaac		(1) 24 June 1837
Myers Elizabeth	Welsh Sylvester	*4 Dec 1826	(4) 3/43
Myers Elizabeth	Welch Sylvester	5 Dec 1826	(6)
Myers Herman A 24	Powell Mollie J 17	28 Oct 1880	(4) 2/14
Myers Isaac Solomon 25	Bowman Martha Ellen 20	31 Mar 1874	(4) 2/6
Myers Jane	Barnhouse M P	24 Oct 1849	(6)
Myers M	Singleton Aaron	1 Nov 1836	(6)
Myers Rachael Eleanor 18	Wallace Rafus Alonzo 22	19 Sept 1895	(4) 2/36
Mytinger Caroline Virginia 23	Athey Thomas Brant 23	28 Nov 1877	(4) 2/10
Mytinger Daniel 62	Newman Maria L 46	27 Oct 1865	(4) 1/1
Mytinger Fannie Hopkins 23	Parker William Clayton 33	31 Mar 1880	(4) 2/14
Mytinger William Machir 27	Stone Anna Evans 28	2 Nov 1886	(4) 2/22
Nally S	McCormick James	24 Sept 1834	(6)
Nally Sarah	Sliger Jacob	20 Oct 1836	(6)
Narvey Drusilla	Lower William	8 Jan 1829	(5)
Naylor Jane	Tapscott Chichester	*6 Oct 1825	(4) 3/66
Naylor Leacy Ann	McDonald Angus	*11 Jan 1827	(4) 3/2
Naylor Robert Cornelius 44	Short Samantha Catherine 22	27 Apr 1892	(4) 2/31
Neal Allen	Endler Luranah	21 Dec 1833	(6)
Nealis Eliza Ann 26	Darr George Philip 26	10 May 1881	(4) 2/16
Nealis Fannie Lorenia 31	Hamilton George Riley 32	8 Dec 1897	(4) 2/39

Name #1	Name #2	Date	Source
Nealis George William 26	Shanholtzer Martha Jane 23	8 Jan 1889	(4) 2/26
Nealis John 31	Clemma Delilah Ann Eliza 21	25 Nov 1884	(4) 2/20
Nealis Joseph 26	Ganoe Mary Jane 21	15 June 1896	(4) 2/37
Nealis Maggie E 22	Grey Jesse Ranson 29	9 Apr 1895	(4) 2/35
Nealis Margaret Elizabeth 28	Foltz Jacob 28	*20 Nov 1880	(4) 2/15
Nealis Mary Matilda 26	Haines John Alexander 28	22 Nov 1882	(4) 2/17
Neel Jerrold Wilber 26	Marshall Florinda Virginia 27	16 Jan 1896	(4) 2/36
Neff Thompson	Alkire Mahala A	15 Nov 1839	(1) 5 Dec 1839
Nelson Alice Virginia 18	Johnson Sol Loundes Vesta 22	15 Oct 1898	(4) 1/41
Nelson Asenath	? Samuel B M	20 Sept 1854	(10)
Nelson Jackson	Slonaker Caroline Virginia 21	10 Nov 1859	(10)
Nelson Jas E 37	Bennett S M J J 31	9 Apr 1868	(4) 1/6
Nelson Joanna S 28	Johnson James W 24	9 Mar 1870	(4) 2/1
Nelson John Edward 23	Selden Charlotte 20	7 Apr 1887	(4) 2/23
Nelson Robert Beauregard 24	Haines Victoria E 15	10 Nov 1885	(4) 2/21
Neman John C	Cade Elizabeth	19 June 1817	(5)
Nesbit Eleanor	Rogers John	3 Aug 1837	(6)
Nesbit Susa	Rogers J L Jr	25 Mar 1841	(6)
Netherton Virginia Bell 18	Whitacre Albert Luther 21	23 Jan 1890	(4) 2/27
Neville H D	Sollars Nancy	19 Dec 1844	(6)
Nevitt Robert Emory 29	Everett Mary Frances 22	23 Sept 1885	(4) 2/21
Newhouse George Washington 20	Cooper Sarah Belle 17	20 Mar 1877	(4) 2/10
Newhouse John	Frazier M J	23 Mar 1842	(6)
Newhouse Mattie 35	Hurshey Auther Wm 26	19 June 1901	(4) 2/44
Newman Catesby	Reed Sarah	*3 Sept 1824	(4) 3/43
Newman John C	Cade Elizabeth	19 June 1817	(6)
Newman Lucindas	Paugh Michael	13 May 1827	(5)
Newman Maria L 46	Mytinger Daniel 62	27 Oct 1865	(4) 1/1
Newman Mary Ann	Walker William C	11 Sept 1852	(2) 7 Oct 1852
Nicewarner Catharine 21	Nixon William Edward 39	20 Apr 1887	(4) 2/23
Nicewoner Priscilla Jane 18	Sirbaugh William Henry 33	29 May 1883	(4) 2/18
Nichols Febe Jane 19	Carder William Baker 28	7 Jan 1896	(4) 2/36
Nichols Isaac Gibson 66	McDonald Celia Ellen 53	27 Jan 1885	(4) 2/20
Nichols Jacob Franklin 22	Timbrook Grace Davis 23	27 Apr 1898	(4) 2/40
Nicholson Elizabeth	Young George	*4 Mar 1824	(4) 3/15
Nicols William Lewellyn 28	Steele Gertrude Maude 27	25 Sept 1890	(4) 2/28
Nixon Ann Elizabeth 30	Brill Harrison 30	*13 Dec 1870	(4) 2/2
Nixon Caudy John 26	Gray Mrs Annie E 33	1 Dec 1887	(4) 2/24
Nixon E	Bracket Apollos	9 Aug 1821	(6)
Nixon Emma E 23	Slonaker James Wm David 31	25 Apr 1894	(4) 2/34
Nixon James E 22	Hardy Martha 21	11 Nov 1872	(4) 2/4
Nixon Jane 47	Gardner Jacob Rosenberger 39	12 Mar 1895	(4) 2/35
Nixon Lemuel 46	Pugh Nancy Jane 30	1 Mar 1866	(4) 1/3
Nixon Nancy	Lanham Dennie	*6 Nov 1826	(4) 3/39
Nixon Rose Ida 28	Pugh John W 59	19 Apr 1887	(4) 2/23
Nixon William Edward 39	Nicewarner Catharine 21	20 Apr 1887	(4) 2/23
Noel Martha Jane	Kerne Elisha	21 Sept 1852	(2) 7 Oct 1852
Noland Cora Lee 18	Alderton Francis Marion 25	18 Mar 1890	(4) 2/27
Noland John William 36	Moore Ann Rebecca 30	15 Nov 1870	(4) 2/2
Noland Robt D 35	Moore Elizabeth J 35	4 Feb 1868	(4) 1/6
Noll Joseph Calvin 25	Abrel Margaret 24	27 Oct 1867	(4) 1/5
Norman Lucy	King John	*17 Oct 1825	(4) 3/68

Name #1	Name #2	Date	Source
Nott Elizabeth	Van Buskirk E	3 Jan 1833	(6)
Oates Eliza Frances 16	Shanholtzer Jacob Anthony 19	1 Dec 1881	(4) 2/16
Oates Elizabeth	Lupton Jesse	7 Sept 1852	(2) 7 Oct 1852
Oates Emma 22	Kump Chas M S 21	6 May 1900	(4) 2/42
Oates Emma V 20	Oates Robt Joshua 26	12 Sept 1900	(4) 2/43
Oates Emma Virginia 21	Oats Algemon 32	2 June 1885	(4) 2/20
Oates George 33	Mitchel Mary Lincoln 26	26 Apr 1893	(4) 2/32
Oates George William 28	Kline Minnie Belle 19	28 Oct 1897	(4) 2/39
Oates James F 26	McKee Verda Alverda Elizabeth 17	20 Apr 1893	(4) 2/32
Oates Robt Joshua 26	Oates Emma V 20	12 Sept 1900	(4) 2/43
Oats ? 19	Arnold John Wesley 22	29 Mar 1860	(10)
Oats Algemon 32	Oates Emma Virginia 21	2 June 1885	(4) 2/20
Oats Amanda 16	Sirbaugh Jonah 18	19 Apr 1881	(4) 2/16
Oats Annie Lee 18	Pugh Edgar Lewis 19	21 Nov 1894	(4) 2/35
Oats Catherine 22	Whistler Uriah 33	1 Oct 1867	(4) 1/5
Oats Christopher 69	Haines Martha 31	11 Feb 1884	(4) 2/19
Oats Daniel 26	Kline Virginia Frances 21	28 Nov 1871	(4) 2/3
Oats Elizabeth Drusilla 16	Haines Noah 28	4 Feb 1879	(4) 2/12
Oats Ella Virginia 28	Ward Edgar Alonzo 40	25 Apr 1894	(4) 2/34
Oats Frances Ellen 27	Mellon Marcus Anthony 25	31 May 1876	(4) 2/8
Oats Frances Virginia 24	Heatwole Marquis Lafayette 23	5 Nov 1884	(4) 2/20
Oats Geo William 38	Mellon Sallie Ester 23	12 Oct 1897	(4) 2/39
Oats George 22	Mauzy Emily 19	8 Apr 1880	(4) 2/14
Oats George Washington 32	Siville Hannah Susan 19	16 Oct 1879	(4) 2/13
Oats Harriet E 25	Hamill Archibald Chisholm 48	26 June 1889	(4) 2/26
Oats Harrison William 25	Swisher Rosa Jane 25	16 Feb 1898	(4) 2/40
Oats Hattie Estella 18	Shanholtzer Albert Wash 24	12 Feb 1901	(4) 2/44
Oats Ira Clay 28	Fletcher Bertha E 21	30 Dec 1895	(4) 2/36
Oats Isaac Edward 22	Oats Maranda Jane 22	3 Apr 1867	(4) 1/5
Oats James Franklin 28	Wise Rebecca 21	24 Nov 1865	(4) 1/1
Oats James Thompson 27	Oats Martha Jane 23	21 Sept 1875	(4) 2/7
Oats Jeanie Dow 20	Gardner Annie Lee 17	8 Nov 1894	(4) 2/35
Oats Jefferson Davis 25	Haines Ida May 24	13 Aug 1896	(4) 2/37
Oats Laura Elnora 21	Oats Lucurgus C 31	27 Apr 1892	(4) 2/31
Oats Lorenzo	Files Barbara Ann	7 Mar 1839	(1) 21 Mar 1839
Oats Lucurgus C 31	Oats Laura Elnora 21	27 Apr 1892	(4) 2/31
Oats Luther Calvin 21	Sirbaugh Ida Virginia 19	19 Oct 1875	(4) 2/7
Oats Malinda Ann 22	Poland John 49	20 Oct 1873	(4) 2/5
Oats Maranda Jane 22	Oats Isaac Edward 22	3 Apr 1867	(4) 1/5
Oats Martha Ann 17	Fletcher Elihu Christy 30	18 Oct 1887	(4) 2/24
Oats Martha Jane 23	Oats James Thompson 27	21 Sept 1875	(4) 2/7
Oats Mary Elizabeth 23	Shivers Jonathan Thomas 26	16 Feb 1869	(4) 1/38
Oats Mollie 22	Fagle Martin B 26	1 Feb 1894	(4) 2/33
Oats Nettie Elizabeth 18	Montgomery Charles Henry 21	5 Oct 1896	(4) 2/37
Oats Retta Alice 19	Pepper Henry Dye 24	28 June 1899	(4) 2/41
Oats Rettie Elizabeth 16	Larrick David Lee 22	19 June 1890	(4) 2/28
Oats Robert Joshua 20	Sirbaugh Sadie Elizabeth 21	*4 June 1894	(4) 2/34
Oats Robert Wm 34	Wilson Louiza 24	24 Sept 1874	(4) 2/6
Oats Sarah Eliz 22	Larrick Frederick 22	28 Aug 1872	(4) 2/3
Oats Theodrick Leath 28	Fishel Margaret Catharine 21	*14 Sept 1887	(4) 2/24
Oats Thomas Edward 25	Baker Mary Eliza Virginia 21	13 Nov 1898	(4) 2/41
Oats Wesley Edgar Lee 22	Lupton Harriett Ettie Lee 20	18 Jan 1888	(4) 2/24

Name #1	Name #2	Date	Source
Oats William Edward 24	Pool Fannie M 23	29 Dec 1896	(4) 2/38
Odass John 34	Taylor R 25	20 Dec 1870	(4) 2/2
Offner Hannah Catharine 24	Dixon James Porter 22	24 Feb 1881	(4) 2/15
Offner James	Grim Catherine	27 Apr 1825	(5)
Offord Sarah	Pugh John	*18 Feb 1828	(4) 3/5
Offutt Ann	Pugh Jonathan	*9 June 1827	(4) 3/36
Offutt Annie 26	Ward James Marion 37	25 Apr 1894	(4) 2/34
Offutt Augusta I 24	Watson Jethro Scott 33	7 Dec 1886	(4) 2/22
Offutt Edith 17	Bloom Thomas D 22	22 Jan 1896	(4) 2/36
Offutt Joseph McKeever 28	Shorb Eliza Lavina 18	7 Feb 1888	(4) 2/24
Offutt Margaret Ellen 26	Hiett Edward P 27	24 Oct 1894	(4) 2/34
Offutt Mary Margaret 40	Keckley Dr Cephas 75	22 Dec 1900	(4) 2/43
Offutt Nancy E 21	Haines Benjamin M 26	1 Jan 1867	(4) 1/4
Offutt Robert James 21	Largent Mary Elizabeth 22	23 Nov 1875	(4) 2/8
Offutt Sarah Gertrude 23	Cooper Edwin Rinehart 22	24 July 1895	(4) 2/35
Offutt Thornton W 44	Moreland Elizabeth 44	*21 Apr 1874	(4) 2/6
Oglesby Daniel Wesley 27	Blaker Portia Jane 23	16 Oct 1873	(4) 2/5
Oglesby John Davis 24	Blaker Matilda Catharine 24	26 Dec 1878	(4) 2/12
Oglisbee Almira Virginia 22	Slonaker George Washington 28	10 Nov 1871	(4) 2/3
Omps Texanna 25	Dehaven Perry Christy 23	25 Nov 1897	(4) 2/39
Orndorf Matilda 17	Davis John 23	27 Dec 1853	(10)
Orndorff Alice 21	Ka? Joseph Robert 21	14 Jan 1901	(4) 2/43
Orndorff Elizabeth Virginia 29	Berkheimer Henry L 50	*4 Nov 1878	(4) 2/12
Orndorff Ella Barbara 25	Kimble Sylvester 25	2 June 1881	(4) 2/16
Orndorff Ellen 22	Corbin Charles 22	24 May 1880	(4) 2/14
Orndorff Frances Elizabeth 21	Cummins George Thomas 26	19 Dec 1883	(4) 2/19
Orndorff George L 24	Dellinger Amanda Virginia 23	11 Apr 1891	(4) 2/29
Orndorff George Edgar 26	Spaid Eliza Ann 18	2 Dec 1880	(4) 2/15
Orndorff Hannah 19	Haines James Henry 22	13 Mar 1860	(10)
Orndorff Harriet Elizabeth 35	Bean John Warren 56	10 Nov 1885	(4) 2/21
Orndorff Henry H	Everett Harriet E	25 Apr 1859	(1) 13 May 1859
Orndorff Henry Hampton	Everett Harriet Elizabeth	25 Sept 1860	(10)
Orndorff Henry J 23	See Sarah 22	25 Oct 1865	(4) 1/1
Orndorff Ida May 21	Miller John William 21	28 Mar 1891	(4) 2/29
Orndorff James H 24	Shanholtzer H E 19	16 Nov 1868	(4) 1/7
Orndorff James Richen 21	French Elizabeth Ellen 19	10 Dec 1884	(4) 2/20
Orndorff John	Short M	28 Nov 1860	(10)
Orndorff Joseph A 45	Farmer Virginia Anne 36	19 Feb 1889	(4) 2/26
Orndorff Joseph Atwell 32	Hemilright Rachel Ann 22	30 Jan 1878	(4) 2/11
Orndorff Joseph William 24	Rosebough Rachel Ann 19	21 Nov 1875	(4) 2/8
Orndorff Joseph Atwell 37	Rudolph Sarah Ellen 34	6 Nov 1879	(4) 2/13
Orndorff Julius Waddle 26	Blaker Mary E 35	12 Oct 1876	(4) 2/9
Orndorff Luther Edward 29	Rudolph Anne Litler 21	4 May 1890	(4) 2/27
Orndorff Mahala 14	Snider Martin 21	18 Jan 1866	(4) 1/2
Orndorff Margaret Elizabeth 18	Haines Isaac Minor 25	17 Mar 1874	(4) 2/6
Orndorff Margaret 26	Roach David 28	18 Nov 1873	(4) 2/5
Orndorff Margaret 25	Sandy William Henry 28	4 Feb 1879	(4) 2/12
Orndorff Margaret 32	Saville Alexander 22	1 Apr 1884	(4) 2/19
Orndorff Marthy E 22	Cheshir Saml B 23	27 June 1868	(4) 1/6
Orndorff Martin Vanburan 45	Hurd Sarah Ann 35	19 Nov 1885	(4) 2/21
Orndorff Mary A	Fishel Jacob	5 Jan 1865	(8)
Orndorff Mary D 28	Ammick Franklin	*3 Spet 1884	(4) 2/19

Name #1	Name #2	Date	Source
Orndorff Mary Elizabeth 19	Brill Robert Franklin 20	19 June 1887	(4) 2/23
Orndorff Mary Magdalen 21	Seibert William Andrew 21	25 Sept 1888	(4) 2/25
Orndorff Mellissa E B 16	Triplett B R 35	22 Mar 1888	(4) 2/24
Orndorff Minerva Ellen 21	Wilson Nimrod 33	22 Oct 1885	(4) 2/21
Orndorff Nancy Jane 45	Tutwiler Martin 57	25 Feb 1875	(4) 2/7
Orndorff Nora Virginia 16	Himelwright John William 25	17 Jan 1889	(4) 2/26
Orndorff Rachele 33	McBride William 43	21 Apr 1875	(4) 2/7
Orndorff Rebecca J 18	Corbin Joseph 53	18 Dec 1866	(4) 1/4
Orndorff Robert Johnson 24	Fishel Frances Jane 18	1 Oct 1891	(4) 2/29
Orndorff Robert Calvin 23	Haines Sarah E 22	21 Apr 1892	(4) 2/30
Orndorff Sarah Jane 16	Davis Samuel Lupton 20	15 Jan 1885	(4) 2/20
Orndorff Simon Peter 22	Short Mary Elizabeth 25	4 Mar 1866	(4) 1/3
Orndorff Stephen 23	Davis Margaret E 18	15 Jan 1873	(4) 2/4
Orndorff William Thompson 29	Albright Sarah Ellen 19	27 Jan 1886	(4) 2/21
Orndorff William Wesley 28	Blaker Ada May 17	28 July 1889	(4) 2/26
Owens Sarah 26	Metcalf Hiram 21	9 Aug 1865	(4) 1/1
Painter E J	Leatherman B F	24 Sept 1846	(5)
Paliner Sarah J	Fishel Isaac	21 June 1863	(8)
Palmer Artona	Merit Rebecca	9 Mar 1845	(6)
Palmer E J	Leatherman B F	24 Sept 1850	(6)
Pancake Andrew 43	High Ann 19	16 Nov 1859	(10)
Pancake Etta Virginia 22	Millar William Charles 22	23 Sept 1890	(4) 2/28
Pancake Frederick S 25	Miller Willie Sarah 21	14 Jan 1886	(4) 2/21
Pancake Hannah	Armstrong Edward		(1) 9 Sept 1837
Pancake James Connar 25	Parker Sarah C 33	9 Mar 1892	(4) 2/30
Pancake John Isaac 26	Millar Mary Decker 32	29 June 1887	(4) 2/23
Pancake John M	Reese Mary B		(1) 14 Apr 1838
Pancake John McNeil	Parsons Parthena	*13 Feb 1826	(4) 3/9
Pancake John Silas 38	Gilkeson Margaret Vance 32	27 Nov 1884	(4) 2/20
Pancake Joseph A 26	Parsons Mary Susan 23	30 Mar 1870	(4) 2/1
Pancake Joseph Samuel 40	Inskeep Sallie Wright 24	3 Mar 1897	(4) 2/38
Pancake Mary McNeil 21	McNeil John William 23	6 Jan 1874	(4) 2/5
Pancake Sallie McNeil 24	Rogers Edward 27	7 Nov 1888	(4) 2/25
Pancake Sarah Maria 27	Parsons James Donaldson 27	19 Apr 1871	(4) 2/2
Pancake Silas Reese 24	Arnold Mary 26	15 Jan 1867	(4) 1/4
Parill Mercy	Thompson Henry	28 Oct 1825	(5)
Paris Elizabeth	Barrack George		(1) 28 Feb 1839
Parish Adam	Ruckman Mary	*31 May 1824	(4) 3/30
Parish George Washington 24	Slonaker Margaret Emma 18	13 Sept 1883	(4) 2/18
Park Alexander 27	Poland Martha Ellen 28	5 Apr 1881	(4) 2/15
Park Anna	Cooper Jacob	*7 Feb 1825	(4) 3/14
Park Ashford 38	Martin Catharine V A 17	1 Sept 1870	(4) 2/2
Park Benjamin 30	Loy Mary Ann 26	29 May 1867	(4) 1/5
Park Elrod 32	Whitlock Elizabeth Maude 17	20 Jan 1898	(4) 2/40
Park George 28	Poland Catherine Ann 21	3 Oct 1867	(4) 1/5
Park George 35	Shanholtzer Mary Henrietta 27	20 Apr 1875	(4) 2/7
Park Geroge	Carder Anna	*8 Oct 1827	(4) 3/51
Park James Ashford 26	Cool Martha Ellen 21	24 Feb 1887	(4) 2/23
Park James Ashford 36	Ruckman Martha Ellen 26	20 Feb 1898	(4) 2/40
Park John	Amon Mary	*18 Aug 1828	(4) 3/21
Park Louisa Jane 25	Brill Isaiah Branson 38	6 Mar 1894	(4) 2/33
Park Mary Ellen 27	Heare Isaac James Todd 43	24 Sept 1867	(4) 1/5

Name #1	Name #2	Date	Source
Park Rebecca	McNemar Wesley B		(1) 30 May 1839
Park Rhoda Ann 31	Combs James Madison 31	16 Apr 1889	(4) 2/26
Park Samuel Imboden 23	Ruckman Lucettie Delinore 19	22 Dec 1886	(4) 2/22
Park Samuel Jr	Horn George	*27 Mar 1824	(4) 3/18
Park Susan 22	Lovett Albert Ottis 24	20 Oct 1869	(4) 2/1
Park William	Brill Susan A	13 Sept 1864	(8)
Park William Early 23	Poland Ivy Melissa 20	23 Jan 1887	(4) 2/23
Parker Adde'm	Hull Eliza J	29 Oct 1846	(6)
Parker Alfred Vause 26	Fox Susan Rebecca 26	6 Nov 1895	(4) 2/36
Parker Benjamin	Long Eliza Jane	*8 Dec 1828	(4) 3/43
Parker Bettie Ward 17	Goldsboro John Thomas 31	26 Nov 1890	(4) 2/28
Parker C E	Levens Caleb	22 Oct 1850	(6)
Parker D E	Herriott J J	12 Sept 1855	(6)
Parker David	Vandiver Elizabeth	1 June 1820	(5)
Parker David	Vandiver Elizabeth	13 Apr 1820	(6)
Parker Eliza	Umstot Amos	1 Apr 1845	(6)
Parker Emily	Davis Jethro	23 Feb 1853	(6)
Parker Idgar Stump 27	Singhass Effie Rush 19	7 Nov 1894	(4) 2/35
Parker Isaac P 50	Kane Lydia I 28	3 Jan 1866	(4) 1/2
Parker Isaac Pierson 21	Carder Verdie Virginia 21	28 Oct 1894	(4) 2/34
Parker Isaac Vance 32	Corbett Gertrude 26	3 Aug 1871	(4) 2/3
Parker Jacob	Ludwick Mary	25 Dec 1823	(6)
Parker James	Rees Jane	28 Nov 1820	(6)
Parker Jas	Whiteman E J	16 Apr 1855	(6)
Parker John	Whiteman Mary Ann	*11 Feb 1826	(4) 3/8
Parker John Edward 37	Condon Sarah Catharine 23	24 Apr 1877	(4) 2/10
Parker John Hite 24	Grace Catherine Brady 20	18 Sept 1867	(4) 1/5
Parker Joseph Foreman 23	Grace M 19	2 May 1860	(10)
Parker Lillian 30	Cookerly John T 21	4 Dec 1899	(4) 2/42
Parker Mary	Higgins Joseph C		(1) 21 Nov 1839
Parker Mary	Rogers Wm	19 May 1836	(6)
Parker Nancy	Arnold Samuel		(1) 20 Jan 1838
Parker Nannie 28	Bauer Frederick William 25	25 Mar 1896	(4) 2/37
Parker R E	Carskadon J H	19 Nov 1846	(6)
Parker Roberta S 22	Hodgson I H W 26	16 Oct 1872	(4) 2/3
Parker S M	Johnson Abram	20 Mar 1844	(6)
Parker Sarah C 33	Pancake James Connar 25	9 Mar 1892	(4) 2/30
Parker Sarah E	Leavens Caleb	22 Oct 1846	(5)
Parker Sarah Elizabeth 22	Butt Leonidas 28	1 Mar 1870	(4) 2/1
Parker Thornton	Sheetz Elizabeth	22 Oct 1818	(6)
Parker Thornton Russell 28	Whiteman Sarah Catherine 26	10 Dec 1881	(4) 2/17
Parker William	Davis Elizabeth	23 Nov 1820	(5)
Parker William Clayton 33	Mytinger Fannie Hopkins 23	31 Mar 1880	(4) 2/14
Parker William Lee 31	Collins Elizabeth Ann 25	22 June 1898	(4) 2/40
Parker Wm	Davis Elizabeth	23 Nov 1820	(6)
Parks George 51	Linthicum Sarah Catharine 25	4 Sept 1889	(4) 2/26
Parks George P 24	Simpson Ida May 20	22 Oct 1890	(4) 2/28
Parmer E	Leatherman J L	2 Oct 1851	(6)
Parmer Eleanor	Leatherman J L	2 Oct 1850	(5)
Parmer J T	Leatherman N J	4 Dec 1850	(5)
Parrell Mary Ann 23	Miller Jeremiah 23	28 Nov 1872	(4) 2/4
Parreot Joseph	Vandiver Hannah	17 Oct 1822	(5)

Name #1	Name #2	Date	Source
Parrill Charles Albert 20	Piles Ellie Margaret 16	20 Apr 1895	(4) 2/35
Parrill Hannah M 19	Baker Jacob V 28	12 Apr 1870	(4) 2/1
Parrill Hugh	Cundiff Lucy	15 Oct 1833	(6)
Parrill John Columbus 38	Carder Sarah Emily 39	4 Sept 1884	(4) 2/19
Parrill John Columbus 28	Hott Matilda Jane 23	24 Nov 1873	(4) 2/5
Parrill Joseph Henry 21	Baker Marg Luc Rosetta L 18	17 Aug 1893	(4) 2/33
Parrill Mary Elizabeth 23	Fediwick John 24	25 Mar 1870	(4) 2/1
Parrill William 19	Moreland Sadie Jane 19	21 Mar 1897	(40 2/38
Parrill William	Ravenscraft Jane	12 Feb 1828	(6)
Parris Adelia	Rafter Jas A	17 May 1849	(6)
Parris Elmira	Brant John G	27 Aug 1852	(6)
Parris Elmira	Michael Joseph	8 Dec 1852	(5)
Parrish Mary 54	Baker Aaron Levi 68	9 Sept 1879	(4) 2/13
Parrot Dennis	Price Louisa	5 Oct 1824	(6)
Parrot James M	Vandiver Hannah	17 Oct 1822	(6)
Parrot Marg	Lynch Sam	17 Mar 1818	(6)
Parrott Dennis M	Price Louisa	*4 Oct 1824	(4) 3/45
Parrott Margaret	Lynch Sam	7 Mar 1818	(5)
Parson Isaac	McCartney R	1 June 1820	(5)
Parsons Adam H 39	Ketterman Barbara A 27	15 Feb 1866	(4) 1/2
Parsons Ann Jemima 32	Vanmeter Solomon 34	31 Dec 1867	(4) 1/6
Parsons David	Mullady Milly	*11 Jan 1827	(4) 3/3
Parsons Edgar Elwood 24	Shannon Hannah Isabel 22	4 May 1886	(4) 2/21
Parsons Edith 33	Waddle Julius Samuel 37	3 June 1891	(4) 2/29
Parsons Francie Curlette 20	Shannon William Andrew 23	27 Nov 1884	(4) 2/20
Parsons Garrett Williams 26	Covell Mary Avery 26	12 Nov 1878	(4) 2/12
Parsons Isaac	McCartney R	1 June 1820	(6)
Parsons Isaac 28	Waddle Emma C 23	12 Nov 1867	(4) 1/5
Parsons James Donaldson 27	Pancake Sarah Maria 27	19 Apr 1871	(4) 2/2
Parsons James G	Curlett Mary	*22 Mar 1825	(4) 3/25
Parsons M C	Bowen Chas G	7 Feb 1853	(6)
Parsons Marshall J 30	Long Mary Christena 22	16 Oct 1878	(4) 2/12
Parsons Mary Catharine 22	Harmison Malcolm Gerstell 24	4 Feb 1891	(4) 2/29
Parsons Mary Susan 23	Pancake Joseph A 26	30 Mar 1870	(4) 2/1
Parsons Parthena	Pancake John McNeil	*13 Feb 1826	(4) 3/9
Paskel M L 29	Hammock B C 26	19 Oct 1868	(4) 1/7
Patch Synthy A	Berry Thomas	13 Nov 1823	(5)
Patengall Mary	Fout Wm	8 May 1832	(6)
Patterson ? 23	Sirbaugh Lucy Virginia 19	15 Nov 1883	(4) 2/18
Patterson Alcinda Ann 22	Carter Jasper Newton 25	11 June 1877	(4) 2/10
Patterson Alverda Baine 24	Sanders Richard Frampton 31	16 Sept 1891	(4) 2/29
Patterson Charles Randolph 50	Alderton Martha Jane 40	5 Sept 1895	(4) 2/36
Patterson Charles 25	Kidwell ? 25	8 Mar 1860	(10)
Patterson Frances Howard 19	Hott Silas Lemuel 32	11 Aug 1878	(4) 2/11
Patterson I H F 38	Burket Mary V 24	7 Dec 1868	(4) 1/7
Patterson Ida Lee 25	Pownall H Harris 22	16 Sept 1891	(4) 2/29
Patterson John 54	Smith Margaret 30	27 Jan 1874	(4) 2/5
Patterson Marian Fernadez 23	Carder Elias Edward 35	31 May 1893	(4) 2/32
Patterson Robert H	Stone Maria	9 May 1839	(1) 16 May 1839
Patterson Samuel	McBride Nancy	*24 Nov 1825	(4) 3/71
Patterson Sarah Ellen 22	Pownall Alonzo Napolen 23	29 Oct 1884	(4) 2/20
Patterson Thomas Ezra 21	Mitchel Ella Bell 20	9 Jan 1890	(4) 2/27

Name #1	Name #2	Date	Source
Patterson Wm E 21	Montgomery Bettie 19	1 July 1892	(4) 2/31
Patterson Zilla Anne 21	Hawkins George C 25	11 Nov 1891	(4) 2/30
Pattie Champ W 30	Harper Nancy M 21	20 Oct 1869	(4) 2/1
Patton Rebecca	Hartman Phil	15 Mar 1828	(6)
Paugh Amanda	Thrush Cornelius	4 July 1859	(6)
Paugh Anna Saville	Thrush Cornelius	4 July 1859	(10)
Paugh Catherine	Sollars Andrew	5 Dec 1848	(6)
Paugh J B	Howard Eveline	19 Sept 1839	(6)
Paugh M	Kitzmiller Lewis	20 Jan 1831	(6)
Paugh Michael	Newman Lucindas	13 May 1827	(5)
Payne Ellen B 19	Boher Richard Singleton 25	27 Sept 1887	(4) 2/24
Payne Fanny Belle 21	Hott David Aaron 24	26 Dec 1894	(4) 2/35
Payne James Edward 23	Messick Minnie Bell 16	11 Dec 1890	(4) 2/28
Payne Nettie Catherine 21	Haines John L 26	13 Dec 1893	(4) 2/33
Payne Travis Fenton 25	Gulick Ivy May 23	23 Sept 1896	(4) 2/37
Peacemaker Alfred P 27	McMannas Catherine L 22	28 Dec 1865	(4) 1/2
Peacemaker Sarah E 31	Clark Sampson B 55	31 Oct 1865	(4) 1/1
Pease John W 28	Hook Laura Virginia 21	9 Nov 1886	(4) 2/22
Peasmaker Isaac Newton 35	Bennett Lucy Maria 28	10 Sept 1885	(4) 2/21
Peasmaker Isaac Newton 43	Lofton Mary Elizabeth 17	10 May 1893	(4) 2/32
Peasmaker Lucy 19	Spurling James 21	20 Dec 1888	(4) 2/26
Peasmaker Susan Frances 32	Haines George M 44	24 Nov 1892	(4) 2/31
Peatt Rachael	Bowman George	*13 Mar 1827	(4) 3/17
Peatt Rachel	Bowman George	15 Mar 1827	(6)
Peer Catharine 30	Poland Isaac 28	19 Oct 1893	(4) 2/33
Peer Charles Tilden 23	Shelly Ellie Virginia 17	29 Aug 1900	(4) 2/43
Peer Elmore Roy 19	Kline Dora 18	22 May 1899	(4) 2/41
Peer Hampton Wesley 22	Haus Sarah Jane 19	12 Sept 1865	(4) 1/1
Peer Herriet 22	Kline John Jr 26	15 Sept 1868	(4) 1/7
Peer James Harrison 25	Lambert Rebecca Wiltmuth 21	7 July 1875	(4) 2/7
Peer Mary Catharine 21	Haines Theodore Bailey 28	21 Mar 1900	(4) 2/42
Peer Mary Lee 20	Bucklew Silas 22	7 Feb 1885	(4) 2/20
Peer Sarah Elizabeth 19	French John William 21	14 Oct 1873	(4) 2/5
Pennington Anna Lee 24	Frank Martin C 23	6 Apr 1897	(4) 2/39
Pennington Elizabeth E 41	Hix John William 30	21 Jan 1884	(4) 2/19
Pennington Frances Mary 17	Funk Andrew Jackson 21	5 Sept 1883	(4) 2/18
Pennington Isaac J 38	Arnold Louisa J 22	10 Jan 1859	(10)
Pennington James	Milslagle Hannah	*14 May 1825	(4) 3/37
Pennington Janie 25	Arnold Albert Smith 30	25 Dec 1895	(4) 2/36
Pennington Jas Franklin 25	Pennington Phoebe Elizabeth 31	16 Aug 1890	(4) 2/28
Pennington Laura Belle 19	Braithwaite Frances Marion 24	18 Apr 1878	(4) 2/11
Pennington Lydia Ann 19	Spaid Tilberry Miles 25	1 Oct 1885	(4) 2/21
Pennington Mary S 24	Pennington Philip M 27	19 Dec 1895	(4) 2/36
Pennington Mary C	Ridgeway William G	25 Dec 1860	(8)
Pennington Norman F 18	B? Elizabeth Adelphia 18	29 Aug 1900	(4) 2/43
Pennington Philip M 27	Pennington Mary S 24	19 Dec 1895	(4) 2/36
Pennington Phoebe Elizabeth 31	Pennington Jas Franklin 25	16 Aug 1890	(4) 2/28
Pennington Saml J 31	Michael Margaret 26	4 Feb 1868	(4) 1/6
Pennington Sarah Jane 21	Brill Elias A 23	13 Nov 1890	(4) 2/28
Pennington William Josephus 25	Ashton Sidney A 20	18 June 1885	(4) 2/20
Pennybaker Mary 32	Shafer David 56	20 Aug 1876	(4) 2/8
Pepper Amanda E 16	Shanholtzer Basil W 21	15 Feb 1872	(4) 2/3

Name #1	Name #2	Date	Source
Pepper Caroline Matilda 45	Buzzard William Grant 57	21 Oct 1892	(4) 2/31
Pepper Charles Mason 34	Pugh Virginia M 22	16 Feb 1897	(4) 2/38
Pepper Frances Emily 29	Carter Calvin Lycurgus 37	11 Oct 1893	(4) 2/33
Pepper Frederick	Slocum Deborah	*13 Jan 1827	(4) 3/5
Pepper Hannah Catharine 40	Deerdurf Benjamin 50	18 Oct 1876	(4) 2/9
Pepper Hattie Jane 23	Frye Robert Lee 28	7 Sept 1892	(4) 2/31
Pepper Henry Dye 24	Oats Retta Alice 19	28 June 1899	(4) 2/41
Pepper Ida Olivancy 27	Shanholtz Daniel Arnold 26	8 Feb 1898	(4) 2/40
Pepper James Anthony 27	Heare Martha Abigail 20	14 Mar 1867	(4) 1/5
Pepper John William 49	Ganoe Rebecca Elizabeth 21	30 Apr 1885	(4) 2/20
Pepper Joseph F 24	Pugh Lucy M 19	27 Aug 1873	(4) 2/4
Pepper Maggie Catherine 19	Wolfe John Sylvester 19	27 Dec 1881	(4) 2/17
Pepper Martha V 28	Pugh Joseph A 30	26 Aug 1873	(4) 2/4
Pepper Mary J	Tharp John 24	27 Oct 1859	(10)
Pepper Mary Jane 24	Spaid ? 25	29 Dec 1859	(10)
Pepper Nancy Jane	Spaid Francis M	5 Jan 1860	(1) 13 Jan 1860
Pepper William H 43	Williams Annie C 40	21 Nov 1882	(4) 2/17
Peppers Juliann	McCauley George	*20 Aug 1827	(4) 3/42
Peppers Sophiah	Carter Robert	*6 June 1825	(4) 3/40
Perkins Jas E	Dawson Avy	14 Apr 1842	(6)
Perrill Edward Ashby 21	Lambert Sallie Ann 23	5 Feb 1883	(4) 2/18
Perrill Isaac Perry 39	Deleplane Mary 22	29 July 1866	(4) 1/3
Perry Charles	Henderson Sarah	27 Mar 1838	(1) 14 Apr 1838
Peter Alice 28	Washington David Bell 30	20 Nov 1889	(4) 1/40
Peter Rachel 19	Loy James William 27	9 Nov 1867	(4) 1/5
Peters ? R 20	Robey Andrew J 23	Nov 1857	(10)
Peters Benjamin F 23	Bruce Minnie B 23	17 July 1886	(4) 1/40
Peters Dora Bell 26	Saville George William 21	3 Apr 1894	(4) 2/34
Peters Emma Florence 19	Ruckman Benjamin 20	7 Nov 1893	(4) 2/33
Peters Harrison 21	Swisher Catharine 30	22 Aug 1871	(4) 2/3
Peters James William 19	Hott Mary Anna 22	31 Oct 1876	(4) 2/9
Peters Lydia	Friddle John	*11 Jan 1827	(4) 3/4
Peters Lydia Ann 24	Wolford ? 35	1859	(10)
Peters Sarah C 17	Ruckman Joseph 23	16 Dec 1854	(10)
Peters Susan Virginia 26	Shank George Washington 22	3 Jan 1880	(4) 2/14
Peterson Andrew Jackson 24	Johnson Anne 21	18 Dec 1889	(4) 1/41
Peterson Andrew 33	Johnson Bessie 22	10 May 1899	(4) 1/42
Peterson Sarah F 22	Combs Jno M 21	22 Feb 1866	(4) 1/2
Pettit Daniel	McKee Mary Margaret	3 Aug 1852	(2) 7 Oct 1852
Pettit Sarah	Everitt Enos	*19 Apr 1824	(4) 3/23
Pickering Hiram	Posey Sarah Ann	*17 Mar 1828	(4) 3/7
Pickering John L	Boley M Ellen 19	7 May 1873	(4) 2/4
Pierce Joseph Wilson 48	Brill Miranda Catharine 38	3 Sept 1885	(4) 2/21
Pifer Barbara 50	Hannum Madison F 65	19 Nov 1895	(4) 2/36
Piles Benjamin 18	Hott Catharine A 21	24 Mar 1896	(4) 2/37
Piles Benjamin Franklin 24	Starkey Catharine J 18	6 Dec 1888	(4) 2/25
Piles Elizabeth	Williams Jno H	*25 Feb 1824	(4) 3/12
Piles Ellie Margaret 16	Parrill Charles Albert 20	20 Apr 1895	(4) 2/35
Piles Fannie J 21	Lee Jesse Washington 21	22 Sept 1898	(4) 2/40
Piles Hannah 39	Kline H Lee 33	11 Apr 1893	(4) 2/32
Piles John	Roberson Jane	14 Jan 1855	(10)
Piles John H	Ruckman Elizabeth	*13 Mar 1824	(4) 3/16

Name #1	Name #2	Date	Source
Piles John William 24	Smith Viola S 18	27 Mar 1899	(40 2/41
Piles Lucille Delma 17	Saville Henry Imboden 23	25 Feb 1886	(4) 2/22
Piles Luther Branson 24	Simmons Matilda Elizabeth 17	2 Aug 1883	(4) 2/18
Piles Rachel Bell 20	Grapes George Walker 29	12 Jan 1887	(4) 2/23
Piles Samuel Jefferson 21	Haines Mary Parker 23	30 Dec 1884	(4) 2/20
Piles Sarah Malinda Alice 18	Smith John William 21	20 Dec 1888	(4) 2/25
Piles Susan F 20	Malick Edward Seymour 23	1 June 1892	(4) 2/31
Plumb John	Fitzergerald Nancy	10 Dec 1826	(5)
Plumb John	Fitzgerald Nancy	*22 Nov 1826	(4) 3/41
Plummer Henry 40	Young Harriet J 26	4 Apr 1868	(4) 1/6
Plush Wm 23	Miers Mary J 48	17 Oct 1865	(4) 1/1
Poland Abner Newton 23	Haines Amanda Milissa 23	16 Oct 1881	(4) 2/16
Poland Aida Louise Elizabeth 17	Iser George Walter 21	14 Nov 1894	(4) 2/35
Poland Amos 22	Marshall Priscilla Barbra 19	30 Jan 1867	(4) 1/4
Poland Amos 75	Brelsford Mary Elizabeth 23	4 Dec 1894	(4) 2/35
Poland Ann Rebecca Susan 23	Craigg Robert Lee 23	7 July 1897	(4) 2/39
Poland Anne Lee Bertie 17	Boyce Noah 23	26 Apr 1898	(4) 2/40
Poland Belle Abigail 18	Haines Jasper Franklin P 28	22 Nov 1881	(4) 2/16
Poland Catherine Ann 21	Park George 28	3 Oct 1867	(4) 1/5
Poland Cedena Catharine 21	Artz James Peter 28	6 Oct 1873	(4) 2/4
Poland Charles Lupton 25	Saville Sarah Frances 25	10 Jan 1897	(4) 2/38
Poland Chloe Jane 17	Shawen Thomas Anthony 20	6 Mar 1889	(4) 2/26
Poland Clerza Ann 20	Loy William Henry 30	18 Dec 1889	(4) 2/27
Poland David Fairfax 34	Haines Anna Jane 33	24 May 1900	(4) 2/42
Poland David Granville 21	Alverson Mary Frances 28	18 July 1881	(4) 2/16
Poland Edward T 23	Hott Mary Elizabeth 21	26 July 1871	(4) 2/3
Poland Elizabeth Marg Susan 16	Combs William Ashby 23	1 Nov 1888	(4) 2/25
Poland Elizabeth Jane 19	Brown Thomas Jefferson 25	4 Aug 1886	(4) 2/21
Poland Emsey Abigail 20	Heishman Angus Wood 32	2 Sept 1886	(4) 2/22
Poland Franklin M 21	Combs Mandy Virginia 18	22 Aug 1878	(4) 2/11
Poland Hannah Susan 28	Iliff Elias Harrison 40	26 May 1874	(4) 2/6
Poland Isaac	Love E		(1) 20 Oct 1838
Poland Isaac 28	Peer Catharine 30	19 Oct 1893	(4) 2/33
Poland Isaac Jackson 29	Wolfe Sarah Ann 27	30 Jan 1877	(4) 2/9
Poland Ivy Melissa 20	Park William Early 23	23 Jan 1887	(4) 2/23
Poland James Henry 26	Rosebrough Sarah Elizabeth 19	23 Dec 1887	(4) 2/24
Poland James Wesley 22	Haines Virginia Isadore 20	26 Dec 1876	(4) 2/9
Poland Jasper Newton 39	Lee Emma Jane 24	19 Apr 1893	(4) 2/32
Poland Jeremiah 23	Lewis Harriete Elizabeth 23	17 Dec 1878	(4) 2/12
Poland John	Carder Mary	*9 Mar 1825	(4) 3/20
Poland John 49	Oats Malinda Ann 22	20 Oct 1873	(4) 2/5
Poland John W 23	Loy Louisa Jane 17	16 Sept 1866	(4) 1/3
Poland Joseph S 25	Haines Susan 25	27 Feb 1866	(4) 1/3
Poland Laura Samantha 19	Richmond Jesse Sylvester 21	21 Nov 1900	(4) 2/43
Poland Lulu Ellen 21	Martin Blakeney Hollis 28	18 May 1898	(4) 2/40
Poland M A	Bauer Peter	13 Apr 1859	(6)
Poland Margaret Ellen 19	Shawen Charles Tilden 21	27 July 1898	(4) 2/40
Poland Martha Ellen 28	Park Alexander 27	5 Apr 1881	(4) 2/15
Poland Martha Jane 21	Heare Jacob W 34	25 Sept 1881	(4) 2/16
Poland Mary	Mullineaux Israel	11 Jan 1821	(6)
Poland Mary C 24	Roberson Amos 34	1 Nov 1866	(4) 1/4
Poland Mary J 26	Millèr W H 23	18 Nov 1868	(4) 1/7

Name #1	Name #2	Date	Source
Poland Peter Duval 23	Tharp Hannah Catherine 19	10 Mar 1880	(4) 2/14
Poland Rebecca 28	Linthicum Benjamin Franklin 33	26 Oct 1881	(4) 2/16
Poland Rebecca Mrs 32	Wolf James Henry 39	21 Nov 1893	(4) 2/33
Poland Richard Henry 48	Ruckman Mary 43	5 July 1881	(4) 2/16
Poland Ruben Franklin 21	Combs Emma Jane 23	18 Mar 1897	(4) 2/38
Poland Sallie Catharine 28	Hott Charles Tilden 24	26 Sept 1900	(4) 2/43
Poland Sarah Ann 40	Loy James William 49	18 Sept 1889	(4) 2/27
Poland William Amos 18	Saville Malinda Margaret 18	4 Feb 1886	(4) 2/21
Poland Zulema Catharine I 20	Brown George Washington 23	1 Nov 1888	(4) 2/25
Poling Daniel 26	White Catharine 20	31 Aug 1892	(4) 2/31
Poling Dora Susan 23	Cornwell George Benjamin 25	11 Nov 1896	(4) 2/38
Poling Eva Virginia 24	Snarr Oliver David 27	1 June 1897	(4) 2/39
Poling George Washington 27	Loy Leah Martha 18	5 Nov 1889	(4) 2/27
Poling Isabella 21	Davis William F 30	30 Mar 1869	(4) 1/38
Poling James Grover 37	Smith Louisa Alice 21	11 Sept 1896	(4) 2/37
Poling James Wm 63	Henderson Virna 40	29 Nov 1899	(4) 2/42
Poling Joseph M 21	Linthicum Margaret M 22	24 June 1872	(4) 2/3
Poling M A	Gannon Strother	3 Apr 1845	(6)
Poling Mitchell Felix 37	Stickley Elizabeth Ann 42	10 Feb 1878	(4) 2/11
Poling Susie A 29	Davis Granvill Wilson 27	3 Apr 1872	(4) 2/3
Pollock Robert Sherrard 33	Grace Emma Virginia 20	11 Nov 1885	(4) 2/21
Polon John	Elifritz Phebe	23 Sept 1830	(6)
Polon Joseph	Wheeler Mary	19 Feb 1835	(5)
Pomeroy Johnson	Johnson Susan	12 June 1860	(10)
Ponifirt Sam	Moreland Eliza	23 June 1840	(6)
Pool Fannie M 23	Oats William Edward 24	29 Dec 1896	(4) 2/38
Pool Joseph Asbury 27	Kimble Clara Eugenie 18	7 Jan 1879	(4) 2/12
Pool Lloyd Logan 24	Kimble Alice Eveline 17	7 Jan 1879	(4) 2/12
Pool Louisa Ella 22	Eskridge Sanford Virgil 20	3 Jun 1897	(4) 2/39
Pool Lyda Hennietta 28	Kerns Frank Perry 27	27 Aug 1889	(4) 2/26
Pool Mary E 21	Markwood George H 22	8 Feb 1866	(4) 1/2
Pool Millie	Welch Thomas	21 Feb 1822	(6)
Pool S A	Markwood John	3 Mar 1850	(6)
Pool Sarah A	Markwood John	4 Mar 1846	(5)
Pool Willie 28	Mauzey William Howard 25	2 Aug 1898	(4) 2/40
Porter Margaret 25	McNeal Benjamin S 57	26 Sept 1865	(4) 1/1
Porter Sarah E 17	Pownell James I 22	12 Oct 1870	(4) 2/2
Portmess John Franklin 26	Milleson Sarah Virg Bell 22	15 Apr 1886	(4) 2/22
Portmess Zoe Etta 19	Ginevan David Jacob 26	12 Jan 1899	(4) 2/41
Posey Sarah Ann	Pickering Hiram	*17 Mar 1828	(4) 3/7
Poston Ashford	McVicker Mary	*19 Nov 1827	(4) 3/55
Poston Delila	Cheshire Samuel	*29 Nov 1824	(4) 3/53
Poston John	McVicker Isabella	*31 Jan 1825	(4) 3/12
Potter Harley E 26	Rodruck Maggie Virginia 19	3 Aug 1881	(4) 2/16
Potts Elizabeth	Mills John	12 Oct 1839	(6)
Potts Elizabeth	Mills John	12 Oct 1840	(5)
Powel Thomas Carskadden 25	Mcloy Jane Susan 19	14 Nov 1865	(4) 1/1
Powell Amanda Virginia 23	Williams Charles McKeever 22	19 Dec 1876	(4) 2/9
Powell Benjamin James 31	Flether Susan Ann 21	9 Apr 1874	(4) 2/6
Powell Clar	Snowden Edgar Jr		(1) 8 May 1857
Powell David Sylvester 28	Milleson Martha 21	20 Feb 1867	(4) 1/4
Powell Elizabeth 16	Barrett Samuel Worthington 23	6 Mar 1877	(4) 2/9

Name #1	Name #2	Date	Source
Powell Elizabeth	Mauzy John	*11 Jan 1825	(4) 3/3
Powell Ettie 22	Dicken Amos Clay 25	17 Aug 1898	(4) 2/40
Powell Henry 23	Richardson Elizabeth 26	3 Jan 1866	(4) 1/2
Powell Isab	Johnson John	30 Apr 1843	(6)
Powell James B	Hays Annie	26 Nov 1845	(5)
Powell James Julius Walter 20	Allender Mary Ellen 18	26 May 1881	(4) 2/16
Powell James L	Jenkins Mary	*13 May 1824	(4) 3/28
Powell Jas H 52	Saville Sarah Ann 27	17 Apr 1866	(4) 1/3
Powell Joanna W	Powell Thornton F	*22 Sept 1827	(4) 3/47
Powell John	Edwards Ann	*5 Apr 1824	(4) 3/21
Powell John	McDonald Susana	*16 Aug 1828	(4) 3/20
Powell John Vernon 22	Slonaker Mary Jane 21	26 Nov 1878	(4) 2/12
Powell Louisa M 23	Haines John Sensery 25	14 Nov 1878	(4) 2/12
Powell Lucinda M 25	Eaton Elijah E 23	29 Mar 1883	(4) 2/18
Powell Mary Alverty 19	Barrett William Scott 17	17 Oct 1876	(4) 2/9
Powell Minnie May 24	Smith Hunter Homer 22	28 Oct 1896	(4) 2/37
Powell Mollie J 17	Myers Herman A 24	28 Oct 1880	(4) 2/14
Powell Nora May 27	Haines Charles William 26	28 May 1900	(4) 2/42
Powell Rebecca Frances 27	Williamson John 31	31 Mar 1874	(4) 2/6
Powell Samuel Dade 60	Saville Belle J 41	17 Oct 1900	(4) 2/43
Powell Susan E 26	Harris Joseph R 21	10 Aug 1876	(4) 2/8
Powell Susan M 19	Buzzard Jasper Newton 24	28 Feb 1867	(4) 1/4
Powell Thornton F	Powell Joanna W	*22 Sept 1827	(4) 3/47
Powell Will Henry 34	Pugh Mary Ella 24	31 Mar 1870	(4) 2/1
Powelson Alvin Judson 26	Lewis Mary Francis 20	6 Feb 1901	(4) 2/44
Powelson Ann E 19	Copelen Moses R 21	11 Dec 1866	(4) 1/4
Powelson Benjamin W 28	Cupp Hannah Elizabeth 35	7 May 1879	(4) 2/13
Powelson Benjamin W 24	Wolford Sarah Elizabeth 19	9 July 1873	(4) 2/4
Powelson Eliza	Heare John L	*20 Oct 1828	(4) 3/33
Powelson Isaiah Francis 25	Shanholtzer Margaret Bell 19	10 Dec 1878	(4) 2/12
Powelson John W 24	Powelson Mary 24	17 July 1868	(4) 1/6
Powelson Mary 24	Powelson John W 24	17 July 1868	(4) 1/6
Powelson Mary A 20	Doman Wm H F 30	21 Oct 1868	(4) 1/7
Powelson Mary Ann	Heare Mathew	*12 Nov 1825	(4) 3/69
Powelson Philip James 27	Wolford Lucy Frances 24	16 June 1874	(4) 2/6
Powelson Robert	Barnes Delilah	*13 June 1825	(4) 3/44
Powelson Rosannah	Ely Benjamin	*29 Mar 1828	(4) 3/8
Powelson William H R 24	Pownell Leacy Ann 18	9 Mar 1859	(10)
Power Edith Virginia 18	Stump Samuel D 22	8 Apr 1888	(4) 2/24
Power Joseph Thompson 21	Wills Sallie 22	28 Mar 1893	(4) 2/32
Power Lillie Florance 18	Hiett Samuel Marion 28	25 May 1893	(4) 2/32
Powers Nora 18	Sowers James Rufus 24	1 Nov 1894	(4) 2/35
Powes Peter	Drace Nancy	30 Dec 1823	(5)
Powleson R J	Welch T A	14 Aug 1845	(6)
Pownal Jasper R	Cheshire Margaret	9 Mar 1859	(10)
Pownal Mary 23	Carder Sanford 30	20 Oct 1859	(10)
Pownall Alonzo Napolen 23	Patterson Sarah Ellen 22	29 Oct 1884	(4) 2/20
Pownall Charles Wilbert 21	Haines Virginia Belle 23	7 Sept 1892	(4) 2/31
Pownall Dora Edith 26	Pultz Charles Michael 37	29 Nov 1893	(4) 2/33
Pownall Elizabeth Jane 23	Carder Benjamin Franklin 31	9 Nov 1880	(4) 2/15
Pownall H Harris 22	Patterson Ida Lee 25	16 Sept 1891	(4) 2/29
Pownall Joann 24	Cowgill W B 20	26 Nov 1868	(4) 1/7

Name #1	Name #2	Date	Source
Pownall John Albert 23	Lewis Parthenia Alice 23	10 Feb 1886	(4) 2/21
Pownall John Daniel 32	Taylor Ella Lee 26	13 Feb 1889	(4) 2/26
Pownall John J	Martin Sarah	*8 Apr 1828	(4) 3/10
Pownall Margaret Ellen 19	Doughtery William H 22	22 Nov 1896	(4) 2/38
Pownall Margaret A 20	Lewis David Harris 24	11 Feb 1885	(4) 2/20
Pownall Maria Edith 26	Rannells Samuel Fahs 31	21 Oct 1896	(4) 2/37
Pownall Martha Elizabeth 22	McDonald Jacob 32	23 Dec 1875	(4) 2/8
Pownall Mary Ann 26	Rannells Charles lee 30	24 May 1893	(4) 2/32
Pownall Melissa Josephine 20	McDonald Thomas Henry 23	15 Dec 1870	(4) 2/2
Pownall Richard Winifield 30	Everett Hester Elizabeth 24	11 Mar 1896	(4) 2/37
Pownall Robert Snyder 29	Rinker Mary Magdalene 19	1 Aug 1893	(4) 2/32
Pownall Robt J 20	Click Susan 22	3 Aug 1868	(4) 1/7
Pownall Rosa Virginia 19	Beatty Isaac 22	9 Feb 1887	(4) 2/23
Pownall Thomas J 26	Scanlan Mary 30	16 Apr 1890	(4) 2/27
Pownall William Marshall 24	Adams Catharine Elizabeth 21	4 Nov 1896	(4) 2/38
Pownell David G 23	Combs Matilda 20	10 Jan 1866	(4) 1/2
Pownell F M 27	Baker Virginia C 24	26 Oct 1868	(4) 1/7
Pownell Florence Woodrow 26	Wolford John Martin 30	16 Jan 1898	(4) 2/40
Pownell James I 22	Porter Sarah E 17	12 Oct 1870	(4) 2/2
Pownell James Marion 24	Cool Eliza Jane 21	15 Dec 1869	(4) 2/1
Pownell Jasper R 38	Gulick Nancy E 22	30 Nov 1865	(4) 1/1
Pownell John Christopher 25	Corbin Mrs Martha Eliza 25	7 Apr 1881	(4) 2/15
Pownell Leacy Ann 18	Powelson William H R 24	9 Mar 1859	(10)
Pownell William A 28	Seeman Hannah Frances 19	15 May 1870	(4) 2/1
Price A H	Miller Elizabeth	16 Apr 1818	(6)
Price Elmira	Keller Charles	*28 Jan 1826	(4) 3/3
Price Louisa	Parrot Dennis	5 Oct 1824	(6)
Price Louisa	Parrott Dennis M	*4 Oct 1824	(4) 3/45
Prickett Levi	Baker Eleanor	*22 Oct 1824	(4) 3/48
Prior Fanny Agnes 29	Kerns Thomas Good 41	3 Apr 1897	(4) 2/35
Probasco Elijah	Probasco Margaret	*16 Dec 1828	(4) 3/48
Probasco Jacob	Frazier Eleanor	*7 July 1825	(4) 3/47
Probasco Margaret	Probasco Elijah	*16 Dec 1828	(4) 3/48
Probst Anna	Kester Elias	17 Dec 1831	(6)
Proctor Clara A 23	Dorsey Ashby Wise 22	13 May 1894	(4) 2/34
Proctor James Monroe 41	Short Catharine Ann 40	18 Oct 1897	(4) 2/39
Proctor Rebecca Frances 18	Kidwell Randolph Hawkins 26	22 May 1877	(4) 2/10
Promfirt Samuel	Moreland Eliza	23 June 1841	(5)
Prye John	Cundiff Catherine Nash	*19 Dec 1825	(4) 3/75
Pugh Albert David 21	Eaton Margaret Laura 20	24 Dec 1891	(4) 2/30
Pugh Amos Luther 24	Garvins Allie Ellen 21	*4 Apr 1877	(4) 2/10
Pugh Ann	Day William	14 June 1824	(4) 3/34
Pugh Artie Virginia 32	Shaffer Samuel Lloyd 37	27 Dec 1899	(4) 2/42
Pugh Azza M 28	Gladstone John E 33	17 Oct 1888	(4) 2/25
Pugh Benjamin 52	Spade Nancy Jane 37	15 June 1869	(4) 2/1
Pugh Charles Newton 24	Hite Lucy Annie Bell 16	18 Nov 1886	(4) 2/22
Pugh David William 30	Taylor Sarah Jane 23	*4 Sept 1879	(4) 2/13
Pugh Derias	Chriswell Elizabeth		(1) 30 May 1839
Pugh Dora C 24	Rinker Charles Frederick 25	25 Oct 1883	(4) 2/18
Pugh Edgar Lewis 19	Oats Annie Lee 18	21 Nov 1894	(4) 2/35
Pugh Effie May 24	Hilbrant John 34	15 May 1894	(4) 2/34
Pugh Ephenia 40	Monroe Alexander 45	26 Jan 1869	(4) 1/38

Name #1	Name #2	Date	Source
Pugh Evan Preston 23	Loy Amanda Jerusha 20	21 Dec 1876	(4) 2/9
Pugh Ezra	Caudy Saray	*13 June 1826	(4) 3/26
Pugh Ezra	McBride Lydia	*15 Jan 1827	(4) 3/7
Pugh Fannie C 17	Scaffenaker Henry B 21	18 Dec 1884	(4) 2/10
Pugh George 53	Anderson Melissa J 29	22 Oct 1896	(4) 2/37
Pugh Hannah	Horn George Jun	27 Dec 1786	(3)
Pugh Hannibal	McNeil Sydney	*29 July 1828	(4) 3/18
Pugh Ida Z 24	Blaker James Fenton 27	16 Oct 1873	(4) 2/5
Pugh James B	Howard Eveline	19 Sept 1840	(5)
Pugh Jesse Webster 20	Berkheimer Lillie Elizabeth 17	30 Aug 1877	(4) 2/10
Pugh John	Guard Sarah	*16 Aug 1824	(4) 3/41
Pugh John	Lockhart Elizabeth	*1 Jan 1825	(4) 3/1
Pugh John	Milleson Elizabeth	21 Feb 1860	(10)
Pugh John	Offord Sarah	*18 Feb 1828	(4) 3/5
Pugh John W 59	Nixon Rose Ida 28	19 Apr 1887	(4) 2/23
Pugh John Wesley 43	Rinker Maggie Elizabeth 28	21 Nov 1887	(4) 2/24
Pugh John Wesley 22	Taylor Caroline 21	9 Jan 1867	(4) 1/4
Pugh Jonathan	Offutt Ann	*9 June 1827	(4) 3/36
Pugh Jonathan L 51	Racey Harriet 51	10 Feb 1874	(4) 2/5
Pugh Joseph A 30	Pepper Martha V 28	26 Aug 1873	(4) 2/4
Pugh Lucy M 19	Pepper Joseph F 24	27 Aug 1873	(4) 2/4
Pugh Margaret	Monroe James	*8 Nov 1827	(4) 3/53
Pugh Margaret Catherine 23	Taylor George 32	16 Dec 1879	(4) 2/14
Pugh Margaret E 26	Monroe Alexander 47	21 Nov 1866	(4) 1/4
Pugh Marion Omer 24	Gill Martha A 24	7 Jan 1897	(4) 2/38
Pugh Martha A 21	Horner William Anderson 31	2 Jan 1901	(4) 2/43
Pugh Martha J B 21	Reed Edward 25	4 Oct 1870*	(4) 2/2
Pugh Martha Jane 22	Florey Newton Brown 23	27 Dec 1876	(4) 2/9
Pugh Mary Ella 24	Powell Will Henry 34	31 Mar 1870	(4) 2/1
Pugh Nancy Jane 30	Nixon Lemuel 46	1 Mar 1866	(4) 1/3
Pugh Robert James 34	Allen Susan Elizabeth 28	4 Oct 1876	(4) 2/9
Pugh Robert Offutt 28	Deaver Sarah Virginia 27	25 Nov 1880	(4) 2/15
Pugh Susan Howard 28	Russell William 32	10 Nov 1880	(4) 2/15
Pugh Virginia Ann 23	Urton Robert Y 22	7 Sept 1869	(4) 2/1
Pugh Virginia M 22	Pepper Charles Mason 34	16 Feb 1897	(4) 2/38
Pugh Walter Lee 22	Haines Susan 25	13 Jan 1897	(4) 2/38
Pugh Zachary Taylor 30	Brook Martha Amanda 22	28 Mar 1877	(4) 2/10
Pultz Albert Fahs 22	Bailey Cora Edith 16	11 May 1893	(4) 2/32
Pultz Charles Michael 37	Pownall Dora Edith 26	29 Nov 1893	(4) 2/33
Pultz John Walker 22	Trenton Mary Florence 19	3 Oct 1871	(4) 2/3
Pultz Leah Margaret 31	Godlove Joseph Rosser 36	9 Apr 1901	(4) 2/44
Pultz Lydia Margaret 22	King Benjamin Franklin 34	10 Feb 1885	(4) 2/20
Pultz Mary Ann 28	Shelly George Warfield 25	25 Feb 1879	(4) 2/12
Pultz Virginia May 21	Mauk Thomas William 24	19 Feb 1896	(4) 2/36
Pumory Ruth	Bosly Adam	13 Sept 1843	(5)
Purgit Edgar C 25	Berry Lessie C 22	26 May 1894	(4) 2/34
Purgit Grace Olive 18	High Cuthbert Elijah 28	24 Oct 1900	(4) 2/43
Purgit Mary Statton 17	Shoemaker Alonzo Tecumsey 19	19 Mar 1896	(4) 2/37
Purgit Minnie Bell 29	Racey Lee Allen 31	20 June 1900	(4) 2/43
Purgit Nashville Summerfield 22	Athey Rachel Virginia 21	10 Apr 1878	(4) 2/11
Purgit Rachael	Sulser Henry	*15 Aug 1825	(4) 3/51
Purgit Susan Jane 39	Kelley Hiram Nelson 52	14 June 1899	(4) 2/41

Name #1	Name #2	Date	Source
Purnel Samuel	Barnhouse L	2 Oct 1851	(6)
Purnel Samuel	Barnhouse Lavina	2 Oct 1850	(5)
Putman Jacob	Flick Magdalene	*24 Mar 1824	(4) 3/17
Pyles Mollie 21	Kidner Wm Franklin 20	1 Nov 1899	(4) 2/42
Quarles Joseph 24	Keys Maria 22	22 Apr 1891	(4) 1/41
Queen Dennis	Farlow Sina	19 Nov 1818	(6)
Queen Elizabeth	Fletcher Elijah	*30 Jan 1826	(4) 3/4
Queen Jane 22	Martin Benj F 22	16 Dec 1866	(4) 1/2
Queen John	Rankins Ellen R	2 Mar 1826	(5)
Queen Margaret Milissa 17	Daugherty Harvey Berry 26	24 Nov 1881	(4) 2/16
Queen Mary 25	Moreland George William 32	3 Sept 1867	(4) 1/5
Queen Stephen	Moreland Mary	*29 Jan 1827	(4) 3/10
Quinn Mary Belle 18	Fisher Z T 25	26 Mar 1867	(4) 1/5
Quisenberry Thomas A 28	Wirgman Emma Maria 29	22 Jan 1890	(4) 2/27
Race Elizabeth	Means Isaac	5 Oct 1826	(6)
Race Sally	Entler William	*3 June 1826	(4) 3/22
Racey Bertie 24	Thomas Orloff Dorsey 24	*28 Dec 1896	(4) 2/38
Racey Calvin Jackson 24	High Cora Sciota 22	21 Aug 1895	(4) 2/36
Racey Harriet 51	Pugh Jonathan L 51	10 Feb 1874	(4) 2/5
Racey John 37	Hamounis ? 28	13 Nov 1855	(10)
Racey John 53	Bumgarner Ellen 47	10 Feb 1870	(4) 2/1
Racey Lee Allen 31	Purgit Minnie Bell 29	20 June 1900	(4) 2/43
Racey Lewis 47	Slonaker Mary D 27	8 Feb 1866	(4) 1/2
Racey Mary J 22	Stevens Jas W 22	17 Feb 1868	(4) 1/6
Racey Olive Bell 19	Kibler Isaac Newton 30	25 May 1896	(4) 2/37
Racey Sarah Jane	Carier Isaac Everett 30	16 Dec 1873	(4) 2/5
Racy Lewis 26	Durst Margaret A 24	26 May 1880	(4) 2/14
Racy Thomas	Brill Diantha	12 Jan 1863	(8)
Rafter Jas A	Parris Adelia	17 May 1849	(6)
Raines Clara Bell 17	Seeders Jonathan Millard 27	12 June 1895	(4) 2/35
Raines Dannie Vanmeter 16	Zirk William Frank 21	23 Feb 1898	(4) 2/40
Raines George Thomas 22	White Sarah 23	9 Nov 1887	(4) 2/24
Raines Isaac Solomon 23	Simpson Martha E E 16	12 July 1893	(4) 2/32
Raines Isabel 18	Bobo George 35	22 Jan 1873	(4) 2/4
Raines Sarah 29	Emsley James Albert 36	30 May 1894	(4) 2/34
Ralston Val	Stullenbarger C	6 June 1847	(6)
Ranck James McNeil 23	Chesnut Charlotte Rebecca 25	17 Jan 1877	(4) 2/9
Randall Thomas	Stewart Priscella C	*24 June 1824	(4) 3/37
Randall Thomas	Stewart Priscilla	1 July 1824	(5)
Randalls Thos	Culp Ann	18 Nov 1830	(6)
Randle David	George Anna	*15 Nov 1824	(4) 3/52
Rankin Ruthy E	Wagoner Henry	23 June 1837	(1) 1 July 1837
Rankins Ellen R	Queen John	2 Mar 1826	(5)
Rannalls Elmira 28	Burkett Jno D 30	21 Sept 1868	(4) 1/7
Rannell Elizabeth	Leatherman Benjamin	9 Feb 1826	(5)
Rannell Elizabeth	Leatherman Benjamin	*6 Feb 1826	(4) 3/6
Rannells Charles lee 30	Pownall Mary Ann 26	24 May 1893	(4) 2/32
Rannells Florence Belle 27	Greenland Nathan 28	7 Feb 1881	(4) 2/15
Rannells John	Miller Kesiah	*12 Nov 1824	(4) 3/51
Rannells John William 31	Cross Elizabeth Susan 20	7 Apr 1881	(4) 2/15
Rannells Louisa Henrietta 19	Taylor Kirk Bride 33	13 Jan 1874	(4) 2/5
Rannells Mary	Wallace John	*3 Nov 1828	(4) 3/37

Name #1	Name #2	Date	Source
Rannells Samuel Fahs 31	Pownall Maria Edith 26	21 Oct 1896	(4) 2/37
Rannells William	Humes Nancy	*20 Sept 1824	(4) 3/44
Rannells William Edward 25	Taylor Addie Elizabeth 20	11 Jan 1899	(4) 2/41
Rase Catharine 18	Durst John L 26	23 Dec 1880	(4) 2/15
Ravencraft Levina	White John	30 Oct 1850	(5)
Ravenscraft Jane	Parrill William	12 Feb 1828	(5)
Ravenscraft Jas	Trenter S	30 Mar 1834	(6)
Ravenscraft Jno D	Culp M	18 Dec 1827	(6)
Ravenscraft John	Culp Maria	*17 Dec 1827	(4) 3/58
Ravenscraft Nancy	Dobbins Thomas	20 Sept 1839	(5)
Ravenscraft Nicholas	Moody Mary	2 Aug 1852	(5)
Ravenscroft John 24	Grayson Cornelia 18	28 Dec 1854	(10)
Ravenscroft N	Dobbins Thor	20 Sept 1838	(6)
Ravenscroft Nich	Moody M	24 Aug 1852	(6)
Ravenscroft Sarah	Dawson Wm	19 Sept 1837	(6)
Rawlines Susan	Shanks John	9 Sept 1823	(5)
Rawling James	Trenter M S	11 Sept 1850	(5)
Rawlings C	Blackburn John	18 Nov 1830	(6)
Rawlings Charles	Rinker N J	29 May 1850	(5)
Rawlings Charles	Walsh Mary	1823	(5)
Rawlings Chas	Rinker N J	29 May 1851	(6)
Rawlings Elizabeth	Miller Mich	19 Feb 1828	(6)
Rawlings Jas	Trenter M S	11 Sept 1851	(6)
Rawlings Julia Ann	Welch Benjamin	23 Aug 1818	(6)
Rawlings M A	Welch Thos S	22 Nov 1855	(6)
Rawlings Mary	Emmit Jas	19 Sept 1844	(6)
Rawlings Peter	Welsh Laurena	26 Sept 1822	(6)
Ray Mary Florence 26	Hannas John D 22	30 Apr 1892	(4) 2/31
Raymond Isabella 40	Woodworth Malcolm W 49	22 Sept 1881	(4) 2/16
Reanser Richard 25	Linaburg Mary C E 23	24 Nov 1870	(4) 2/2
Redman Barnet	Lett Stacy	4 Sept 1823	(5)
Redman Isaac	Lowry Betsy	23 Nov 1832	(5)
Redmond James Sanford 23	Allen Kitty 47	23 Sept 1880	(4) 1/40
Reed Anthony 24	Watkins Louisa V 17	21 Nov 1866	(4) 1/4
Reed Azariah Pugh 28	Wilson Esther Sophia 27	*20 Aug 1877	(4) 2/10
Reed Cora Maude 21	Stickley Rufus William 27	3 Feb 1897	(4) 2/38
Reed David Riley 22	Haines Ollie 19	27 May 1890	(4) 2/28
Reed Edward 25	Pugh Martha J B 21	4 Oct 1870*	(4) 2/2
Reed Edwin Summerfield 22	Chaney Alice Maria 24	25 Dec 1878	(4) 2/12
Reed Quinites H 20	Edwards Harriette E 35	15 Nov 1881	(4) 2/16
Reed Sarah	Newman Catesby	*3 Sept 1824	(4) 3/43
Reede Maria	Bruner George	*30 Apr 1827	(4) 3/31
Rees Jane	Parker James	28 Nov 1820	(6)
Reese Elenomy	Welch J G	19 Jan 1858	(6)
Reese Eliza	Herriott Ephraim	*10 Nov 1827	(4) 3/54
Reese Eliza	Herriott Ephraim	13 Nov 1827	(6)
Reese Frances	Tasker John	28 Apr 1842	(6)
Reese Hannah	Emmerson James	13 Sept 1827	(6)
Reese Hannah	Emmerson James	*12 Sept 1827	(4) 3/45
Reese Lydia	Rogers John	*20 Oct 1828	(4) 3/34
Reese Mary B	Pancake John M		(1) 14 Apr 1838
Reese Mary Elizabeth 33	Alkire Nimrod 51	5 Sept 1865	(4) 1/1

Name #1	Name #2	Date	Source
Reese Thomas	Umpstott Catherine	*26 Dec 1827	(4) 3/61
Reese Wm D	Johnson H A	4 Sept 1845	(6)
Reese, Ele'r	Flannigan John	4 June 1835	(6)
Reid Cordelia Theresa 26	Farmer George William 30	*19 Feb 1877	(4) 2/9
Reid Frances V A 29	Frank Andrew J 37	22 Dec 1870	(4) 2/2
Reigner Electa 16	Cowgill James William 23	9 Nov 1879	(4) 2/13
Reynolds Augusta Virginia 22	Scanlon Maurice 21	26 Oct 1881	(4) 2/16
Reynolds James Howard 37	Dyre Elizabeth 25	3 Oct 1865	(4) 1/1
Reynolds Margaret C 19	Miller Jacob 21	4 Feb 1866	(4) 1/2
Reynolds William Frank 28	Kenney Virginia Ann 22	18 Jan 1877	(4) 2/9
Rhinehart Ellis	Hollenbach Mariah	17 July 1823	(5)
Rhoderick Futah C 20	Likens James 25	13 Feb 1866	(4) 1/2
Rhumsberg George Washington 21	Stewart Matilda Jane 21	10 Dec 1874	(4) 2/6
Rice Mary Jane 35	Johnson Jesse 47	May 1, 1871	(4) 2/2
Richard Isiah 21	Sechrist Jane E 24	1 July 1855	(10)
Richardson Elizabeth 26	Powell Henry 23	3 Jan 1866	(4) 1/2
Richardson Henry Harrison 26	Jackson Mary V 21	15 Oct 1885	(4) 1/40
Richardson John	Heitt Osie	31 Aug 1834	(5)
Richmond Catharine Ann 20	Richmond Robert Wm 24	30 Aug 1877	(4) 2/10
Richmond Jesse Sylvester 21	Poland Laura Samantha 19	21 Nov 1900	(4) 2/43
Richmond Lucy Edmonia Belle 21	Shanholtzer George William 22	13 Nov 1884	(4) 2/20
Richmond Mary Jane 35	Sirbaugh Aaron 45	22 Aug 1878	(4) 2/11
Richmond Rebecca E 25	Light John W 35	21 Aug 1884	(4) 2/19
Richmond Robert Wm 24	Richmond Catharine Ann 20	30 Aug 1877	(4) 2/10
Richmond Samuel Patton 34	Wolford Ettie Beall 21	24 Feb 1892	(4) 2/30
Richmond Sidney Elizabeth 19	Brelsford James William 23	24 Mar 1881	(4) 2/15
Richmond Susan Bell 15	Whitacre Henry Carson 22	30 Jan 1898	(4) 2/40
Ridgeway Jacob	High Nancy	15 Sept 1839	(1) 26 Sept 1839
Ridgeway William G	Pennington Mary C	25 Dec 1860	(8)
Riding Peter	Dayton Elizabeth	27 Aug 1841	(5)
Ridings M A	Brant John G	27 Aug 1852	(5)
Rieley Elizabeth Jane 22	Fletcher Joseph 22	15 Aug 1869	(4) 2/1
Rietbrook Henry 36	Monroe Hannah 29	Oct 1854	(10)
Riggle Catherine	Brill Isaac	*21 Mar 1825	(4) 3/24
Riggleman Ella 35	Spurling William 48	13 Dec 1897	(4) 2/39
Riggleman John Robert 19	Heare Emsey Jane 25	6 Jan 1878	(4) 2/11
Riggleman Joseph 21	Heare Abigail Virginia 23	8 Nov 1877	(4) 2/10
Riggs Jas	Vandiver Matilda	14 Oct 1830	(6)
Riley Alex	Kelly Isabel	26 Mar 1827	(6)
Riley Alexander	Kelley Isabelle	29 Mar 1827	(5)
Riley Alexander	Kelly Isabella	*19 Mar 1827	(4) 3/19
Riley Alonzo Vandorn 22	Clark Gracie Valarie 19	18 July 1900	(4) 2/43
Riley Fenton Butler 32	Hook Martha Anne E 22	21 Aug 1890	(4) 2/28
Riley Frances Catharine 32	Eaton Levi James 24	28 Sept 1882	(4) 2/17
Riley George William 28	Hawkins Elizabeth Jane 21	14 Oct 1891	(4) 2/29
Riley J C	Arnold J S	20 Dec 1854	(6)
Riley James Robert 31	Kidwell Mary Ellen 24	15 Mar 1877	(4) 2/10
Riley Jane	Smoot Josiah	*19 Feb 1827	(4) 3/13
Riley Lucy Jane 21	Serbaugh Harrison 22	14 Sept 1875	(4) 2/7
Riley Mary Cordelia 19	Hott George 27	21 Oct 1880	(4) 2/14
Riley Ollie Venetta 17	Shanholtzer Taylor 21	30 Sept 1894	(4) 2/34
Riley Robert Fenton 29	Schnibbe Margaret Dorothy 19	31 Oct 1889	(4) 2/27

Name #1	Name #2	Date	Source
Riley Sarah M 21	? Isaac 23	3 July 1859	(10)
Rinehart Ellis	Hollenback E	26 June 1823	(6)
Rinehart Margaret Ann 19	Moreland William Franklin 31	22 Feb 1887	(4) 2/23
Rinehart Stephen Chandler 46	Herriott Mary Isabell 32	13 Jan 1867	(4) 1/4
Rinehart Virginia Bell 16	Moreland William Edward 22	17 Feb 1881	(4) 2/15
Rineheart Jeremiah 27	Kerns Mary Jane 21	3 July 1873	(4) 2/4
Ringer George Washington 27	Heare Augusta Florence 27	2 Nov 1892	(4) 2/31
Rinker Ann Jemima 29	High Alonzo Tecumseh 31	4 Feb 1883	(4) 2/18
Rinker Annie 22	Biser John Wesley 25	8 Feb 1893	(4) 2/32
Rinker Charles Frederick 25	Pugh Dora C 24	25 Oct 1883	(4) 2/18
Rinker Christina	Stewart Sam	17 Feb 1831	(6)
Rinker Daniel	Taylor Jane	7 Oct 1824	(5)
Rinker Elizabeth	Rotruck John	10 Dec 1850	(6)
Rinker Elizabeth	Rotruck John	10 Dec 1846	(5)
Rinker Elizah	Hendrixon Eliz	10 Sept 1835	(5)
Rinker Hester	Clark Hendrix	4 June 1828	(5)
Rinker Joshua 35	High Susan Elizabeth 17	24 Oct 1867	(4) 1/5
Rinker Maggie Elizabeth 28	Pugh John Wesley 43	21 Nov 1887	(4) 2/24
Rinker Mary Magdalene 19	Pownall Robert Snyder 29	1 Aug 1893	(4) 2/32
Rinker N J	Rawlings Charles	29 May 1850	(5)
Rinker N J	Rawlings Chas	29 May 1851	(6)
Rinker Rebecca 21	Fergusen William 23	5 Sept 1865	(4) 1/1
Rinker Sam'l	High Emely	18 Oct 1836	(6)
Rinker Samuel 45	Flemming Nancy 28	5 Oct 1879	(4) 2/13
Rinker Susan Rebecca 33	Fleming Joseph 53	9 Oct 1890	(4) 2/28
Rinker Sylvester 25	High Emily 28	19 June 1878	(4) 2/11
Rives Robert William 48	Emmart Mrs Barbara Ann 48	17 Sept 1889	(4) 2/27
Rizer Matthias	Earsom Nancy	14 Nov 1839	(1) 21 Nov 1839
Roach David 28	Orndorff Margaret 26	18 Nov 1873	(4) 2/5
Roach Eliza E 26	Bloss William G 21	20 Sept 1900	(4) 2/43
Roadcap Columbia Elizabeth 17	Bobo Herman Faulkner 21	1 Oct 1898	(4) 2/40
Roadcap John 27	Shoemaker Mary Ann 21	30 Dec 1875	(4) 2/8
Roberson Amos 34	Poland Mary C 24	1 Nov 1866	(4) 1/4
Roberson Belle June 26	Saville Robert Wise 29	21 Feb 1888	(4) 2/24
Roberson Fannie Eleanora 23	Bean Edward Thomas 28	27 Dec 1893	(4) 2/33
Roberson James William 27	Saville Laura Catherine 28	29 Dec 1896	(4) 2/38
Roberson Jane	Piles John	14 Jan 1855	(10)
Roberson John Alexander 23	Alkire Jennie Lee 23	15 Aug 1888	(4) 2/25
Roberson Lewis Ashby 24	Malick Eva Irene 16	16 Oct 1894	(4) 2/34
Roberson Margaret Ellen 20	Wolford Jacob Webster 23	30 Dec 1886	(4) 2/23
Roberson Rachael 24	McDonald Archibald 26	Feb 1866	(4) 1/2
Roberson Rebecca Ann 35	Bennett Silvanus 36	29 Jan 1867	(4) 1/4
Roberson Rebecca Frances 22	Malick William Reese 27	2 Mar 1899	(4) 2/41
Roberson Sanford Taylor 21	Yost Susan Ann 22	29 Jan 1874	(4) 2/5
Roberson Sarah Ann 23	Friddle John Samuel 26	19 Dec 1899	(4) 2/42
Robert Benjamin	Leatherman Polly	3 Jan 1826	(5)
Robert J L	Rotruck E J	7 May 1846	(5)
Roberts Ann	Miller Jacob	28 Oct 1830	(6)
Roberts B	Leatherman Polly	3 Jan 1826	(6)
Roberts Benjamin	Leatherman Polly	*28 Dec 1825	(4) 3/76
Roberts Dorcas	Hunter John	24 May 1827	(5)
Roberts Eleanor	Bean Andrew	24 Feb 1820	(6)

Name #1	Name #2	Date	Source
Roberts Elizabeth J	Martin George S	13 June 1861	(6)
Roberts Elizabeth	Bosley Tobias	1840	(5)
Roberts Elizabeth	Roberts Moses	26 Feb 1835	(6)
Roberts Hannah	Jenkins H P	3 Sept 1850	(5)
Roberts Hannah	Jinkins H P	3 Sept 1851	(6)
Roberts J L	Rotruck E J	27 May 1850	(6)
Roberts John	Bosley Nancy	11 June 1829	(6)
Roberts John 25	Durst Susan Catherine 19	22 Dec 1881	(4) 2/17
Roberts Margaret Louise 20	Shannon Edgar Wilson 20	7 Aug 1893	(4) 2/32
Roberts Martha	Smith Soloman	*18 Aug 1825	(4) 3/54
Roberts Mary	Colbert Jonathan	24 Feb 1823	(5)
Roberts Moses	Roberts Elizabeth	26 Feb 1835	(6)
Roberts Susan	Davis Minert	31 May 1849	(6)
Roberts Thomas	Leatherman Sarah	5 Dec 1843	(5)
Roberts William Wesley 21	Fisher Louisa Walton 21	26 Sept 1877	(4) 2/10
Robertson N	McNary Nim	24 June 1833	(6)
Robey Andrew J 23	Peters ? R 20	Nov 1857	(10)
Robey Rebecca 21	Bobo William H 21	17 June 1860	(10)
Robinson Elizabeth	White James	9 Oct 1834	(6)
Robinson Ellen Comfort 42	Stewart John William 27	14 Sept 1882	(4) 2/17
Robinson John Wesley 58	Holt Phillis 40	11 Feb 1885	(4) 1/40
Robinson Mary Catharine 24	Godlove William Tucker 42	26 Mar 1899	(4) 2/41
Robinson Soloman	Ruckman Hannah	*7 Feb 1825	(4) 3/13
Robinson William 24	Cool Mary Matilda 22	21 June 1870	(4) 2/2
Robison Jacob R 30	Laudaen Hannah 25	12 Dec 1865	(4) 1/2
Roby Isaac	Cole Mary	19 Jan 1837	(5)
Roderick Abraham 58	Arnold Rebecca 43	27 Mar 1866	(4) 1/3
Roderick Nancy C 24	Stonebraker David T 23	11 Jan 1866	(4) 1/2
Rodruck Maggie Virginia 19	Potter Harley E 26	3 Aug 1881	(4) 2/16
Roetruck Peter	Miller Catherine	20 Aug 1816	(5)
Rogers Edgar 21	Whiteman Hannah 19	8 Feb 1899	(4) 2/41
Rogers Edward 27	Pancake Sallie McNeil 24	7 Nov 1888	(4) 2/25
Rogers Isaac 21	Thompson Malissa Isabell 23	3 June 1874	(4) 2/6
Rogers J L Jr	Nesbit Susa	25 Mar 1841	(6)
Rogers James	Ellifritz Angelina	30 Oct 1845	(6)
Rogers John	Nesbit Eleanor	3 Aug 1837	(6)
Rogers John	Reese Lydia	*20 Oct 1828	(4) 3/34
Rogers John Benjamin 22	Keckley Rosa C Catharine 21	26 May 1892	(4) 2/31
Rogers John Henry 19	Thompson Margaret Jane 21	26 Sept 1867	(4) 1/5
Rogers John Thomas 24	McDonald Rebecca 22	18 Oct 1898	(4) 2/41
Rogers M E	McDowell Thomas	9 Feb 1859	(6)
Rogers Martha Ann	Taylor Daniel	*25 Oct 1824	(4) 3/49
Rogers Soloman 21	Thompson Sarah Virginia 20	26 Sept 1867	(4) 1/5
Rogers Wm	Parker Mary	19 May 1836	(6)
Rogers Wm Henry 24	Grapes M B 23	18 Nov 1896	(4) 2/38
Roice William H 25	Whitacre Anne Elizabeth 21	6 Mar 1889	(4) 2/26
Rolls David Powel 27	Bruce Florence Bell 28	28 Apr 1897	(4) 1/41
Rolls Eveline 30	Ruckner David 59	25 Nov 1875	(4) 1/39
Rolls George B 23	Lowe Mary 16	24 May 1877	(4) 1/39
Rolls Henry Wm 24	Thornton Lucy Jane 21	7 Jan 1874	(4) 1/38
Rolls Sallie 36	Fairfax ? 38	24 Mar 1874	(4) 1/38
Rolls Taylor Burton 23	Magruder Minnie 17	10 Feb 1892	(4) 1/41

Name #1	Name #2	Date	Source
Rolon Evan J	Dawson Eliz	6 Nov 1845	(6)
Roomsberg George Washington 36	Stewart Sarah Virginia 30	29 July 1886	(4) 2/22
Roomsburgh Samantha Belle 17	Shanholtzer Charles William 24	10 June 1894	(4) 2/34
Rorabough Daniel	Snyder Rebecca		(1) 1 Dec 1838
Rosebaugh Harriet 27	Conrad George 20	22 Nov 1865	(4) 1/1
Rosebough John M 41	Funk Marian 33	28 July 1873	(4) 2/4
Rosebough Joseph Philip 33	Davey Margaret Ellen 21	10 Oct 1900	(4) 2/43
Rosebough Rachel Ann 19	Orndorff Joseph William 24	21 Nov 1875	(4) 2/8
Rosebrock Mariah Isabel 23	Strosnyder George Washington 23	*6 July 1881	(4) 2/16
Rosebrough Sallie Rebecca 22	Baker Charles 20	9 Apr 1897	(4) 2/39
Rosebrough Sarah Elizabeth 19	Poland James Henry 26	23 Dec 1887	(4) 2/24
Rosebugh Mary Elizabeth 24	Mauk John Frederick 23	15 Feb 1883	(4) 2/18
Ross Abraham Isaac	Hayden Annie	17 Apr 1884	(4) 1/40
Ross Mary	Davis Miner	14 Jan 1830	(6)
Ross Mary 22	Green Jacob 21	9 May 1878	(4) 1/39
Rotruck B L	Sollars Susan	5 Dec 1844	(6)
Rotruck E	Greenwalt John	31 Oct 1844	(6)
Rotruck E	Leatherman Dan	28 Dec 1846	(6)
Rotruck E J	Robert J L	7 May 1846	(5)
Rotruck E J	Roberts J L	27 May 1850	(6)
Rotruck Hannah	Likins George	14 Apr 1841	(5)
Rotruck Ida May 18	Messick James Albert 24	1 Jan 1884	(4) 2/19
Rotruck J M	Greenwait Mar	12 Sept 1839	(6)
Rotruck Jacob	Likens Mary	1 Apr 1851	(6)
Rotruck Jacob	Likins Mary	1 Apr 1846	(5)
Rotruck Jacob M	Grenwade Margaret	12 Sept 1840	(5)
Rotruck John	Rinker Elizabeth	10 Dec 1846	(5)
Rotruck John	Rinker Elizabeth	10 Dec 1850	(6)
Rotruck M	Bailey Thornton	4 Dec 1856	(6)
Rotruck Peter	Miller Catherine	20 Aug 1816	(6)
Rotruck Polly	George John	8 July 1834	(5)
Rotruck Polly	Taylor Robert	23 Sept 1824	(5)
Rotruck Robert Elmer 27	High Martha I 21	15 Nov 1899	(4) 2/42
Rotruck S C	Blackburn Jas	26 Dec 1842	(6)
Rotruck S M	Blackburn E G	19 Sept 1839	(6)
Rotruck Sarah	Likins James	3 Nov 1836	(5)
Rotruck Susan M	Blackburn E G	19 Sept 1840	(5)
Rowzee Isaac Newton 20	Doman Sallie B 29	9 Feb 1898	(4) 2/40
Rowzee Mary Elizabeth 22	Haines Stephen Wheeler 26	6 Apr 1884	(4) 2/19
Rowzee Samuel Atwell 47	Malcolm Martha Jane 38	6 May 1883	(4) 2/18
Royce Anne Virginia 25	Henderson Richard Thomas 45	31 Dec 1889	(4) 2/27
Royce Frederick 35	Critton Phoebe 35	27 Nov 1860	(10)
Ruckman Albert 21	Wolford Alverda Melissa 18	15 Apr 1885	(4) 2/20
Ruckman Ann 25	Saville Walker 21	18 Dec 1866	(4) 1/4
Ruckman Arthur Jackson 23	Keister Emma Elizabeth 22	3 Mar 1896	(4) 2/37
Ruckman Benjamin 20	Peters Emma Florence 19	7 Nov 1893	(4) 2/33
Ruckman Eliza	Trentor William L	*14 Mar 1825	(4) 3/21
Ruckman Elizabeth	Piles John H	*13 Mar 1824	(4) 3/16
Ruckman Emily	Evans Caleb 25	1854	(10)
Ruckman Frances Elmira 27	Compton Henry C 24	5 May 1885	(4) 2/20
Ruckman Gibson	Harmon Catherine	22 Aug 1854	(10)
Ruckman Gibson	? Elizabeth	22 Aug 1854	(10)

Name #1	Name #2	Date	Source
Ruckman Granville Armstrong 30	Bowles Carrie Belle 19	12 Feb 1878	(4) 2/11
Ruckman Hannah	Robinson Soloman	*7 Feb 1825	(4) 3/13
Ruckman Hannah 19	Birch Samuel 22	16 Nov 1868	(4) 1/7
Ruckman Harriet Jane 23	Doyle Matthew 33	23 Mar 1882	(4) 2/17
Ruckman Jacob Calvin 27	McDonald Martha Jane 22	13 Nov 1895	(4) 2/36
Ruckman James	Fahs Caroline		(2) 14 May 1857
Ruckman James Gibson 19	Combs Mary Jane 22	3 Feb 1870	(4) 2/1
Ruckman Jas J 27	Starkey Jemima E 23	20 Feb 1866	(4) 1/2
Ruckman John	Henline Sari	6 Oct 1853	(6)
Ruckman John William 23	Wolford Margaret Catherine 18	27 Dec 1866	(4) 1/4
Ruckman Joseph 23	Peters Sarah C 17	16 Dec 1854	(10)
Ruckman Lucettie Delinore 19	Park Samuel Imboden 23	22 Dec 1886	(4) 2/22
Ruckman Margaret Ellen 22	Swisher Vincent Markwood 24	29 May 1884	(4) 2/19
Ruckman Martha Ellen 26	Park James Ashford 36	20 Feb 1898	(4) 2/40
Ruckman Martha E 22	Heare Paran 23	1 Dec 1869	(4) 2/1
Ruckman Martha Rosetta 20	Loy Edgar Johnson 23	30 Apr 1891	(4) 2/29
Ruckman Mary	Parish Adam	*31 May 1824	(4) 3/30
Ruckman Mary 43	Poland Richard Henry 48	5 July 1881	(4) 2/16
Ruckman Mary Ann	Blue Zachariah	*20 Feb 1826	(4) 3/11
Ruckman Mary Elizabeth 21	Wolfe George W 28	30 May 1878	(4) 2/11
Ruckman Robt James 25	Schnibbe Mary Catharine 20	27 Nov 1895	(4) 2/36
Ruckman Samuel	Watkins Elizabeth	*8 Sept 1828	(4) 3/26
Ruckman Sarah Ann 21	Shanholtzer Jacob Larkin 19	15 July 1874	(4) 2/6
Ruckman Sarah Virginia 23	Henderson Laskin Harris Lane 26	16 Dec 1879	(4) 2/14
Ruckman Thomas	Carmichael Nancy	4 Jan 1838	(1) 20 Jan 1838
Ruckman Thomas McDonald 33	Haines Salema Jane 29	3 Dec 1878	(4) 2/12
Ruckman William 20	Swisher Margaret Millisa 16	29 May 1884	(4) 2/19
Ruckman Wilson	Hannas Charity	*14 Oct 1828	(4) 3/31
Ruckman Wright Welton 26	Heare Lucy Catharine Imboden 17	6 Sept 1880	(4) 2/14
Ruckner David 59	Rolls Eveline 30	25 Nov 1875	(4) 1/39
Rudolph ? 26	Albright Lewis 23	24 Nov 1860	(10)
Rudolph Adam 67	Evans Sarah Amanda 25	10 Apr 1867	(4) 1/5
Rudolph Anne Litler 21	Orndorff Luther Edward 29	4 May 1890	(4) 2/27
Rudolph Barbara A	Gray James	22 Nov 1866	(9)
Rudolph Barbara A 24	Gray Jas K 22	22 Nov 1866	(4) 1/4
Rudolph Cora Victoria 24	Lynn John Henry 28	14 June 1900	(4) 2/43
Rudolph David William 28	Cole Jane Eliza Robertson 27	11 Mar 1880	(4) 2/14
Rudolph Emanda E 22	Baylis Sanford 37	13 Mar 1869	(4) 1/38
Rudolph George Adam 41	Wilson Rachel 31	25 June 1896	(4) 2/37
Rudolph Jacob	Bowers R I E Melchora	4 Oct 1864	(8)
Rudolph Margaret Frances 34	Kump Benjamin Franklin 35	15 June 1875	(4) 2/7
Rudolph Rebecca Susan 42	Bloxham James William 52	6 Oct 1897	(4) 2/39
Rudolph S 26	Taylor Sarah 19	8 Mar 1859	(10)
Rudolph Sarah Amanda 30	Yost James Henry 25	7 Mar 1880	(4) 2/14
Rudolph Sarah Ellen 34	Orndorff Joseph Atwell 37	6 Nov 1879	(4) 2/13
Rudolph Streit Perry 44	Brill Rachel Ann 28	9 Apr 1891	(4) 2/29
Rudy Joshua	Baker Miller	21 Feb 1819	(6)
Rummer Martha E 27	Sherwood A J 42	*1 Aug 1900	(4) 2/43
Rumsburg Sarah Lucinda 16	Shelley James Luther 24	24 Apr 1892	(4) 2/30
Runnells Jacob	Young Sarah	*31 Dec 1824	(4) 3/56
Runyon Levi Ashby 21	Lambert Catharine Regina 24	28 May 1885	(4) 2/10
Rush Mary 38	Combs John Jos 59	13 Oct 1874	(4) 2/6

Name #1	Name #2	Date	Source
Russell Ellen 21	Gibson Mel 31	22 Nov 1883	(4) 1/40
Russell M Edith 21	Strock David F 24	23 Apr 1895	(4) 2/35
Russell William 32	Pugh Susan Howard 28	10 Nov 1880	(4) 2/15
Ryan James	Barrick Caroline	3 Oct 1860	(5)
Ryan Jas	Barrick Caroline	3 Oct 1859	(6)
Ryan William	Bean Rebecca	3 August 1837	(1) 19 Aug 1937
Sailor Wm	Hull Ruth	19 Feb 1847	(6)
Salters John	Berry Hannah	11 Apr 1832	(6)
Salts Catherine	Bruce William	9 Nov 1828	(6)
Sanders Alexander Thomas 29	Cummins Alverda Lee 22	16 Dec 1885	(4) 2/21
Sanders John Henry 26	Haines Ellen Elizabeth 19	1 Mar 1877	(4) 2/9
Sanders Margaret Elizabeth 22	Cummins Edward Beall 25	2 Dec 1885	(4) 2/21
Sanders Mary Susan 21	Carder Lafaette Ashby 25	23 Oct 1889	(4) 2/27
Sanders Mayberry G 30	Heatwole Barbara Etta 20	28 Dec 1887	(4) 2/24
Sanders Milissa Kereebeck 28	Bailey James Peter 32	18 Sept 1894	(4) 2/34
Sanders Richard Frampton 31	Patterson Alverda Baine 24	16 Sept 1891	(4) 2/29
Sanders Vallie Rosa 17	Gulick William Taylor 25	23 Sept 1896	(4) 2/37
Sands Hannah	Elifritz Sol	20 Jan 1824	(6)
Sands James	Steerman Catherine	25 Aug 1825	(6)
Sandy Margaret Ann Virginia 20	McBride John Alexander 23	5 Nov 1878	(4) 2/12
Sandy Sarah Belle 21	Wright James Francis 26	27 Dec 1886	(4) 2/23
Sandy William Henry 28	Orndorff Margaret 25	4 Feb 1879	(4) 2/12
Santemires Emanuel T 22	Allen Elizabeth 21	4 Oct 1877	(4) 2/10
Savill Abraham	Haines Eliza	*9 June 1827	(4) 3/35
Savill John Judson 22	Swisher Rebecca Jane 21	22 Aug 1867	(4) 1/5
Savill Mariah Margaret 18	Hammock William 45	17 Feb 1869	(4) 1/38
Saville Alexander 22	Orndorff Margaret 32	1 Apr 1884	(4) 2/19
Saville Amanda Florence 23	Vanpelt Charles Thompson 27	15 Oct 1891	(4) 2/30
Saville Ann Mariah 23	Brill Richard 27	13 Oct 1881	(4) 2/16
Saville Annie Elizabeth Mrs 40	Sutherland James H Anderson 23	14 May 1890	(4) 2/28
Saville Belle J 41	Powell Samuel Dade 60	17 Oct 1900	(4) 2/43
Saville Catharine 69	Malick Aaron 78	9 Oct 1879	(4) 2/13
Saville Charles Harbert 28	Doman Ida Malinda 27	15 Sept 1897	(4) 2/39
Saville Charles Andrew 23	Shanholtzer Ida May 21	4 Aug 1892	(4) 2/31
Saville Druzilla Ann 23	Cline Madison Rector 21	22 Oct 1879	(4) 2/13
Saville Eliza 19	Kline James N 24	22 Sept 1885	(4) 2/21
Saville Eliza Elizabeth 19	Shanholtzer Benjamin 24	22 Apr 1875	(4) 2/7
Saville Eliza Jane 33	Smith William 37	9 Feb 1870	(4) 2/1
Saville Eliza Margaret 17	Shanholtzer Lemuel Silas 20	24 Dec 1889	(4) 2/27
Saville George Washington 24	Shanholtzer Ann Elizabeth 23	27 Jan 1870	(4) 2/1
Saville George William 21	Peters Dora Bell 26	3 Apr 1894	(4) 2/34
Saville Gustavis M 24	Streby Clara Matilda 22	14 Apr 1897	(4) 2/39
Saville Harriet Jane 17	Kirby Edward Walter 27	28 Sept 1886	(4) 2/22
Saville Henry Imboden 23	Piles Lucille Delma 17	25 Feb 1886	(4) 2/22
Saville Hider Washington 28	Messick Emma Susan 20	1 Mar 1899	(4) 2/41
Saville Isaac H 23	Bowman Mary Jane 19	11 Apr 1872	(4) 2/3
Saville Isaac Johnson 25	Barnes Oceanna 21	30 May 1888	(4) 2/25
Saville Isaac Newton 21	Miles Martha Ellen Virginia 18	28 Aug 1884	(4) 2/19
Saville Jefferson Davis 27	Moreland Sarah Ellen 20	28 May 1890	(4) 2/28
Saville Joel Jackson 22	McCauley Rosetta Florence 21	16 Jan 1883	(4) 2/18
Saville John 27	Shanholtzer Sarah 26	24 July 1866	(4) 1/3
Saville John 33	Sheckle Rebecca 23	16 July 1857	(10)

Name #1	Name #2	Date	Source
Saville John Abraham	Simmons Sarah D 32	6 Aug 1884	(4) 2/19
Saville John Benjamin 21	Loy Sedema Catharine 17	21 Oct 1886	(4) 2/22
Saville John David 23	Martin Virginia Bell 21	18 Dec 1889	(4) 2/27
Saville John Letcher 24	Miller Rosa Verena 23	26 Jan 1886	(4) 2/21
Saville Joseph 21	Hott Rachel 20	29 May 1860	(10)
Saville Laura Catherine 28	Roberson James William 27	29 Dec 1896	(4) 2/38
Saville Lavina Catherine 28	Wolford Granville Harper 26	12 May 1891	(4) 2/29
Saville Lucinda Catherine 18	Hott George Wash Jefferson 23	30 Aug 1883	(4) 2/18
Saville Lucy Ann 16	Lear Jefferson Davis 22	28 Feb 1884	(4) 2/19
Saville Malinda Margaret 18	Poland William Amos 18	4 Feb 1886	(4) 2/21
Saville Maria Elizabeth 17	Heare David Hott 25	11 Dec 1873	(4) 2/5
Saville Mary Catherine 24	Swartz Samuel 36	*8 Oct 1878	(4) 2/12
Saville Mary Catharine Mrs 53	Huffman Amos 64	8 Aug 1889	(4) 2/26
Saville Mary Jane 18	Simmons Samuel 23	2 Aug 1877	(4) 2/10
Saville Mary Jane 23	Grapes George Wesley 26	10 Oct 1889	(4) 2/27
Saville Mary Jane 16	Kline Edward Luther 25	7 Feb 1889	(4) 2/26
Saville Nancy Irene 18	Arnold Joseph Robert 29	18 Sept 1895	(4) 2/36
Saville Oliver 30	Combs Elizabeth 18	2 May 1860	(10)
Saville Peter Oliver 34	Everett Lorany Florence 24	5 Jan 1898	(4) 2/40
Saville Peter Oliver 27	Shank Caroline Vina 27	13 Dec 1887	(4) 2/24
Saville Philip 60	Malick Hannah Catharine 44	31 Oct 1876	(4) 2/9
Saville Philip Holland 31	Malick Mallissa Arabel 24	26 July 1892	(4) 2/31
Saville Rachel C 21	Yost Robert J 27	17 Apr 1873	(4) 2/4
Saville Rebecca Ann 21	Baker Hezekiah Clagett 24	29 Jan 1874	(4) 2/5
Saville Robert Wise 29	Roberson Belle June 26	21 Feb 1888	(4) 2/24
Saville Sarah Ann 27	Powell Jas H 52	17 Apr 1866	(4) 1/3
Saville Sarah Catharine 20	Kline John 27	11 Apr 1889	(4) 2/26
Saville Sarah Elizabeth 21	Largent Joseph Sanford 22	1 Jan 1867	(4) 1/4
Saville Sarah Frances 25	Poland Charles Lupton 25	10 Jan 1897	(4) 2/38
Saville Virginia Price 22	Cheshire ? Granville 27	11 Mar 1880	(4) 2/14
Saville Walker 21	Ruckman Ann 25	18 Dec 1866	(4) 1/4
Saville William Ridgeley 26	Loy Minnie Belle 20	18 July 1900	(4) 2/43
Saville William Van Kirk 21	Moore Myrtle V 18	22 June 1898	(4) 2/40
Saville William H 23	Moreland Chloe E 21	31 Jan 1868	(4) 1/6
Saville William Henry	Shanholtzer Sarah Virginia 21	25 June 1874	(4) 2/6
Saville Wm Taylor 24	Wolford Hattie Elizabeth 22	23 Feb 1892	(4) 2/30
Scaffenaker Henry B 21	Pugh Fannie C 17	18 Dec 1884	(4) 2/10
Scamp Abraham	Hopkins Maria		(1) 1 July 1837
Scanlan Elizabeth Ellen 21	Alkire Hiram Welton 24	24 Dec 1878	(4) 2/12
Scanlan Ella Pauline 26	Heiskell Edgar Sensency 40	22 Apr 1891	(4) 2/29
Scanlan Mary 30	Pownall Thomas J 26	16 Apr 1890	(4) 2/27
Scanlen Samuel 20	Watson Minerva Frances 18	1 Dec 1875	(4) 2/8
Scanlon Anna 24	Swisher James Larimore 34	7 July 1886	(4) 2/22
Scanlon Maurice 21	Reynolds Augusta Virginia 22	26 Oct 1881	(4) 2/16
Schaffer Oliver Wellington 23	Lupton Kate Parsons 19	15 June 1881	(4) 2/16
Schaffnaker John Frederick 21	Anderson Martha M 21	31 Dec 1890	(4) 2/28
Schaffnaker L Nathaniel 22	Gardner Nora Lee 19	12 Dec 1893	(4) 2/33
Schaitepfield Sibil	Leise Thomas	28 May 1827	(4) 3/34
Schnibbe George Wesley 22	Keister Minnie 21	6 May 1890	(4) 2/28
Schnibbe Lewis 24	Albin Elizabeth 25	11 Oct 1866	(4) 1/3
Schnibbe Margaret Dorothy 19	Riley Robert Fenton 29	31 Oct 1889	(4) 2/27
Schnibbe Mary Catharine 20	Ruckman Robt James 25	27 Nov 1895	(4) 2/36

Name #1	Name #2	Date	Source
Schockey Joseph	Hartman Margaret	*1 Nov 1828	(4) 3/36
Schoroley Mary 28	Allender Thomas Neavitt 22	20 Oct 1896	(4) 2/37
Schrock Geo	Inskeep Rachel	27 Sept 1832	(6)
Schultze Eliza J 29	White Christian S 27	25 July 1867	(4) 1/5
Scott David	Edwards Martha	*17 Apr 1826	(4) 3/16
Scott James	Doran Rebecca	3 Jan 1837	(5)
Scott Jemima 25	Harris Sanford Simmons 27	24 Sept 1865	(4) 1/1
Scott Maria	Thomas Samuel	9 May 1839	(5)
Scott Mary E	Thompson John A	13 Nov 1838	(1) 1 Dec 1838
Scritchfield Sarah	Lees Thos	31 May 1827	(6)
Scruggs Henry 28	Hammack Ella 34	29 Aug 1889	(4) 2/26
Scruggs William Franklin 30	Keister Katie 22	5 May 1887	(4) 2/23
Sea Adam	Heinzman Elizabeth	*6 Jan 1825	(4) 3/4
Seaton Elizabeth 31	Simpson Thomas 26	12 Aug 1868	(4) 1/7
Seaton Emily Alice Frances 16	Whitacre Jacob W 25	7 June 1887	(4) 2/23
Seaton K 48	Kerns A 24	6 Feb 1859	(10)
Sechrist Jane E 24	Richard Isiah 21	1 July 1855	(10)
Sechrist Margaret C 49	Batt John W 52	30 June 1898	(4) 2/40
Sechrist Mary Ellen 34	Simmons John William 30	30 Dec 1886	(4) 2/22
Sechrist Nancy 48	Brill Thomas Benton 34	28 Aug 1884	(4) 2/19
Secord Samuel Franklin 38	Corbin Parthenia 23	13 Apr 1892	(4) 2/30
Secrist William Miller 30	Farmer Frances Virginia 27	15 Oct 1885	(4) 2/21
Seders John S	Montgomery ?	20 Dec 1855	(10)
Seders Mary Ann 17	Crawfis Robert R 25	10 Jan 1878	(4) 2/11
See Jennie 18	Whitacre John 18	20 Sept 1894	(4) 2/34
See Sarah 22	Orndorff Henry J 23	25 Oct 1865	(4) 1/1
Seeders Ebenezer	Baker Sarah Ellen	19 Mar 1857	(1) 27 Mar 1857
Seeders Ebenezer 22	Baker Sarah Ellen 19	Mar 1857	(10)
Seeders George Washintgon 31	Baker Mary Catherine 35	14 Aug 1867	(4) 1/5
Seeders George Washington 52	Vaughn Sarah 48	16 Oct 1887	(4) 2/24
Seeders Jonathan Millard 27	Raines Clara Bell 17	12 June 1895	(4) 2/35
Seeders Martha Jane 20	Garland Baltzer 22	8 Oct 1891	(4) 2/29
Seeman Hannah Frances 19	Pownell William A 28	15 May 1870	(4) 2/1
Seibert William Andrew 21	Orndorff Mary Magdalen 21	25 Sept 1888	(4) 2/25
Selden Charlotte 20	Nelson John Edward 23	7 Apr 1887	(4) 2/23
Selden William Henry 23	Bean Christian 20	10 Apr 1888	(4) 2/25
Seldon Frederick John 26	Gill Isadore 22	5 May 1897	(4) 2/39
Seleleton Archibald H 23	Jackson Sarah 23	18 Dec 1886	(4) 1/40
Self Maggie E 23	Wilson Abraham 37	1 Sept 1869	(4) 2/1
Sellers Tobitha	Smith William	4 Sept 1823	(5)
Selvey Harrison 26	Johnson Susan Jane 24	5 Sept 1890	(4) 2/28
Serbaugh ? 24	McDonald Esther 20	10 Sept 1857	(10)
Serbaugh Arminta Belle 22	Eaton James William 20	16 Mar 1898	(4) 2/40
Serbaugh Charles Edward 36	Brill Amanda Jane 23	13 Aug 1874	(4) 2/6
Serbaugh Emma Almira 22	McDonald Alvin Elzey 22	25 Dec 1889	(4) 2/27
Serbaugh Harrison 22	Riley Lucy Jane 21	14 Sept 1875	(4) 2/7
Serbaugh Mary Catharine 27	McKeever Elias 29	3 Feb 1874	(4) 2/5
Serbaugh Sarah Alverda 22	Clark James Madison 22	26 Mar 1889	(4) 2/26
Seville William 25	Hott Elizabeth 19	24 Mar 1859	(10)
Sexton Patrick 45	Davis Charity 40	30 Jan 1876	(4) 2/8
Seymour Belzara 22	Lewis James William 22	12 Jan 1898	(4) 2/40
Seymour Caroline 21	Brady Jno Copsey 22	15 Nov 1865	(4) 1/1

Name #1	Name #2	Date	Source
Shadwell Jennie 21	Constable Thomas Franklin 45	24 Aug 1890	(4) 2/28
Shafer David 56	Pennybaker Mary 32	20 Aug 1876	(4) 2/8
Shafer Hannah	Hamilton Samuel	*29 Sept 1825	(4) 3/62
Shaffer Samuel Lloyd 37	Pugh Artie Virginia 32	27 Dec 1899	(4) 2/42
Shall Daniel James William 31	Wolford Etta Virginia Beall 19	10 Dec 1878	(4) 2/12
Shambaugh Jos Jasper Mathew 38	Kerns Rachel C 28	24 Apr 1901	(4) 2/44
Shane Charles Wesley 22	Hott Laura Ann 18	6 Nov 1879	(4) 2/13
Shane Edward F 22	Shanholtzer Lydia Maria 17	3 Apr 1884	(4) 2/19
Shanholtz Benj 26	Daugherty N I 22	22 Sept 1868	(4) 1/7
Shanholtz Benjamin Thomas 18	Davis Emily Susan 21	6 May 1867	(4) 1/5
Shanholtz Daniel Arnold 26	Pepper Ida Olivancy 27	8 Feb 1898	(4) 2/40
Shanholtz Minor 32	Shouse Jane 17	16 Nov 1868	(4) 1/7
Shanholtzer Abigal Catharine 21	Combs Andrew Gibson 20	2 Feb 1882	(4) 2/17
Shanholtzer Albert Wash 24	Oats Hattie Estella 18	12 Feb 1901	(4) 2/44
Shanholtzer Amanda E 19	Foltz Joshua I 24	17 Dec 1872	(4) 2/4
Shanholtzer Ann Elizabeth 23	Saville George Washington 24	27 Jan 1870	(4) 2/1
Shanholtzer Annie Bell 22	Ganoe Berzelius 22	24 Nov 1897	(4) 2/39
Shanholtzer Anthony 27	Alkire Sarah 26	20 Apr 1871	(4) 2/2
Shanholtzer Basil W 21	Pepper Amanda E 16	15 Feb 1872	(4) 2/3
Shanholtzer Benjamin 43	Doman Etta Virginia 33	25 Apr 1894	(4) 2/34
Shanholtzer Benjamin Lee 22	Hott Nora Jemima C 18	31 Dec 1891	(4) 2/30
Shanholtzer Benjamin 24	Saville Eliza Elizabeth 19	22 Apr 1875	(4) 2/7
Shanholtzer Charles W 22	Alkire Elizabeth M 35	29 Oct 1895	(4) 2/36
Shanholtzer Charles Lupton 21	Arnold Laura Catharine 18	2 Jan 1889	(4) 2/26
Shanholtzer Charles William 24	Roomsburgh Samantha Belle 17	10 June 1894	(4) 2/34
Shanholtzer Chloe Margaret 23	Haines Ambrose Clayton 27	11 Mar 1884	(4) 2/19
Shanholtzer Christopher 40	Crock Mary Jane 35	23 Feb 1875	(4) 2/6
Shanholtzer Cora Bell 19	Speelman Bradford 23	9 Jan 1901	(4) 2/43
Shanholtzer Daniel Tucker 25	Haines Rebecca Frances 22	21 Jan 1869	(4) 1/38
Shanholtzer Della May 20	French Charles Edgar 25	26 Mar 1901	(4) 2/44
Shanholtzer E I 21	Grovner William H 22	9 May 1868	(4) 1/6
Shanholtzer Eliza Jane 26	Haines Samuel Taylor 28	7 Feb 1878	(4) 2/11
Shanholtzer Elizabeth 29	Hott William 68	31 Jan 1871	(4) 2/2
Shanholtzer Fannie B A 23	Starns Thomas J 23	25 Sept 1873	(4) 2/4
Shanholtzer George William 22	Kidwell Malinda Jane 22	25 Mar 1886	(4) 2/22
Shanholtzer George William 22	Richmond Lucy Edmonia Belle 21	13 Nov 1884	(4) 2/20
Shanholtzer H E 19	Orndorff James H 24	16 Nov 1868	(4) 1/7
Shanholtzer Hamilton Temple 23	Haines Bertha Frances 24	12 June 1901	(4) 2/44
Shanholtzer Ida May 21	Saville Charles Andrew 23	4 Aug 1892	(4) 2/31
Shanholtzer Jacob Anthony 19	Oates Eliza Frances 16	1 Dec 1881	(4) 2/16
Shanholtzer Jacob Larkin 19	Ruckman Sarah Ann 21	15 July 1874	(4) 2/6
Shanholtzer James Fahs 23	Cheshire Mary Susan 30	2 Nov 1898	(4) 2/41
Shanholtzer James R Luther 20	Moreland Delcie L 20	24 Mar 1901	(4) 2/44
Shanholtzer John Newton 38	Carder Martha Jane 28	20 Nov 1889	(4) 2/27
Shanholtzer John Edward 19	Shank Lacey Ellen 21	13 Dec 1887	(4) 2/24
Shanholtzer John E 22	Shank Margaret R 20	2 Mar 1869	(4) 1/38
Shanholtzer John Martin 21	Shingleton Anner Maria 20	13 May 1875	(4) 2/7
Shanholtzer John Wesley 23	Wolford Emily Price 17	17 Dec 1879	(4) 2/14
Shanholtzer Jos Dan Bueguard 19	Whitacre Harriet Elizabeth 19	21 June 1882	(4) 2/17
Shanholtzer Joseph M 20	Shingleton Mary Susan 19	31 Jan 1884	(4) 2/19
Shanholtzer Lemuel Silas 20	Saville Eliza Margaret 17	24 Dec 1889	(4) 2/27
Shanholtzer Linnie 19	McDonald William 20	18 Aug 1891	(4) 2/29

Name #1	Name #2	Date	Source
Shanholtzer Lorenza Edgar 29	Barnes Mary Elizabeth 20	24 Apr 1901	(4) 2/44
Shanholtzer Lula Bertha 23	Gray William Bruce 30	14 Dec 1898	(4) 2/41
Shanholtzer Lydia Marg Ann 19	Carlyle Isaac Newton 24	29 Sept 1870	(4) 2/2
Shanholtzer Lydia Maria 17	Shane Edward F 22	3 Apr 1884	(4) 2/19
Shanholtzer Maggie Diadem 20	Wolford Granvill Harper 23	5 Apr 1899	(4) 2/41
Shanholtzer Marg Melissa 17	Foltz Benjamin Price 26	7 Jan 1879	(4) 2/12
Shanholtzer Margaret Rose 18	Haines Benjamin Taylor 28	25 Feb 1879	(4) 2/12
Shanholtzer Marg L Catherine 17	Kidwell Albert R 24	25 Aug 1893	(4) 2/33
Shanholtzer Margaret Bell 19	Powelson Isaiah Francis 25	10 Dec 1878	(4) 2/12
Shanholtzer Martin 28	Barrett Rebecca Elizabeth 19	17 Feb 1869	(4) 1/38
Shanholtzer Martha Jane 23	Nealis George William 26	8 Jan 1889	(4) 2/26
Shanholtzer Mary Martha Jane 22	Bohrer Anthony 23	19 Oct 1893	(4) 2/33
Shanholtzer Mary Ann 20	Hannas Solomon 28	31 Jan 1888	(4) 2/24
Shanholtzer Mary 35	Kerns Lewis Kennison 33	25 Dec 1873	(4) 2/5
Shanholtzer Mary Catharine 21	Moorehead Robt Wm 19	19 Oct 1865	(4) 1/1
Shanholtzer Mary Henrietta 27	Park George 35	20 Apr 1875	(4) 2/7
Shanholtzer Mary Frances 17	Whitacre Aquilla McCarsen 21	11 Sept 1884	(4) 2/19
Shanholtzer Miranda Catharine 19	Haines Benjamin Franklin 24	10 Jan 1878	(4) 2/11
Shanholtzer Noah 28	Bedinger Christina Margaret 20	17 Nov 1873	(4) 2/5
Shanholtzer P 32	Vanhorn A J 25	17 Nov 1868	(4) 1/7
Shanholtzer Philip Lemuel 23	Daugherty Harriet Elizabeth 18	19 Aug 1875	(4) 2/7
Shanholtzer Philip Solomon 22	Grapes Emma Irene 21	12 Aug 1888	(4) 2/25
Shanholtzer Philip Absalon 26	McCauley Mary Ellen 23	12 Nov 1878	(4) 2/12
Shanholtzer Phoebe Jane 31	Haines Charles Henry 27	3 Mar 1886	(4) 2/22
Shanholtzer Robert Harris 24	Hawkins Martha Virginia 20	15 May 1889	(4) 2/26
Shanholtzer Rosa Lucinda 21	Williams John Worthington 25	18 Jan 1891	(4) 2/29
Shanholtzer Sarah Emily Margaret 18	Bucklew William Jasper 21	24 Sept 1891	(4) 2/29
Shanholtzer Sarah 18	Hott Fowler Canfield 23	26 Mar 1874	(4) 2/6
Shanholtzer Sarah 32	Martin John Robert 33	23 Dec 1879	(4) 2/14
Shanholtzer Sarah 26	Saville John 27	24 July 1866	(4) 1/3
Shanholtzer Sarah Virginia 21	Saville William Henry	25 June 1874	(4) 2/6
Shanholtzer Silas L 25	Watson Mariah S 23	17 Mar 1868	(4) 1/6
Shanholtzer Solomon Jonathan 26	Wilson Virginia Catharine 19	2 Nov 1884	(4) 2/20
Shanholtzer Taylor Franklin 19	Haines Alcinda 19	10 Mar 1870	(4) 2/1
Shanholtzer Taylor 21	Riley Ollie Venetta 17	30 Sept 1894	(4) 2/34
Shanholtzer Theresa Jane 33	Foltz Smith Loy 33	20 Apr 1890	(4) 2/28
Shanholtzer William Jasper 28	Arnold Sarah Jane 19	14 Mar 1878	(4) 2/11
Shanholtzer William Robert 21	Henderson Elizabeth Caroline 19	26 Sept 1870	(4) 2/2
Shank Abraham 25	Hott Eliza Jane 22	6 Dec 1874	(5) 2/6
Shank Anne Lucinda 23	Smith Franklin Lee 25	12 Dec 1892	(4) 2/31
Shank Caroline Vina 27	Saville Peter Oliver 27	13 Dec 1887	(4) 2/24
Shank Cordelia 25	Housell John Luther 23	25 Apr 1900	(4) 2/42
Shank David 69	Hott Rachel Susan 29	20 Dec 1885	(4) 2/21
Shank Dugle 25	Starnes Oty 19	6 Apr 1898	(4) 2/40
Shank Frances Elizabeth 21	Maphis Jacob Anthony 18	28 Feb 1884	(4) 2/18
Shank George Washington 22	Peters Susan Virginia 26	3 Jan 1880	(4) 2/14
Shank John Harbert 28	Haines Julia Ann 20	27 Nov 1884	(4) 2/20
Shank John Lonas 25	Carder Sarah Elizabeth 24	18 Mar 1891	(4) 2/29
Shank Julia Ann 19	Simpson George Thomas 23	22 Oct 1891	(4) 2/30
Shank Lacey Ellen 21	Shanholtzer John Edward 19	13 Dec 1887	(4) 2/24
Shank Laura Francis 21	Wolford Harvey Clinton 28	29 Dec 1880	(4) 2/15
Shank Lucretia 20	Haines John Henry 26	13 Nov 1873	(4) 2/5

Name #1	Name #2	Date	Source
Shank Margaret Ann 35	Wolford ? 39	13 Dec 1859	(10)
Shank Margaret R 20	Shanholtzer John E 22	2 Mar 1869	(4) 1/38
Shank Melissa 21	Hines James Randolph 21	18 Apr 1877	(4) 2/10
Shank Oliver Holland 26	Sulser Laura Alice 23	20 Dec 1882	(4) 2/18
Shank Philip S 25	Hines Rebecca C 26	15 Jan 1872	(4) 2/3
Shank Rachel Ann 18	Emsley James Albert 26	10 Apr 1883	(4) 2/18
Shank William Edgar 22	Mayer Minnie Bell 20	31 Mar 1897	(4) 2/38
Shank Wm E	Gilbert S H	19 Jan 1854	(6)
Shanks John	Rawlines Susan	9 Sept 1823	(5)
Shannon Andrew	Smith Rebecca	*21 Dec 1826	(4) 3/48
Shannon Edgar Wilson 20	Roberts Margaret Louise 20	7 Aug 1893	(4) 2/32
Shannon Emily W 33	Towers Charles Henry 29	12 Aug 1890	(4) 2/28
Shannon Hannah Isabel 22	Parsons Edgar Elwood 24	4 May 1886	(4) 2/21
Shannon Jeremiah Chadwick 25	Bryan Florence 22	14 Nov 1871	(4) 2/3
Shannon William Andrew 23	Parsons Francie Curlette 20	27 Nov 1884	(4) 2/20
Shannon William Walker 36	Shouse Edith May 27	2 Dec 1890	(4) 2/28
Sharf George	Edwards Ann		(1) 13 Jan 1838
Sharp Thomas Elwell 44	Huffman Mary Catharine 34	25 Dec 1878	(4) 2/12
Sharpless A	Abernathy Robert	21 July 1842	(6)
Sharpless E	Harvey J W	9 Dec 1847	(6)
Sharpless H	Anderson Lloyd	28 Jan 1841	(6)
Sharpless Missouri	Mills Seth	20 Nov 1850	(6)
Sharpless Missouri	Mills Seth	20 Nov 1846	(5)
Sharpless Sarah	Kite Henry	20 Aug 1816	(5)
Sharpless Sarah	Kite Henry	20 June 1816	(6)
Sharpless Wm	Harvey Susan	14 Oct 1841	(6)
Sharps Wash	Kite Nancy	19 Jan 1843	(6)
Sharrest M C	Wallace R J	22 Aug 1846	(5)
Sharretts M C	Wallace R J	22 Aug 1850	(6)
Shawen Charles Tilden 21	Poland Margaret Ellen 19	27 July 1898	(4) 2/40
Shawen Daniel M 22	Larrimore Jane 25	1857	(10)
Shawen James Ashby 25	Haines Laura Belle Ella 21	24 Nov 1886	(4) 2/22
Shawen Lydia Bell 18	Haines Charles Page 21	24 Aug 1898	(4) 2/40
Shawen Mary E C 19	Messick Charles Ward 19	10 Sept 1895	(4) 2/36
Shawen Thomas Anthony 20	Poland Chloe Jane 17	6 Mar 1889	(4) 2/26
Shawin Annie Bell 23	Cheshire George Washington 23	19 Nov 1878	(4) 2/12
Shawn Daniel R 20	Wolf J Elizabeth 22	*19 Apr 1869	(4) 2/1
Shawn Daniel R 20	Wolford Elizabeth J 22	*19 Apr 1869	(4) 1/38
Shearer William	Asbury Mary	*1 Mar 1824	(4) 3/14
Shears Godfrey	Shears Mary	28 Oct 1845	(6)
Shears Isaac	Stonebreaker Catherine	20 Feb 1831	(5)
Shears Jacob	Steel Elizabeth	23 Apr 1833	(5)
Shears Mary	Shears Godfrey	28 Oct 1845	(6)
Shears William	Steel Lucindas	27 Aug 1827	(5)
Shearwood Ida 20	Beaver John E 25	8 Sept 1886	(4) 2/22
Sheckle Rebecca 23	Saville John 33	16 July 1857	(10)
Sheets James	Blackburn M	30 Mar 1837	(6)
Sheetz Daniel Benjamin 31	Doyle Zulemma Margaret 30	21 Aug 1889	(4) 2/26
Sheetz Edward Blackburn 25	Snyder Kate Lavinia 22	20 Feb 1867	(4) 1/4
Sheetz Elizabeth	Parker Thornton	22 Oct 1818	(6)
Sheetz Frederick Warin 26	Davis Susan Mary 23	14 Nov 1865	(4) 1/1
Sheetz Jacob Dice 29	Fletcher Margaret 23	30 May 1877	(4) 2/10

Name #1	Name #2	Date	Source
Sheetz James 53	Harper Myra Ann 27	15 June 1869	(4) 2/1
Sheetz Mary Elizabeth	McCarty Aquilla B		(1) 10 June 1853
Sheetz Mary Virginia 30	Blue Michael M 47	15 Sept 1886	(4) 2/22
Sheetz Sallie Ann 28	Bowman George Washington 27	17 Oct 1871	(4) 2/3
Shell Cathleen	Tucker Joseph	28 Nov 1827	(5)
Shell Clara	George Joseph	23 Dec 1842	(5)
Shell Lucretia	Mooreland Walter	10 Jan 1836	(5)
Shelley Hannah May 18	Jackson Henry Byrne 23	22 Dec 1891	(4) 2/30
Shelley James Luther 24	Rumsburg Sarah Lucinda 16	24 Apr 1892	(4) 2/30
Shelley Philip 45	Hott Susan Ann 30	6 Mar 1877	(4) 2/9
Shelly Charles William 23	Lewis Maria Catharine 18	29 Dec 1886	(4) 2/23
Shelly Ellie Virginia 17	Peer Charles Tilden 23	29 Aug 1900	(4) 2/43
Shelly George Warfield 25	Pultz Mary Ann 28	25 Feb 1879	(4) 2/12
Shelly John Melausthon 18	Clem Laura Christina 17	29 June 1896	(4) 2/37
Shelly Laura Ellen 24	Davis Robert P 38	29 Jan 1895	(4) 2/35
Shelly Maggie B 20	Arnold Geo Benjamin 22	16 Aug 1870	(4) 2/2
Shelly Priscilla C 23	McCauly Andrew W 23	3 Dec 1867	(4) 1/6
Shelton John N	Busby Ann	*29 Oct 1828	(4) 3/35
Shelton Margaret Ann 30	Keller Peter 45	*29 Nov 1871	(4) 2/3
Shelton Mary Jane 30	Lambert Abraham H 42	25 Mar 1869	(4) 1/38
Shereman Dorothy C 17	Wilkins Matthais 49	8 Mar 1866	(4) 1/3
Sheridan Campbell 50	Linton Elizabeth H 50	4 Aug 1892	(4) 2/31
Sheriff Nancy V 20	Kline James 35	29 June 1868	(4) 1/6
Sherrard William	McDonald Millicent S	*24 May 1825	(4) 3/38
Shers Frances Ellen 30	Utt Richard Henry Levi 25	18 Oct 1894	(4) 2/34
Sherwood A J 42	Rummer Martha E 27	*1 Aug 1900	(4) 2/43
Shewalter Marietta 21	Athey Newton David 30	20 Dec 1876	(4) 2/9
Shields John	Shillingburg Mary	3 Mar 1831	(5)
Shields M J	Bosley Daniel	6 Apr 1848	(6)
Shields Mary	Kitzmiller William H	27 Nov 1836	(5)
Shillinburg W	Burgess C	17 Aug 1852	(6)
Shillingburg Eliz	Bean Sol	19 Jan 1837	(6)
Shillingburg Mary	Shields John	3 Mar 1831	(5)
Shillingburg Margaret	Smith Thomas	28 Oct 1842	(5)
Shillingburg S	Harvey Sam	22 Nov 1821	(6)
Shillingburg Sarah	Harvey Sam	2 Nov 1821	(5)
Shillingburg Wash	Burgess Caroline	15 Aug 1852	(5)
Shillingburg Washington	Evans Nancy	19 Sept 1842	(5)
Shingleton Absalom Lee 28	Ganoe Mary Victoria 18	23 Aug 1893	(4) 2/33
Shingleton Absalom 36	Haines Nancy 28	1856	(10)
Shingleton Absalon Lee 21	Messick Elizabeth Jane 16	19 Jan 1887	(4) 2/23
Shingleton Anner Maria 20	Shanholtzer John Martin 21	13 May 1875	(4) 2/7
Shingleton Catharine 21	Cheshire Burr William 19	7 Dec 1898	(4) 2/41
Shingleton Elihue Pownell 23	McDonald Rebecca Josaphine 18	22 Dec 1880	(4) 2/15
Shingleton Elizabeth 33	Beatty Abraham 32	8 Nov 1899	(4) 2/42
Shingleton Elizabeth Mrs 53	Messick Thomas Harrison 62	7 Oct 1897	(4) 2/39
Shingleton James Raymond 44	Haines Elizabeth 42	11 Feb 1886	(4) 2/21
Shingleton James Holister 28	Hott Ora E 18	14 Dec 1898	(4) 2/41
Shingleton Jemima 20	Bowman George 27	19 Sept 1872	(4) 2/3
Shingleton Job Jeremiah 26	Timbrook Sarah Selana 17	25 Oct 1876	(4) 2/9
Shingleton Joseph Sibert 23	McDonald Rachel Catharine 25	25 Mar 1884	(4) 2/19
Shingleton Mariah 23	McDonald Jared Andrew 24	22 Dec 1880	(4) 2/15

Name #1	Name #2	Date	Source
Shingleton Mary Susan 19	Shanholtzer Joseph M 20	31 Jan 1884	(4) 2/19
Shingleton Minnie Florence 22	Fletcher Alvin M 20	3 Sept 1895	(4) 2/36
Shingleton Rebecca Ann 23	Timbrook John David 22	20 Mar 1884	(4) 2/19
Shingleton Rebecca Josephine 33	Timbrook John David 34	8 Apr 1896	(4) 2/37
Shingleton William Jackson 28	Moyer Anna Rebecca 19	21 Apr 1897	(4) 2/39
Shipe Isaac Robert 22	Sulser Sarah Tabitha Inskeep 20	14 July 1880	(4) 2/14
Shipman ? 36	Bumgarner Elizabeth Ann 21	22 Dec 1859	(10)
Shireman Anne M	Timbrook Philip	28 Sept 1893	(4) 2/33
Shirly James	McNemar Lurana	3 Mar 1853	(5)
Shivers John	Barrott Rhoda	*17 Jan 1825	(4) 3/9
Shivers Jonathan Thomas 26	Oats Mary Elizabeth 23	16 Feb 1869	(4) 1/38
Shoaf Thomas	Spencer Ruth	3 Apr 1823	(6)
Shockey Job	Ludwick Emily J	24 Sept 1853	(5)
Shockey Lydia	Ferryman Francis	*29 Oct 1827	(4) 3/52
Shockey Margaret 24	Spurling James 23	1855	(10)
Shockey Sam V	Liller M V	24 July 1845	(6)
Shockey Susan	Liller Thomas	28 Oct 1845	(6)
Shoemaker Alonzo Tecumsey 19	Purgit Mary Statton 17	19 Mar 1896	(4) 2/37
Shoemaker Anna 18	Barb Franklin Columbus 22	8 Dec 1880	(4) 2/15
Shoemaker Archibald Jerome 21	Liller Clara Elizabeth 20	22 Mar 1893	(4) 2/32
Shoemaker Charles Wallace 21	Haggerty Mary Bell 15	17 June 1884	(4) 2/19
Shoemaker Edward Holland 26	Arnold Hester A 22	20 Mar 1877	(4) 2/10
Shoemaker Elijah 59	Huffman Catharine 44	17 July 1887	(4) 2/23
Shoemaker Eliza Ellen 18	Anderson James H 24	4 Apr 1877	(4) 2/10
Shoemaker Emma Catherine 20	Baily Edward Wright 23	7 Feb 1894	(4) 2/33
Shoemaker Gerta May 24	Stickley Tobias Taylor 26	9 Aug 1893	(4) 2/32
Shoemaker Hannah Catharine 20	Taylor Julius Waddle 27	21 Mar 1877	(4) 2/10
Shoemaker James Beckwith 32	Brown Hattie Jane 20	7 Jan 1885	(4) 2/20
Shoemaker Jasper 22	Arnold Mary Susan 21	14 Sept 1866	(4) 1/3
Shoemaker John	Kelly E	26 Mar 1856	(6)
Shoemaker John 22	Kelley Elizabeth 20	26 Mar 1857	(10)
Shoemaker Lionel Franklin 21	High Dorothy Ann 19	2 June 1891	(4) 2/29
Shoemaker M J	Davy John	20 May 1838	(6)
Shoemaker Maggie A 19	Arnold Robert H 24	4 July 1872	(4) 2/3
Shoemaker Martha Virginia 20	Ludwig Sanford Romanus 30	18 Sept 1889	(4) 2/27
Shoemaker Mary Ann 21	Roadcap John 27	30 Dec 1875	(4) 2/8
Shoemaker Mary Elizabeth 19	Barb William Henry 26	31 Dec 1891	(4) 2/30
Shoemaker Rosetta E 18	Merritt George Washington 28	27 Nov 1889	(4) 2/27
Shoemaker S	High Jonathan	15 Sept 1836	(6)
Shoemaker Sarah Catherine 26	Helman Frederick Hinnbiord 24	*15 Sept 1875	(4) 2/7
Shoemaker Sarah Frances 29	Miller Charles F 23	10 Oct 1877	(4) 2/10
Shoemaker T	Arnold Rob't	14 Feb 1839	(6)
Shoemaker Thomas Nicholas 22	Jewell Mary C 18	1 Aug 1893	(4) 2/32
Shoemaker Tirzah	Arnold Robert	14 Feb 1840	(5)
Shoemaker W H	Kelly S A	29 June 1848	(6)
Shope Elias	Iliff Margaret	*5 Apr 1824	(4) 3/20
Shorb Eliza Lavina 18	Offutt Joseph McKeever 28	7 Feb 1888	(4) 2/24
Shorb Florence Lee 28	Haines William Davis 28	21 Sept 1892	(4) 2/31
Shore Margaret	McGraw Samuel	7 Feb 1826	(6)
Shores Ev	Walburn Reuben	3 Oct 1850	(6)
Shores Evelin	Walburn Reuben	3 Oct 1846	(5)
Shores Margaret	McGraw Samuel	*6 Feb 1826	(4) 3/5

Name #1	Name #2	Date	Source
Short Caroline Virginia 17	Bowley James 22	5 Feb 1880	(4) 2/14
Short Catharine Ann 40	Proctor James Monroe 41	18 Oct 1897	(4) 2/39
Short George	Cogle Ann E		(1) 13 May 1859
Short George	McBride Martha	*29 Dec 1828	(4) 3/49
Short Hannah Miranda 22	? 32	8 Nov 1883	(4) 2/18
Short Isaac	Vandegrift Mary	*24 Jan 1827	(4) 3/9
Short J Wesley 54	Hiett Anne Bell 35	13 Mar 1900	(4) 2/42
Short James D 21	Baker Amanda F 18	Jan 1857	(10)
Short John William 26	Moore Anna Dawson 35	3 Feb 1881	(4) 2/15
Short Joseph Calvin 34	Benear Belle 31	5 Aug 1891	(4) 2/29
Short M	Orndorff John	28 Nov 1860	(10)
Short Martha Ellen 23	Dunn Francis Marion 29	27 Feb 1881	(4) 2/15
Short Mary Elizabeth 25	Orndorff Simon Peter 22	4 Mar 1866	(4) 1/3
Short Samantha Catherine 22	Naylor Robert Cornelius 44	27 Apr 1892	(4) 2/31
Short William	Baker Lucy	*31 July 1827	(4) 3/40
Shouse Edith May 27	Shannon William Walker 36	2 Dec 1890	(4) 2/28
Shouse Jane 17	Shanholtz Minor 32	16 Nov 1868	(4) 1/7
Showalter Annie Bell 23	Snyder John Wesley 29	10 Apr 1895	(4) 2/35
Showalter Lydia A 25	Carter John W 22	15 Feb 1868	(4) 1/6
Showalter Rebecca 35	Stickley Geo 51	23 Mar 1868	(4) 1/6
Showalter Samuel Brown 36	Malcom Elmira Jane 28	*17 Apr 1871	(4) 2/2
Shrout Margaret 31	Stonebraker John P 46	13 Jan 1866	(4) 1/2
Shrout Nancy	Dayton Valentine	7 Jan 1852	(6)
Shrout William Lewis 25	Kesner Mahala Jane 17	7 Nov 1891	(4) 2/30
Shull Florence Minnie May 18	Haines William Hill 25	23 Feb 1898	(4) 2/40
Shultz Bessie J 29	White C S 27	25 July 1867	(4) 2/1
Shurley Lazarus	Flemming Anne	*14 Mar 1825	(4) 3/23
Shurs Harriet 21	Burgess John 30	20 Feb 1866	(4) 1/2
Sibole ? 32	Bowman George 31	4 Sept 1860	(10)
Sickafoos John	McFarland Catherine	*26 July 1826	(4) 3/30
Sigcafoose John	McFarling Cathaleen	6 Aug 1826	(5)
Simmons Annie 29	Cleve John Michael 31	6 Oct 1897	(4) 2/39
Simmons E A	Wilson Wm	14 Dec 1834	(6)
Simmons Estella May 18	Lough Charles 28	22 Oct 1899	(4) 2/42
Simmons John Henry 25	Darr Annie Lee 16	25 Dec 1888	(4) 2/25
Simmons John William 30	Sechrist Mary Ellen 34	30 Dec 1886	(4) 2/22
Simmons Josiah	Hilky Elizabeth	4 Nov 1844	(5)
Simmons Matilda Elizabeth 17	Piles Luther Branson 24	2 Aug 1883	(4) 2/18
Simmons Maude McClung 19	Cupp William Arthur 23	1 Dec 1897	(4) 2/39
Simmons Pene	Douthit Jas	24 Sept 1835	(6)
Simmons Samuel 23	Saville Mary Jane 18	2 Aug 1877	(4) 2/10
Simmons Sarah D 32	Saville John Abraham	6 Aug 1884	(4) 2/19
Simmons William M	Fisher Ann Jemima		(1) 6 June 1839
Simmons? Millie Dorothy 21	Jenkins William Henry 22	*26 Dec 1892	(4) 2/31
Simmures? Daniel Harrison 23	Steward Sarah Virginia 18	6 Sept 1893	(4) 2/33
Simpson C Ann 33	Bradfield Jas 40	27 Feb 1868	(4) 1/6
Simpson George Thomas 23	Shank Julia Ann 19	22 Oct 1891	(4) 2/30
Simpson Hannah Catharine 22	Arnold George Statton 28	8 Mar 1876	(4) 2/8
Simpson Hugh Soloman 24	Chaney Nancy Ann 25	9 June 1880	(4) 2/14
Simpson Ida May 20	Parks George P 24	22 Oct 1890	(4) 2/28
Simpson Jane	Spotz Joseph	*13 Nov 1828	(4) 3/40
Simpson Jane 21	Cool John Wesley 29	19 Dec 1875	(4) 2/8

Hampshire County Marriage Records

Name #1	Name #2	Date	Source
Simpson John	McCauley Rebecca	*11 Dec 1826	(4) 3/45
Simpson Martha E E 16	Raines Isaac Solomon 23	12 July 1893	(4) 2/32
Simpson Mary Ellen 22	Hoke John Levi 37	14 Sept 1884	(4) 2/19
Simpson Samuel A 35	Everett A Frances 18	18 Aug 1896	(4) 2/37
Simpson Thomas 26	Seaton Elizabeth 31	12 Aug 1868	(4) 1/7
Sims Rebecca F 24	Bowens Joseph 25	15 Oct 1874	(4) 2/6
Sinclair John M 22	Hull Sarah Catharine 17	1 Mar 1866	(4) 1/3
Sine Albert A 20	Whitacre N M 16	14 Apr 1896	(4) 2/37
Sine Alfred L 33	Kelsoe Lillie B 34	6 Mar 1895	(4) 2/35
Sine Christy	Cackley Margaret	*27 Apr 1825	(4) 3/32
Sine Floyd Holmes 27	Baker Sarah Rebecca 20	24 Mar 1897	(4) 2/38
Sine Mary 40	Smith Jefferson 46	18 Oct 1865	(4) 1/1
Sine William H 38	Catlett Zina 27	30 Dec 1882	(4) 2/18
Sine William Henry 24	Whitaker Nancy Virginia 21	13 July 1875	(4) 2/7
Singhass Effie Rush 19	Parker Idgar Stump 27	7 Nov 1894	(4) 2/35
Singleton Aaron	Myers M	1 Nov 1836	(6)
Singleton Alexander 25	Banks Emily 24	16 June 1874	(4) 1/39
Singleton Alexander 20	Brown Lula 22	6 July 1896	(4) 1/41
Singleton Wilburn	Ludwick Catherine	23 Aug 1860	(5)
Sion Adam	Latherman Susan	6 Oct 1840	(5)
Sion Adam	Leatherman Susan	6 Oct 1839	(6)
Sirbaugh ? 19	Whitacre ? 21	31 Dec 1857	(10)
Sirbaugh Aaron 45	Richmond Mary Jane 35	22 Aug 1878	(4) 2/11
Sirbaugh Annie Cyrena 17	Eaton John Willaim 21	30 May 1878	(4) 2/11
Sirbaugh Chas Lemuel 25	McDowell Jennie A 19	4 July 1899	(4) 2/41
Sirbaugh Frances Ellen 21	McKee Edward Tollison 22	22 May 1890	(4) 2/28
Sirbaugh Ida 20	Hutcheson Jonathan 30	23 Jan 1901	(4) 2/43
Sirbaugh Ida Virginia 19	Oats ? 21	19 Oct 1875	(4) 2/7
Sirbaugh Jacob 30	Frank Ellen 22	24 Dec 1879	(4) 2/14
Sirbaugh James 19	Keller Maggie Bell 19	22 Feb 1899	(4) 2/41
Sirbaugh Jonah 18	Oats Amanda 16	19 Apr 1881	(4) 2/16
Sirbaugh Julia Virginia 23	Sirbaugh Robert Baxter 24	29 Nov 1899	(4) 2/42
Sirbaugh Julius A 18	Hawkins Mary A 19	25 Dec 1877	(4) 2/11
Sirbaugh Lucy S 18	McDonald Charles H 22	23 Jan 1901	(4) 2/43
Sirbaugh Lucy Virginia 19	Patterson ? 23	15 Nov 1883	(4) 2/18
Sirbaugh Mary Elizabeth 18	Barr John Martin 23	21 Aug 1888	(4) 2/25
Sirbaugh Mary Elizabeth 21	Miller Amos Wm 21	24 Mar 1878	(4) 2/11
Sirbaugh May Catharine 18	Deats Joseph Jefferson 25	*5 Sept 1875	(4) 2/7
Sirbaugh Olivia Catharine 23	Whitacre Arthur Clark 25	25 Jan 1894	(4) 2/33
Sirbaugh Robert Baxter 24	Sirbaugh Julia Virginia 23	29 Nov 1899	(4) 2/42
Sirbaugh Sadie Elizabeth 21	Oats Robert Joshua 20	*4 June 1894	(4) 2/34
Sirbaugh Samuel Harvey 25	Kackley Minnie Bell 21	26 Dec 1889	(4) 2/27
Sirbaugh Samuel Harvey 37	McKeever Margery Ann 27	24 May 1900	(4) 2/42
Sirbaugh Uriah Offutt 24	Brannon Frances Elizabeth 22	30 Aug 1893	(4) 2/33
Sirbaugh Vernie 20	Milleson John 35	8 Aug 1892	(4) 2/31
Sirbaugh William Henry 33	Nicewoner Priscilla Jane 18	29 May 1883	(4) 2/18
Sirbaugh Wm Joshua 24	Kerns Elizabeth Florence 20	25 Feb 1892	(4) 2/30
Sirbough Servanah 17	Laurence John Thomas 23	27 Jan 1881	(4) 2/15
Sirk Rosa Florence 21	Crites Allen 23	26 Dec 1899	(4) 2/42
Sites John 31	Merygold Mary Jane 26	14 Dec 1865	(4) 1/2
Sivel James 21	Youse Caroline 22	30 Nov 1854	(10)
Siville Hannah Susan 19	Oats George Washington 32	16 Oct 1879	(4) 2/13

Name #1	Name #2	Date	Source
Slane Annie 21	Deaver Howell Hook 27	13 Nov 1878	(4) 2/12
Slane Benjamin	Cheshire Delilah	*7 June 1824	(4) 3/31
Slane Daniel Webster 24	Wolford Mary Esther 18	11 Dec 1884	(4) 2/20
Slane Harriett	Milleson Silas	*19 Feb 1827	(4) 3/12
Slane Julia Ann 26	Kidwell George Washington 28	12 Apr 1876	(4) 2/8
Slane Lucinda 26	? Isaac 29	15 Oct 1872	(4) 2/3
Slane Lucy Ellen 20	Wolford George T 22	27 July 1882	(4) 2/17
Slane Maria	Fahs Joseph	*2 Apr 1827	(4) 3/25
Slane Milly	Barrott Samuel	*23 Aug 1825	(4) 3/55
Slane Nancy	Winckelblick Philip	*25 Dec 1826	(4) 3/49
Slane Nancy E 20	Alderton Edward 23	31 May 1876	(4) 2/8
Slane Rebecka	Blackman David	*3 Jan 1825	(4) 3/2
Sliger Jacob	Nally Sarah	20 Oct 1836	(6)
Sloan Eliz	Stump W B	20 Apr 1858	(6)
Sloan Mary	Wright Dr F M	30 Oct 1859	(6)
Sloan Mary	Wright M F Dr	30 Oct 1860	(5)
Sloan Sarah	Arnold Michael	*16 Feb 1828	(4) 3/3
Sloane Elizabeth	Arnold Joseph	*20 Jan 1827	(4) 3/8
Slocum Deborah	Pepper Frederick	*13 Jan 1827	(4) 3/5
Slonacre Margaret May 19	Whitacre Burton Walter 23	14 Mar 1893	(4) 2/32
Slonaker Alice Belle 14	Whitacre Archibald Vanderbilt 20	29 Dec 1896	(4) 2/38
Slonaker Arthur Clinton 23	Harloe Laura Rebecca 21	24 Mar 1881	(4) 2/15
Slonaker Caroline Virginia 21	Nelson Jackson	10 Nov 1859	(10)
Slonaker Clara Elizabeth 23	Billmyre Richard Dabney 27	7 June 1883	(4) 2/18
Slonaker Dora E 22	Knee E Lester 28	10 Oct 1900	(4) 2/43
Slonaker Emily Frances 16	Whitacre Jackson 26	17 Oct 1893	(4) 2/33
Slonaker George Washington 28	Oglisbee Almira Virginia 22	10 Nov 1871	(4) 2/3
Slonaker James Wm David 31	Nixon Emma E 23	25 Apr 1894	(4) 2/34
Slonaker Laura Roselle 17	Spaid Amos Josephus 23	19 Jan 1893	(4) 2/32
Slonaker Lettie 23	Bunner James Alexander 35	8 Sept 1895	(4) 2/36
Slonaker Louisa L 25	Hawkins Henry 35	3 Mar 1868	(4) 1/6
Slonaker Margaret Emma 18	Parish George Washington 24	13 Sept 1883	(4) 2/18
Slonaker Mary D 27	Racey Lewis 47	8 Feb 1866	(4) 1/2
Slonaker Mary Jane 21	Powell John Vernon 22	26 Nov 1878	(4) 2/12
Slonaker Michael	Barrett Eleanor	*16 aPR 1827	(4) 3/26
Slonaker Molly Delila 22	Kelso Mahlon Lore 30	22 Dec 1891	(4) 2/30
Slonaker Olive Edith 17	Hiett Samuel Leonidas 24	28 Nov 1892	(4) 2/31
Slonaker Wesley 48	Heatwole Laura Louisa 24	4 Apr 1882	(4) 2/17
Slonaker Wesley Luther 25	McBee Alice Maretta 22	5 Oct 1886	(4) 2/22
Slonaker William 24	Haines Hariett Elizabeth 17	14 Apr 1859	(10)
Smaltz Lewella 32	Hook Isaiah Proctor 60	1 Jan 1901	(4) 2/43
Smaltz Robert Lee 24	Haines Mary E 20	10 Apr 1901	(4) 2/44
Smar Eliza	McCullough John		(1) 18 Aug 1838
Smarr James Lawrence 22	Bowman Hannah Elizabeth 26	22 Feb 1877	(4) 2/9
Smarr P	Leatherman Peter	16 May 1833	(6)
Smellie James Wilson 47	Harness Annie Pearl 25	14 Apr 1897	(4) 2/39
Smeltz William	Boley Catherine	2 Nov 1822	(5)
Smith ? 40	Wolford Sarah Ellen 21	10 Sept 1859	(10)
Smith Aaron Clarence 23	McDonald Anne Bell 20	9 Mar 1892	(4) 2/30
Smith Abraham I	White Sarah	*3 Oct 1825	(4) 3/64
Smith Abram	White Sarah	4 Oct 1825	(6)
Smith Andrew 23	Lewis Mary Alberta 22	31 Aug 1896	(4) 1/41

Name #1	Name #2	Date	Source
Smith Angeline	Bacon?art Charles	16 Sept 1852	(2) 7 Oct 1852
Smith Ann 22	Sutton William 25	25 Dec 1867	(4) 1/6
Smith Anna Mariah	Cedars Thomas	25 Aug 1822	(6)
Smith Annie Lee 18	Hiett Evan Peter 26	23 Aug 1899	(4) 2/41
Smith Asa 23	Buckaloo Rebecca C 24	11 Oct 1857	(10)
Smith B Jetson 29	Wilson Lucy Jane 26	24 Mar 1897	(4) 2/38
Smith Benjamin Taylor 23	Haines Chloe Margaret 18	28 Feb 1877	(4) 2/9
Smith Benjamin Wesley 23	Corbin Martha Jane 18	31 Oct 1883	(4) 2/18
Smith Boyd 23	Williams Mary 21	1 Jan 1891	(4) 1/41
Smith Calvin M 48	Spurling Rebecca 29	29 Sept 1891	(4) 2/29
Smith Charles Henry 20	Davis Virginia 22	22 Sept 1875	(4) 2/7
Smith Charles Milton 25	McBride Virginia Bell 21	11 Apr 1895	(4) 2/35
Smith Charles William 31	Hiett Laura Ann 25	4 June 1895	(4) 2/35
Smith Charlotte 30	Colley Jacob 27	23 Nov 1886	(4) 1/40
Smith Clara Cristena 17	Spurling Isaac 34	8 Nov 1882	(4) 2/17
Smith Cutbert	Steele Sarah	19 Oct 1844	(5)
Smith Cuthbert	Thrasher	16 June 1833	(5)
Smith Daniel Victor 29	Liller Maggie Lee 21	24 May 1883	(4) 2/18
Smith Dorcas	Welch Isaac	24 Aug 1820	(6)
Smith Eliz	Junkins Thoas	24 Apr 1849	(6)
Smith Elizabeth	Moreland Sam	20 Jan 1831	(6)
Smith Ellen 40	Bias Joseph 26	13 Apr 1871	(4) 1/38
Smith Franklin Lee 25	Shank Anne Lucinda 23	12 Dec 1892	(4) 2/31
Smith George Renic 31	Kelley Etta Fanny 31	3 Oct 1900	(4) 2/43
Smith Giles Jenkins 40	Hiett Dorothy 35	30 Mar 1875	(4) 2/7
Smith Greenbury	Hendrixon Margaret	17 Mar 1836	(5)
Smith Henrietta 18	Bowles Stewart B 26	15 Apr 1868	(4) 1/6
Smith Henry Baker 24	Anderson Mary Jane 23	13 Dec 1892	(4) 2/31
Smith Hunter Homer 22	Powell Minnie May 24	28 Oct 1896	(4) 2/37
Smith Isabel	Smith Philip	22 Nov 1848	(6)
Smith Jacob	Entler Nancy	*17 Sept 1828	(4) 3/27
Smith Jacob	Grimm Susan	4 Mar 1841	(6)
Smith James Franklin 26	Kendall Laura Lowring 19	10 Oct 1881	(4) 2/16
Smith James Renza 25	Swisher Nola May 18	1 Mar 1899	(4) 2/41
Smith James William 21	Grapes Margaret Ann 20	16 Oct 1879	(4) 2/13
Smith Jefferson 46	Sine Mary 40	18 Oct 1865	(4) 1/1
Smith Jemima	High William H 54	17 Feb 1892	(4) 2/30
Smith John	Ganoe Elizabeth	*15 Dec 1828	(4) 3/47
Smith John	Hiper Elizabeth	12 Aug 1832	(5)
Smith John Wesley 23	Collins Susanna 19	28 Aug 1890	(4) 2/28
Smith John William 21	Piles Sarah Malinda Alice 18	20 Dec 1888	(4) 2/25
Smith Joseph 71	Bloxham Mahala 52	19 Apr 1866	(4) 1/3
Smith Joseph M 21	Baker Sarah 19	5 Jan 1860	(10)
Smith Laura Bell 24	Lewis Enoch Bert 26	16 Dec 1882	(4) 2/18
Smith Louisa Alice 21	Poling James Grover 37	11 Sept 1896	(4) 2/37
Smith Lousia	Michael John	1 Nov 1843	(5)
Smith Maggie Francis 29	Bucklew Elzy Flournoy 19	5 Nov 1895	(4) 2/36
Smith Margaret 18	Stonebraker Isaac Taylor 21	12 Nov 1896	(4) 2/38
Smith Margaret 18	Williams Abram 24	23 Sept 1865	(4) 1/1
Smith Margaret 30	Patterson John 54	27 Jan 1874	(4) 2/5
Smith Margaret Ann 19	Godlove Isaac Calvin 24	13 Feb 1876	(4) 2/8
Smith Margaret C 23	Ambler James 35	19 Dec 1865	(4) 1/2

Name #1	Name #2	Date	Source
Smith Martha Susan Elizabeth 17	Duckworth Andrew Marvell 28	30 Nov 1887	(4) 2/24
Smith Mary	Lyon John	*12 Mar 1827	(4) 3/16
Smith Mary	Steerman Wm	22 Apr 1830	(6)
Smith Mary	Wolford ?	June 1859	(10)
Smith Mary Ann	Baker Joshua	5 Mar 1829	(5)
Smith Mary Elizabeth 36	Hinkle Mausie Lewis Davis 50	3 Jan 1867	(4) 1/4
Smith Mary Elizabeth 19	Sowers John Newton 29	23 Oct 1888	(4) 2/25
Smith Mary Jane 20	Hoopengarner Samuel Sheridan 25	1 Jan 1889	(4) 2/26
Smith Mary Jane 20	Kuykendall Joseph 26	2 Dec 1900	(4) 2/43
Smith Millie	Baker Joseph	19 Jan 1837	(6)
Smith Nancy C 19	Carder Raliegh 26	25 Aug 1875	(4) 1/39
Smith Nathaniel Seymour 22	Godlove Lydia Abigail Pownall 20	* Sept 1879	(4) 2/13
Smith Nimrod	Thrasher Jane	18 Sept 1836	(5)
Smith Peter	Barrick Susan	20 Mar 1817	(6)
Smith Philip	Smith Isabel	22 Nov 1848	(6)
Smith R	Barnhouse Andrew	17 Nov 1831	(6)
Smith Rebecca	Campbell George	21 Feb 1819	(6)
Smith Rebecca	Shannon Andrew	*21 Dec 1826	(4) 3/48
Smith Rebecca E 22	McBrid Eli 25	3 Feb 1868	(4) 1/6
Smith Rosa 23	Bartlett John 24	3 Feb 1875	(4) 1/39
Smith Rosa Lee 24	Hardy Boyd 27	2 Aug 1887	(4) 1/40
Smith Sarah	Dawson William O	9 Aug 1860	(5)
Smith Sarah	Mills Isaac	28 Nov 1840	(5)
Smith Sarah	Mills Isaac	28 Nov 1839	(6)
Smith Sarah 21	Millburn George Henry 23	30 Dec 1875	(4) 1/39
Smith Sarah C	Davis Felix	*25 July 1825	(4) 3/52
Smith Sarah C 19	Haines Jno W 22	13 Sept 1866	(4) 1/3
Smith Sarah Catharine 50	St Myer Andrew Alexander 65	24 Oct 1895	(4) 2/36
Smith Sarah Francis 22	Lear Jefferson Davis 30	21 June 1892	(4) 2/31
Smith Sarah Jane 32	Dawson William D 57	9 Aug 1860	(10)
Smith Sarah Jane 22	Swisher Benjamin F 24	20 Oct 1859	(10)
Smith Sol	Janney Rachel	19 Dec 1840	(5)
Smith Sol	Janney Rachel	19 Dec 1839	(6)
Smith Soloman	Roberts Martha	*18 Aug 1825	(4) 3/54
Smith Sylves	Crosley Joanna	1 Oct 1844	(6)
Smith Thomas	Shillingburg Margaret	28 Oct 1842	(5)
Smith Viola S 18	Piles John William 24	27 Mar 1899	(40 2/41
Smith Virginia S 19	Frye Benjamin Hanson 25	15 June 1876	(4) 2/8
Smith William	Sellers Tobitha	4 Sept 1823	(5)
Smith William 37	Saville Eliza Jane 33	9 Feb 1870	(4) 2/1
Smith William Brown 28	Keys Edith 23	30 Nov 1894	(4) 1/41
Smith William George 23	High Francis 23	7 Aug 1889	(4) 2/26
Smoot Addie Mabell 21	Foltz John Wesley 26	3 Jan 1888	(4) 2/24
Smoot Charles Middleton 35	Foltz Elizabeth 25	10 Jan 1897	(4) 2/38
Smoot John William 21	Ganoe Maggie Jane 20	21 Jan 1895	(4) 2/35
Smoot John William 20	Hardy Sarah Elizabeth 21	30 Oct 1873	(4) 2/5
Smoot Josiah	Riley Jane	*19 Feb 1827	(4) 3/13
Smoot Judson 21	Foltz May 16	24 Feb 1891	(4) 2/29
Smoot Mariah	Burkitt John	*19 Jan 1824	(4) 3/7
Smoot Norman	Betterton Margaret	*16 Aug 1825	(4) 3/53
Smoot Rebecca A	Alkire Peter	20 Apr 1853	(1) 29 Apr 1853
Smoot Samuel	Hoffman Elizabeth	*24 May 1825	(4) 3/41

Name #1	Name #2	Date	Source
Snapp James C 46	Monroe Malinda 35	25 Oct 1860	(10)
Snapp Mariah	Wolverton Isaac	*15 May 1826	(4) 3/19
Snarr Oliver David 27	Poling Eva Virginia 24	1 June 1897	(4) 2/39
Sneathen R	Buzzard ?	1 Dec 1857	(10)
Snider Anna M 21	Arnold David A 24	21 Nov 1877	(4) 2/10
Snider Martin 21	Orndorff Mahala 14	18 Jan 1866	(4) 1/2
Snigers Milly 19	Bias Joseph 21	21 Oct 1865	(4) 1/1
Sniggers Anne 31	Cison Charles Henry 25	29 Dec 1885	(4) 1/40
Snodgrass Eliza C	Coyner David H		(1) 28 Mar 1839
Snowden Edgar Jr	Powell Clar		(1) 8 May 1857
Snyder Anna 26	Blanton Erastus See 27	21 Dec 1869	(4) 2/1
Snyder Benjamin Franklin 24	Miller Mary Elizabeth 21	2 June 1886	(4) 2/22
Snyder Cordelia May 20	Timbrook Isaac Hunter 23	13 Sept 1899	(4) 2/41
Snyder Hariete	Welton Alonzo	*21 Feb 1825	(4) 3/16
Snyder Ida Elizabeth Powell 18	Deaver Howell Foote 40	11 Oct 1892	(4) 2/31
Snyder John M 49	Kidd Virginia B 35	28 Aug 1873	(4) 2/4
Snyder John Wesley 29	Showalter Annie Bell 23	10 Apr 1895	(4) 2/35
Snyder Joseph Sylvester 30	Thomas Emma Jane 21	22 Nov 1893	(4) 2/33
Snyder Kate Lavinia 22	Sheetz Edward Blackburn 25	20 Feb 1867	(4) 1/4
Snyder Lizzie 19	Straw Merritt S 30	11 Oct 1899	(4) 2/42
Snyder Martin Luther 22	Miller Ellen 22	1 Sept 1881	(4) 2/16
Snyder Mary Elizabeth 18	Ullery Alfred L 32	7 Sept 1875	(4) 2/7
Snyder Mary Rebecca Melissa 18	Loy James Mordicai 24	20 Aug 1899	(4) 2/41
Snyder Peter 23	Wolford Rebecca	1855	(10)
Snyder Rebecca	Rorabough Daniel		(1) 1 Dec 1838
Snyder Richard Martin 23	Kerns Laura Belle 22	8 Nov 1888	(4) 2/25
Snyder Samuel A 21	Malcolm Laura E 19	27 Dec 1893	(4) 2/31
Snyder Virginia Ashley 20	Marpole James Madison 27	20 Apr 1882	(4) 2/17
Soles Edward Eli 30	Keller Sarah Catharine 30	9 Mar 1881	(4) 2/15
Sollars Andrew	Paugh Catherine	5 Dec 1848	(6)
Sollars Eliz	Blackburn Jas	8 Oct 1840	(6)
Sollars Mary	Kitzmiller Joseph	20 Jan 1831	(6)
Sollars Nancy	Neville H D	19 Dec 1844	(6)
Sollars Susan	Rotruck B L	5 Dec 1844	(6)
Sowers Ellen B 17	Daugherty Daniel Ashby 20	20 Dec 1882	(4) 2/18
Sowers James Rufus 24	Powers Nora 18	1 Nov 1894	(4) 2/35
Sowers John Newton 29	Smith Mary Elizabeth 19	23 Oct 1888	(4) 2/25
Sowers Martha Susan 21	Hott James Henry 24	26 Sept 1876	(4) 2/8
Sowers Sarah Margaret 43	Abe John Adam 53	25 Nov 1897	(4) 2/39
Spade E A V 18	Davis Jno W 23	19 Dec 1868	(4) 1/7
Spade Frances V 24	Chamberline J A R 25	19 Dec 1868	(4) 1/7
Spade John	Leatherman Elizabeth	24 Nov 1836	(6)
Spade Mahalah	Arnold William	*31 Dec 1827	(4) 3/63
Spade Nancy Jane 37	Pugh Benjamin 52	15 June 1869	(4) 2/1
Spaid ? 25	Pepper Mary Jane 24	29 Dec 1859	(10)
Spaid Amos Josephus 23	Slonaker Laura Roselle 17	19 Jan 1893	(4) 2/32
Spaid Ann Maria 19	Brill Wm Paul 25	13 Dec 1866	(4) 1/4
Spaid Christina Adaline 21	Swisher Perry Franklin 25	*8 Jan 1877	(4) 2/9
Spaid Elin May 20	Kelso Carter Gilbert 24	19 Mar 1891	(4) 2/29
Spaid Elisabeth	Kline Philip	*21 Feb 1827	(4) 3/15
Spaid Eliza Ann 18	Orndorff George Edgar 26	2 Dec 1880	(4) 2/15
Spaid Fannie Hayes 25	Brill Lewis Walter 24	14 Nov 1894	(4) 2/35

Name #1	Name #2	Date	Source
Spaid Flavius J 21	Wilson Mary Elizabeth 23	28 Nov 1867	(4) 1/5
Spaid Francis M	Pepper Nancy Jane	5 Jan 1860	(1) 13 Jan 1860
Spaid Frederick M 24	Brill Margaret C 22	13 Dec 1866	(4) 1/4
Spaid Hannah Caroline 24	Davis George Franklin 24	11 Dec 1873	(4) 2/5
Spaid Jacob Franklin 35	Brill Lydia Catharine 23	11 Jan 1894	(4) 2/33
Spaid Jeremiah James 25	Lafollette Gegirtha Frances 18	12 Apr 1899	(4) 2/41
Spaid John H	Miller Mary Virginia	16 Apr 1857	(10)
Spaid John W	Brill Margaret E	2 Mar 1865	(8)
Spaid Luther B 24	Lupton Martha Lizzie 18	29 Sept 1897	(4) 2/39
Spaid Margaret	Goos John D	23 Sept 1852	(2) 7 Oct 1852
Spaid Mariah Elizabeth 21	Brill Al? Luther 24	12 Nov 1896	(4) 2/37
Spaid Martha 21	Heishman Abraham Lincoln 27	13 Oct 1892	(4) 2/31
Spaid Nellie Love 19	Brill George Clarence 23	28 Feb 1900	(4) 2/42
Spaid Nicholas Leatherman 27	Anderson Sarah Angelina 21	26 Mar 1874	(4) 2/6
Spaid Regina Susanna 34	Gray Henry Newton 35	28 Dec 1893	(4) 2/33
Spaid Sarah Eleanora 19	Brill Lernon Hilkie 21	3 Mar 1887	(4) 2/23
Spaid Tilberry Miles 25	Pennington Lydia Ann 19	1 Oct 1885	(4) 2/21
Speelman Bradford 23	Shanholtzer Cora Bell 19	9 Jan 1901	(4) 2/43
Speelman David	Hagar Susan	14 Nov 1822	(5)
Speelman Mollie V 18	Kremes George Thomas 22	10 Aug 1871	(4) 2/3
Speelman William 23	Miller Claudia Shelton 23	11 Jan 1897	(4) 2/38
Spencer Arthur	Lees Catherine	9 Dec 1819	(6)
Spencer C C	McKenzie A	26 Aug 1849	(6)
Spencer Eliz	Flick Jacob	4 May 1837	(6)
Spencer Eliza	Blackburn W H	24 Mar 1853	(6)
Spencer John	Miller Mary	*10 Nov 1824	(4) 3/50
Spencer Julia	Dawson Jacob	23 Nov 1854	(6)
Spencer Julia	Miller Peter	26 Feb 1824	(6)
Spencer Julia Ann	Miller Peter	*21 Feb 1824	(4) 3/11
Spencer Mary	Flick Isaac	6 Mar 1828	(6)
Spencer Rachel	Fleek Peter	*29 Jan 1828	(4) 3/2
Spencer Rachel	Flick Peter	31 Jan 1828	(6)
Spencer Ruth	Shoaf Thomas	3 Apr 1823	(6)
Spencer Susan	Urice Peter	25 Apr 1822	(6)
Spencer Susan E	Blackburn James	20 Jan 1853	(6)
Sperrow Bertha Evaline 16	Houser Charles Stewart 24	30 Jan 1895	(4) 2/35
Sperrow Charles O 20	Thomas Ellen Elizabeth 17	26 Nov 1895	(4) 2/36
Spicer Ruth	McClure James	28 Sept 1826	(6)
Spielman John William 20	Wright Sarah Catharine 19	12 Feb 1874	(4) 2/5
Spotz Joseph	Simpson Jane	*13 Nov 1828	(4) 3/40
Spurling Ellen Ashby 25	Doman Thomas Lee 25	25 Nov 1888	(4) 2/25
Spurling Harriet 26	Davey Edward 28	2 June 1877	(4) 2/10
Spurling Isaac 34	Smith Clara Cristena 17	8 Nov 1882	(4) 2/17
Spurling James 21	Peasmaker Lucy 19	20 Dec 1888	(4) 2/26
Spurling James 23	Shockey Margaret 24	1855	(10)
Spurling Luke 22	Davy Mary 24	7 Sept 1865	(4) 1/1
Spurling Luther 28	Doman Elizabeth Catherine 21	10 May 1887	(4) 2/23
Spurling Margaret Lane 23	Allender John William 21	3 Oct 1888	(4) 2/25
Spurling Mary Catharine 22	Michael John Henry 20	28 May 1879	(4) 2/13
Spurling Rebecca 29	Smith Calvin M 48	29 Sept 1891	(4) 2/29
Spurling Reuben 33	Liller Elizabeth Belle 22	24 Sept 1889	(4) 2/27
Spurling Robert 30	Madera Anna Bell 21	14 Feb 1883	(4) 2/18

Name #1	Name #2	Date	Source
Spurling Sarah Ann 20	Corbin ? 22	3 Nov 1857	(10)
Spurling Sidney Jane 28	White Madison 26	14 Feb 1879	(4) 2/12
Spurling William 39	Lear Mary Catharine 20	24 Mar 1886	(4) 2/22
Spurling William 51	Merritt Hannah 31	27 Aug 1857	(10)
Spurling William 48	Riggleman Ella 35	13 Dec 1897	(4) 2/39
St Clair Marjory	King Wesley	16 Nov 1820	(5)
St Clair Nancy	Davis Joseph	10 Nov 1833	(6)
St Myer Andrew Alexander 65	Smith Sarah Catharine 50	24 Oct 1895	(4) 2/36
Stackhouse Stephen P 38	Beall Ella V 27	31 Oct 1871	(4) 2/3
Stafford Eliza	Wiley Zale		(1) 19 Sept 1839
Stagg Delilah	Flick Wm S	19 Sept 1854	(6)
Stagg Elizabeth	Leatherman Dan	25 Aug 1822	(6)
Stagg Frank	Leatherman D	1 Feb 1844	(6)
Stagg Isabel Lauretta 17	Flick John William 25	22 Oct 1878	(4) 2/12
Stagg M A	Urice John	3 Mar 1859	(6)
Stagg M A	Urice Sam	24 Apr 1856	(6)
Stagg William	Thrash Mary	*7 Jan 1828	(4) 3/1
Staggs John	Whiteman M	26 Nov 1840	(6)
Staggs John	Whiteman Margaret	26 Nov 1841	(5)
Staggs Mary	Mudy James	15 Aug 1844	(6)
Staggs Mary Ann	Urice John 35	13 Mar 1859	(10)
Staggs Mary Elizabeth 18	Biser Silas 21	18 Feb 1874	(4) 2/5
Staggs William	Thrush Martha	10 Jan 1828	(5)
Staggs Wm	Thrush Mary	10 Jan 1828	(6)
Stall Peter	Van Buskirk Sarah	20 Oct 1841	(5)
Stall Peter	Van Buskirk Sarah	20 Oct 1840	(6)
Stallaberger Mathew	Hayes Rebecca	*18 Dec 1826	(4) 3/46
Staouther Ann	Davy Washington	8 Dec 1838	(1) 22 Dec 1838
Starkey Catharine J 18	Piles Benjamin Franklin 24	6 Dec 1888	(4) 2/25
Starkey Jemima E 23	Ruckman Jas J 27	20 Feb 1866	(4) 1/2
Starkey John	Combs Sarah	*Jan/Feb 1824	(4) 3/8
Starkey John Frederick 20	Chaney Mary Elizabeth 28	25 Dec 1876	(4) 2/9
Starkey Rebecca 20	Loy William 24	27 Dec 1866	(4) 1/4
Starn Grace Charlotte 20	Yost Robert Branson 25	29 July 1891	(4) 2/29
Starne Machir I 22	Albright Sarah S A 16	4 Dec 1872	(4) 2/4
Starne Thomas	Burner Ruth	*27 Dec 1824	(4) 3/55
Starnes John Thomas 36	Carder Rebecca Leath 27	26 Apr 1899	(4) 2/41
Starnes John William 23	Cheshire Maltilda Jane 20	15 Oct 1867	(4) 1/5
Starnes Martha A 28	Yost Granville Armstrong 26	2 Jan 1890	(4) 2/27
Starnes Mary H 23	Cheshire James 19	4 July 1889	(4) 2/26
Starnes Oty 19	Shank Dugle 25	6 Apr 1898	(4) 2/40
Starnes Sarah 21	Carter Frederick 34	27 Feb 1866	(4) 1/3
Starnes William Absalom 32	Hannas Sarah Elizabeth 20	23 Feb 1887	(4) 2/23
Starns Abigal A 20	Haines Geo M 20	10 Feb 1868	(4) 1/6
Starns Bettie Parker 19	Wagoner Edmond Berkeley 22	28 Dec 1880	(4) 2/15
Starns Isaac Parsons 23	Cheshire Louisa Virginia 18	18 May 1880	(4) 2/14
Starns Mary Parker 22	Haines David E 26	26 Oct 1881	(4) 2/16
Starns Nancy Ann 21	Beatty Hugh 25	20 Feb 1878	(4) 2/11
Starns Thomas J 23	Shanholtzer Fannie B A 23	25 Sept 1873	(4) 2/4
Statton N G	Taylor Aseneth	18 Jan 1854	(6)
Staup Christopher 35	Lore Catharine 42	17 Feb 1870	(4) 2/1
Steally Jacob	Wilson Ellen	15 Apr 1824	(6)

Name #1	Name #2	Date	Source
Steel Elizabeth	Shears Jacob	23 Apr 1833	(5)
Steel Lucinda	Frantz Adam	26 Feb 1828	(5)
Steel Lucindas	Shears William	27 Aug 1827	(5)
Steele Catharine 32	White C S 33	26 May 1873	(4) 2/4
Steele Gertrude Maude 27	Nicols William Lewellyn 28	25 Sept 1890	(4) 2/28
Steele Sarah	Smith Cutbert	19 Oct 1844	(5)
Steele Thomas 40	Tutwiler Caroline Frances 24	20 Jan 1886	(4) 2/21
Steerman Catherine	Sands James	25 Aug 1825	(6)
Steerman Dan	Davis Rebecca	21 Sept 1830	(6)
Steerman Rich	Burnet M	4 Nov 1836	(6)
Steerman Wm	Smith Mary	22 Apr 1830	(6)
Steinback Sarah	Burns Morgan	*20 July 1824	(4) 3/40
Stemple Sarah Elizabeth	Bizer John	10 Mar 1859	(1) 1 Apr 1859
Stephens Beverly Nash 29	King Emily Laura 21	20 Oct 1896	(4) 1/41
Stephens Lillie B 24	Lafollette Mullen 25	16 Apr 1895	(4) 2/35
Stephens Margaret Ellen 21	Brill Champion Trone 40	4 Mar 1896	(4) 2/37
Stephens Sarah 19	Keckley Harrison Lot 29	26 Dec 1888	(4) 2/26
Stern George	Hoover Sarah	*2 Sept 1828	(4) 3/23
Stevens Jas W 22	Racey Mary J 22	17 Feb 1868	(4) 1/6
Stevens Malinda 21	Edmondson Oswell 21	25 Jan 1888	(4) 1/40
Stevenson Mary A 48	Mills Thomas Thompson 45	24 May 1892	(4) 2/31
Steward Elihu G 29	Haines Flora Margreat 17	*4 Mar 1892	(4) 2/30
Steward Sarah Virginia 18	Simmures? Daniel Harrison 23	6 Sept 1893	(4) 2/33
Stewart Amanda 18	Lee John David 38	29 Dec 1887	(4) 2/24
Stewart Benjamin Franklin 21	Moreland Martha Virginia 18	22 Dec 1881	(4) 2/17
Stewart Edna Earl 18	Brown Francis Marion 24	13 Nov 1891	(4) 2/30
Stewart Edward 21	Everett Elizabeth Catharine 21	16 July 1879	(4) 2/13
Stewart Elizabeth 28	Brooks Charles 45	9 Oct 1873	(4) 2/4
Stewart George W	Yost ?	2 Feb 1860	(10)
Stewart H M	Flick Thorn	27 Nov 1855	(6)
Stewart Henry Michael 31	Davey Lucy Lee 24	23 Jan 1901	(4) 2/43
Stewart James	Bizer Mary	*23 June 1826	(4) 3/28
Stewart James Henry 25	Jane Moreland 26	16 Feb 1869	(4) 1/38
Stewart James Henry 51	Milslagle Flora Belle 28	11 Oct 1893	(4) 2/33
Stewart John William 40	Didawick Mary Aida 18	30 Mar 1893	(4) 2/32
Stewart John William 35	Haws Lydia Ann 18	12 July 1888	(4) 2/25
Stewart John William 27	Robinson Ellen Comfort 42	14 Sept 1882	(4) 2/17
Stewart Lula 19	Ludwig John William 28	31 May 1897	(4) 2/39
Stewart Margaret Elizabeth 40	Kline Julius Calvin 28	30 Dec 1880	(4) 2/15
Stewart Matilda Jane 21	Rhumsberg George Washington 21	10 Dec 1874	(4) 2/6
Stewart P	Randall Thomas	1 July 1824	(6)
Stewart Priscella C	Randall Thomas	*24 June 1824	(4) 3/37
Stewart Robert Smith 25	Wolford Hannah Catharine 23	3 Feb 1881	(4) 2/15
Stewart Sam	Rinker Christina	17 Feb 1831	(6)
Stewart Sarah Virginia 30	Roomsberg George Washington 36	29 July 1886	(4) 2/22
Stewart William Jefferson 29	Wolford Mary Margaret 28	26 July 1871	(4) 2/3
Stickley ? Tobias 22	Kerns Nancy Elizabeth 22	24 Feb 1874	(4) 2/5
Stickley Benjamin	McDonald Eleanor	21 Sept 1826	(5)
Stickley Elizabeth Ann 42	Poling Mitchell Felix 37	10 Feb 1878	(4) 2/11
Stickley Gabriel Tobias 33	Malcolm Ann Alice 24	28 June 1885	(4) 2/20
Stickley Geo 51	Showalter Rebecca 35	23 Mar 1868	(4) 1/6
Stickley Jane	Caldwell Samuel		(1) 5 Dec 1839

Name #1	Name #2	Date	Source
Stickley John A 26	Taylor Gracie A 18	19 Dec 1865	(4) 1/2
Stickley Joseph Riley 22	Whiteman Gertrude May 21	28 June 1894	(4) 2/34
Stickley Mariah J 22	Greitzner Christian 23	18 Mar 1869	(4) 1/38
Stickley Mary Margaret 22	Kelly Joseph A 23	18 June 1867	(4) 1/5
Stickley Rufus William 27	Reed Cora Maude 21	3 Feb 1897	(4) 2/38
Stickley Sarah Virginia 22	Blue Kirk 23	30 June 1889	(4) 2/26
Stickley Tobias 64	Cummins Mary Ann 54	23 Sept 1869	(4) 2/1
Stickley Tobias Taylor 26	Shoemaker Gerta May 24	9 Aug 1893	(4) 2/32
Stickley Tobias Marion 23	Taylor Sarah Ellen 27	5 Apr 1881	(4) 2/15
Stily Jacob	Wilson Elen	*13 Apr 1824	(4) 3/22
Stine Mary E	Bovey Henry A	14 May 1857	(1) 22 May 1857
Stingley Lydia	Lyon Thomas	6 Mar 1823	(5)
Stingley William	Tucker Nancy	27 May 1824	(5)
StMyer John 23	Allen Margaret 22	21 Aug 1884	(4) 2/19
Stockslager Jacob	Bull Mary	*3 Nov 1826	(4) 3/38
Stone Anna Evans 28	Mytinger William Machir 27	2 Nov 1886	(4) 2/22
Stone Maria	Patterson Robert H	9 May 1839	(1) 16 May 1839
Stonebraker David T 23	Roderick Nancy C 24	11 Jan 1866	(4) 1/2
Stonebraker Isaac Taylor 21	Smith Margaret 18	12 Nov 1896	(4) 2/38
Stonebraker John P 46	Shrout Margaret 31	13 Jan 1866	(4) 1/2
Stonebreaker	McDonald Anthony	18 Sept 1836	(5)
Stonebreaker Catherine	Shears Isaac	20 Feb 1831	(5)
Stonebreaker Ruth	Jones Jesse	21 May 1834	(5)
Stottlemyer James 23	Clingerman Mollie 22	*27 Aug 1888	(4) 2/25
Strauderman Elizabeth 23	Baker ? 38	21 Nov 1883	(4) 2/18
Strauther Liddie 50	Unger Joseph Montgomery 50	11 Apr 1901	(4) 2/44
Straw Merritt S 30	Snyder Lizzie 19	11 Oct 1899	(4) 2/42
Strawden Geo W 27	Jackson Mary 17	20 May 1884	(4) 1/40
Strawder Wm A 39	Harper Eliza Jane 21	1 Jan 1866	(4) 1/2
Strawer Julia Ann	Belt James S		(1) 29 Sept 1838
Streby Clara Matilda 22	Saville Gustavis M 24	14 Apr 1897	(4) 2/39
Streby Joseph Clarence 23	Heiskell Eleanora Grace 23	10 June 1891	(4) 2/29
Street S H 21	Woods John H 22	22 Jan 1868	(4) 1/6
Streets Elizabeth	Murphy John	5 Dec 1844	(6)
Streets John William 22	Fairfax Bertie 17	26 Nov 1889	(4) 1/41
Streets Mary 21	Martin Henry 23	9 May 1878	(4) 1/39
Streits Sara 21	Gilicrist James H 24	8 Oct 1879	(4) 1/39
Strieby Sadie A 34	Swisher James R 35	29 Mar 1899	(4) 2/41
Strock David F 24	Russell M Edith 21	23 Apr 1895	(4) 2/35
Strosnyder George Washington 23	Rosebrock Mariah Isabel 23	*6 July 1881	(4) 2/16
Strother Walter Spencer 21	Davis Nora Clifton 17	16 Oct 1895	(4) 2/36
Stuckey Benjamin Allen 28	Leith Sarah Winiford 23	27 Oct 1881	(4) 2/16
Stullenbarger C	Ralston Val	6 June 1847	(6)
Stullenbarger Mat	Hays R	19 Dec 1826	(6)
Stump Elizabeth D W	Abernathy William	*8 Jan 1825	(4) 3/5
Stump Elizabeth Catharine 20	Ginivan Morris Newton 29	21 Feb 1872	(4) 2/3
Stump Jacob 29	Thompson Evelina 21	17 Feb 1859	(10)
Stump James Adam 25	Hass Sarah Arnold 27	4 Aug 1886	(4) 2/22
Stump Joseph 42	Miller Nancy 26	13 Jan 1870	(4) 2/1
Stump Lena Elizabeth 23	Harmison Charles Chilton 31	12 Oct 1892	(4) 2/31
Stump Mary Ann 29	Doman John B 29	5 Jan 1886	(4) 2/21
Stump Peter	Caudy Margaret	*3 May 1827	(4) 3/32

Name #1	Name #2	Date	Source
Stump Rebecca	Stump William	*17 July 1826	(4) 3/29
Stump Samuel D 22	Power Edith Virginia 18	8 Apr 1888	(4) 2/24
Stump Sarah	Moore Abraham	*1 Oct 1828	(4) 3/29
Stump W B	Sloan Eliz	20 Apr 1858	(6)
Stump William	Stump Rebecca	*17 July 1826	(4) 3/29
Stump William 25	Brice Nellie Lewis 19	29 July 1894	(4) 2/34
Stump Wm Baldwin 40	Arnold Charlotte 37	17 Mar 1875	(4) 2/7
Stuttenbarger E	Kitzmiller H	8 May 1856	(6)
Sulser Henry	Purgit Rachael	*15 Aug 1825	(4) 3/51
Sulser Laura Alice 23	Shank Oliver Holland 26	20 Dec 1882	(4) 2/18
Sulser Mary Jamima 19	Arnold Benjamin Franklin 22	9 Feb 1881	(4) 2/15
Sulser Mortimer 53	Iser Rachel J 48	2 Mar 1892	(4) 2/30
Sulser Mortimore 44	Ludwick Elizabeth Jane 37	11 Oct 1881	(4) 2/16
Sulser Sarah Tabitha Inskeep 20	Shipe ? 22	14 July 1880	(4) 2/14
Sulser William Henry 23	Bowman Margaret Frances 16	*14 Nov 1879	(4) 2/13
Sulser William Henry 23	Bowman Margaret Frances 18	17 Sept 1881	(4) 2/16
Summers John	Bobo Rebecca	* 18 Feb 1828	(4) 3/4
Susan White 34	High Elijah 63	18 Mar 1869	(4) 1/38
Sutherland James H Anderson 23	Saville Mrs Annie Elizabeth 40	14 May 1890	(4) 2/28
Sutherland Louisa 17	Boyce Charles Edward 23	4 July 1896	(4) 2/37
Sutton Charlotte 35	Johnson Abraham 30	30 Nov 1865	(4) 1/1
Sutton F Annie 37	Gardner James 46	28 June 1881	(4) 1/40
Sutton Jane	Whiting Saul	12 Jan 1835	(6)
Sutton William 25	Smith Ann 22	25 Dec 1867	(4) 1/6
Swainy Thomas 25	Lyons Darkas Ann 18	23 Sept 1869	(4) 2/1
Swartz Samuel 36	Saville Mary Catherine 24	*8 Oct 1878	(4) 2/12
Swartz Sarah Catharine 26	Boone James Daniel 32	24 Apr 1892	(4) 2/30
Sweltz Wm	Bosley Catherine	28 Nov 1822	(6)
Swier Catharine	Corbin David	*7 Feb 1826	(4) 3/7
Swier David	McBride Louiza	*15 Sept 1828	(4) 3/26
Swisher ?	Burkett John Thomas	28 Feb 1860	(10)
Swisher Ann Rebecca 35	Kline Philip 50	2 Nov 1873	(4) 2/5
Swisher Ann Ziletta 23	Adams George W 32	28 Apr 1875	(4) 2/7
Swisher Asa Sine 22	Allemong Martha Jane 22	*20 Nov 1880	(4) 2/15
Swisher Benjamin F 24	Smith Sarah Jane 22	20 Oct 1859	(10)
Swisher Catharine 30	Peters Harrison 21	22 Aug 1871	(4) 2/3
Swisher Catherine	Cokenow Henry	*19 Mar 1827	(4) 3/Page Torn
Swisher Cora Florence 20	McDonald John William 24	2 Sept 1891	(4) 2/29
Swisher David Edward 22	Miller Agnes Jannetta 21	21 Dec 1887	(4) 2/24
Swisher Dorthy Ann 18	Wolf James H 32	21 Apr 1885	(4) 2/20
Swisher Harriet 30	Doyle Matthew 60	19 Oct 1865	(4) 1/1
Swisher Henry	Hoffman Sarah	*12 Feb 1827	(4) 3/11
Swisher James Larimore 34	Scanlon Anna 24	7 July 1886	(4) 2/22
Swisher James R 35	Strieby Sadie A 34	29 Mar 1899	(4) 2/41
Swisher Jane Annis 22	Tutwiler Jonathan Foxter 24	8 Jan 1878	(4) 2/11
Swisher John Arnold Harris 26	McGill Ella C 22	17 Oct 1883	(4) 2/18
Swisher John Henry 27	Taylor Carrie Vance 29	30 June 1891	(4) 2/29
Swisher John Wesley 24	Allamong Lewella Elizabeth 29	16 June 1895	(4) 2/35
Swisher Joseph Anthony 58	Mauk Martha Jane 26	1 Nov 1892	(4) 2/31
Swisher Kessiah 27	Taylor James 25	30 Oct 1877	(4) 2/10
Swisher Margaret Millisa 16	Ruckman William 20	29 May 1884	(4) 2/19
Swisher Mary Alice 22	Lee John David 26	26 Oct 1876	(4) 2/9

Name #1	Name #2	Date	Source
Swisher Mary Belle 25	Vandervort Virgil 30	3 June 1885	(4) 2/20
Swisher Mary Virginia 21	Jordan Robert 35	15 Feb 1866	(4) 1/2
Swisher Mary Virginia 21	Gray Benjamin Franklin 23	16 June 1895	(4) 2/35
Swisher Minnie L 21	Householder William Robert 24	27 Dec 1894	(4) 2/35
Swisher Nettie Rebecca 21	Lewis Philip Alexander 27	28 Feb 1894	(4) 2/33
Swisher Nola May 18	Smith James Renza 25	1 Mar 1899	(4) 2/41
Swisher Perry Franklin 25	Spaid Christina Adaline 21	*8 Jan 1877	(4) 2/9
Swisher Philip Mathew 30	McDonald Sarah Jane 38	9 Nov 1882	(4) 2/17
Swisher Philip Matthew 23	Cool Louisa Catharine 22	2 Nov 1876	(4) 2/9
Swisher Pruda Dara D 15	Kline Joseph 28	31 Dec 1876	(4) 2/9
Swisher Rebecca Ann 36	Watson John Gordy 32	23 Feb 1882	(4) 2/17
Swisher Rebecca Jane 21	Savill John Judson 22	22 Aug 1867	(4) 1/5
Swisher Rosa Jane 25	Oats Harrison William 25	16 Feb 1898	(4) 2/40
Swisher Sarah Belle 17	Kline John Wesley 24	1 Sept 1881	(4) 2/16
Swisher Stephen 24	Hott Catharine 21	29 May 1860	(10)
Swisher Susan Virginia 21	Ewers Luther Carson 21	1 Dec 1875	(4) 2/8
Swisher Vincent Markwood 24	Ruckman Margaret Ellen 22	29 May 1884	(4) 2/19
Syms Jas	Brown Parthenia	6 June 1848	(6)
Tabb Dougal C	McDowell Matilda Woodie		(1) 13 May 1859
Tabb Harlan Page 29	Vandiver Sarah Frances 23	29 Mar 1871	(4) 2/2
Tacker Isaac	Barnhouse Mariam	15 Oct 1840	(5)
Tapscott Chichester	Naylor Jane	*6 Oct 1825	(4) 3/66
Tapscott Newton	Fairfax Louisa W	*3 Mar 1825	(4) 3/17
Tarr Oliver Harrison 27	High Mary Susan 33	13 Sept 1893	(4) 2/33
Tasker George	Junkins Mary	29 Sept 1825	(6)
Tasker George	Jenkins Mary	*26 Sept 1825	(4) 3/60
Tasker George	Davis Aseneth	5 Apr 1832	(6)
Tasker H F	Harvey Mariah	4 Feb 1836	(6)
Tasker Isaac	Barnhouse M	15 Oct 1839	(6)
Tasker John	Reese Frances	28 Apr 1842	(6)
Tasker L S	Knight Caleb	30 Oct 1851	(6)
Tasker L S	Kight Caleb	25 Dec 1850	(5)
Tasker M C	Kalbaugh Alex	8 Oct 1850	(6)
Tasker M J	Barrick Jacob	29 Nov 1848	(6)
Tasker Millie	Trenter Joshua	20 Aug 1816	(6)
Tasker Mynta	Brown James	30 Nov 1820	(6)
Tasker Nancy	Thrasher Abram	Feb 1820	(5)
Tasker Nancy	Thrasher A	2 Mar 1820	(6)
Tasker Sarah	Wilson William	8 Sept 1818	(6)
Tate James	Flick Elizabeth	29 Jan 1839	(6)
Tate James	Flick Elizabeth	29 Jan 1840	(5)
Tawzer Wilber Irvin 22	Dicken Viola Myrtle 14	26 July 1896	(4) 2/37
Taylor Addie Elizabeth 20	Rannells William Edward 25	11 Jan 1899	(4) 2/41
Taylor Alberta Lee 22	Harwood William Green 27	20 Jan 1885	(4) 2/20
Taylor Ann	Ludwick Joseph	*10 Sept 1825	(4) 3/59
Taylor Ann Cecilia 25	Wills Silas Grayson 23	17 Oct 1876	(4) 2/9
Taylor Aseneth	Statton N G	18 Jan 1854	(6)
Taylor Caroline 21	Pugh John Wesley 22	9 Jan 1867	(4) 1/4
Taylor Carrie Vance 29	Swisher John Henry 27	30 June 1891	(4) 2/29
Taylor Catherine	Brown John	*13 Sept 1828	(4) 3/25
Taylor Charles 27	Washington Bessie 19	3 Sept 1891	(4) 1/41
Taylor Charles M 35	Murphy Mary E 32	18 Jan 1866	(4) 1/2

Name #1	Name #2	Date	Source
Taylor Charles S	Higgins Patsy	*10 June 1826	(4) 3/24
Taylor D Dawson 33	Thompson Jemima 31	24 June 1893	(4) 2/32
Taylor Daniel	Rogers Martha Ann	*25 Oct 1824	(4) 3/49
Taylor Dora D 40	Herbaugh Ettie 23	25 Jan 1899	(4) 2/41
Taylor Ella Lee 26	Pownall John Daniel 32	13 Feb 1889	(4) 2/26
Taylor Francis Lemuel 26	Light Ethel Minerva 21	10 Sept 1900	(4) 2/43
Taylor George 32	Pugh Margaret Catherine 23	16 Dec 1879	(4) 2/14
Taylor Gracie A 18	Stickley John A 26	19 Dec 1865	(4) 1/2
Taylor Hannah Elizabeth 26	French Charles Montgomery 32	18 Nov 1873	(4) 2/5
Taylor Hannah Lawson 19	Long Uriah 27	8 Mar 1893	(4) 2/32
Taylor Harriet Ellen 25	Williams Samuel Holland 42	6 Dec 1882	(4) 2/18
Taylor Hattie A 24	Long William 33	4 Mar 1884	(4) 2/18
Taylor Isaac 22	Brown Mary 21	20 Sept 1879	(4) 1/39
Taylor Isaac 25	Arnold Hannah Catharin 20	8 Sept 1875	(4) 2/7
Taylor Isaac 29	Kuykendall Fannie B 24	5 Mar 1867	(4) 1/4
Taylor J Wm 24	Click Emma F 21	24 Aug 1868	(4) 1/7
Taylor Jacob Thomas 41	Fellers Jennie 27	14 Feb 1893	(4) 2/32
Taylor James 25	Swisher Kessiah 27	30 Oct 1877	(4) 2/10
Taylor Jane	Rinker Daniel	7 Oct 1824	(5)
Taylor Jemima 26	Carter John William 27	5 Mar 1873	(4) 2/4
Taylor John Edward 31	Wilson Annie Smith 21	7 Mar 1877	(4) 2/9
Taylor John of Thos 37	Kreemer Emma Catharine 26	28 Oct 1886	(4) 2/22
Taylor Joseph	High Miss		(1) 22 Dec 1838
Taylor Joseph 27	Mills Sarah Catharine 20	7 Jan 1874	(4) 2/5
Taylor Julius Waddle 27	Shoemaker Hannah Catharine 20	21 Mar 1877	(4) 2/10
Taylor Kirk Bride 33	Rannells Louisa Henrietta 19	13 Jan 1874	(4) 2/5
Taylor Lelia Clyde 22	Wirgman Charles Thornton 24	17 Apr 1889	(4) 2/26
Taylor Lesizah 21	Markwood Jno W 24	18 Apr 1866	(4) 1/3
Taylor Maggie Elizabeth 23	Berry William Richard 28	22 Feb 1882	(4) 2/17
Taylor Maggie Jane 18	George William Henry 23	31 Aug 1898	(4) 2/40
Taylor Mary Elizabeth 26	Mercer Bertram Longfellow 25	4 Sept 1895	(4) 2/36
Taylor Mary Ellen 30	Hite George William 35	19 May 1885	(4) 2/20
Taylor Mary Ellen 18	Kessel Charley Anderson 23	27 Feb 1895	(4) 2/35
Taylor Mary Susan 20	French Charles Montgomery 34	16 Feb 1876	(4) 2/8
Taylor Nancy	Dye J W	19 Dec 1859	(6)
Taylor Nancy	Dye J W	19 Dec 1860	(5)
Taylor Parentha	Brown Jno	13 Sept 1828	(6)
Taylor R 25	Odass John 34	20 Dec 1870	(4) 2/2
Taylor Robert	Kail Elizabeth	*30 Jan 1825	(4) 3/11
Taylor Robert	Rotruck Polly	23 Sept 1824	(5)
Taylor Sallie A	Thrush Peter	8 Mar 1842	(6)
Taylor Sarah 19	Rudolph S 26	8 Mar 1859	(10)
Taylor Sarah Ellen 27	Stickley Tobias Marion 23	5 Apr 1881	(4) 2/15
Taylor Sarah Jane 23	Pugh David William 30	*4 Sept 1879	(4) 2/13
Taylor Seymour Rudolph 30	Hoffman Martha Ann 23	16 May 1888	(4) 2/25
Taylor Simon	Davis Margaret		(1) 21 July 1838
Taylor Simon D 33	Murphy Sarah M 26	1 Nov 1865	(4) 1/1
Taylor Susan	French William	*28 May 1825	(4) 3/39
Taylor W J	High M A	26 Oct 1853	(6)
Taylor Wm F 31	Blue Mrs Susan 29	18 Dec 1877	(4) 2/10
Templar John L	Keiter Esther	29 Mar 1838	(1) 7 Apr 1838
Tevalt Isaac	Bosly Phebe	25 Oct 1832	(5)

Name #1	Name #2	Date	Source
Tharp Ann	Evans Alexander	*2 Jan 1826	(4) 3/1
Tharp Hannah Catherine 19	Poland Peter Duval 23	10 Mar 1880	(4) 2/14
Tharp Jackson 28	Johnson Lena 21	25 Aug 1897	(4) 2/39
Tharp John 24	Pepper Mary J	27 Oct 1859	(10)
Tharp Samuel Isaac 45	Combs Anne 40	13 Jan 1885	(4) 2/20
Tharp Wilber L 28	Monroe Ellen 22	29 Nov 1899	(4) 2/42
Thatcher Sarah	Harper Rhody	18 Apr 1816	(5)
Thatcher Sarah	Harper R	14 Apr 1816	(6)
Thomas Adda Salina 21	Miller ? 25	*29 Aug 1882	(4) 2/17
Thomas Albt	Lett Cabel	1 Jan 1835	(5)
Thomas David 23	Dicken Flora Frances 17	8 June 1887	(4) 2/23
Thomas Ellen Elizabeth 17	Sperrow Charles O 20	26 Nov 1895	(4) 2/36
Thomas Emma Jane 21	Snyder Joseph Sylvester 30	22 Nov 1893	(4) 2/33
Thomas George H 26	Washington Margaret Esther 22	25 July 1893	(4) 2/32
Thomas Jane	Doll Abraham	*11 June 1827	(4) 3/37
Thomas Jane	Doll Abram	14 June 1827	(6)
Thomas Mary Florence 22	Emmart Morgan 28	8 Feb 1893	(4) 2/32
Thomas Orloff Dorsey 24	Racey Bertie 24	*28 Dec 1896	(4) 2/38
Thomas Samuel	Scott Maria	9 May 1839	(5)
Thompson Charles Taylor 22	Martin Estella May 21	*9 May 1901	(4) 2/44
Thompson Charles Eugene 26	Gill Lucretia 25	19 Feb 1880	(4) 2/14
Thompson Elijah	Kail Christiana	*4 Apr 1825	(4) 3/28
Thompson Ellen	Martin John	*19 Feb 1827	(4) 3/14
Thompson Emily Maria 20	Godlove Joseph Rosser 25	19 Mar 1890	(4) 2/27
Thompson Eva Jane 17	Godlove Isaac Calvin 27	21 Jan 1880	(4) 2/14
Thompson Evelina 21	Stump Jacob 29	17 Feb 1859	(10)
Thompson Henry	Parill Mercy	28 Oct 1825	(5)
Thompson Jemima 31	Taylor D Dawson 33	24 June 1893	(4) 2/32
Thompson John 74	Iser Etta 19	17 Oct 1894	(4) 2/34
Thompson John A	Scott Mary E	13 Nov 1838	(1) 1 Dec 1838
Thompson John Harris 25	Ewers Catharine Frazier 18	8 Dec 1869	(4) 2/1
Thompson Malinda Ann 48	Flanagan William Lambert 49	27 Jan 1897	(4) 2/38
Thompson Malissa Isabell 23	Rogers Isaac 21	3 June 1874	(4) 2/6
Thompson Margaret Jane 21	Rogers John Henry 19	26 Sept 1867	(4) 1/5
Thompson Mary	Carter Albert	*6 June 1825	(4) 3/42
Thompson Mary Alwilda 17	Godlove William Henry Tucker 23	29 Oct 1879	(4) 2/13
Thompson Ruth	Wise Nimrod	5 July 1838	(1) 14 July 1838
Thompson Sarah Virginia 20	Rogers Soloman 21	26 Sept 1867	(4) 1/5
Thompson Sarah Virginia 19	Abrell George William 23	5 May 1891	(4) 2/29
Thornton Belle 21	Coleman Johnson 21	10 July 1879	(4) 1/39
Thornton Lucy Jane 21	Rolls Henry Wm 24	7 Jan 1874	(4) 1/38
Thornton Samantha 40	Allen Jacob 62	2 Mar 1898	(4) 1/41
Thrash Margaret	Bane George	*23 June 1828	(4) 3/16
Thrash Mary	Stagg William	*7 Jan 1828	(4) 3/1
Thrash Michael	Umpstott Catherine	1 Mar 1824	(4) 3/13
Thrasher	Smith Cuthbert	16 June 1833	(5)
Thrasher Abram	Tasker Nancy	2 Mar 1820	(6)
Thrasher Jane	Smith Nimrod	18 Sept 1836	(5)
Thresher Mary	Crosley Joseph	11 June 1822	(6)
Thrush Cornelius	Paugh Amanda	4 July 1859	(6)
Thrush Cornelius	Paugh Anna Saville	4 July 1859	(10)
Thrush John	Umstot Rachel	18 Dec 1823	(5)

Name #1	Name #2	Date	Source
Thrush John	Umstot Rachel	20 Nov 1823	(6)
Thrush Martha	Staggs William	10 Jan 1828	(5)
Thrush Mary	Bane Geo	26 June 1828	(6)
Thrush Mary	Staggs Wm	10 Jan 1828	(6)
Thrush Mich	Umstot Catherine	4 Mar 1824	(6)
Thrush Peter	Taylor Sallie A	8 Mar 1842	(6)
Thrush Sarah	Hull William H	27 Oct 1850	(5)
Thrush Sarah	Hull Wm F	27 Oct 1851	(6)
Timbrook Benjamin Harrison 23	Davey Elizabeth 26	27 Nov 1884	(4) 2/20
Timbrook Cora Lee 19	Haines William Lupton 21	18 Dec 1890	(4) 2/28
Timbrook Francis Elijah 28	Cowgill Carrie Jane 20	20 May 1891	(4) 2/29
Timbrook Gibson 45	Haines Mary 30	18 Mar 1875	(4) 2/7
Timbrook Grace Davis 23	Nichols Jacob Franklin 22	27 Apr 1898	(4) 2/40
Timbrook Hannah Tabitha 19	Messick Uriah Oliver 25	10 Mar 1887	(4) 2/23
Timbrook Hannah Catharine 20	Davis John William 22	27 Aug 1874	(4) 2/6
Timbrook Hanson	Lockmiller Eliza	31 May 1853	(1) 10 June 1853
Timbrook Isaac Franklin 27	Frye Sarah Elizabeth 30	9 Sept 1897	(4) 2/39
Timbrook Isaac Hunter 23	Snyder Cordelia May 20	13 Sept 1899	(4) 2/41
Timbrook John David 22	Shingleton Rebecca Ann 23	20 Mar 1884	(4) 2/19
Timbrook John David 34	Shingleton Rebecca Josephine 33	8 Apr 1896	(4) 2/37
Timbrook Julia Ann 23	McDonald Jared Andrew 28	5 Mar 1885	(4) 2/20
Timbrook Maggie E 17	Corbin John Snyder 20	24 Oct 1894	(4) 2/35
Timbrook Malinda Melissa 20	Heltzel Franklin Davis 25	14 Nov 1878	(4) 2/12
Timbrook Martha Elizabeth 20	Hott Benjamin Franklin 25	16 Feb 1888	(4) 2/24
Timbrook Mary Catharine 18	Loy Lemuel Johnson 20	27 Dec 1883	(4) 2/19
Timbrook Mary Susan 19	Doyle James Philip 35	27 Dec 1888	(4) 2/26
Timbrook Philip	Shireman Anne M	28 Sept 1893	(4) 2/33
Timbrook Sarah M Virginia 22	Loy Morgan Randolph 21	26 Dec 1878	(4) 2/12
Timbrook Sarah Selana 17	Shingleton Job Jeremiah 26	25 Oct 1876	(4) 2/9
Timbrook Susie M 21	Davis Dora Edward 20	17 Mar 1897	(4) 2/38
Timbrook Thomas Wesley 21	Fout Lydia 20	1 June 1892	(4) 2/31
Timbrook Virginia Margaret 25	Wilson William Calvin 22	13 Feb 1883	(4) 2/18
Toliver Sarah Frances 35	Morgan Samuel 44	*27 Mar 1871	(4) 1/38
Tower Lidia Frances 21	Boley John William 25	30 Mar 1880	(4) 2/14
Towers Charles Henry 29	Shannon Emily W 33	12 Aug 1890	(4) 2/28
Tracy Samuel	Athey Amy		(1) 8 Sept 1838
Trenter Cathleen	Hershey James	11 Jan 1838	(5)
Trenter Joshua	Tasker Millie	20 Aug 1816	(6)
Trenter M S	Rawling James	11 Sept 1850	(5)
Trenter M S	Rawlings Jas	11 Sept 1851	(6)
Trenter Poland	Davis R C	3 July 1856	(6)
Trenter S	Ravenscraft Jas	30 Mar 1834	(6)
Trenton ? 23	Davis Catherine 21	3 July 1857	(10)
Trenton Emily Jane 21	Hardy Albert Franklin 22	27 Mar 1867	(4) 1/5
Trenton Mary Florence 19	Pultz John Walker 22	3 Oct 1871	(4) 2/3
Trentor Harriet A 19	Ashfield John H 25	19 Jan 1866	(4) 1/2
Trentor Joshua	Tasker Millie	20 Aug 1816	(5)
Trentor M C	Kalbauga Alex	8 Oct 1846	(5)
Trentor Samuel	Mintsligie Nancy		(1) 29 July 1837
Trentor William L	Ruckman Eliza	*14 Mar 1825	(4) 3/21
Trevett Joseph	Brookhart Rhody	*9 Sept 1825	(4) 3/58
Triplett B R 35	Orndorff Mellissa E B 16	22 Mar 1888	(4) 2/24

Name #1	Name #2	Date	Source
Triplett Bush 26	Himelwright Jane C 22	2 Sept 1875	(4) 2/7
Triplett Margaret	Arnold Solomon	9 Apr 1833	(5)
Trout James Henry 31	Caldwell Susan Jane 20	2 Aug 1865	(4) 1/1
Truax William 50	Davilbliss Martha 37	1 Oct 1888	(4) 2/25
Tucker Caroline Matilda 22	Dean Jeremiah 22	10 Oct 1865	(4) 1/1
Tucker Daniel	Ward Susan	24 May 1842	(6)
Tucker Eliza C 23	High Jno C 23	16 Dec 1868	(4) 1/7
Tucker Hannah	Linthicum William	24 June 1824	(5)
Tucker Isaac	Athey Susanna	24 Mar 1830	(5)
Tucker Jacob	Head Martha	10 May 1848	(6)
Tucker Joseph	Shell Cathleen	28 Nov 1827	(5)
Tucker Nancy	Stingley William	27 May 1824	(5)
Tucker William	Athey Elizabeth	5 Apr 1827	(5)
Turley Charles William 20	Corbin Sarah 21	15 May 1887	(4) 2/23
Tutwiler Caroline Frances 24	Steele Thomas 40	20 Jan 1886	(4) 2/21
Tutwiler Jonathan Foxter 24	Swisher Jane Annis 22	8 Jan 1878	(4) 2/11
Tutwiler Joseph Henry 28	Miller Alverda 28	10 Dec 1889	(4) 2/27
Tutwiler Martin 57	Orndorff Nancy Jane 45	25 Feb 1875	(4) 2/7
Tutwiler Mary Ann Keys 26	Arnold Daniel 41	10 Mar 1880	(4) 2/14
Tutwiler Samuel Benjamin 32	Buzzard Mary Rebecca 29	16 Aug 1899	(4) 2/41
Tytus Margaret	Collins Moses	*4 Jan 1826	(4) 3/2
Tyzert Lucinda	Bruce Upton	8 Aug 1843	(5)
Ulery Martha Elizabeth 20	Malcom Robert Gorden 29	16 Apr 1867	(4) 1/5
Ullery Alfred L 32	Snyder Mary Elizabeth 18	7 Sept 1875	(4) 2/7
Ullery Jacob Lemuel 21	Coxe Bathsheba Ellen 21	15 Jan 1870	(4) 2/1
Umpstott Catherine	Thrash Michael	1 Mar 1824	(4) 3/13
Umpstott Catherine	Reese Thomas	*26 Dec 1827	(4) 3/61
Umstot Amos	Parker Eliza	1 Apr 1845	(6)
Umstot Eliz	Flick Arthur	8 May 1845	(6)
Umstot Peter	Urice Elizabeth	7 Nov 1844	(6)
Umstot Rachel	Thrush John	18 Dec 1823	(5)
Umstot Rachel	Thrush John	20 Nov 1823	(6)
Umstot Simon	Elifritz Kesia	6 Sept 1851	(6)
Umstot Simon	Elifritz Kesia	6 Sept 1850	(5)
Umstott ?	Hollenback Catharine 23	1 Aug 1860	(10)
Umstott Samuel	Hollenbach Catherine	23 Aug 1860	(5)
Unger Joseph Montgomery 50	Strauther Liddie 50	11 Apr 1901	(4) 2/44
Unglesby Rebecca	Alloway Hiram	*29 Mar 1827	(4) 3/24
Urice Elizabeth	Umstot Peter	7 Nov 1844	(6)
Urice Elizabeth	Miller Peter	28 May 1841	(5)
Urice Elizabeth	Miller Peter	28 May 1840	(6)
Urice Geo	Arnold Mary	22 Dec 1841	(6)
Urice John	Stagg M A	3 Mar 1859	(6)
Urice John 35	Staggs Mary Ann	13 Mar 1859	(10)
Urice Marg	Martin Francis	22 Dec 1836	(6)
Urice Peter	Spencer Susan	25 Apr 1822	(6)
Urice Sam	Stagg M A	24 Apr 1856	(6)
Urice Sarah	Flick E H	27 Aug 1846	(6)
Urice Solomon	Waxler Sarah	1 Sept 1844	(6)
Urton Bersheba	Moorhead James		(1) 6 Oct 1838
Urton Robert Y 22	Pugh Virginia Ann 23	7 Sept 1869	(4) 2/1
Urton William	Moorhead Martha		(1) 23 May 1839

Name #1	Name #2	Date	Source
Utla Catherine	Hull Stephen	15 Feb 1835	(6)
Utt Richard Henry Levi 25	Shers Frances Ellen 30	18 Oct 1894	(4) 2/34
Van Buskirk E	Nott Elizabeth	3 Jan 1833	(6)
Van Buskirk M J	Likins Michael	11 May 1862	(5)
Van Buskirk M J	Likens M	11 May 1865	(6)
Van Buskirk S	Likens Wm	28 Jan 1863	(6)
Van Buskirk Sarah	Likins William	20 Jan 1862	(5)
Van Buskirk Sarah	Stall Peter	20 Oct 1840	(6)
Van Buskirk Sarah	Stall Peter	20 Oct 1841	(5)
Van Buskirk V	Welch T S	14 Apr 1859	(6)
Van Meter Ann R	Head Geo	18 May 1848	(6)
Vance James	Heiskell Catherine	*31 July 1826	(4) 3/31
Vance John Thomas 36	Inskeep Mary Elizabeth 28	20 Oct 1869	(4) 2/1
Vance Kitty Campbell 27	Zimmerman Joshua Soule 26	10 Oct 1900	(4) 2/43
Vandegraft John 38	Miles Sarah Ann 36	8 Jan 1880	(4) 2/14
Vandegrift Mary	Short Isaac	*24 Jan 1827	(4) 3/9
Vandergriff Jno 22	Miller Elizabeth 21	16 Sept 1868	(4) 1/7
Vandergrift William Gerard 26	Watson Mary Hester 20	31 Oct 1867	(4) 1/5
Vandergrift Wm Leonard 36	Haines Margaret Ann 21	29 May 1879	(4) 2/13
Vandervort Virgil 30	Swisher Mary Belle 25	3 June 1885	(4) 2/20
Vandiver Arch	Williams Rebecca	14 Mar 1837	(5)
Vandiver Elizabeth	Parker David	1 June 1820	(5)
Vandiver Elizabeth	Parker David	13 Apr 1820	(6)
Vandiver Hannah	Parreot Joseph	17 Oct 1822	(5)
Vandiver Hannah	Parrot Jas	17 Oct 1822	(6)
Vandiver Jeannie Baird 26	Wirgman Wilbur Fisk 29	9 Feb 1881	(4) 2/15
Vandiver John	Blackburn N	19 May 1831	(6)
Vandiver Matilda	Riggs Jas	14 Oct 1830	(6)
Vandiver Nancy Mrs	Blake Samuel V		(2) 9 Apr 1857
Vandiver Sarah	Ward John	18 Dec 1817	(6)
Vandiver Sarah Frances 23	Tabb Harlan Page 29	29 Mar 1871	(4) 2/2
Vandiver Susan	Holliday Angus M D	*20 Dec 1824	(4) 3/54
Vanhorn A J 25	Shanholtzer P 32	17 Nov 1868	(4) 1/7
Vanmeter Solomon 34	Parsons Ann Jemima 32	31 Dec 1867	(4) 1/6
Vanosdall Rebecca F 16	Alderton Wm H 23	20 July 1868	(4) 1/6
Vanosdel Martha Ann 21	King Thomas Earl 26	23 Dec 1875	(4) 2/8
Vanpelt Charles Thompson 27	Saville Amanda Florence 23	15 Oct 1891	(4) 2/30
Vaughn Sarah 30	Merritt William 58	*8 Mar 1873	(4) 2/4
Vaughn Sarah 48	Seeders George Washington 52	16 Oct 1887	(4) 2/24
Veach Abel Seymour 25	High Christena Kale 17	17 Oct 1878	(4) 2/12
Veach Henson W 25	Leatherman Maggie J 20	18 Apr 1887	(4) 2/23
Vermillion Mary Ellen 17	Messick William Harrison 22	4 Mar 1886	(4) 2/22
Violet Della Roberson 21	Hamilton James William 24	26 Jan 1887	(4) 2/23
Violett James Edmond 46	Funk Mary Susan 21	7 Nov 1884	(4) 2/20
Vishon Whitley 30	Kuhn John 26	8 Mar 1866	(4) 1/3
Waddle Alice henderson 25	Cook John Wesley 30	6 Sept 1883	(4) 2/18
Waddle Emma C 23	Parsons Isaac 28	12 Nov 1867	(4) 1/5
Waddle Julius Samuel 37	Parsons Edith 33	3 June 1891	(4) 2/29
Waggoner Martha Ann 21	Dohrman Herman H 26	25 Jan 1866	(4) 1/2
Wagoner Edmond Berkeley 22	Starns Bettie Parker 19	28 Dec 1880	(4) 2/15
Wagoner Elizabeth 55	Kirby William 56	10 July 1894	(4) 2/34
Wagoner George Henry 25	Haines Ella 22	1 Apr 1891	(4) 2/29

Name #1	Name #2	Date	Source
Wagoner Henry	Rankin Ruthy E	23 June 1837	(1) 1 July 1837
Wagoner Julian	Hinkle Lewis	2 Aug 1838	(1) 11 Aug 1838
Wagoner Mora Lin 29	Glaize Mary E 28	30 May 1893	(4) 2/32
Walaker Mary Catherine 20	Hill William Barger 24	8 Mar 1866	(4) 1/3
Walburn Reuben	Shores Ev	3 Oct 1850	(6)
Walburn Reuben	Shores Evelin	3 Oct 1846	(5)
Walker Amanda Jane 28	Miller Uriah Lease 38	27 June 1893	(4) 2/32
Walker David Frederick 21	Biser Amanda Jane 16	30 Jan 1881	(4) 2/15
Walker David Shelby 60	Duncan Elizabeth 26	15 July 1875	(4) 2/7
Walker James Wright 25	Gettys Sarah Febia 24	2 Mar 1875	(4) 2/7
Walker Philip Washington 27	Combs Nancy 24	17 Oct 1875	(4) 2/7
Walker William C	Newman Mary Ann	11 Sept 1852	(2) 7 Oct 1852
Walker William Laurens 27	Dailey Nelia Dupuy 23	1 Nov 1900	(4) 2/43
Wallace Charles	Bartlow Eunice	21 Aug 1822	(6)
Wallace John	Rannells Mary	*3 Nov 1828	(4) 3/37
Wallace R J	Sharretts M C	22 Aug 1850	(6)
Wallace R J	Sharrest M C	22 Aug 1846	(5)
Wallace Rafus Alonzo 22	Myers Rachael Eleanor 18	19 Sept 1895	(4) 2/36
Walsh Mary	Rawlings Charles	1823	(5)
Walton Louisa A	Cherry James		(1) 1855
Ward Abigal	Johnson William	*17 Jan 1825	(4) 3/10
Ward Charles 22	Day Nannie 25	28 Sept 1893	(4) 1/41
Ward Cornelia Gertrude 26	Coffroth Alex Hamilton Jr 37	5 May 1886	(4) 2/22
Ward Edgar Alonzo 40	Oats Ella Virginia 28	25 Apr 1894	(4) 2/34
Ward Elizabeth	Jones Thomas	17 July 1823	(6)
Ward Elizabeth	Athey John W		(1) 3 Feb 1838
Ward Elizabeth	Jones Thomas	22 Aug 1823	(5)
Ward James Marion 37	Offutt Annie 26	25 Apr 1894	(4) 2/34
Ward Jesse	Cundiff Sarah D	13 Oct 1829	(6)
Ward John	Kelly Isabelle	27 Nov 1828	(6)
Ward John	Grymm Isabella	*25 Nov 1828	(4) 3/42
Ward John	Vandiver Sarah	18 Dec 1817	(6)
Ward Margaret E 36	Hall William 48	23 Dec 1873	(4) 2/5
Ward Millie	Kitzmiller Gasper	13 Dec 1821	(6)
Ward Minnie	Kitzmiller Gasper	13 Dec 1821	(5)
Ward Susan	Tucker Daniel	24 May 1842	(6)
Ward Wm Henry 23	Coleman Ellen Jane 22	19 Feb 1875	(4) 1/39
Warner William 25	Austin Violet Fleming 16	24 Feb 1874	(4) 1/38
Warnick Henry	Demmett S	7 Feb 1843	(6)
Warrens John 30	Bragg Maria 41	6 Mar 1877	(4) 1/39
Washington Bessie 19	Taylor Charles 27	3 Sept 1891	(4) 1/41
Washington Bettie M 23	Inskeep John J 24	4 Mar 1869	(4) 1/38
Washington Carson 29	Washington Virginia 22	26 Oct 1884	(4) 1/40
Washington David Bell 30	Peter Alice 28	20 Nov 1889	(4) 1/40
Washington Edna 29	Miller Gilbert Proctor 32	19 Apr 1899	(4) 2/41
Washington Fanny 23	Hamilton Wilber 22	8 Dec 1883	(4) 1/40
Washington George 23	Inskeep Ann Elizabeth 19	4 Oct 1870	(4) 2/2
Washington Henry W 21	Anderson Amanda V 22	20 Aug 1888	(4) 1/40
Washington Hite 21	McGruder Martha L E 16	26 Aug 1899	(4) 1/42
Washington John 25	Bank Rhoda 26	14 Aug 1880	(4) 1/39
Washington John Henry 21	Washington Martha 18	27 Aug 1879	(4) 1/39
Washington Jos C 23	Dandridge Isadore 21	3 Dec 1883	(4) 1/40

Name #1	Name #2	Date	Source
Washington Lewis 45	Jackson Kate 19	*23 June 1869	(4) 1/38
Washington Margaret Esther 22	Thomas George H 26	25 July 1893	(4) 2/32
Washington Martha 18	Washington John Henry 21	27 Aug 1879	(4) 1/39
Washington Mary Frances 18	Williams James Thomas 20	29 Sept 1897	(4) 1/41
Washington Mary 24	Campbell Henry Wilson 33	19 Sept 1888	(4) 2/25
Washington Miranda 27	Mathews James 42	3 Oct 1894	(4) 2/34
Washington Rebecca Cordelia 18	Jacob Granville 23	13 Jan 1880	(4) 1/39
Washington Sarah Gertrude 26	Blue James Henry 33	29 Nov 1881	(4) 2/17
Washington Smith 22	Dandridge Rebecca 20	31 Jan 1871	(4) 1/38
Washington Virginia 22	Washington Carson 29	26 Oct 1884	(4) 1/40
Wasson Nancy	George Silas	*19 July 1824	(4) 3/39
Watkins Elizabeth	Ruckman Samuel	*8 Sept 1828	(4) 3/26
Watkins Harriet J 20	McBride Alpheus 22	10 Apr 1866	(4) 1/3
Watkins Harrison	Arnold Catherine	*23 Apr 1824	(4) 3/26
Watkins Lorenzo Edward 22	Davis Eleanor Jane 22	1 Apr 1888	(4) 2/24
Watkins Louisa V 17	Reed Anthony 24	21 Nov 1866	(4) 1/4
Watsen Gordon John 38	Doman Martha 28	15 Jan 1890	(4) 2/27
Watson Agnes Elenora 22	Light Charles Holliday 22	19 Feb 1874	(4) 2/5
Watson Alb	McNemar Anna	10 Oct 1830	(6)
Watson Albert Taylor 24	Ewers Mary Agnes 22	9 May 1882	(4) 2/17
Watson Elizabeth Jane 18	Carder Albert Lee 26	19 Apr 1894	(4) 2/34
Watson Emily Jane 18	Ginevan Thomas 27	25 Oct 1860	(10)
Watson Jane	Malcom James	*14 Oct 1828	(4) 3/30
Watson Jethro Scott 33	Offutt Augusta I 24	7 Dec 1886	(4) 2/22
Watson John Gordy 32	Swisher Rebecca Ann 36	23 Feb 1882	(4) 2/17
Watson Mariah S 23	Shanholtzer Silas L 25	17 Mar 1868	(4) 1/6
Watson Mary Hester 20	Vandergrift William Gerard 26	31 Oct 1867	(4) 1/5
Watson Minerva Frances 18	Scanlen Samuel 20	1 Dec 1875	(4) 2/8
Waxler Lethy A	Davis Mivert	7 Feb 1861	(5)
Waxler Sarah	Urice Solomon	1 Sept 1844	(6)
Weaver Franklin	Ellis Elize	*7 Apr 1828	(4) 3/9
Webster Harriet 41	Brown Frank 47	16 Sept 1889	(4) 1/40
Webster John 29	Hardy Harriett 27	25 Dec 1872	(4) 1/38
Webster John 33	Hall Harriett 34	10 Nov 1885	(4) 1/40
Webster Joseph 25	Bigan Esther Jane 21	22 Apr 1875	(4) 1/39
Webster Nancy Jane 23	Gardner Esau 23	25 June 1874	(4) 1/39
Welch ? 26	? Virginia 22	Oct 1859	(10)
Welch B B	Welch Elizabeth	5 Oct 1848	(6)
Welch Benjamin	Rawlings Julia Ann	23 Aug 1818	(6)
Welch Beu Ann	Welch R S	29 Feb 1844	(6)
Welch E	Kuykendall Luke	13 Nov 1828	(6)
Welch Elizabeth	Welch B B	5 Oct 1848	(6)
Welch Elizabeth	Kuykendall Luke	*10 Nov 1828	(4) 3/38
Welch Harriet C	Long J W	6 Sept 1849	(6)
Welch Isaac	Smith Dorcas	24 Aug 1820	(6)
Welch J G	Reese Elenomy	19 Jan 1858	(6)
Welch Laureana	Rawlings Peter	26 Sept 1822	(6)
Welch Lucy	Welch Sylvester	14 Sept 1843	(6)
Welch Nancy	Maddox Thos	12 Feb 1831	(6)
Welch R S	Welch Beu Ann	29 Feb 1844	(6)
Welch S M	Welch Wm B	29 Sept 1842	(6)
Welch Sarah	Welch Thos	11 Sept 1817	(6)

Name #1	Name #2	Date	Source
Welch Susan	Ludwick Fred	21 Sept 1841	(6)
Welch Susan	Leright Edm	17 Mar 1835	(6)
Welch Sylvester	Myers Elizabeth	5 Dec 1826	(6)
Welch Sylvester	Welch Lucy	14 Sept 1843	(6)
Welch T A	Powleson R J	14 Aug 1845	(6)
Welch T S	Van Buskirk V	14 Apr 1859	(6)
Welch Thos	Welch Sarah	11 Sept 1817	(6)
Welch Thos	Pool Millie	21 Feb 1822	(6)
Welch Thos S	Rawlings M A	22 Nov 1855	(6)
Welch William	Clipstine Mary Jane	27 Aug 1838	(1) 8 Sept 1838
Welch William	George Sarah	11 Dec 1844	(5)
Welch Wm B	Welch S M	29 Sept 1842	(6)
Welsh Sylvester	Myers Elizabeth	*4 Dec 1826	(4) 3/43
Welton Aaron 26	Welton Mary E 22	4 Jan 1866	(4) 1/2
Welton Alonzo	Snyder Hariete	*21 Feb 1825	(4) 3/16
Welton Ann Elizabeth	Harness Joseph		(1) 11 Nov 1837
Welton F B	Cunningham Jane		(1) 14 Nov 1839
Welton Mary E 22	Welton Aaron 26	4 Jan 1866	(4) 1/2
Welton Wright	Johnson E	31 May 1836	(6)
West Margaret Catharine 26	Hartman George Thomas 23	22 Sept 1880	(4) 2/14
Whalen Thomas Edward 23	Alexander Mary E 20	15 June 1895	(4) 1/41
Wheeler Mary	Polon Joseph	19 Feb 1835	(5)
Whetzel Anthony 30	Hartman Phoebe Jane 19	4 Feb 1895	(4) 2/35
Whip Elizabeth	Bane Abner	*21 Feb 1826	(4) 3/13
Whip Elizabeth A	Bailey J W	15 June 1848	(6)
Whip M L	Leatherman Geo W	30 July 1857	(6)
Whip Sarah	Baxter R B	23 Sept 1851	(6)
Whipp Sarah	Baxter R B	23 Sept 1850	(5)
Whistler Uriah 33	Oats Cathcrine 22	1 Oct 1867	(4) 1/5
Whitacre ? 21	Sirbaugh ? 19	31 Dec 1857	(10)
Whitacre ?lorence Edward 21	Lupton Rebecca Artiminsta 17	10 June 1900	(4) 2/42
Whitacre Albert Luther 21	Netherton Virginia Bell 18	23 Jan 1890	(4) 2/27
Whitacre Alice Virginia 22	Kave James Albert 29	*14 Nov 1895	(4) 2/36
Whitacre Alpheus Jerome 26	Abe Lacey Ann 26	25 Mar 1896	(4) 2/37
Whitacre Amos Bushrod Currell 25	Harmison Lucy Ellen 25	3 June 1885	(4) 2/20
Whitacre Ann Z 20	Abrill William E 25	28 Mar 1867	(4) 1/5
Whitacre Anne Elizabeth 21	Roice William H 25	6 Mar 1889	(4) 2/26
Whitacre Aquilla McCarsen 21	Shanholtzer Mary Frances 17	11 Sept 1884	(4) 2/19
Whitacre Archibald Vanderbilt 20	Slonaker Alice Belle 14	29 Dec 1896	(4) 2/38
Whitacre Arthur Clark 25	Sirbaugh Olivia Catharine 23	25 Jan 1894	(4) 2/33
Whitacre Benjamin Franklin 24	Wilson Margaret Jane 22	5 Feb 1874	(4) 2/5
Whitacre Bessie Fernon 15	Brooks Jeremiah Calvin 21	1 July 1900	(4) 2/42
Whitacre Burton Walter 23	Slonacre Margaret May 19	14 Mar 1893	(4) 2/32
Whitacre Eliza Jane 30	Fuller William 48	20 Nov 1870	(4) 2/2
Whitacre Elizabeth Ellen 43	Bennett Job 41	24 Mar 1890	(4) 2/27
Whitacre George William 24	Abrell Emma M 19	25 Sept 1894	(40 2/34
Whitacre Harriet Elizabeth 19	Shanholtzer Joseph Daniel Bueguard 19	21 June 1882	(4) 2/17
Whitacre Harrison Randolph 24	Catlett Ellen 25	24 Mar 1896	(4) 2/37
Whitacre Henry Carson 22	Richmond Susan Bell 15	30 Jan 1898	(4) 2/40
Whitacre Jackson 26	Slonaker Emily Frances 16	17 Oct 1893	(4) 2/33
Whitacre Jacob W 25	Seaton Emily Alice Frances 16	7 June 1887	(4) 2/23
Whitacre John 18	See Jennie 18	20 Sept 1894	(4) 2/34

Name #1	Name #2	Date	Source
Whitacre Jordon 31	Eaton Eliza Ann 17	21 Dec 1871	(4) 2/3
Whitacre Lycurgus M 23	Abrill Amanda Elizabeth 25	21 Nov 1895	(4) 2/36
Whitacre Lydia F 24	Kelley Isaac Patrick 32	12 Feb 1884	(4) 2/19
Whitacre Mary E 16	Bennett Philip Emanuel 24	22 Mar 1896	(4) 2/37
Whitacre Mary Matilda 30	Keplinger Christian 36	31 Aug 1874	(4) 2/6
Whitacre N M 16	Sine Albert A 20	14 Apr 1896	(4) 2/37
Whitacre Phoebe Ann Catharine 17	Gess Wm Perry 23	11 June 1874	(4) 2/6
Whitacre Rhoda Ann 25	Moreland Bazil Newton 28	7 Mar 1880	(4) 2/14
Whitacre Rhoda Ellen 20	Kelley Edward 22	6 June 1876	(4) 2/8
Whitacre Robert Calhoun 25	Wolford Leanna 16	26 Oct 1893	(4) 2/33
Whitacre Sarah E 18	Abrell Lemuel 21	22 Nov 1866	(4) 1/4
Whitacre Silas Jeremare 20	Bonney Martha Jane 24	3 June 1899	(4) 2/41
Whitacre Sydnon McClellan 27	Howard Helen Frances 19	31 Oct 1889	(4) 2/27
Whitacre Theresa 21	Whitlock Risus 24	13 Sept 1870	(4) 2/2
Whitacre Vance Elwood 23	Haines Mary Ellen 17	27 Mar 1901	(4) 2/44
Whitacre Virginia 23	Kerns Robert W 45	21 Aug 1898	(4) 2/40
Whitacre William Washington 23	Kackley Minnie G 17	21 May 1896	(4) 2/37
Whitaker Amanda L 23	Doman Jasper W 23	3 July 1873	(4) 2/4
Whitaker Nancy Virginia 21	Sine William Henry 24	13 July 1875	(4) 2/7
White Abram	Ferriman H	13 Sept 1846	(6)
White Alberta Lee 23	McDonald John Snyder 30	12 Dec 1893	(4) 2/33
White Arther Little 20	Digman Ellen C 20	31 Aug 1870	(4) 2/2
White Betsey	Black John	*27 Sept 1825	(4) 3/61
White C S 27	Shultz Bessie J 29	25 July 1867	(4) 2/1
White C S 33	Steele Catharine 32	26 May 1873	(4) 2/4
White Catharine 20	Poling Daniel 26	31 Aug 1892	(4) 2/31
White Christena 28	Martin William Franklin 35	did not marry	(4) 2/39
White Christian S 27	Schultze Eliza J 29	25 July 1867	(4) 1/5
White Christina 30	Iser Silas 53	20 Jan 1898	(4) 2/40
White Emma Jane Victoria 19	Millison Jesse Benjamin 28	22 Nov 1899	(4) 2/42
White Frances Ann 30	Flournoy Samuel Lightfoot 28	8 Apr 1875	(4) 2/7
White Geo Willaim 22	Wolford Aldeah Florence 21	18 May 1876	(4) 2/8
White George Solomon 22	Biser Laura Edna 21	31 Oct 1898	(4) 2/41
White George W	Ganoe Hester E	13 Apr 1859	(1) 13 May 1859
White George W 21	? Mary	30 Sept 1860	(10)
White Henry	Harvey Eliza	24 Mar 1836	(6)
White Indiana 18	Loy Charles Nixon 25	3 Feb 1892	(4) 2/30
White James	Robinson Elizabeth	9 Oct 1834	(6)
White John	Ravencraft Levina	30 Oct 1850	(5)
White John K	Jewett Ellen M	19 Nov 1839	(1) 5 Nov 1839
White Lettie 34	Williams Douglas 36	16 Aug 1876	(4) 1/39
White Lucy 26	Ferguson Robert Gallier 25	27 Jan 1876	(4) 2/8
White Madison 26	Spurling Sidney Jane 28	14 Feb 1879	(4) 2/12
White Mary 27	Mayhew Benjamin 35	11 May 1854	(10)
White Mary Elizabeth Ann 24	Anderson Daniel Luther 25	1 May 1883	(4) 2/18
White Pathenia	Corbin Cornelius	*29 Aug 1825	(4) 3/56
White Robert	Liller Elizabeth	7 Nov 1844	(6)
White Robert Norvell	McBride Matilda	13 Feb 1824	(4) 3/10
White Sarah	Smith Abraham I	*3 Oct 1825	(4) 3/64
White Sarah	Smith Abram	4 Oct 1825	(6)
White Sarah 23	Raines George Thomas 22	9 Nov 1887	(4) 2/24
White Thomas Edward 24	Kidwell Alice Jane 15	30 Dec 1873	(4) 2/5

Name #1	Name #2	Date	Source
White Virginia M 19	Longacre Isaac N 26	8 Mar 1866	(4) 1/3
White William Chester 28	Finley Nannie Edwards 25	1 Dec 1886	(4) 2/22
Whiteman Anne Elizabeth 26	Huffman Daniel Frederick 27	28 Feb 1900	(4) 2/42
Whiteman Annie Virginia 19	Arnold George Edward 26	9 May 1888	(4) 2/25
Whiteman Charles David 29	High Sarah Louisa 26	20 Jan 1886	(4) 2/21
Whiteman Charles Bradford 35	Bean Chloa Ann Virginia 24	18 May 1892	(4) 2/31
Whiteman Cora Ada 19	Leatherman John Frederick 21	12 Aug 1891	(4) 2/29
Whiteman E J	Parker Jas	16 Apr 1855	(6)
Whiteman Edward W 25	Bizer Julia Ann 17	6 Nov 1872	(4) 2/4
Whiteman Edward F 41	Carrol Hannah C 21	12 Sept 1871	(4) 2/3
Whiteman Francis High 20	Huffman John Samuel 28	25 Nov 1891	(4) 2/30
Whiteman Gertrude May 21	Stickley Joseph Riley 22	28 June 1894	(4) 2/34
Whiteman Hannah 19	Rogers Edgar 21	8 Feb 1899	(4) 2/41
Whiteman Hattie Ethel 21	Huffman Jacob Seymour 25	25 May 1900	(4) 2/42
Whiteman John Henry 22	Leatherman Jane Ann 24	31 Nov 1867	(4) 1/6
Whiteman M	Staggs John	26 Nov 1840	(6)
Whiteman Margaret	Staggs John	26 Nov 1841	(5)
Whiteman Margaret Isabel 28	Klinedinsts Augustive 42	21 May 1879	(4) 2/13
Whiteman Mary Ann	Parker John	*11 Feb 1826	(4) 3/8
Whiteman Robert Elijah 26	Bean Vinora 18	30 July 1890	(4) 2/28
Whiteman S A	Buzzard J N	3 Apr 1854	(6)
Whiteman Sallie 21	Hoopingarner Wilson 21	*3 May 1879	(4) 2/13
Whiteman Sarah Ann 24	Buzzard Jacob N 30	Apr 1854	(10)
Whiteman Sarah Catherine 26	Parker Thornton Russell 28	10 Dec 1881	(4) 2/17
Whiteman Sarah Elizabeth 26	Greenwalt William Henry 25	25 June 1891	(4) 2/29
Whitfield John Amos 23	Allen Jane 26	23 Sept 1880	(4) 1/40
Whiting Alfred 37	Banlon Ann Eliz 26	23 Nov 1865	(4) 1/1
Whiting Saul	Sutton Jane	12 Jan 1835	(6)
Whitlock Darius Minor 49	Barrett Florence C 28	19 Sept 1895	(4) 2/36
Whitlock Edward Augustus 21	Chilcott Anne 20	13 Dec 1896	(4) 2/38
Whitlock Elizabeth Maude 17	Park Elrod 32	20 Jan 1898	(4) 2/40
Whitlock Lottie Gertrude 19	Bennett John Brundell 29	23 Oct 1890	(4) 2/28
Whitlock Lydia Jane 22	Eaton Balam 36	28 Mar 1867	(4) 1/5
Whitlock Margaret Catharine 23	McCauley Jesse F 24	12 Feb 1896	(4) 2/36
Whitlock Mary Laney 21	McKee Hiram Addison 27	28 Jan 1876	(4) 2/8
Whitlock Risus 24	Whitacre Theresa 21	13 Sept 1870	(4) 2/2
Whitlock William Braxton 22	Eaton Sophia Rosella 16	31 Oct 1890	(4) 2/28
Wigfield Henry Wm 29	Dicken Alverretta Clemmons 21	24 Oct 1876	(4) 2/9
Wiley Zale	Stafford Eliza		(1) 19 Sept 1839
Wilkins Matthais 49	Shereman Dorothy C 17	8 Mar 1866	(4) 1/3
Wilkins Silas 24	Davis Sarah Ellen 30	3 Apr 1892	(4) 2/30
Williams Abram 24	Smith Margaret 18	23 Sept 1865	(4) 1/1
Williams Addie 21	Davis Hampton Ashby 30	4 Jan 1893	(4) 2/32
Williams Annie C 40	Pepper William H 43	21 Nov 1882	(4) 2/17
Williams Charles McKeever 22	Powell Amanda Virginia 23	19 Dec 1876	(4) 2/9
Williams Douglas 36	White Lettie 34	16 Aug 1876	(4) 1/39
Williams Frances 32	McIlwee Charles Ashby 26	8 Sept 1887	(4) 2/23
Williams H B 26	McKee Mary Ida 18	6 Oct 1897	(4) 2/39
Williams Isaac Welton 24	Deats Martha 15	*5 Sept 1875	(4) 2/7
Williams James Thomas 20	Washington Mary Frances 18	29 Sept 1897	(4) 1/41
Williams Jno H	Piles Elizabeth	*25 Feb 1824	(4) 3/12
Williams John Worthington 25	Shanholtzer Rosa Lucinda 21	18 Jan 1891	(4) 2/29

Name #1	Name #2	Date	Source
Williams Mary 21	Smith Boyd 23	1 Jan 1891	(4) 1/41
Williams Rebecca	Vandiver Arch	14 Mar 1837	(5)
Williams Samuel Holland 42	Taylor Harriet Ellen 25	6 Dec 1882	(4) 2/18
Williams Sarah E 23	Johnson Henry 27	23 Aug 1866	(4) 1/3
Williams Susan	Kuykendall Isaac	29 Sept 1852	(2) 7 Oct 1852
Williams Thomas 23	Brumback Mandy Jane 21	19 Oct 1869	(4) 1/38
Williamson Benjamin	Millison Martha	*21 Nov 1827	(4) 2/57
Williamson John 31	Powell Rebecca Frances 27	31 Mar 1874	(4) 2/6
Williamson Mary Ann 45	Burnside John Robert 47	4 Apr 1886	(4) 2/22
Williamson Mary	Berry William	*20 Dec 1827	(4) 3/59
Williamson Nannie M 36	Hoffman Martie Rizer 38	12 Sept 1876	(4) 2/8
Williamson Otis 21	Hott Ollie Vernon 18	11 Nov 1896	(4) 2/38
Williamson Silas William 33	Hiett Allis Jane 27	19 Feb 1874	(4) 2/5
Willison Emma B 22	Chaney William J 25	24 Jan 1895	(4) 2/35
Wills Clara Belle 19	Bullett Frank 18	13 Dec 1883	(4) 1/40
Wills Jane 26	Hiett John Luther 25	23 Mar 1871	(4) 2/2
Wills Minnie Virginia 21	Wolfe Ferman Edward 27	12 Sept 1894	(4) 2/34
Wills Sallie 22	Power Joseph Thompson 21	28 Mar 1893	(4) 2/32
Wills Silas Grayson 23	Taylor Ann Cecilia 25	17 Oct 1876	(4) 2/9
Wilson Abraham 37	Self Maggie E 23	1 Sept 1869	(4) 2/1
Wilson Alexander	Yost Margaret	*24 Apr 1827	(4) 3/28
Wilson Annie Smith 21	Taylor John Edward 31	7 Mar 1877	(4) 2/9
Wilson Elen	Stily Jacob	*13 Apr 1824	(4) 3/22
Wilson Elizabeth	Harvey William	11 Sept 1823	(5)
Wilson Ellen	Steally Jacob	15 Apr 1824	(6)
Wilson Emma 26	Cheshire Uriah Benj 29	9 Nov 1869	(4) 2/1
Wilson Esther Sophia 27	Reed Azariah Pugh 28	*20 Aug 1877	(4) 2/10
Wilson Hannah A A 29	Brill Dorsey Clenton 26	30 Sept 1886	(4) 2/22
Wilson Jas	Junkins Lucinda	25 Dec 1832	(6)
Wilson John	Hamilton Mary	11 Nov 1841	(6)
Wilson Joseph	Fitzgerald Maria	*15 Sept 1826	(4) 3/34
Wilson Louiza 24	Oats Robert Wm 34	24 Sept 1874	(4) 2/6
Wilson Lucy Jane 26	Smith B Jetson 29	24 Mar 1897	(4) 2/38
Wilson Margaret Jane 22	Whitacre Benjamin Franklin 24	5 Feb 1874	(4) 2/5
Wilson Martha F 21	Larrick Theodore F 23	14 Dec 1872	(4) 2/4
Wilson Mary Elizabeth 23	Spaid Flavius J 21	28 Nov 1867	(4) 1/5
Wilson Mary Elizabeth 51	Hartman David Columbus 51	24 Nov 1897	(4) 2/39
Wilson Mary Taylor 30	Miller Dr Joseph M 47	14 Nov 1900	(4) 2/43
Wilson Nancy	Leatherman John	23 Apr 1829	(6)
Wilson Nat	Davis Mary	2 Dec 1816	(6)
Wilson Nathan	Davis Rebecca	2 Dec 1816	(5)
Wilson Nimrod 33	Orndorff Minerva Ellen 21	22 Oct 1885	(4) 2/21
Wilson Peter	Hull Louisa	29 Jan 1843	(6)
Wilson Rachel 31	Rudolph George Adam 41	25 June 1896	(4) 2/37
Wilson Reb'a	Maxwell John	27 Dec 1836	(6)
Wilson Rebecca 28	Haines William Henry 35	13 Dec 1896	(4) 2/38
Wilson S 23	Fisher Emma Lillian 18	30 Oct 1879	(4) 2/13
Wilson Sarah Jane 16	Larrick Zachariah Taylor 23	16 June 1870	(4) 2/2
Wilson Thomas	Dixon Elizabeth	16 July 1829	(5)
Wilson Thos	Dixon Elizabeth	16 June 1829	(6)
Wilson Virginia Catharine 19	Shanholtzer Solomon Jonathan 26	2 Nov 1884	(4) 2/20
Wilson Virginia 18	Maphis George Washington 22	17 Aug 1865	(4) 1/1

Name #1	Name #2	Date	Source
Wilson William	Tasker Sarah	8 Sept 1818	(5)
Wilson William Calvin 22	Timbrook Virginia Margaret 25	13 Feb 1883	(4) 2/18
Wilson Wm	Simmons E A	14 Dec 1834	(6)
Wilson Wm	Tasker Sarah	8 Sept 1818	(6)
Wilson Zacharia L	Maphis Rachel	13 Sept 1864	(7)
Wilt John M	Baker Rebecca	11 Sept 1845	(6)
Wince Benjamin F 23	Lewis Ann F 25	19 Aug 1873	(4) 2/4
Winckelblick Philip	Slane Nancy	*25 Dec 1826	(4) 3/49
Windle Mary Susan 26	Butler John Franklin 28	12 Aug 1891	(4) 2/29
Wine Susan	Arnold Solomon	17 Jan 1839	(1) 1 Feb 1839
Wineow John	Duling Catherine M	21 June 1837	(1) 1 July 1837
Winfield Minnie 20	Fishell Jacob David 22	7 Oct 1896	(4) 2/37
Wingfield Susannah	Mutte Archibald	*18 Apr 1826	(4) 3/17
Wintling Charles Edward 21	Dicken Miranda Catherine 21	14 Aug 1879	(4) 2/13
Wirgman Charles Thornton 24	Taylor Lelia Clyde 22	17 Apr 1889	(4) 2/26
Wirgman Emma Maria 29	Quisenberry ?Thomas A 28	22 Jan 1890	(4) 2/27
Wirgman James Jr 32	Munday Anna Belle 26	24 Feb 1892	(4) 2/30
Wirgman Wilbur Fisk 29	Vandiver Jeannie Baird 26	9 Feb 1881	(4) 2/15
Wise Barbara	Gray William	8 Dec 1866	(9)
Wise Nimrod	Thompson Ruth	5 July 1838	(1) 14 July 1838
Wise Rebecca 21	Oats James Franklin 28	24 Nov 1865	(4) 1/1
Withers Chas B 24	Fox Rebecca 24	15 Nov 1865	(4) 1/1
Withers Henry Clay 24	Miller Ann Eliza 18	26 Aug 1880	(4) 2/14
Wolf Elta Lyda 23	Frye Edward Powell 27	2 Feb 1888	(4) 2/24
Wolf J Elizabeth 22	Shawn Daniel R 20	*19 Apr 1869	(4) 2/1
Wolf James H 32	Swisher Dorthy Ann 18	21 Apr 1885	(4) 2/20
Wolf James Henry 39	Poland Mrs Rebecca 32	21 Nov 1893	(4) 2/33
Wolf L A	Metcalf Fenton	2 Nov 1826	(6)
Wolf Lacy Ann	Medcalf Fenton	*28 Oct 1826	(4) 3/37
Wolfe Alexander Jackson 31	Haines Mary 32	7 Dec 1890	(4) 2/28
Wolfe Catharine 33	Gray Morgan 31	6 Oct 1870	(4) 2/2
Wolfe Daisey E 16	Davey Robert Gideon 24	28 Apr 1901	(4) 2/44
Wolfe Ferman Edward 27	Wills Minnie Virginia 21	12 Sept 1894	(4) 2/34
Wolfe George W 28	Ruckman Mary Elizabeth 21	30 May 1878	(4) 2/11
Wolfe John Sylvester 19	Pepper Maggie Catherine 19	27 Dec 1881	(4) 2/17
Wolfe Sarah Ann 27	Poland Isaac Jackson 29	30 Jan 1877	(4) 2/9
Wolford ?	Smith Mary	June 1859	(10)
Wolford ? 35	Peters Lydia Ann 24	1859	(10)
Wolford ? 39	Shank Margaret Ann 35	13 Dec 1859	(10)
Wolford Aldeah Florence 21	White Geo Willaim 22	18 May 1876	(4) 2/8
Wolford Alice Belle 21	Fletcher Emanuel Lupton 19	1 Aug 1898	(4) 2/40
Wolford Alverda Melissa 18	Ruckman Albert 21	15 Apr 1885	(4) 2/20
Wolford Anne Belle 22	Hiett Zebulon Montgomery 30	13 Nov 1888	(4) 2/25
Wolford Annie Rebecca 24	Wolford Samuel Isaiah 25	28 June 1892	(4) 2/31
Wolford Benjamin Franklin 21	Flory Mary Virginia 21	12 Apr 1880	(4) 2/14
Wolford Benjamin Thomas 23	Davey Lotty Ann 22	2 Mar 1897	(4) 2/38
Wolford Benjamin Franklin 22	Wolford Francis Ellen 23	9 Feb 1890	(4) 2/27
Wolford Charles C 21	Martin Annie L 22	25 Sept 1894	(4) 2/34
Wolford Charles Edward 29	Wolford Sarah C 21	1 Aug 1889	(4) 2/26
Wolford Charles William 21	Wolford Ida O 19	24 July 1888	(4) 2/25
Wolford Chas E 20	Godlove Rebecca Virginia 22	30 Nov 1880	(4) 2/15
Wolford David Markwood 27	Arnold Laura May 18	12 Feb 1888	(4) 2/24

Name #1	Name #2	Date	Source
Wolford Elizabeth	McDonald Samuel	7 June 1859	(10)
Wolford Elizabeth J 22	Shawn Daniel R 20	*19 Apr 1869	(4) 1/38
Wolford Emily Price 17	Shanholtzer John Wesley 23	17 Dec 1879	(4) 2/14
Wolford Etta Virginia Beall 19	Shall Daniel James William 31	10 Dec 1878	(4) 2/12
Wolford Ettie Beall 21	Richmond Samuel Patton 34	24 Feb 1892	(4) 2/30
Wolford Fannie Maria 17	Cowgill Alexander C 20	11 June 1873	(4) 2/4
Wolford Francis Ellen 23	Wolford Benjamin Franklin 22	9 Feb 1890	(4) 2/27
Wolford George F 29	Wolford Laura 37	17 Mar 1892	(4) 2/30
Wolford George T 22	Slane Lucy Ellen 20	27 July 1882	(4) 2/17
Wolford Granville Harper 26	Saville Lavina Catherine 28	12 May 1891	(4) 2/29
Wolford Granvill Harper 23	Shanholtzer Maggie Diadem 20	5 Apr 1899	(4) 2/41
Wolford Hannah Catharine 23	Stewart Robert Smith 25	3 Feb 1881	(4) 2/15
Wolford Hannah Catharine 20	Wright Albert Lee 22	14 Nov 1889	(4) 2/27
Wolford Harvey Clinton 28	Shank Laura Francis 21	29 Dec 1880	(4) 2/15
Wolford Hattie Elizabeth 22	Saville Wm Taylor 24	23 Feb 1892	(4) 2/30
Wolford Ida O 19	Wolford Charles William 21	24 July 1888	(4) 2/25
Wolford Isabella	Bennett William	*4 Oct 1827	(4) 3/50
Wolford Jacob Webster 23	Roberson Margaret Ellen 20	30 Dec 1886	(4) 2/23
Wolford John Martin 21	Albright Lydia Adeline 20	26 Feb 1889	(4) 2/26
Wolford John Martin 30	Pownell Florence Woodrow 26	16 Jan 1898	(4) 2/40
Wolford John William 22	Allamong Fannie Lynch 17	9 Nov 1885	(4) 2/21
Wolford John William 35	Martin Lizzie Lee 18	31 Oct 1899	(4) 2/42
Wolford Jonathan	Foltz Mary Ann	11 Jan 1866	(4) 1/2
Wolford Joseph Marion 19	Haines Mary Elizabeth 22	27 Nov 1890	(4) 2/28
Wolford Laura 37	Wolford George F 29	17 Mar 1892	(4) 2/30
Wolford Leanna 16	Whitacre Robert Calhoun 25	26 Oct 1893	(4) 2/33
Wolford Leonard Harper 25	Martin Lillie May 22	6 Mar 1895	(4) 2/35
Wolford Leonard Harper 21	Michael Virginia May 17	3 Mar 1891	(4) 2/29
Wolford Lucinda Elizabeth 18	Haines James Edward 19	19 Nov 1876	(4) 2/9
Wolford Lucy Ellen 30	McBride John William 26	29 July 1896	(4) 2/37
Wolford Lucy Frances 24	Powelson Philip James 27	16 June 1874	(4) 2/6
Wolford Lutetia 24	Corbin Oscalosa 27	13 Oct 1894	(4) 2/34
Wolford Malinda Catherine 18	Combs Philip 25	9 Jan 1876	(4) 2/8
Wolford Malinda Jane 17	Martin Richardson Rufus 22	17 June 1874	(4) 2/6
Wolford Margaret Catherine 18	Ruckman John William 23	27 Dec 1866	(4) 1/4
Wolford Mary Elizabeth 25	Wolford William Holland 20	4 Dec 1888	(4) 2/25
Wolford Mary Esther 18	Slane Daniel Webster 24	11 Dec 1884	(4) 2/20
Wolford Mary Margaret 28	Stewart William Jefferson 29	26 July 1871	(4) 2/3
Wolford Matilda Virginia 21	Baker Berzealious Honian 23	20 Nov 1873	(4) 2/5
Wolford Rebecca	Snyder Peter 23	1855	(10)
Wolford Richard Nixon 25	Gray Ida May 20	18 Apr 1894	(4) 2/34
Wolford Robert James 22	Bucklew Mary Catherine 25	15 Oct 1876	(4) 2/9
Wolford Robert Richardson 24	Carlyle ? May 18	3 Mar 1897	(4) 2/38
Wolford Rosa Lee 23	Bowman J Edward 23	19 Sept 1894	(4) 2/34
Wolford Samuel Isaiah 25	Wolford Annie Rebecca 24	28 June 1892	(4) 2/31
Wolford Sarah C 21	Wolford Charles Edward 29	1 Aug 1889	(4) 2/26
Wolford Sarah Ellen 21	Smith ? 40	10 Sept 1859	(10)
Wolford Sarah Elizabeth 19	Powelson Benjamin W 24	9 July 1873	(4) 2/4
Wolford Sarah Elizabeth 22	Brelsford George Washington 19	2 Feb 1887	(4) 2/23
Wolford Sarah Lurena 19	Grapes John Thomas 23	30 Oct 1883	(4) 2/18
Wolford Sarah Virginia 19	Hiett Evan Terrin 23	11 Dec 1873	(4) 2/5
Wolford Sidney Sophia 23	Moreland James Jackson 24	25 Apr 1882	(4) 2/17

Name #1	Name #2	Date	Source
Wolford William 54	Brill Emma Pheby 36	2 May 1878	(4) 2/11
Wolford William Ryland 23	Haws Euphennia 18	26 Aug 1884	(4) 2/19
Wolford William Lock 23	Loy Alverda Catharine 18	4 Jan 1887	(4) 2/23
Wolford William Holland 20	Wolford Mary Elizabeth 25	4 Dec 1888	(4) 2/25
Wolverton Isaac	Snapp Mariah	*15 May 1826	(4) 3/19
Wood Daniel 66	Howard Clemy 65	19 Aug 1865	(4) 1/1
Woods Catharine Emily 24	Edmondson Robert Allen 23	16 Dec 1877	(4) 1/39
Woods Ellen 42	Johnson Henry 65	25 July 1891	(4) 1/41
Woods John H 22	Street S H 21	22 Jan 1868	(4) 1/6
Woodward George 34	Arnold Abigail 22	Jan 1859	(10)
Woodward George W	Arnold Abigail	17 Jan 1859	(5)
Woodworth Malcolm W 49	Raymond Isabella 40	22 Sept 1881	(4) 2/16
Worden Horatia N 24	Keller Martha V 22	14 Mar 1866	(4) 1/3
Worman William	Cundiff Nancy	* 2 Apr 1825	(4) 3/26
Worman Wm	Cundiff Nancy	7 Apr 1825	(6)
Worth Maria Louisa	Michael David	19 Sept 1837	(1) 7 Oct 1837
Worth Rebecca Anne	Michael Moses	19 Sept 1837	(1) 7 Oct 1837
Wotring James Abraham 28	Hook Florence Virginia 24	9 Feb 1886	(4) 2/21
Wright Albert Lee 22	Wolford Hannah Catharine 20	14 Nov 1889	(4) 2/27
Wright F M Dr	Sloan Mary	30 Oct 1859	(6)
Wright James Francis 26	Sandy Sarah Belle 21	27 Dec 1886	(4) 2/23
Wright M F Dr	Sloan Mary	30 Oct 1860	(5)
Wright Margaret Ellen 21	Hannas Charles Dougal 22	29 Oct 1891	(4) 2/30
Wright Mary Cordelia 16	Kerns Samuel Nathan 30	5 June 1894	(4) 2/34
Wright Sarah Catharine 19	Spielman William 20	12 Feb 1874	(4) 2/5
Wycoff Moses	Harvey D	1 May 1828	(6)
Yates Elenor	Davis James	*26 Apr 1825	(4) 3/31
Yokum Mary Jane 23	Judy Adam 22	21 Mar 1866	(4) 1/3
Yokum Riley	Drace Agnes	22 Feb 1832	(5)
Yost ?	Stewart George W	2 Feb 1860	(10)
Yost Elizabeth Ann 25	Loy Samuel 40	27 Nov 1866	(4) 1/4
Yost Emma Lee 20	Bryan James Abernathy 35	1 May 1889	(4) 2/26
Yost Granville Armstrong 26	Starnes Martha A 28	2 Jan 1890	(4) 2/27
Yost Henry 60	Carder Rebecca 40	3 Feb 1878	(4) 2/11
Yost James Henry 25	Rudolph Sarah Amanda 30	7 Mar 1880	(4) 2/14
Yost John 25	Yost Rachel	18 Aug 1859	(10)
Yost Margaret	Wilson Alexander	*24 Apr 1827	(4) 3/28
Yost Maria Flory 18	Kerns John Lewis 25	15 Oct 1867	(4) 1/5
Yost Mary Elizabeth 22	Edwards Francis Taylor 25	24 Dec 1876	(4) 2/9
Yost Rachel	Yost John 25	18 Aug 1859	(10)
Yost Robert Branson 25	Starn Grace Charlotte 20	29 July 1891	(4) 2/29
Yost Robert J 27	Saville Rachel C 21	17 Apr 1873	(4) 2/4
Yost Susan Ann 22	Roberson Sanford Taylor 21	29 Jan 1874	(4) 2/5
Young George	Nicholson Elizabeth	*4 Mar 1824	(4) 3/15
Young Harriet J 26	Plummer Henry 40	4 Apr 1868	(4) 1/6
Young Sarah	Runnells Jacob	*31 Dec 1824	(4) 3/56
Youse Caroline 22	Sivel James 21	30 Nov 1854	(10)
Zeiler Edward Newton 29	Anderson Delilah M 20	24 Sept 1891	(4) 2/29
Zimmerman Joshua Soule 26	Vance Kitty Campbell 27	10 Oct 1900	(4) 2/43
Zirk William Frank 21	Raines Dannie Vanmeter 16	23 Feb 1898	(4) 2/40
?	McBride Samuel 30	19 Dec 1854	(10)
? 22	Loy Sarah Catharine 23	3 Dec 1883	(4) 2/18

Name #1	Name #2	Date	Source
? 25	Anderson Gertrude Frances 23	20 Dec 1883	(4) 2/18
? 32	Short Hannah Miranda 22	8 Nov 1883	(4) 2/18
? Elizabeth	Ruckman Gibson	22 Aug 1854	(10)
? Ellen 23	Brill William M	22 Feb 1860	(10)
? Harriett	Arnold Jacob M 30	1 May 1873	(4) 2/3
? Isaac 23	Riley Sarah M 21	3 July 1859	(10)
? Martha 38	Duling Edmond 39	24 Oct 1860	(10)
? Mary	White George W 21	30 Sept 1860	(10)
? Samuel B M	Nelson Asenath	20 Sept 1854	(10)
? Soloman J 29	McDonald Margaret 23	18 Mar 1860	(10)
? Virginia 22	Welch ? 26	Oct 1859	(10)